Interpreting Eden

"This is not the usual book on Genesis 1–3. It takes up many of the same problems other books do (such as the length of the creation days), but it expects you to think much harder about them than you were expecting to. Perhaps, for example, you might approach this book looking for arguments defending literal interpretation. Well, Poythress will tell you that the term *literal* has at least five meanings, so theses about literal versus figurative interpretation generally need more careful formulation than we usually give them. But none of these careful distinctions has the aim of compromising the inerrancy of Scripture as God's Word. Indeed, you will emerge from this book with a greater sense of how Genesis really is the Word of God. Indeed, you will learn much about how, as Poythress says, we should 'read the Word of God in the presence of God.' This is how biblical and linguistic expertise ought to be used in expounding the Bible."

John M. Frame, Professor of Systematic Theology and Philosophy Emeritus, Reformed Theological Seminary, Orlando

"This new book by Vern Poythress is a remarkably wise and comprehensive analysis of multiple recent approaches to interpreting Genesis 1–3. Drawing on several decades of detailed biblical research, Poythress effectively answers modern views that simplistically attribute 'scientific error' to Genesis, and he demonstrates convincingly that Genesis 1–3 must be understood as prose narrative that purports to describe actual events, not as fictional or allegorical literature. But he also wisely cautions against 'overinterpreting' Genesis 1–3 by claiming that it contains scientific information that was not the intention of either its human or divine author. Highly recommended!"

Wayne Grudem, Distinguished Research Professor of Theology and Biblical Studies, Phoenix Seminary

"We always owe our thanks to Vern Poythress for his characteristic of careful and thoughtful engagement with the biblical text and with other interpreters; how much more on these texts and topics! Besides attention to linguistic details, Poythress always draws the reader to the bigger issues connected to interpretation and to the Christian worldview. This will be worth your time to read, study, consider, and digest."

C. John Collins, Professor of Old Testament, Covenant Theological Seminary; author, *Did Adam and Eve Really Exist?*; Old Testament editor, *ESV Study Bible*

"Poythress is a genius of our time. *Interpreting Eden* tackles massively complex issues (some far more complex than I had initially thought) and points a way forward. From this point on, no interpreter of the creation narratives can avoid interacting with this book."

Derek W. H. Thomas, Chancellor's Professor, Reformed Theological Seminary; Teaching Fellow, Ligonier Ministries; Senior Minister, First Presbyterian Church, Columbia, South Carolina

"This is a fascinating, helpful, and well-written book. Vern Poythress has managed to engage in a meaningful way with the serious questions raised today about reading Genesis 1–3 carefully, with hermeneutical finesse, and, at the same time, has interacted with related modern scientific theories with discernment. One does not need to agree with all his conclusions to learn from his way of treating questions, discussions, and competing views fairly and with wisdom. This book helps us think more clearly and deeply about some of the issues that concern us the most."

Richard E. Averbeck, Director of the PhD in Theological Studies and Professor of Old Testament and Semitic Languages, Trinity Evangelical Divinity School

Interpreting Eden

A Guide to Faithfully Reading and Understanding Genesis 1–3

Vern S. Poythress

CROSSWAY®

WHEATON, ILLINOIS

Library of Congress Cataloging-in-Publication Data

Names: Poythress, Vern S., author.
Title: Interpreting Eden: a guide to faithfully reading and understanding Genesis 1–3 / Vern S. Poythress.
Description: Wheaton, Illinois: Crossway, 2019. | Includes bibliographical references and index.
Identifiers: LCCN 2018029010 (print) | LCCN 2018051949 (ebook) | ISBN 9781433558740 (pdf) | ISBN 9781433558757 (mobi) | ISBN 9781433558764 (epub) | ISBN 9781433558733 (tp) | ISBN 9781433558764 (ePub) | ISBN 9781433558757 (Mobipocket)
Subjects: LCSH: Eden. | Bible. Genesis, I–III—Criticism, interpretation, etc.
Classification: LCC BS1237 (ebook) | LCC BS1237 .P69 2019 (print) | DDC 222/.1106—dc23
LC record available at https://lccn.loc.gov/2018029010

Contents

Tables and Illustrations

Tables

Illustrations

Foreword

Some topics are notoriously complex, and few, if any, are more complex than the doctrine of creation. This complexity springs in large part from the wide array of disciplines that impinge on the topic: exegesis of the opening chapters of Genesis and of other biblical passages that talk about creation; questions of literary genre; hermeneutical principles; the interface between Scripture and contemporary science (with its many compartmentalized disciplines, from cosmology to thermodynamics to biology and geology); reception theory, which wrestles with the history of the interpretation of these chapters across many centuries and even more cultures; epistemology; the implications of working with God-inspired texts; the dogmatism of various theological cliques on the left hand and on the right; the nature of history; literary structure; and the place of analogy when talking about God. And that list is certainly not exhaustive, but merely suggestive.

Enter Vern Poythress. Not every New Testament scholar begins his academic career with a PhD in mathematics from Harvard or writes across an extraordinarily wide range of theological topics: baptism, science, providence, accommodation, translation theory, the Trinity, inerrancy, hermeneutics, spiritual gifts, literary genre, typology, eschatology, apocalyptic, sociology, and, of course, creation. In the more than forty years I have known him, Dr. Poythress has kept pushing back the frontiers in a widening range of important subjects; it is hard to keep up with all his work. And that is the first reason why he is as qualified as anyone, and more qualified than most, to wrestle with what the Bible says about creation: he has spent his life interacting intelligently with many of the related fields. Indeed, informed readers will find echoes of some of his earlier work in this study, as the panoply of his previous efforts comes together in this combination of analysis and synthesis.

The second and third reasons why Dr. Poythress is the person to write this work hang together: he simultaneously espouses a very high view of Scripture and classic confessionalism. Some adopt the former but know little of the latter: they tend toward a mere proof-texting exegesis, unable to see the forest as they fasten on a knot in the third branch of the sixteenth tree from the right. One remembers the insight of Francis Schaeffer, writing forty-five years ago (in *Genesis in Space and Time*). He set out to unpack not everything he could possibly find in Genesis 1–11, but everything in those chapters that must be true for the rest of the Bible to be coherent and faithful. Dr. Poythress is not so restrictive, but he has a fine instinct for what is most important. Others loudly avow their commitment to historic confessionalism, but are either unwilling or unable to engage in careful exegesis. Dr. Poythress wants to hold these polarities together.

The fourth reason that qualifies Dr. Poythress to write this work is that, despite the complexities and subtleties of the issues, he writes with rare clarity and simplicity.

And finally, Dr. Poythress has an extraordinarily supple and creative mind. Not infrequently, scholars who have been shaped by Reformed confessionalism can manage no more than the faithful articulation of that heritage (which, of course, is no small virtue), while scholars who owe intellectual allegiance to very little can put forward many stimulating and creative proposals even while they ride right off the range. But Dr. Poythress manages to maintain the theological "thickness" of a rich tradition while venturing unafraid into many creative suggestions and postures. That is one of the reasons why it is a delight to read what he writes: I am invariably stimulated, challenged, egged on to think my way again through something I mistakenly thought I understood adequately.

That is a large part of the valuable contribution that Vern Poythress makes in this work. I read him with pleasure not because I think he is always right, and therefore doing no more than reinforcing my biases, but because as far as I can see he is far more likely to be right than not, and in any case he stimulates me to think within the matrix of profoundly Christian commitments. In a few areas, I think he is wrong: for example, the way he sets up the weighted contributions of the divine author and the human author is bold, but finally unconvincing. But even where I think he is wrong, he teaches me to shore up my own position with more care.

Be that as it may, books that I can recommend because I agree with them have their own easy usefulness; books that I recommend because they wrestle in a highly informed and stimulating way with biblical texts, whether I agree with them or not, are even more useful. Take it up, and read.

D. A. Carson

Acknowledgment

I am grateful to the *Westminster Theological Journal* for granting permission for me to reuse articles that originally appeared there in some of the chapters of this book. I have revised these articles and sometimes rearranged pieces from them so that they would fit coherently into this book. The following articles are used:

"Rethinking Accommodation in Revelation." *Westminster Theological Journal* 76, no. 1 (2014): 143–56.

"A Misunderstanding of Calvin's Interpretation of Genesis 1:6–8 and 1:5 and Its Implications for Ideas of Accommodation." *Westminster Theological Journal* 76, no. 1 (2014): 157–66.

"Three Modern Myths in Interpreting Genesis 1." *Westminster Theological Journal* 76, no. 2 (2014): 321–50.

"Correlations with Providence in Genesis 1." *Westminster Theological Journal* 77, no. 1 (2015): 71–99.

"Rain Water versus a Heavenly Sea in Genesis 1:6–8." *Westminster Theological Journal* 77, no. 2 (2015): 181–91.

"Correlations with Providence in Genesis 2." *Westminster Theological Journal* 78, no. 1 (2016): 29–48.

"Dealing with the Genre of Genesis and Its Opening Chapters." *Westminster Theological Journal* 78, no. 2 (2016): 217–30.

"Genesis 1:1 Is the First Event, Not a Summary." *Westminster Theological Journal* 79, no. 1 (2017): 97–121.

"Time in Genesis 1." *Westminster Theological Journal* 79, no. 2 (2017): 213–41.

Introduction

The Need

How can we faithfully interpret Genesis 1–3?[1] There are many controversies about the meaning of the early chapters of Genesis. How
do we find our way through them? Thinking about sound principles
for interpreting the Bible can help set us on a solid path. That is what
we will do in this book. We will focus on biblical truths that offer us
a basis for sound interpretive principles. These principles, in turn, will
lead to faithful interpretation of Genesis 1–3.

Many of the controversies over Genesis 1–3 have a connection
with claims from modern science. Mainstream cosmologists claim,
for example, that the universe developed over billions of years, while
Genesis 1 says that God's creative acts took six days. How do we
deal with such discrepancies? To evaluate various scientific claims in
detail would take a book in itself.[2] For readers whose primary question is whether Genesis 1–3 can be harmonized with modern science,
let me reassure you that there are answers. But we must be patient in

---

1. The literary break in Genesis comes at the end of Genesis 4 rather than the end of Genesis 3,
which is why C. John Collins includes Genesis 4 in his book *Genesis 1–4: A Linguistic, Literary,
and Theological Commentary* (Phillipsburg, NJ: P&R, 2006). We must certainly pay attention
to the literary organization of Genesis. But in this book, we focus more narrowly on chaps. 1–3
of Genesis because of their theological implications and their connections with scientific claims.
Collins's book offers a supplement to this one through its inclusion of Genesis 4. See also C. John
Collins, *Reading Genesis Well: Navigating History, Poetry, Science, and Truth in Genesis 1–11*
(Grand Rapids, MI: Zondervan, 2018).
2. I try to offer a beginning in *Redeeming Science: A God-Centered Approach* (Wheaton,
IL: Crossway, 2006). For up-to-date critiques of Darwinism, including its scientific weaknesses,
see Michael Denton, *Evolution: Still a Theory in Crisis* (Seattle: Discovery Institute, 2016); J. P.
Moreland, et al., eds., *Theistic Evolution: A Scientific, Philosophical, and Theological Critique*
(Wheaton, IL: Crossway, 2017).

the process of working them out. We must be patient because we are traveling a route that involves a number of distinct issues. Some of our observations will be at odds with widespread assumptions among the elites of Western culture. Some assumptions within the prevailing cultural atmosphere need to be challenged.

Among other things, we will consider to some extent how science fits into a biblically based view of the world (see especially chaps. 1, 2, and 4). Science as a human endeavor can have some wonderful fruits. But it can also have biases and make assertions that later turn out to be untrue or not the whole truth.

Nevertheless, our focus in this book is primarily on Genesis 1–3, not on scientific claims. Why Genesis 1–3? These early chapters, and the book of Genesis as a whole, have a significant role within the whole of Scripture because they give us the beginning of history. The beginning and the end of history both have an important influence on how we understand the middle period of time, the time in which we live. Disputes in interpreting Genesis become more vigorous because some of them make a difference, maybe even a big difference, in how we construe the middle.

In a broad sense, the middle includes us, as well as almost all the events about which the Bible talks. It includes the central events of redemption—preeminently, the life, death, resurrection, ascension, and reign of Christ. The biblical account of the creation and the fall offers the largest backdrop against which we are supposed to understand the middle. But just what do the Bible as a whole and Genesis in particular say about the creation and the fall?

Creation and Fall—in the Context of Sciences

Interpreting the first three chapters of Genesis involves many kinds of questions. Within a single book, we cannot devote equal attention to all of them. There are questions about: (1) theology, such as the doctrine of creation, the doctrine of human nature, the doctrine of sin, and the meaning of human sexuality; (2) themes, such as light, order and disorder, fruitfulness, and dominion, and how these themes relate to the rest of the Bible; and (3) the relation of Genesis 1–3 to modern scientific claims. We will focus primarily on this third set of questions.

Some of the disputes in interpreting Genesis 1–3 are clearly related to modern scientific assertions about earlier phases of the development of the universe. People also look at issues connected to the standard mainstream neo-Darwinian account concerning the origin of living things. How did the present diversity in species of plants and animals come about? Was it by random processes without design or by God's design?

We also encounter discussions about Adam and Eve. How, if at all, does the account of the creation of Adam and Eve in Genesis 2 relate to mainstream scientific claims about the origin of humanity? Was there a single original pair? In what sense were they original? Did they come from earlier hominids by natural processes?[3]

On each of these questions, some people are willing to reject mainstream scientific assertions and hold to their interpretation of Genesis 1–3. Others reject the biblical account and hold to their understanding of the claims of modern science. And then there are those in between, holding a number of different positions. Some people propose harmonizations between Genesis and science. Some propose to reinterpret Genesis, some to reinterpret or redo the scientific material. It is well to recognize that the dominant viewpoint among scientists is not the only one. There are various minority viewpoints, represented by qualified scientists, but these viewpoints are largely suppressed by majority voices, by active persecution, and by selective reporting in the media.

More detailed questions about science and Genesis 1–3 also have a larger context. What is the nature of science? What is the nature of the Bible? Either of these questions could lead to a whole book.[4] In this book, we will have to be content with a short summary so that we may have space for a close look at Genesis 1–3.

Interpretive Principles

Some of these questions are difficult. Why? Taken by itself, Genesis 1–3 does not provide direct answers to all the questions that we

---

3. For a survey of many such questions, see Kenneth D. Keathley and Mark F. Rooker, *40 Questions about Creation and Evolution* (Grand Rapids, MI: Kregel, 2014).
4. See Vern S. Poythress, *Redeeming Science: A God-Centered Approach* (Wheaton, IL: Crossway, 2006); Vern S. Poythress, *God-Centered Biblical Interpretation* (Phillipsburg, NJ: P&R, 1999); Vern S. Poythress, *Inerrancy and Worldview: Answering Modern Challenges to the Bible* (Wheaton, IL: Crossway, 2012). A more specialized supplement to the last of these is found in Vern S. Poythress, *Inerrancy and the Gospels: A God-Centered Approach to the Challenges of Harmonization* (Wheaton, IL: Crossway, 2012).

might have. But it does have something to say. How do we interpret what it says? Much depends on how we interpret any biblical passage.

To some extent, the questions become *more* difficult because sin creeps into the process of interpretation. Not all interpretations of the Bible or all interpretations of Genesis 1–3 are morally innocent. In fact, sin can creep in unawares even when we feel sincere in our desire to understand Genesis 1–3 responsibly. Sin has effects on the mind. We need to "be transformed by the renewal of [our] mind" (Rom. 12:2).

Genesis 1–3 remains the same text it has been for centuries. But the disputes do not go away. They are not being settled to everyone's satisfaction. When disputes continue, it can be useful to attend to principles of interpretation, that is, to hermeneutical issues, in hopes of gaining more clarity and moving forward. That is what we propose to do in this book: to consider Genesis 1–3 afresh in the light of certain interpretive principles. So our focus is on the process of interpretation and its assumptions, not just on the question of what Genesis 1–3 says or its implications.[5]

In particular, within the scope of this book, we cannot definitively settle all the possible questions about Adam and Eve. Whole books have been written on that subject.[6] It is an important subject, partly because of the way in which the beginning of the human race affects our view of what it means to be human and partly because of the specific way in which the New Testament draws a parallel between Adam and Christ (Rom. 5:12–21; 1 Cor. 15:21–22, 44–49). The parallel depends on the assumption that Adam was a real person. How can it be that we and the whole human race "died" in Adam if Adam was not actually there as the locus for this death (1 Cor. 15:22; Rom. 5:12, 16–18)?

Though we cannot present full arguments for all conclusions, we hope to make progress in providing a hermeneutical framework in which gradually to proceed toward answers.

---

5. For a focus on linguistic and literary principles, see Collins, *Reading Genesis Well.*

6. See Ann Gauger, Douglas Axe, and Casey Luskin, *Science and Human Origins* (Seattle: Discovery Institute, 2012); Hans Madueme and Michael Reeves, eds., *Adam, the Fall, and Original Sin: Theological, Biblical, and Scientific Perspectives* (Grand Rapids, MI: Baker, 2014). For a spectrum of views, see Matthew Barrett and Ardel B. Caneday, eds., *Four Views on the Historical Adam* (Grand Rapids, MI: Zondervan, 2013). An important exegetical and theological contribution is found in J. P. Versteeg, *Adam in the New Testament: Mere Teaching Model or First Historical Man?* (Phillipsburg, NJ: P&R, 2012).

When a lot is at stake, we must be patient both with ourselves and with others. We must acknowledge that sins in the arena of interpretation are not easy to root out—among us or among others. Every sinful human being has the temptation to read the Bible the way he wants it to speak rather than the way that it actually does speak according to the meaning and power of the Holy Spirit.

We must also be patient concerning the state of our knowledge. God has chosen to provide some answers in the Bible, but he has not given all the answers to questions about which we might be curious. Our knowledge of the societies of the ancient Near East is fragmentary. And work in science continues. Science is a "work in progress," and we cannot always tell beforehand where there may be radical changes in interpreting evidence.

PART 1

BASIC INTERPRETIVE PRINCIPLES

1

God

Let us begin with some basic interpretive principles.

Behind all of the particular questions about various verses of Genesis 1–3, and behind most of the interpretive issues as well, we find the question of God. Understanding who God is influences our interpretation of Genesis 1–3. In fact, the question of God is all-important for interpreting the Bible as a whole. Indeed, it is the most important question for Western civilization today. Apart from a significant minority, elite culture within Western civilization has given up on the idea that God is the Trinitarian deity described in the Bible. Education, media, and the arts travel in other directions.

One direction that is being explored is materialism or naturalism. The philosophy of materialism says that the world is composed of matter in motion. That is all that there is at the bottom of the world and the foundation of human experience. All the complexity that we see has built up gradually out of simpler constituents of matter. In particular, there is no God. Genesis 1–3 is viewed as one of many made-up stories of origins. (Note that philosophical materialism has its own story of origins. See Fig. 1.1.)

But is philosophical materialism really viable? If matter is all that there is, it would seem that our thoughts and ideas are not real. They are illusions. Some materialists do say that consciousness is an illusion. But if that is so, the ideas of materialist philosophy are also illusory. So it seems that materialist philosophy cannot give a coherent account of its own basis.

Fig. 1.1: Philosophical Materialism versus Biblical Theism

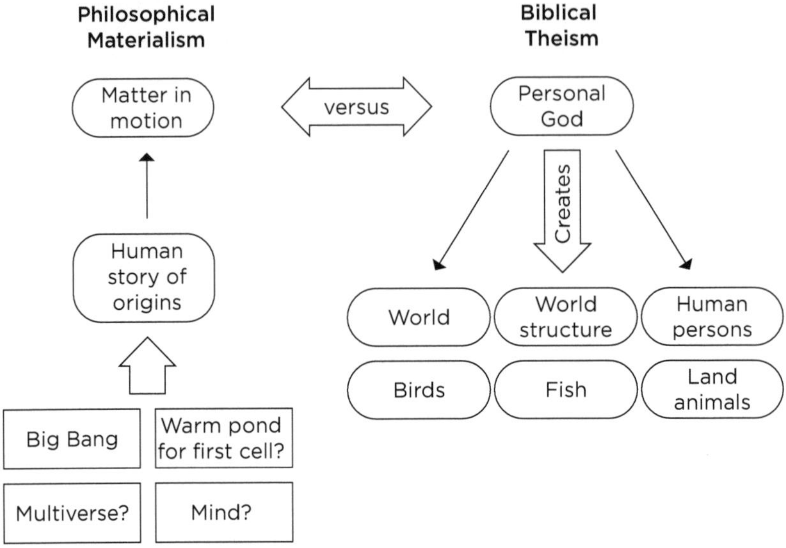

Not everyone is a materialist these days. Pure materialism seems too grim. Therefore, some people edge closer to pantheism, which says that everything is god. Though this position is "spiritual" in a sense, it radically disagrees with Genesis 1–3. It discards Genesis 1–3 or treats it as a confused reaction to the actual reality that everything is divine.

The question of God is important because God himself is important. But the question is also important because it has implications for morality and human living. What does it mean for an action to be morally right or wrong? Does morality have its root in the moral character of God? And if God exists, does he have purposes for human living, purposes that tell us who we really are?

Suppose we think that there is no God. Is morality no more than a personal, subjective preference, like regarding chocolate ice cream as better than vanilla? Is morality merely the product of mindless, unguided, random evolution? If so, it would seem to follow that everyone's notions of morality are equally products of evolution. So the desire to help others has the same standing as the desire to steal from others. There is no real basis to consider one person's moral preferences to be superior to another's.

Since the question of God is important, Genesis 1–3 is important. It is one of the central texts in the Bible that tell us about God.

Who Is God?

From the standpoint of the elite in Western culture, maybe God exists and maybe he does not. But life goes on. According to this kind of thinking, life can be conducted mostly without reference to God. If someone wants to add a religious dimension in his private life, that is up to him. And, indeed, many people think of themselves as "spiritual" in some sense. They are seeking contact with something transcendent. But many of them are not really seeking the God described in the Bible. They are seeking a substitute elsewhere, in meditation, in communion with nature, in spiritualism, or in reading and listening to a host of sources.

The Bible is at odds with this atmosphere. God is at the center of its message. And God has particular characteristics. There is only one true God (Deut. 4:35, 39). And because he alone is God, it is fitting to worship him alone. He requires exclusive allegiance, by analogy with the exclusive allegiance that a man and a woman used to be expected to give to each other in marriage. This requirement of exclusive allegiance sounds oppressive to many modern people, but that is because they do not understand either God or themselves. They do not understand that they have been created for communion with God, and that such communion alone fulfills their true natures. They have lost communion through human rebellion.

So not just any idea of God and any kind of response to the transcendent is adequate. We must come to know about *this particular God* and resist the temptation to bring in all kinds of other ideas as to what we would like God to be.

Miracles

When we actually pay attention to the Bible, we find out what it says about God. This God, it turns out, works miracles when he wishes. The four Gospels all indicate that Jesus worked miracles. And the greatest miracle was that Jesus was raised from the dead by the power of God: "But God *raised him* from the dead, and for many days he appeared to those who had come up with him from

Galilee to Jerusalem, who are now his witnesses to the people" (Acts 13:30–31). The Old Testament contains other striking instances of miracles. God appeared to Abraham in human form (Gen. 18:1–2). God rained fire and sulfur on Sodom and Gomorrah (19:24). God divided the waters of the Red Sea (Ex. 14:21). God spoke in an audible voice to Israel from the top of Mount Sinai (Exodus 19). God through Elijah raised from the dead the widow of Zarephath's son (1 Kings 17:21–22).

Many Western people today are skeptical of such claims. But if we ask why, we soon confront the fact that Western culture has already given up on the idea of such a God *before* reading any passage from the Bible. Allegedly, "modern science" has shown that miracles are impossible. But the empirical investigations that scientists conduct can only uncover *regularities*, to which scientists give the name of "law." They cannot rightly say that there can be no exceptions. People say that there are no exceptions because they are already influenced by a philosophy that says that God does not exist, that the world is run by mechanism, and that therefore there can be no exceptions.[1] (See Fig. 1.2.)

Fig. 1.2: Miracles according to Mechanism versus the God of the Bible

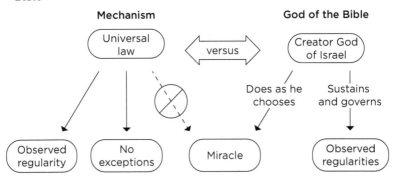

God's Rule over All

But miracles are only the beginning of the ways in which we must reckon with God. The Bible indicates that God is intimately involved

---

1. For further discussion, see Vern S. Poythress, *Redeeming Science: A God-Centered Approach* (Wheaton, IL: Crossway, 2006), chap. 1.

in the events of the world. He is involved not only in extraordinary, exceptional events, but in the most ordinary events. In his sovereign rule, he controls events both big and small, both natural and human. For a thorough confirmation of the reality of God's control, readers may go to whole books devoted to the subject.[2] Here, we may be content to cite a sampling of verses:

> You cause the grass to grow for the livestock
>   and plants for man to cultivate,
> that he may bring forth food from the earth. (Ps. 104:14)

> The lot is cast into the lap,
>   but its every decision is *from the* LORD. (Prov. 16:33)

> But if God so *clothes the grass* of the field, which today is alive and tomorrow is thrown into the oven, will he not much more clothe you, O you of little faith? (Matt. 6:30)

> For the Son of Man goes as it has been *determined*, but woe to that man by whom he is betrayed! (Luke 22:22)

> For truly in this city there were gathered together against your holy servant Jesus, whom you anointed, both Herod and Pontius Pilate, along with the Gentiles and the peoples of Israel, to *do whatever your hand and your plan had predestined to take place.* (Acts 4:27–28)

We also have verses that proclaim the comprehensive character of God's control in general terms:

> Who has spoken and it came to pass,
>   unless the Lord has commanded it?
> Is it not from the mouth of the Most High
>   that *good and bad* come? (Lam. 3:37–38)

> In him we have obtained an inheritance, having been predestined according to the purpose of him who *works all things* according to the counsel of his will. (Eph. 1:11)

---

2. John M. Frame, *The Doctrine of God* (Phillipsburg, NJ: P&R, 2002); Loraine Boettner, *The Reformed Doctrine of Predestination* (Grand Rapids, MI: Eerdmans, 1936); Vern S. Poythress, *Chance and the Sovereignty of God: A God-Centered Approach to Probability and Random Events* (Wheaton, IL: Crossway, 2014).

Principles such as these do not appear in only one or two books of the Bible, but in many.[3] They occur in both the Old Testament and the New Testament. They occur on the lips of Jesus as well as others.

This idea of the comprehensive rule of God contrasts with several alternatives that are common today. It contrasts with philosophical materialism, which believes that God does not exist. It contrasts with pantheism, which identifies the world with god ("The world is god."). It contrasts also with deism.

Deism was a popular view in the eighteenth century. In its classical form, it postulated that God created the world but was thereafter uninvolved. This contrasts with the continuous involvement described in the Bible.

Among people who claim to be Christian, something akin to deism still exists in our time. (For convenience, we will use the word deism to cover a broader field of views.) This broadened deism consists in the idea that, in most cases, created things are sufficient in themselves to develop under their own power. In other words, God is basically uninvolved in detailed development. A view of this kind does not completely deny the occurrence of miraculous intervention at key times— for example, in the resurrection of Christ. And it may affirm that God is continuously involved in sustaining each created thing *in being*. For example, it is surely correct that God sustains the existence of grass. But that is a minimal affirmation. The Bible says that "you cause the grass to grow for the livestock" (Ps. 104:14). God is causing the grass to grow, not just sustaining its existence. Or consider another illustration. The deistic view affirms that God sustains the existence of the wind and the water. Psalm 147:18 says that "he makes his wind blow and the waters flow." This psalm depicts a far more vigorous and intimate involvement by God with specific events than what deistic views hold.

Science and Modern Deistic Thinking

In our time, deistic views are influenced by the predominance of science and its technological benefits. Science, it is thought, shows us what the world is like. And the world that it shows us is one in which most things undergo causal developments under their own power.

---

3. In narrative books in the Bible, the principles often reside in the background—it is assumed that the events are being worked out according to God's purposes.

That is, our world is either a world completely without God or a deistic world, in which God mostly leaves the world to its own inner working.

But such thinking is a product not of the scientific data, but of analyzing the scientific data in a deistic way. In other words, deism is built into the implicit framework that people assume and use when thinking about science. They interpret the process of causation as self-sufficient, ignoring the presence of God working all things according to his will (Eph. 1:11). They assume self-sufficiency rather than demonstrate it. By contrast, the person who genuinely believes that God is intimately involved in growing grass and making the winds blow sees scientific data as a description of the faithfulness of God. God is so faithful in the ways in which he makes grass grow and the winds blow that we can give detailed descriptions of the regularities. Scientists at their best are merely describing some of the regular ways that God comprehensively rules the world.

We may illustrate with an analogy. Let us suppose that a scientist undertakes to observe the patterns in my life and my wife's. Every morning we get up at about seven thirty. This pattern continues for months. So the scientist formulates a law: these people get up at seven thirty. It seems to be a perfectly sound law, with no exceptions. But then one morning we get up at five thirty. Is this a "miracle"? Our rising at this hour certainly may seem exceptional, strange, and unaccountable. But then the scientist finds out that we got up at that hour because we had an early flight to catch. Our personal purposes, which normally involve regular hours of sleep, can be overridden at any point by *other*, more specialized personal purposes that deal with a situation that is important to us and for which it makes sense to deviate from our normal behavior. So it is with God. The consistency and "normality" of his rule over all things gives us the basis for our ability to predict the future and to live normal lives in a dependable world around us. The sun rises every day. There are indeed what theologians call "secondary causes," as when one billiard ball knocks another ball and causes it to move, or when wind blows down a house (Job 1:19). God in his plan specifies these causal relations. But because God is personal, with personal purposes, the ties between his purposes and special situations can be the occasion for deviation from what we are accustomed to see. Personal rule is different from impersonal mechanism, though people may not always easily notice the difference.

Yes, people can tell themselves the tale that the regularities found by scientists are part of an impersonal mechanism rather than an expression and display of the faithfulness of God in his rule over all. But the tale is false. And it can be shown to be false, because the regularities themselves are rational and language-like, testifying to the personal nature of the God who specifies them.

We cannot dwell on these matters without a much more expansive explanation, which belongs to another book.[4] For the moment, we can take note of the fact that modern deistic views differ radically from what the Bible depicts about God's involvement. (See Fig. 1.3.)

Fig. 1.3: The Deistic View versus the God of the Bible in His Involvement

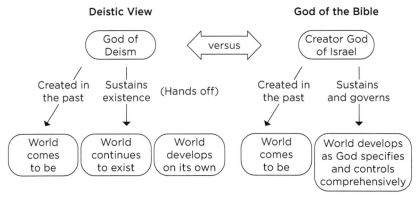

The Implications of God's Rule

What do we think? What is God like? Is he like the descriptions in the Bible? I believe so. If we do not follow the Bible, we will, in the end, be making up our own view of God.

The teachings in the Bible pose a fundamental challenge not only to individuals but to the whole of Western civilization. Western civilization was once heavily influenced by biblical teaching, but is rapidly losing that influence. Such a situation leads to the question, "Does God in fact exist, and is he the *kind* of God who rules over everything,

---

4. Poythress, *Redeeming Science*, especially chap. 1.

as the Bible describes?" Is he a God who "makes his wind blow and the waters flow" (Ps. 147:18)? If he is, then many things in Western civilization have to be rethought and retooled.

Such rethinking would not mean that we would *reject* everything from the present and the past. God has blessed every culture with much good (Acts 14:17). We call such blessings "common grace." They are "common" because God gives these blessings to people all over the world, in all cultures and in all religions.[5] But if God exists, we have to rethink what is actually good and what is a corruption or distortion of the truth. False beliefs about God and false allegiances to false gods have an effect.

True and False Religion

We may also raise the question of what God himself thinks about people's conceptions about the spiritual realm and the realm of transcendence. The Bible has teaching about that too. It says that God detests false worship, which includes any kind of substitution of a false god or false object of worship for the true God. The Old Testament says clearly that it is detestable to worship other gods, such as Chemosh, the god of Moab, or Molech, the god of the Ammonites:

> Then Solomon built a high place for Chemosh the *abomination* of Moab, and for Molech the *abomination* of the Ammonites, on the mountain east of Jerusalem. And so he did for all his foreign wives, who made offerings and sacrificed to their gods.
>
> And the LORD was *angry* with Solomon, because his heart had turned away from the LORD, the God of Israel, who had appeared to him twice and had commanded him concerning this thing, that he should not go after other gods. But he did not keep what the LORD commanded. (1 Kings 11:7–10)
>
> For all the gods of the peoples are worthless *idols*,
>   but the LORD made the heavens. (Ps. 96:5)

This kind of exclusive claim for the God of Israel is in sharp contrast to the modern idea that all religions are basically equal and that they all represent legitimate ways to access the divine. (See Fig. 1.4.)

---

5. Vern S. Poythress, *The Lordship of Christ: Serving Our Savior All of the Time, in All of Life, with All of Our Heart* (Wheaton, IL: Crossway, 2016), 53–59.

Fig. 1.4: Affirmation of Religions versus One Exclusive God

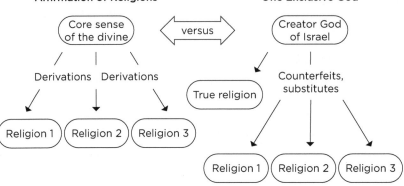

The alternatives to worshiping the true God include modern substitutes as well as the ancient ones. The god that deism has invented is a false god. The alternatives also include cases in which people see something impersonal as ultimate. That impersonal ultimate can be nature, matter, fate, or something they desire, such as money or sex. It can be an impersonal conception of the scientific laws that govern everything.[6] On this level of analysis, the alternatives are not religion and secularism, that is, no religion. Rather, everyone treats something as ultimate. Each postulated ultimate thing functions in place of God. At this level, everyone has a "religion." Even the philosophical materialist has a religion when he postulates that matter is ultimate. Matter is his god. He views matter as self-sufficient and eternal, which are characteristics of God. (See Fig. 1.5.)

Fig. 1.5: What Is Ultimate?

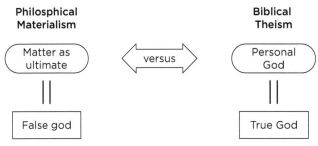

---

6. This view is critiqued in Poythress, *Redeeming Science*, chap. 1.

The decision confronts us in our day just as it did in the days of Joshua: whom will we serve (Josh. 24:15)? Will we serve the Lord, the God of Israel, or counterfeit gods that human imagination makes? It will not work for us to divide our allegiance:

> But Joshua said to the people, "You are not able to serve the LORD, for he is a holy God. He is a jealous God; he will not forgive your transgressions or your sins. If you forsake the LORD and serve foreign gods, then he will turn and do you harm and consume you, after having done you good." (Josh 24:19–20)

Fig. 1.6: False Gods versus True God

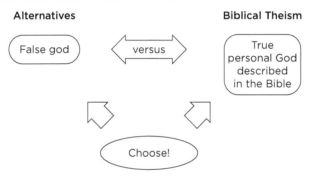

In sum, interpreting Genesis 1–3 depends on who we think God is. We need to interpret it bearing in mind that there is one true God, who created everything, who rules everything, and who can work miracles whenever he chooses.

2

Interpretive Implications
of God's Activity

The God of the Bible is the only true God. If we decide to serve him, we must serve him alone. And the implications of the truth about God are extraordinarily wide-ranging. In this chapter, I sketch out preliminary implications for how we interpret the relation of the Bible to the ancient Near East, to language, and to modern science.

God's Involvement

Let us consider how God is involved in this world. In his providential rule, God is intimately involved in everything, from the biggest wars to the movement of every ant in an anthill. He is involved in all human affairs, including all the affairs of the mind—all academic subjects. As C. S. Lewis found out by experience, God makes a radical difference:

> In one night the Landlord—call him by what name you would—had come back to the world, and filled the world, quite full without a cranny. His eyes stared and His hand pointed and His voice commanded in everything that could be heard or seen, even from this place where John sat, to the end of the world: and if you passed the end of the world He would be there too. . . . All things said one word: CAUGHT—Caught into slavery again, to walk

warily and on sufferance all his days, never to be alone; never the master of his own soul, to have no privacy, no corner whereof you could say to the whole universe: This is my own, here I can do as I please. Under that universal and inspecting gaze, John cowered like some small animal caught up in a giant's hands and held beneath a magnifying-glass.[1]

Lewis's description sounds grim, as indeed it might seem to a person who wakes up and finds that God is bigger and more terrifying than what he expected. But Lewis goes on to tell about the grace and mercy of God found in Christ. In the end, it is not at all grim—it is glorious.

How We Understand the Ancient Near East

If the truth about God has implications for every "cranny" of the world, it has implications for interpretation—many implications. We may begin with the last point from the previous chapter. God is a "jealous" God (Ex. 20:5). True service offered to the true God matters. God is distinct from all the false gods: "For all the gods of the peoples are *worthless idols*" (Ps. 96:5). If that is so, we can no longer read the information about the ancient Near East as it tends to be read in circles of modern critical scholarship.

The scholar wants to use the tools of modern scholarship, and these include tools of modern sociology, religious studies, and historiography. Many insights result by virtue of common grace. But we must also reckon with the possibility of distortion arising through the use of modern tools. The atmosphere of these tools is one in which religions are treated as human products created to respond, in some vague way, to the realm of the transcendent. All religions are fundamentally on a level. But are they? Or is there one God who denounces all false worship, even among his chosen people, Israel? Is Israel really distinct from every other people on the face of the earth by the very fact that God chose her to be his own? (See Fig. 2.1.)

---

1. C. S. Lewis, *The Pilgrim's Regress: An Allegorical Apology for Christianity, Reason, and Romanticism*, 3rd ed. (Grand Rapids, MI: Eerdmans, 1943), 147. Lewis offers us an "allegorical apology," but a good many pieces within it correspond vaguely to his own experience on the path to becoming a Christian.

Fig. 2.1: Analyzing Religions of the World

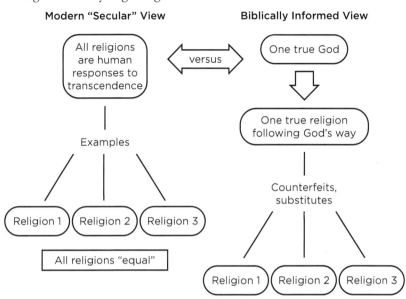

The truth about God has implications about how we interpret Genesis 1–3 within the larger environment of the ancient Near East. Is Genesis 1–3 merely one document among many ancient Near Eastern poems, myths, and traditions about the remote past? Is it one imaginary story among many about how the world gradually came to its present shape and humanity came to its present state of affairs? If God does not exist, or if he is not uniquely involved with Israel, it might seem reasonable to treat Genesis 1–3 as just one more document. (See Fig. 2.2)

But what if God does exist? What if God caused Genesis 1–3 to be written as his own communication to Israel? Can we conclude that he merely fell in with existing ways of thinking? Some people who claim to believe in the God of the Bible seem to think so. They affirm, of course, that Genesis 1–3 is monotheistic. It talks about only one great God, who made everything. It is different *theologically* from the polytheism in the ancient Near East. But does this one difference propagate into everything and make everything different in the end? By telling us later in the Bible about his "jealousy," God indicates that he is contrasting himself with all traditions everywhere that involve false gods. How do we deal with this key principle? Do we say that the key for interpreting Genesis 1–3 is to set it in its own ancient context? Well, yes, God crafted it first of all for that ancient context. But he could say something different from and contrasting with that context. And according to his purpose, he *also* crafted his words so that they would continue to speak relevantly to all future generations of his people and to us (Deut. 31:9–13, 24–29; Rom. 15:4).

Fig. 2.2: Genesis as Fitting in or Distinct

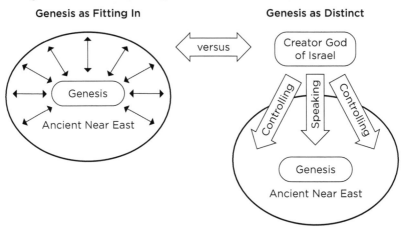

We must also reckon with how the presence of God affects our interpretation of religions in the ancient Near East. Religions are not all equal. Neither are they all innocent. Either people serve the true God or they have counterfeits. The counterfeits have fragments of the truth, but they substitute for the real thing (Rom. 1:23). They are idols. The process of counterfeiting can operate in cultural ideas about creation. The ancient Near East had counterfeit gods in counterfeit creation stories. Of course, there were similarities with the real thing, the creation story in Genesis 1–2. The counterfeit had to be near to the truth to be effective in holding people's allegiance. This idea of counterfeiting, when applied to the ancient Near East, differs from a sociology-of-religion approach that tries to be "neutral" in its analysis of all religions.

In sum, we have to rethink our principles for sociological analysis, for history, and for analyzing every single document from the past as well as the present. Putting God into the picture is radically disruptive, like putting Mount Everest in the middle of a flood plain. At the same time, we can affirm and appreciate that many piecemeal insights can arise in modern analyses by virtue of common grace. We have to be discerning.

How We Understand Language

Genesis is written in Hebrew, and Hebrew is a language. What is human language? Is it *merely* human? If so, is a book written in Hebrew never able to rise above the limitations of the merely human? Or is Genesis divine speech?

Here also God makes a difference. Did God really speak and say, "Let there be light," before any human being existed (Gen. 1:3)? Did God really speak in an audible voice to the people of Israel from the top of Mount Sinai (Ex. 20:18–19; Deut. 5:22)? Or is language merely a human construct, the limits of which then become the limits of our "world"? According to the Bible, God himself is the origin of language.[2] Our view of language affects how we view God's speeches, such as "Let there be light." And it affects how we view Genesis 1–3 as a whole—whether we treat it as the word of God or merely human words somehow reaching out toward a divine unknown. (See Fig. 2.3.)

Fig. 2.3: Two Views of Communication about God

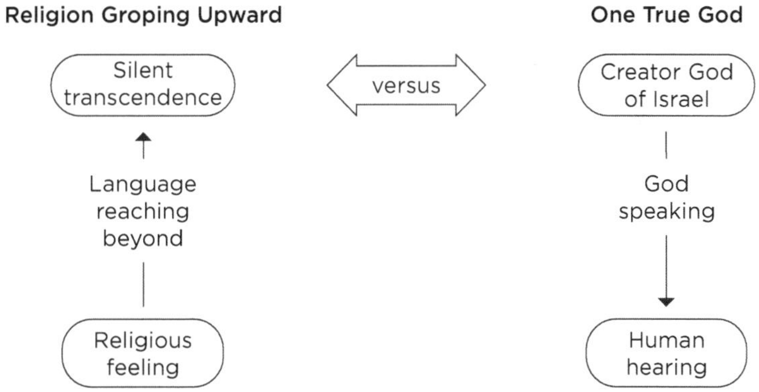

How We Understand Genesis 1

Believing in the God of the Bible also radically affects our understanding of Genesis 1. This God of the Bible can do as he pleases (Ps. 115:3).

---

2. Vern S. Poythress, *In the Beginning Was the Word: Language—A God-Centered Approach* (Wheaton, IL: Crossway, 2009).

It really is the case that, if he says "Let there be light," there is light (Gen. 1:3). Events can take place that are radically different from what we experience today if God is pleased to cause them.

The modern West tends to take the existing order of things as a fixed point. It approaches Genesis 1 within that kind of framework. And so, the thinking goes, Genesis 1, if it is to be more than fanciful fiction, must be primarily about this existing order. Therefore, it is some kind of vaguely poetic account concerning God's relation to that order. It is only a short step to conclude that Genesis 1 is theological *in contrast to* being about space-time events that happened once in a particular temporal order in the distant past. But if God is God, we cannot make assumptions merely on the basis of the present order of things, as if that were eternal. (To make the present order eternal is actually to begin to produce a substitute god in the form of a second eternity, the eternity of the present order.)

How We Understand God's Speech

The presence of God also affects how we understand God's speech. We cannot have an extended discussion of this point, but we can at least make a beginning.[3] The God of the Bible rules the world by speaking:

> By the *word* of the LORD the heavens were made,
>   and by the *breath* of his mouth all their host. (Ps. 33:6)

Scientists are made in the image of God, and they can think God's thoughts after him on a creaturely level. They can make their best guesses about the laws of the universe. But the real law, the law that actually governs the universe, is the speech of God.[4] It is personal speech, not an impersonal mechanism. God is so faithful to his own commitments that scientists can confidently make predictions. God's faithfulness is so consistent that it may seem to an unbelieving scientist that he is dealing merely with a mechanism. But that is an illusion, an illusion that is contradicted by miracles and will receive a yet greater refutation when Christ returns and God creates a new heaven and a new earth (Rev. 21:1).

---

3. See Vern S. Poythress, *Redeeming Science: A God-Centered Approach* (Wheaton, IL: Crossway, 2006).
4. Poythress, *Redeeming Science*, chap. 1.

How We Understand Modern Science

So there are two conceptions of science, not one. In the Christian conception, God rules the universe by his words of command:

> He sends out *his command* to the earth;
> *his word* runs swiftly.
> He gives snow like wool;
> he scatters frost like ashes. (Ps. 147:15–16)

According to the second conception, the "laws of nature" are just out there, as an impersonal something, like a mechanism. (See Fig. 2.4.)

Fig. 2.4: Two Conceptions of Scientific Law

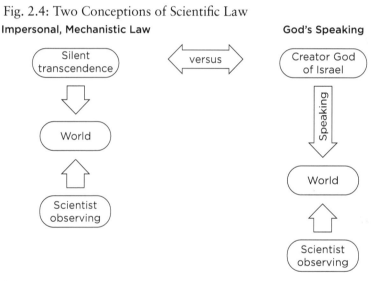

This second conception is *close* to the truth. God does maintain the world in a very regular way, according to his faithfulness. The result is that science is possible. In a great many ways, non-Christian, agnostic, and atheistic scientists can proceed with their work. They can give us solid insights. At the same time, this mechanistic view is a substitute for the truth about God's personal rule. It substitutes the impersonal for the personal. In this respect, it is a counterfeit. It is a substitute god.

Scientists constantly depend on God's faithfulness. They depend as well on their minds being made in the image of God, so that they have hope of understanding the speech by which he rules. At the same time, they produce in their minds a substitute, in the form of an impersonal conception of scientific law. At a fundamental level, this use of a substitute is just as idolatrous as the worship of the statues ancient people produced as representations of their gods.

So a good deal of modern science is simultaneously helpful and corrupt. It is helpful because it relies on the faithfulness of God and the regularity of his rule. It has a conception of law that is close to the truth. At the same time, it is corrupt because of the religious corruption present in the idea that law is impersonal. Therefore, we cannot naively trust it. We have to appreciate the positive contributions science makes due to common grace. At the same time, we have to understand the way in which it often lets religious corruption sneak in.

The interpretation of Genesis 1–3 goes together with numerous attempts in our day to relate Genesis 1–3 to modern science. There is nothing wrong with undertaking a dialogue. But near the beginning of the conversation, some of the attempts assume that science has "got it right"—not just that we have insights from science, but that science gives us the right answer all the time and in every respect. And there may also be the assumption that scientific endeavor is "religiously neutral," that it has no bias or corruption.

I have seen advertisements for meetings for dialogues between science and faith. Most of the time, it sounds as if these dialogues are arranged asymmetrically. The idea is that theologians and biblical scholars will talk to scientists and hear what the scientists have discovered. Then the theologians and biblical scholars will go home and assess how their former ideas need to be revised in the light of science. It is assumed that biblical scholars and theologians will change, while the scientists do not need to change. That is because, within their field of specialization, they supposedly already have it right.

There are things to be learned in this process. By common grace, scientists may discover beautiful things of great value. But how often do we find a conference where the theologians are permitted to talk about the question of whether modern science has been corrupted by an idolatrous distortion in the very concept of scientific law? Such discussion is less likely, because we—the Western world—feel secure in our modernity. The accusation is too outlandish.

My claim is that this sense of security is illusory. Apart from marginalized minority voices, the elites in the Western world have, without realizing it, rejected the very possibility that there could be a God such as the Bible describes. To accept that possibility would be too spiritually painful because it would require a reassessment of everything achieved in the West since the Enlightenment and a loss of the security in our "civilization."

But we actually are not talking about the mere possibility that this God exists. He does exist. All of Western civilization, to which I have alluded, is depending day by day on him (Acts 17:28). He is inescapably here, and we know that he is here. But we suppress this truth (Rom. 1:18) and tell ourselves stories to try to conceal our dependence. We cannot pursue here this whole line of reasoning, which would take a book to develop.[5] My point is that when we begin seriously to take God into account, it changes some important hermeneutical principles for interpreting Genesis 1–3. In fact, it changes every hermeneutical principle under the sun, because they are all affected by God's presence.[6]

Reading Genesis with God in Mind

Today we can read many interpretations of the book of Genesis, and even more interpretations focused on Genesis 1–3 or part of it. The interpretations do not agree. Should we be surprised? Not really. Genesis 1–3 does not contain enough information to answer completely all the questions that we may address to it. When we press into some questions in detail, we run into uncertainties. People may understandably disagree about matters that are intrinsically uncertain in our present state of knowledge.

In addition, interpretations do not take place in a vacuum. People already have commitments due to past training, as well as heart commitments. A person without a rich and complex past is like an infant, who has no ability to interpret any text. So, yes, interpreters come with a past. They are not necessarily slaves to their past, but they do have a past.

---

5. Poythress, *Redeeming Science*; subordinately, Vern S. Poythress, *Redeeming Sociology: A God-Centered Approach* (Wheaton, IL: Crossway, 2011).

6. Vern S. Poythress, *Reading the Word of God in the Presence of God: A Handbook for Biblical Interpretation* (Wheaton, IL: Crossway, 2016).

What is in this past for each potential interpreter of Genesis 1–3? Much is involved. Among those things in the past is the challenge of religious commitment. Does the interpreter believe in the God who is described in the Bible or not? If he does not, he has to have some substitute. After all, he has to depend on regularities that he did not invent, regularities in history, society, language, the natural world, and his own mental apparatus and memory. Without those things, he can do nothing; he cannot begin. So he does rely on those things. Does he hold to them as manifestations of the faithfulness of God and his sovereign sustaining power? Does he thank God for them? Or are they just there, as impersonal rules independent of God? And from whom has he learned? From all sorts of sources. But what commitments do those sources have to God or to counterfeit gods, that is, lying substitutes?

Many interpreters undertake to interpret without dwelling for long on the question of interpretive principles. That might seem to be a convenient strategy, because we have a natural eagerness to get on with discussing the text itself, Genesis 1–3. Moreover, the interpreters who bring to Genesis 1–3 different religious commitments may still offer positive insights by common grace. The impulse to proceed quickly is understandable. But if we go that way, we run the danger of not understanding why the interpretations sometimes differ widely. Some differences are minor ones concerning some detail. We may find that in our existing state of knowledge we cannot confidently draw conclusions concerning a minor difference. But, of course, with Genesis 1–3, the differences are sometimes major. Some interpreters, for example, think that Genesis 1–3 is not about events that actually happened long ago, in time and space, but only about a poetic or theological interpretation of the Israelites and their situation. So it pays to ask our interpreters, if we may, "What do you think about God?"

If you claim to believe in the God described in the Bible, have you thought through how radically different that belief is from the typical religious assumptions among the elite groups in our civilization? Have you thought through how that belief is going to recast every hermeneutical principle that you hold and carry into practice? Have you thought through the implications for how we view the ancient Near East, language, and modern scientific claims?

If you do not believe in the God described in the Bible, you have some substitute, and that affects your interpretation. There can be ten thousand substitutes, varying in their details. That means there can be ten thousand interpretations of Genesis 1–3. But in the end, it means nothing. Of course, if a person goes astray about such a fundamental reality as the meaning of the presence of God, his results down the line will show the influence of that fateful move. As usual, insights still arise by common grace in spite of bad religious commitments. Conversely, failures in insight can arise in spite of good religious commitments. We live in a world of mental struggle.

Some modern interpretations, including ones that discount any reference to actual events of long ago, claim to be Christian interpretations. It sounds nice to say that, but by itself it does not mean much, because the word *Christian* can be used very loosely. It is better to ask, "Do you believe in the God about whom Jesus Christ taught while he was on earth and about which he commissioned his apostles to speak?" On the fundamental issue of who God is, Jesus Christ claimed to know: "All things have been handed over to me by my Father, and no one knows the Son except the Father, and no one knows the Father except the Son and anyone to whom the Son chooses to reveal him" (Matt. 11:27). The Father about whom Jesus speaks is recognizably the same God who is described in the Old Testament. He works miracles; he cares for the tiniest things, like sparrows and hairs on the head (10:29–30); he determined beforehand the events of the crucifixion and the resurrection (Luke 22:22).

The issue of who God is will not go away, even if some biblical interpreters choose not to attend to it. It is crucial. There are not many alternatives for how we deal with the issue.

1. If a person thinks that Jesus is teaching us accurately, he must accept that God is the God that we have been describing, based on Scripture. And that leads to reconfiguring everything that he has inherited from modern Western culture. He can no longer interpret Genesis in the same way.

2. If a person thinks Jesus was mistaken in his view of God, his authority as a religious teacher is broken, and historic Christianity is destroyed.

3. A person could think that the Gospels give a mistaken impression as to what Jesus taught. But if the Gospels were mistaken on such a fundamental point, they would be essentially worthless in giving us access to the core of Jesus's religious teaching. So no one could really know what he thought about God, and his importance would be undermined.

4. Finally, if a person thinks that the whole Bible is just one more religious document, why bother with it, since it is so unacceptable to modern people, not merely at some peripheral point, but at the heart, in its teaching about God?

The way in which an interpreter responds to the question of God makes a particular difference in interpreting Genesis 1. This chapter is about the question in dispute. It shows the sovereignty of God over the world that he made. It does so not so much by directly *teaching* the doctrine of the sovereignty and presence of God, but by *showing* his sovereignty through its description of the particular events that took place by the command of God and according to his plan.[7] By its contents, it raises the same question: "Is God this kind of God or not?" If he is, we are obliged to interpret Genesis 1 itself, along with all the rest of the Bible, using hermeneutical principles in harmony with who God is. If, on the other hand, Genesis 1 is wrong about such a fundamental thing as its presentation of who God is, we should not expect it to be of outstanding religious value in other respects. It loses interest, except as an antiquarian record.

Of course, interpreters can still produce interpretations of Genesis 1 that offer other, alternative views of God himself. Once Genesis 1 is set in a context outside the Bible and outside the teaching of Jesus, many possible meanings can be ascribed to it. But why should we choose one meaning over others, except to please our own fancy?

So we might pose to ourselves a challenge similar to what Elijah gave in his time: "How long will you go limping between two differ-

---

7. On the difference between "showing" and "telling" in Hebrew narrative, see C. John Collins, *Genesis 1–4: A Linguistic, Literary, and Theological Commentary* (Phillipsburg, NJ: P&R, 2006), 11–12, citing other sources, including V. Philips Long, *The Reign and Rejection of King Saul: A Case for Literary and Theological Coherence* (Atlanta: Scholars Press, 1989), 31–34. See also C. John Collins, *Did Adam and Eve Really Exist? Who They Were and Why You Should Care* (Wheaton, IL: Crossway, 2011), 60–64, 164–65; C. John Collins, *Reading Genesis Well: Navigating History, Poetry, Science, and Truth in Genesis 1–11* (Grand Rapids, MI: Zondervan, 2018), 46–47. We will address this issue again in chap. 6.

ent opinions? If the LORD is God, follow him; but if Baal, then follow him" (1 Kings 18:21). The elite cultures in the modern West do not worship Baal, but they have their own alternatives. Choose! It is interesting that Elijah set up the two alternatives in the context of a test by miracle. "The God who answers by fire, he is God" (v. 24).

Fig. 2.5: Baal versus the God of Israel

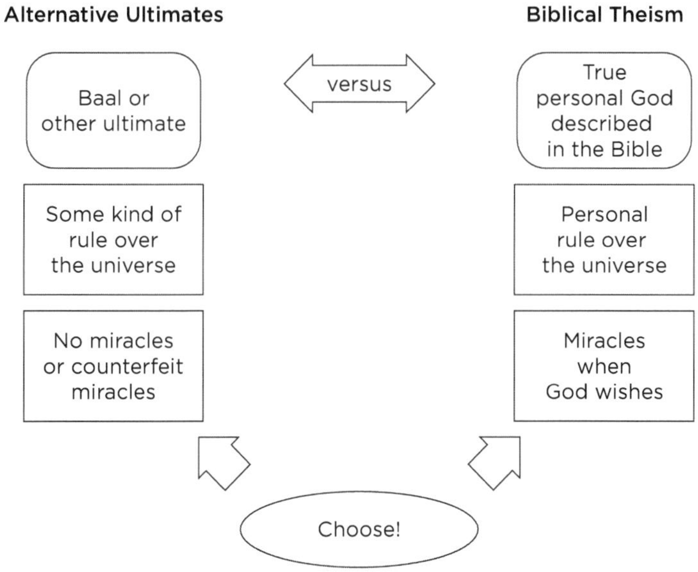

Alternative Ultimates   **Biblical Theism**

Baal or other ultimate	versus	True personal God described in the Bible
Some kind of rule over the universe		Personal rule over the universe
No miracles or counterfeit miracles		Miracles when God wishes

Choose!

The elite cultures of the modern West do not believe in this God. Thus, they do not believe in miracles either. So when they look at 1 Kings 18, they already have a definite interpretive strategy in place. They have taught themselves to see the narrative as an exaggerated tradition or legend rather than an actual account of a miracle. But in doing so, they are clearly cutting against the grain of the Bible itself. The Bible at this point makes the question of God hang on the reality of a miracle. So 1 Kings 18 confronts us with the same question about the existence and nature of God that we have already seen. The typical scholar immersed in Western culture simply evades the question. He assumes that he is right and that the Bible is wrong rather than letting the question engage his heart.

For my part, I am with Elijah. To the modern Western interpreter, I want to pose the same question that Elijah posed: "How long will you go limping between two different opinions?" And if you choose to follow Baal—or his modern analogue in the form of philosophical materialism, a mechanistic conception of scientific law, or a form of pantheism or postmodernism, to which might be added some source for ethical principles—you should just be done with the Bible as a religious authority. After all, you have decided that it is full of religious falsehood *at a fundamental level*. Do not fool yourself as well as others by treating it as if it were still a source of religious authority.[8] Yes, any of us could draw nice-sounding religious lessons from verses here and there. But we would be picking and choosing, and our real basis for authority in religion would be elsewhere.

But there is also Elijah's alternative. God, the God and Lord of Israel, exists, the same God as described in the Bible. That is the presupposition that we should have when we come to Genesis. But if that is true, we will go in a very different direction than many modern interpretations of Genesis—even some that claim to be "Christian."

Choosing this different direction does not guarantee that we will get everything right in our interpretation. All human knowledge is finite and subject to corruption by sin. Sincerity does not guarantee solidity in knowledge. It is worth reminding ourselves of these things. Therefore, I do not claim that what I say is a final answer to all questions, but a step along the way.

---

8. J. Gresham Machen made a similar point decades ago in *Christianity and Liberalism* (originally published, New York: Macmillan, 1923; new ed., Grand Rapids, MI: Eerdmans, 2009).

3

The Status of the Bible

One more question remains concerning fundamental hermeneutical commitments. It is the question of the status of the Bible itself. What is the Bible? What is the book of Genesis within it? Genesis is a literary corpus of words. But how does this literary corpus, this book, relate to the God about whom we have been speaking?

The Bible Is the Word of God

We can pursue a number of questions. Does the true God speak? Genesis 1:3 says that he does: "And God said, 'Let there be light,' and there was light." Does God speak to human beings? He does: "And the LORD God commanded the man, saying, 'You may surely eat of every tree of the garden, but of the tree of the knowledge of good and evil you shall not eat, for in the day that you eat of it you shall surely die'" (Gen. 2:16–17). Did God undertake, in the course of history, to begin to produce a permanent written record of his verbal communication to Israel? He did, in the form of the Ten Commandments: "And the LORD gave me the two tablets of stone written with the *finger* of God, and on them were all the words that the LORD had spoken with you on the mountain out of the midst of the fire on the day of the assembly" (Deut. 9:10; compare Ex. 31:18).

All of these texts and others in the Bible lead us into a consideration of the biblical teaching that the texts in the Bible are themselves the very Word of God, gathered according to the providence of God into a permanent canon. Here we have a cluster of important issues. If God exists and he speaks to us, it is important that we recognize that he is speaking and respond with all the submission that he deserves. The Bible's claim to be the Word of God is backed up by accompanying miracles, by prophecies that were given centuries before the events that they predicted, and also by the Bible's own attestation to itself. Furthermore, the Holy Spirit of God convicts people that they are hearing the Word of God.

But how can the Bible be the Word of God if it contains contradictions between Genesis 1 and 2, or between Genesis 1–3 and modern science, as some affirm? We will address these concerns later in the book. We may anticipate those parts of the book by saying that there are no contradictions, though there may be difficulties about which we as human beings do not yet have full answers.

We cannot here undertake a full defense of the divine inspiration of the Bible. I concur with the books, some centuries old and some more recent, that defend this point of view.[1] That will obviously make a difference in how we interpret Genesis as a whole and Genesis 1–3 in particular.

It is worth noting what Jesus says in Matthew 19:4–5:

> He answered, "Have you not read that *he who created them* from the beginning made them male and female, and *said*, 'Therefore a man shall leave his father and his mother and hold fast to his wife, and the two shall become one flesh'?"

Jesus cites Genesis 2:24. He indicates that it is what God said. Within the context of Genesis 2, verse 24 is simply one verse in the

---

1. This point of view can be found in Augustine (*The Harmony of the Evangelists*), in John Calvin, and in many ancient writers, as confirmed by John D. Woodbridge, *Biblical Authority: A Critique of the Rogers/McKim Proposal* (Grand Rapids, MI: Zondervan, 1982). More recent defenses include Archibald A. Hodge and Benjamin B. Warfield, *Inspiration*, with introduction by Roger R. Nicole (Grand Rapids, MI: Baker, 1979); Benjamin Breckinridge Warfield, *The Inspiration and Authority of the Bible*, ed. Samuel G. Craig (Philadelphia: Presbyterian and Reformed, 1967); N. B. Stonehouse and Paul Woolley, eds., *The Infallible Word: A Symposium by Members of the Faculty of Westminster Theological Seminary*, 3rd rev. printing (Philadelphia: Presbyterian and Reformed, 1967); D. A. Carson and John D. Woodbridge, eds., *Scripture and Truth* (Grand Rapids, MI: Baker, 1992); John M. Frame, *The Doctrine of the Word of God* (Phillipsburg, NJ: P&R, 2010); Kevin DeYoung, *Taking God At His Word: Why the Bible Is Knowable, Necessary, and Enough, and What That Means for You and Me* (Wheaton, IL: Crossway, 2014); Peter A. Lillback and Richard B. Gaffin, Jr., eds., *Thy Word Is Still Truth: Essential Writings on the Doctrine of Scripture from the Reformation to Today* (Philadelphia: Westminster Seminary Press; Phillipsburg, NJ: P&R, 2013). See also Vern S. Poythress, *Inerrancy and Worldview: Answering Modern Challenges to the Bible* (Wheaton, IL: Crossway, 2012).

narrative. So by implication, Jesus is saying that the whole of Genesis is what God said. In this and in other ways, Jesus confirms that the Old Testament is the Word of God.[2]

What about Transmission and Sources?

The books of the Bible have been transmitted by copying over a period of centuries.[3] The process of transmission makes a fascinating study. Transmission has an obvious role to play in our interpretation of the Bible, because it allows us to access the message of the original through examining the copies.

But what about the sources *behind* the texts in the Bible, sources that various authors of the books of the Bible may have used? Some of the biblical books show that their authors were aware of earlier sources (e.g., Luke 1:1; 2 Sam. 1:18; 1 Kings 11:41). Among biblical scholars, one popular point of view with respect to Genesis and the other books of the Pentateuch is the "documentary hypothesis." This hypothesis has several forms, with differences in detail. But the most well known, since the nineteenth century, says that there are four main sources behind the Pentateuch, typically labeled J, E, D, and P. These four sources have differing dates, and differing and allegedly sometimes contradictory content. Many books defend this point of view, and many books criticize it.[4] My own opinion is that it is not sound. But we cannot pursue all the details here. Those who hold to JEDP, and also some who hold to other theories about sources, often interpret Genesis 1–3 by interpreting the sources behind the text we now have. In particular, the documentary hypothesis alleges that Genesis 1–2 contains two distinct creation narratives, Genesis 1:1–2:4a and 2:4b–25, deriving from the P source and the J source respectively, and that these two do not agree.

Contrary to this approach, sources make little *direct* contribution to our understanding of the meaning of the autographic text. Even in a text that has only a human author, the author may choose to mean

---

2. See especially John Murray, "The Attestation of Scripture," in *The Infallible Word*, 1–42.

3. For a short discussion of transmission from the time of the autographs, see John H. Skilton, "The Transmission of the Scriptures," in *The Infallible Word*, 141–95.

4. For example, T. D. Alexander, *From Paradise to Promised Land: An Introduction to the Pentateuch*, 2nd ed. (Grand Rapids, MI: Baker, 2002), 3–82. One of the marks against JEDP is that the theory has internal problems, and many scholars can see that it is not as plausible as it appeared to be in the nineteenth century.

something different from the sources that he uses. We must attend to what the author says and what he means by it, not to his sources. (See Fig. 3.1.)

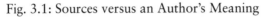

Fig. 3.1: Sources versus an Author's Meaning

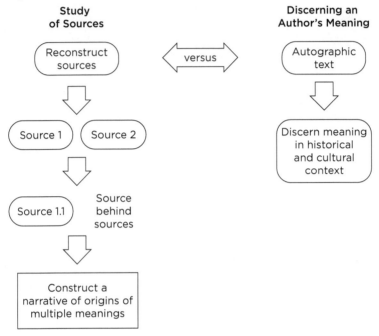

The problem with sources is, of course, compounded by the fact that for the books of the Bible, we do not have confident knowledge about the sources. We may make an exception in the case of 1–2 Chronicles. It seems clear that the human author of 1–2 Chronicles used 1–2 Samuel and 1–2 Kings. But he also may have used other sources that we do not have now (1 Chron. 9:1; 2 Chron. 24:27). Luke may have used the Gospel of Mark. This is the majority opinion, but it too is disputed. With respect to other books of the Bible, we have even less confidence about sources because those possible sources are no longer with us. Trying to reconstruct sources in such circumstances is guesswork. We do not know when we may have succeeded. And even if we do succeed, we still have the difficulty that the writer of the book we have before us might mean something different from the source. His meaning might be subtly different or radically different.

Such is particularly true with respect to most reconstructions at-tempted by the historical-critical approach to the Bible. When it is alleged that a source behind the Bible had a different theology or a different picture of the history of a particular episode, are we going to say that this different (and nonavailable) view overrides the text that we have? My answer is no. Some texts, namely, the texts of the canon, have divine authority. Other texts or oral traditions do not.

When we undertake to interpret Genesis, we shall therefore inter-pret Genesis, not its putative sources. In particular, we will interpret Genesis 1–3 as a continuous literary whole, not, as is alleged, as a composite document that must be decomposed into two contradictory creation accounts in Genesis 1 and 2.

A similar principle holds with respect to alleged parallels be-tween Genesis and texts and customs in the ancient Near East. When God speaks or writes, he does so as one who is absolute mas-ter of language. He is also master of the environment, linguistic, historical, and cultural, into which he sends his word. All interpre-tation should therefore take into account who he is, as master of context. We take into account context because he himself has taken it into account.[5] Taking into account contexts is very different from *leveling* all pieces of language and culture into one homogeneous whole, so that the verbal communication in the Bible cannot mean anything different from the surrounding instances of communica-tion and the surrounding cultures. Even human speakers can have new ideas and speak new thoughts. They are, after all, made in the image of God. How much more can God speak beyond the bounds of what has been said previously in human discourses. We must allow, therefore, that God speaks in a way that meshes with the surrounding context, and also that he can say what he wishes to say, distinct from the context.

A Summary

In short, in interpreting Genesis 1–3, we should take into account that Genesis is the very speech of God. That implies also that we should focus on what it says, rather than on possible sources, in order to receive sound instruction.

---

5. See Poythress, *Inerrancy and Worldview*, especially chap. 11.

4

Interacting with Scientific Claims

How do we handle the relation of the early chapters of Genesis to modern scientific claims? A number of interpreters have pointed out that claims from sciences can serve as an occasion for reexamining whether we have interpreted the Bible accurately. But that is quite different from saying that we put the Bible and sciences side by side as "equal authorities."[1] How do we deal with the authority of the Bible in relation to the authority claimed for modern scientific pronouncements?

Scientific Claims as Occasions for Reexamining Interpretation

The history of Copernican theory is more complex than usually realized, but it can still serve as a hypothetical example. Copernican theory says that the earth rotates and travels around the sun. So is this theory in tension with biblical passages that speak of the earth as not moved (Ps. 93:1; 96:10; 104:5)?[2] A reexamination of the biblical passages may conclude that they are not propounding an astronomical theory, but are making poetic statements tied to ordinary human observation. The earth is stable from the standpoint of the people who stand on it.

In this scenario, Copernican theory has stimulated people to ask fresh questions about the Bible. But if all goes well, the resulting

---

1. For helpful discussion, see James N. Anderson, "Can We Trust the Bible over Evolutionary Science?" *Reformed Faith & Practice* 1, no. 3 (December 2016): 6–23, http://journal.rts.edu/article /can-we-trust-the-bible-over-evolutionary-science/.
2. See also my discussion of Copernican theory in chap. 5.

answer about the meaning of the passages is one that could have been seen by asking questions *even with no knowledge of Copernican theory*. The real turning point in interpretive understanding comes not from Nicolaus Copernicus but from observing the kind of text and genre that we have in the Psalms. The Psalms are poetic songs. And they are addressing ordinary people, not technical specialists in astronomy. The focus is on admiring God and trusting him for his faithfulness, as illustrated by the stability of the earth beneath.

We could put it another way. The world that God created is rich, with many aspects to it. Technical scientific theories can be wonderful in their own way, but they are only one way, or several ways, out of a multitude of ways to explain the world. Ordinary human experience still has a role in helping us understand the world, and still gives us one aspect of reality.[3] So encounter with Copernican theory or some other scientific theory that *appears* to conflict with the Bible can legitimately be an occasion for growing in our understanding of the *kind* of communication and reality on which biblical communication focuses.

Scientific Claims as Trump Cards

But we have a different kind of interaction between the Bible and science if we treat them as equal authorities. And realistically, such is a temptation in our time. The prestige of science and admiration for scientific achievements has had such an influence that, for many people, scientific claims have become a trump card that exceeds all other authorities. If the Bible appears to disagree, so much the worse for the Bible. (See Fig. 4.1.)

And if someone nevertheless feels that he must continue to attribute some kind of authority to the Bible, he must do whatever it takes to make the Bible's affirmations fit in with the claims of scientists. So he must cast about to find some interpretation that will head off the conflict. Perhaps the offending individual verses will be reinterpreted. Or perhaps the reinterpretation will be more global: a person will propose that the Bible is about who and why,

---

3. Vern S. Poythress, *Redeeming Science: A God-Centered Approach* (Wheaton, IL: Crossway, 2006), chap. 16.

while science is about how, and so the two sources can never actually disagree.[4]

Fig. 4.1: Science as a Trump Card

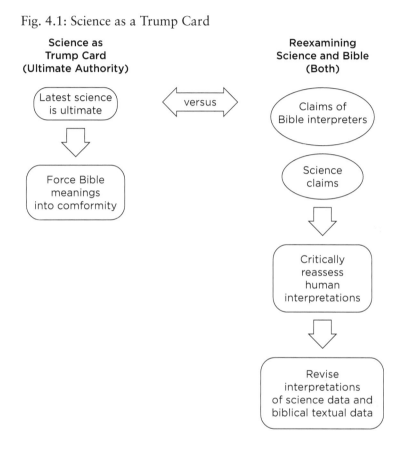

But several things are wrong with this scenario. First, in such a situation, there is enormous pressure on the person to distort interpretation in the direction of harmonization with scientific claims. Genuine biblical authority is in fact being dissolved.

Second, scientific claims are not sacrosanct. Scientists, after all, are human. Scientific investigation is a complex, many-dimensional affair, and there are many ways in which it is subject to lapses, even when conducted by people of sincere good will.[5] Scientific theories that once

---

4. Though there is a grain of truth here, I discuss and reject this formula in Poythress, *Redeeming Science*, 107–8.

5. We may cite Thomas S. Kuhn, *The Structure of Scientific Revolutions* (Chicago: University of Chicago Press, 1970) as a key influential work focusing on some of the human and social

appeared to be well established and permanent have been replaced. A prominent example can be found in the transition from nineteenth- to twentieth-century physics. In the nineteenth century, following the lead of earlier work going back to Isaac Newton, most physicists felt that the nature of space, time, and motion under the influence of physical forces was well understood. They had developed a picture of absolute space and time in which physical objects moved. This picture appeared to be irreplaceable. And yet it was replaced, not by one but by two different twentieth-century developments—the theory of relativity and quantum mechanics.

Practical achievements in technology make the average person feel that science must be fairly secure because it is successful. But success depends more on some theories than on others. And like nineteenth-century physics, a theory can be "successful" in practical terms even when it needs replacement.

Moreover, the conduct of science has a social and even a political dimension. We might like it to be otherwise, but ambitious people can put their own pride and glory above the search for truth and the practice of fairness. There can be backstabbing and manipulation behind the scenes. Scientific consensus can sometimes be the product of group thinking.

Third, scientific work can be corrupted by idolatry. And in our day, it is. I mentioned earlier the difference between (1) understanding the laws of the universe as the speech of God, who is personal, and (2) understanding laws as impersonal, as mechanistic. The second conception is an idolatrous corruption of the first. We need to be aware of that difference and to reckon with the potential for that difference to propagate into the work of scientists and to influence the larger directions of scientific investigation.

Let us also observe that in our day, quite a bit of Western intellectual discourse supposes that the progress of science supports philosophical materialism, that is, the view that the world is nothing but matter, energy, and motion. (Some forms of materialism deny the reality of human consciousness, free will, moral standards, and beauty. Others, more circumspectly, say only that these latter are extra layers

---

dimensions of the conduct of science. Much literature has subsequently grown up around Kuhn's work, in critique, in affirmation, and in modification.

that somehow have spontaneously arisen from matter, energy, and motion alone.) Philosophical materialism has an influence on scientists' conception of what they are doing, and what sorts of questions, procedures, and hypotheses are appropriate. So scientific investigation is not in fact conducted in a neutral arena, untouched by philosophical convictions and commitments. Such influences are seldom noted or overtly discussed in the technical work of practicing scientists because they are understandably hastening onward to do the detailed work that they love. But the influences can still be there, as an overall atmosphere.

In fact, these observations hold with special force with respect to neo-Darwinism as a totalizing framework for biology. Neo-Darwinism has considerable difficulty in dealing with evidence for enormous complexity in living cells and for the stability of basic biological "types." For instance, when people breed dogs, they get dogs and never cats. When they artificially produce mutations in a genus of fruit flies (genus Drosophila), they may get a lot of dead flies, but they never arrive at anything except more of the same genus of flies.[6]

But there is no alternative theory in sight that is compatible with philosophical materialism. Even apart from strict materialism, if a theorist believes that the laws of the universe are impersonal and mechanical, allowing for no exceptions, and no presence and interference from a divine power, there is essentially no alternative to the story that life derived by gradual steps from previous life. So the theorist assumes that some form of such a story *must* be true, whether or not evidence currently supports it.

We need to ask hard questions. How far is neo-Darwinism actually supported by evidence, and what sort of evidence? What evidence is available that is actually difficult to integrate into the theory? How far is the theory maintained because of philosophical commitments to an impersonal conception of law or to materialism, or because of the lack of an equally materialistic alternative theory?[7]

---

6. See, for example, Michael Denton, *Evolution: Still A Theory in Crisis* (Seattle: Discovery Institute, 2016).

7. I am thinking particularly of work done by advocates of intelligent design, such as Michael J. Behe, *The Edge of Evolution: The Search for the Limits of Darwinism* (New York: Free Press, 2007); Stephen C. Meyer, *Signature in the Cell: DNA and the Evidence for Intelligent Design* (New York: HarperOne, 2009); Meyer, *Darwin's Doubt: The Explosive Origin of Animal*

The Bible and Science in Relation to Each Other

In addition to these difficulties, it is fairly easy to see that the Bible and scientific claims do not belong on the same level. Our human interpretation of the Bible is fallible. And our interpretation of scientific data is fallible. So apparent tensions can always be an occasion to reassess both (not just our interpretation of the Bible!). But the Bible is the Word of God, and it has been given to us with verbal structure and verbal meanings that make specific claims.

We can contrast the verbal character of the Bible with the situation that scientists examine. The world that God has given us is ruled by his governing word of power. But apart from a few exceptions, such as Genesis 1:3, we do not have those words of his in verbally explicit form. Scientists make guesses about the laws, that is, about the words of God governing the world. But their guesses are not identical with the Word of God. So it is a mistake to see scientific claims as infallible, but it is not a mistake to see the Bible's discourses as infallible. (See Fig. 4.2.)

It is also the case that, according to the Bible, God speaks to us through the revelation in the Bible precisely for the purpose of giving us the message of salvation, reconciling us to himself, and setting us on the path of obedience to his commands. It has a central role in the remedy for sin. Since sin contaminates everything, including the life of the mind, the Bible is a necessary help in cleansing our minds.

More could be said about the process of interaction between interpreting the Bible and interpreting scientific data, and readers may wish to pursue the question in fuller discussions elsewhere.[8] For our purposes, we must let this summary suffice.

Our purpose in the rest of the book is not mainly to interact in detail with scientific claims about the past. Other books do that. It is to look at interpretive issues that affect how we see the meaning of Genesis in relation to scientific claims. When we do that, we will see that it brings us closer to answers concerning the relation of the Bible to scientific claims.

Life and the Case for Intelligent Design (New York: HarperOne, 2013); and J. P. Moreland et al., eds., *Theistic Evolution: A Scientific, Philosophical, and Theological Critique* (Wheaton, IL: Crossway, 2017).

8. Poythress, *Redeeming Science*, chaps. 2–3.

Fig. 4.2: Interpreting Scientific Claims and the Bible

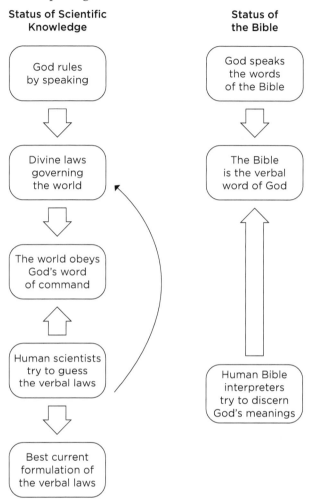

A Summary

In sum, the Bible and science do not have equal roles. Each functions as a source of instruction. But the Bible has primacy for two reasons. First, it is God's verbal discourse, while science is a fallible human account of what human beings think are natural laws. Second, God uniquely designed the Bible to give us guidance. He gives guidance primarily concerning how we can have our guilt removed and be reconciled to him. But then, as a fruit of that reconciliation, he gives us guidance that transforms our thinking about all of life.

5

Three Modern Myths in Interpreting Genesis 1

We may continue to examine the influence of modern frameworks of assumptions on interpretation. In this chapter, our purpose is to develop a sound approach for assessing how information from the broader environment of the ancient Near East should influence our interpretation of Genesis. To do so, we will look critically at modern ideas about what kind of world we live in and how we should understand distant cultures such as those of the ancient Near East. Assumptions about such issues affect the interpretation of Genesis 1–3, but especially Genesis 1.[1]

Three modern myths often interfere with understanding Genesis 1. I propose to uncover these myths in order to remove obstacles to understanding Genesis 1.

Rather than beginning with the myths immediately, let us first consider one strand in contemporary interpretation of Genesis 1. This approach begins by reading Genesis 1 within its ancient Near Eastern context. It compares and contrasts Genesis 1 with ancient Near Eastern myths. By so doing, it endeavors to show that many modern readers misread Genesis 1. They read with scientific assumptions and questions in mind, and they may easily project onto Genesis 1 detailed scientific information that is

---

1. Apart from the introductory paragraph, this chapter is a revision of Vern S. Poythress, "Three Modern Myths in Interpreting Genesis 1," *Westminster Theological Journal* 76, no. 2 (2014): 321–50. Used with permission.

not there. Depending on what they read in, they may find that Genesis 1 does or does not agree with modern science. But the whole procedure is mistaken, because it involves misinterpretation. Readers should not seek for scientific teaching in Genesis 1, but treat it for what it is, a document that comes from another culture than our own.

The Idea of Outmoded Cosmology

There is much to be said in favor of this kind of approach because the interference of modern assumptions generates misunderstanding among both defenders and critics of Genesis 1. Yet for our long-run spiritual health, a great deal depends on just *how* the interpretive task is accomplished. It is not always accomplished well. Some books and articles tell us that Genesis 1 naturally and understandably contains outmoded and erroneous cosmological notions common to the ancient Near East because it was written within that cultural milieu. For instance, scholars may say that Genesis 1:6–8 refers to a solid dome of sky ("the expanse") and a heavenly sea held in by the dome ("the waters that were above the expanse").[2]

Such claims have been around for more than a century among liberal scholars, but now they are cropping up in some broadly evangelical circles as well. People who think that erroneous cosmological ideas occur in the Bible might still say that they want to affirm the divine authority of the Bible. For instance, they might say that Genesis 1 contains erroneous cosmology without any compromise to its divine authority because the authorial intent is to teach theology, not science or ancient cosmology. Here is their thinking:

> The cosmological trappings are only the vehicle, while the "cargo" that the vehicle carries consists in the theological content of the passage. More specifically, the cargo of Genesis 1 consists in the theological affirmation that God is the only God and the unique Creator. The cargo is what the passage intends to teach theologically. The vehicle is the culturally conditioned, limited, erroneous

---

2. The idea of a solid dome holding in a heavenly sea appears in numerous places in Old Testament scholarly literature, such as T. H. Gaster, "Cosmogony," in *Interpreter's Dictionary of the Bible*, ed. George Arthur Buttrick (New York: Abingdon, 1962), 1.703, 704, and has made its way into lexicons, such as Francis Brown, S. R. Driver, and Charles A. Briggs, *A Hebrew and English Lexicon of the Old Testament* (Oxford: Oxford University Press, 1953), 956, רָקִיעַ sense 2. For a better approach, see C. John Collins, *Genesis 1–4: A Linguistic, Literary, and Theological Commentary* (Phillipsburg, NJ: P&R, 2006), 45–46, and the sequel chapters to this one.

cosmology that finds expression in Genesis 1. The vehicle is in service for the sake of delivering the cargo. But the vehicle is not what the passage intends to teach.

Consequently, according to this approach, Genesis 1 contains no errors in its *teaching*. In fact, its teaching harmonizes well with modern science, because when rightly understood, Genesis 1 is not teaching anything directly *about* science or anything that *could* contradict science. For convenience, I will call this kind of approach the *vehicle-cargo approach*. How people construe the distinction between the cargo (the core teaching) and the vehicle leads to important debates, which we cannot pursue here.[3]

Fig. 5.1: Vehicle-Cargo Approach versus Classical Understanding of the Bible

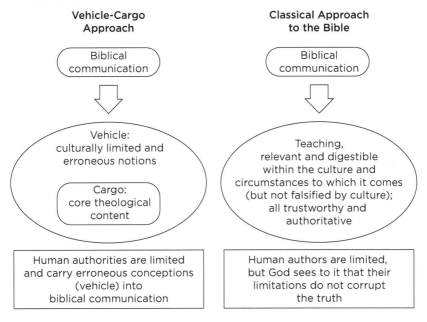

The vehicle-cargo approach can say that God "accommodates" himself to the erroneous views of ancient addressees and allows

3. See Noel Weeks, "Cosmology in Historical Context," *Westminster Theological Journal* 68, no. 2 (2006): 283–93; Weeks, "The Ambiguity of Biblical 'Background,'" *Westminster Theological Journal* 72, no. 2 (2010): 219–36; Vern S. Poythress, "Problems for Limited Inerrancy," *Journal of the Evangelical Theological Society* 18, no. 2 (1975): 93–102.

such views to find a place in the Bible. But we must be careful. The word *accommodation* has several usages. Several kinds of "accommodation" have occurred through the history of the church. In the ancient church, the classical doctrine of accommodation said that Scripture spoke in a way that took into account finite human capacities. But it maintained that Scripture did *not* "accommodate" error. By contrast, a more recent concept of accommodation, associated with biblical criticism, allows for the inclusion of error, and that is the decisive difference.[4] In addition to these usages, interpreters have sometimes spoken of progressive revelation as a form of accommodation, since the revelation given at earlier times is suitable for or "accommodated" to the earlier redemptive-historical epoch and the capacity of people at that time.[5] The word *accommodation* could also be applied to God's redemptive acts in distinction from his speech: God's fatherly care takes into account the weaknesses of his people.[6]

We meet still further complexities about accommodation because in the last few decades, some writers have interpreted statements from Martin Luther, John Calvin, and earlier figures as though these statements used a vehicle-cargo distinction (or something like it). I do not agree with these interpretations, but it is not my purpose here to engage in a complicated historical discussion.[7] Even if, for the sake of argument, we were to suppose that a vehicle-cargo approach appears in premodern interpretations in orthodox circles, it would only mean that we need to inspect carefully the older ideas along with the newer ones.

As I have said, a number of modern writings use a hermeneutical distinction between vehicle and cargo (without using these specific labels). These writings are not all the same. It is unfair to lump them all together. But to treat each one individually would go far beyond the scope of this chapter. And more writings of a

---

4. See Richard A. Muller, *Dictionary of Latin and Greek Theological Terms: Drawn Principally from Protestant Scholastic Theology* (Grand Rapids, MI: Baker, 1985), 19.

5. L. M. Sweet and G. W. Bromiley, "Accommodation," in *The International Standard Bible Encyclopedia* (Grand Rapids, MI: Eerdmans, 1979), 1.25.

6. Jon Balserak, "The God of Love and Weakness: Towards an Understanding of God's Accommodating Relationship with His People," *Westminster Theological Journal* 62, no. 2 (2000): 177–95.

7. See, for example, the critique in Vern S. Poythress, "A Misunderstanding of Calvin's Interpretation of Genesis 1:6–8 and 1:5 and Its Implications for Ideas of Accommodation," *Westminster Theological Journal* 76, no. 1 (2014): 157–66, reproduced in Appendix C, p. 341.

similar kind continue to appear. Consequently, I do not want to single out any particular one. My point is that there seem to be common patterns. Among these patterns is the idea that Genesis 1 includes pieces of erroneous ancient cosmology.[8] For convenience, I will address only this one idea, for which I will use the label "the vehicle-cargo approach"—though this label does not do justice to the variations.

For my limited purpose, I propose to focus on three traps into which a vehicle-cargo approach may fall. All three traps have to do with the challenges in understanding documents from other cultures. When we try to bridge cultures, one of the greatest hindrances lies in the hidden assumptions that we carry with us from our native cultures. The vehicle-cargo approach sees well enough that many people are falling into traps due to the influence of modern science when they read Genesis 1. Unfortunately, and somewhat paradoxically, the vehicle-cargo approach may fall into traps of its own due to the presence of at least three modern myths.

But as we proceed in the analysis, we must be careful and charitable. I am not saying that everyone who adopts a vehicle-cargo approach falls prey to the myths. I want only to show that readers of Genesis 1 and readers of the modern writings need to guard against the myths in order to head off misunderstandings.

The Myth of Scientistic Metaphysics

The first myth concerns the ways in which the knowledge from modern science surpasses the knowledge of the ancient world and tribal cultures that have no contact with modern civilization.

The stock example of this improvement in knowledge has to do with the sun. It goes like this:

The ancient world thought that the earth did not move and that the sun, moon, and stars moved around it. Nicolaus Copernicus

---

8. As a sample, we may mention Peter Enns, *Inspiration & Incarnation: Evangelicals and the Problem of the Old Testament* (Grand Rapids, MI: Baker, 2005), 25–27, 49–56; Kenton Sparks, *God's Word in Human Words: An Evangelical Appropriation of Critical Biblical Scholarship* (Grand Rapids, MI: Baker, 2008), 231–36; Denis O. Lamoureux, *I Love Jesus & I Accept Evolution* (Eugene, OR: Wipf & Stock, 2009), 46–70; John H. Walton, *The Lost World of Genesis One: Ancient Cosmology and the Origins Debate* (Downers Grove, IL: InterVarsity Press, 2009), 55–57; Walton, *Genesis 1 as Ancient Cosmology* (Winona Lake, IN: Eisenbrauns, 2011), 155–61.

showed that the sun did not move and that the earth rotated and moved around the sun. Ever since, we have known that the ancients were wrong. The sun does not rise; rather, the earth rotates. Consequently, the Bible contains demonstrable errors in cosmology. Jesus himself talks about the sun rising (Matt. 5:45). He does not correct the erroneous cosmology, but uses it as a vehicle to express spiritual truth. The doctrinal teaching concerning God's love and mercy is true; the statement about the sun is false, but it is not part of the teaching. This is no error in the teaching, because Jesus does not intend to teach us that the sun rises.

For a long time, some interpreters approached the issue about the sun in a different way. They contented themselves with the principle that the Bible describes things as they *appear*. Calvin speaks this way in discussing Genesis 1:

> For, to my mind, this is a certain principle, that nothing is here [in Genesis 1] treated of but the *visible form* of the world. . . .
>
> It must be remembered, that Moses does not speak with philo-sophical acuteness on occult mysteries, but relates those things which are everywhere *observed*, even by the uncultivated, and which are in common use. . . .
>
> Moses makes two great luminaries [sun and moon]; but astronomers prove, by conclusive reasons, that the star [i.e., planet] of Saturn, which, on account of its great distance, ap-pears the least of all, is greater than the moon. Here lies the difference; Moses wrote in a popular style things which, with-out instruction, all ordinary persons, endued with common sense, are able to understand; but astronomers investigate with great labour whatever the sagacity of the human mind can com-prehend. . . . If the astronomer inquires respecting the actual dimensions of the stars, he will find the moon to be less than Saturn; but this is something abstruse, for *to the sight it ap-pears* differently. Moses, therefore, rather adapts his discourse to common usage.[9]

---

9. John Calvin, *Commentaries on the First Book of Moses Called Genesis* (Grand Rapids, MI: Baker, 1979), 1.79 [on Gen. 1:6], 1.84 [on Gen. 1:14], 1.86–87 [on Gen. 1:16] (emphasis added). For Calvin on Genesis 1:6, see Poythress, "Misunderstanding," found in Appendix C in the present book, p. 341.

Bernard Ramm, writing in 1954, includes a discussion of *phenomenal language*, that is, language describing how things appear to ordinary human observation.[10] The Bible characteristically uses phenomenal language. Once we recognize it, many of the elementary problems dissolve.

But this approach does not seem to please everyone today. People continue to bring up the topic of the sun. They are clearly not satisfied with the well-known appeal to phenomenal language. Why not?

The issue of the sun's rising comes up not because it is so bothersome in itself, but because it is thought to illustrate the way our interpretations of the Bible must be adjusted more widely. That is, more is at stake. What more? The vehicle-cargo approach claims that the Bible contains erroneous cosmology, not merely phenomenal language.[11]

Accordingly, the vehicle-cargo approach may press the point that the church was wrong about Copernicus, and that even the language in Scripture about the sun rising and the earth not moving (Pss. 93:1; 96:10) is erroneous. It does so in order that we may reassess the actual character of Scripture. As a result of the reassessment, we will no longer bring Scripture into conflict with modern science. (And, in addition to science, some advocates of the vehicle-cargo approach want to extend their principles to other areas of potential conflict, such as history or ethics.)

This route of harmonization is understandable, but it depends on a myth with regard to Copernicus, a myth propagated by the popularization of science in modern culture. The myth has several distinct elements, not all of which are always present. The first and least

---

10. Bernard Ramm, *The Christian View of Science and Scripture* (Grand Rapids, MI: Eerdmans, 1954), 67–68, quoting from John H. Pratt, *Scripture and Science Not at Variance*, 7th ed. (London: Hatchards, 1872), 24–29, with various reprints. See also Collins, *Genesis 1–4*, 46n23, 264–65.

Almost all of the events described in Genesis 1 took place before any human being existed to observe them. But Genesis 1 as a written description is addressed to human beings, including those without contact with modern science. Quite appropriately, it describes the events in a manner pertinent to what would have been observable by a human being, and in a manner analogous to present providential events that are regularly observed ("phenomena"). Calvin's discussion of Genesis 1 understands this point. In a similar manner, Job 38:27 describes grass sprouting "where no man is." No human being observes this grass. But it is easy for a human reader to understand what is happening. The grass is really there in various desert places. A human being knows what it *would* be like to see the grass (phenomenally). A later chapter in this book picks up on this positive aspect in the descriptions of Genesis 1.

11. For points complementary to mine, see C. John Collins, *Reading Genesis Well: Navigating History, Poetry, Science, and Truth in Genesis 1–11* (Grand Rapids, MI: Zondervan, 2018), chap. 9.

important element concerns the story of Copernicus himself.[12] Sometimes people have the impression that Copernicus *demonstrated* that the earth moved. Actually, he knew that it could not be easily demonstrated, because both the earlier Ptolemaic mathematical model and Copernicus's own sun-centered model could account for the main astronomical observations. Allowing for some margin of error, both models made the same predictions about the positions of the sun, moon, and planets in the sky. Copernicus's model had the virtue of greater simplicity.[13]

A second mythic element says that the sun does not move. But according to Isaac Newton's theory of gravitation (which came later than Copernicus), it does move in one obvious sense. The sun and Jupiter both move in orbits around their common center of gravity. Because the sun is more massive, the movements of the sun are much smaller, but still significant.

The third mythic element is more subtle. It lies in the popular assumption that the language about motion is unambiguous. Either the sun moves or it does not. But the assumption breaks down immediately when we ask, "Moves with respect to what?" From a suitably chosen observational standpoint in a neighboring galaxy, it could be seen that the sun is moving in a huge orbit around the center of the Milky Way Galaxy. From the standpoint of the sun itself, it is not moving at all, but that is trivial. Likewise, from the standpoint of the earth, the earth is not moving. Scientists who work in pertinent specialized areas know all this very well, but it is not part of the popularized view concerning the sun and the earth. My point is partly to make plain the flawed character of popularized knowledge of science.

The fourth mythic element involves the assumption that one observational standpoint is the original or right one. Albert Einstein's general theory of relativity places observers in accelerated systems on the same mathematical level with all other observers. An observer standing still on earth is one such observer. From the point of view

---

12. We cannot enter into the details of the history (see Thomas S. Kuhn, *The Copernican Revolution: Planetary Astronomy in the Development of Western Thought* [Cambridge: Harvard University Press, 1992]) or the mistaken reactions to Copernicus on the part of some theologians and philosophers of the day. Our discussion of myth is in part relevant to them as well.

13. There was also a third model, by Tycho Brahe, according to which the moon and sun revolved around the earth while the other planets revolved around the sun.

of this scientific theory, the statement that the earth is moving is not intrinsically better than the statement that it is not. Both statements are ambiguous until we specify the observational standpoint. Either statement may be true, depending on what observational standpoint we specify. Equations of transformation allow us to move from one standpoint to the other.[14]

Once we recognize the mythic character of elements three and four, the modern critique of the rising of the sun threatens to disintegrate. The problem is with modern myth, not with the Bible or the ancient Near East.

The vehicle-cargo approach might undertake a repair job by insisting that the problem with the ancient Near East is that the people thought that the sun *really* rose, not just that it *appeared* to rise. They thought this because they did not have our modern sophistication about observational standpoints.[15] To this attempted repair the simplest reply might be, "Perhaps they thought as they did because it was true. Given their observational standpoint, the sun did rise (and still does)." The vehicle-cargo approach appeals to the contrast between "reality" and mere "appearance." This appeal illustrates that the modern approach has still not grasped that it is caught in a myth. It speaks as if we could settle what "really" is the case. But we could do that only if we eliminated what it thinks is the unenlightened observational standpoint of the ancient observer. However, as the theory of relativity has made amply evident, to eliminate the observational standpoint is to eliminate the very ability to talk coherently about motion and rest.

So we may let the vehicle-cargo approach try again. "What I mean," the advocate might say, "is that the ancient people carried along a raft of assumptions about the cosmos, and that we now know that those assumptions were wrong. For instance, they thought that the earth was at the center in an absolute sense." Well, perhaps they did. And perhaps they did not. Might it just be the case that the average Israelite did not worry about complicated physical and

14. Readers for whom these ideas are new may receive a clear introductory explanation from the originator: Albert Einstein, *Relativity: The Special and General Theory* (New York: Henry Holt, 1920).

15. Actually, it was quite easy for an ordinary ancient observer to see that the world looks different from inside a house or a tent than from outside, and different from the top of a hill than from the bottom of a valley.

mathematical systems for describing motions of the heavenly bodies? Maybe he just thought that the sun rose, because it did (given his standpoint). Maybe he also thought that it rose because God made it rise, as Jesus says (Matt 5:45).[16] He could have had those thoughts without having any scientific theory at all. He just described what he saw, and knew that God brought it about. *How* God brought it about, and what later scientific theories might say about the underlying mathematical system for the solar system, were simply outside the range of his concerns.

It is possible that, accustomed as we are to having a huge framework of popularized science in the back of our minds (including mythic elements generated in the process of popularization), we project such a science-like interest onto ordinary Israelites, and we suppose that they must have had a false kind of science in their minds, substituting for the true science that we have now. Instead, ordinary Israelites may not have had any "theory" at all.

Finally, let us suppose for the sake of argument that the Israelites did have false assumptions about the cosmos in their minds. The Bible does not endorse their assumptions merely by saying that the sun rises. It simply does not speak to such questions. Ramm made the point that *"the language of the Bible is non-postulational with reference to natural things."* That is, it does not postulate any particular scientific cosmology. It lacks *"theorizing."*[17] Instead, it describes the world as seen by the naked eye. The vehicle-cargo approach is correct in implying that the Bible does not immediately correct all possible false assumptions about cosmology, biology, or any other field of specialized knowledge. The dispute is not about that, but about what it means for communication to be truthful. It can be truthful if it does not speak about such false assumptions. It cannot be truthful if it actively endorses the assumptions or clearly presupposes them.[18]

---

16. The last point presupposes a distinction between God as primary cause and secondary causes within creation. For discussion, consult Vern S. Poythress, *Redeeming Science: A God-Centered Approach* (Wheaton, IL: Crossway, 2006), chap. 1.

17. Ramm, *Christian View of Science*, 69 (emphasis original).

18. Interested readers can pursue further discussions and illustrations of this point in Vern S. Poythress, *Inerrancy and Worldview: Answering Modern Challenges to the Bible* (Wheaton, IL: Crossway, 2012), especially chaps. 3–4, 8–13. In addition, questions could be raised about a mental-picture theory of truth; see Poythress, *Inerrancy and the Gospels: A God-Centered Approach to the Challenges of Harmonization* (Wheaton, IL: Crossway, 2012), chap. 7. A mental-

The four small mythic elements dealing with Copernicus contribute to a much larger myth that has little to do with him. The grand popular myth is that modern science exposes the way things "really are," as opposed to the mistaken character of appearances. According to this grand myth, the "reality" is that the earth moves, and only falsely "appears" to be unmoving. A solid-looking table is mostly empty space[19] between elementary particles, and only falsely appears to be solid. A rainbow is really light waves of various frequencies, and only *appears* to be beautiful colors to our eyes. Our minds are really the electrical and chemical firing of neurons, and only appear to have thoughts.

This grand myth constitutes an extended metaphysical statement about what is real and what is not. According to this myth, current science allegedly provides ultimate metaphysical answers. We may call this the myth of *scientistic metaphysics*.[20]

To refute this grand myth takes metaphysical reflection, more than we can do here.[21] But we can at least observe that the grand myth is ill-grounded. The work in specialized sciences uncovers additional "layers" of meaning of which we were previously unaware—for example, the microscopic level, the macro level of astronomy and cosmology, and layers in biology, geology, meteorology, chemistry, and physics. That in itself does not imply that the initial, "phenomenal" layers of ordinary observation are "unreal." The "unreality" of appearances follows only if we have a metaphysical principle of reductionism,

---

picture theory confuses the meaning of the text with the mental picture produced in readers' minds. When this theory is present, any mistaken pictures of the cosmos present among Israelite readers get read back into the text as if the pictures were part of the meaning.

19. There is some irony here in the fact that the popularized picture of particles with empty space in between has been qualified in its turn by quantum field theory, a mathematical theory that has no accurate intuitive representation by means of three-dimensional space. The mathematics uses complex infinite dimensional vector space (Hilbert space), and suggests as a simplified model that "empty" space is a sea of virtual particles, especially virtual photons that mediate the electromagnetic force within and between atoms. Thus, the confident assurance that the table is mostly empty space is itself one of the popular myths left over from earlier forms of physics (e.g., the Rutherford model of the atom).

I have no objection to simplified models, including the Rutherford model of empty space, as long as we understand that the model explicates one "layer" of reality. When, however, a person uses such a model to teach the unreality of ordinary experience, his arrogance and bad metaphysics are showing, and then it seems to me that it is fair to criticize both.

20. Note that scientistic metaphysics is *not* the same as philosophical materialism. Philosophical materialism says that there is nothing besides matter, motion, and energy. Scientistic metaphysics says that science shows us the deepest realities, while ordinary experience provides merely appearances that are unreal.

21. Poythress, *Redeeming Science*, chaps. 15–16; Poythress, *Redeeming Philosophy: A God-Centered Approach to the Big Questions* (Wheaton, IL: Crossway, 2014), parts II–IV.

which says that science gets to the "bottom," the "real" foundation of being, and that everything above the bottom is unreal in relation to the bottom. (See Fig. 5.2.)

Fig. 5.2: Two Views of What Is Real

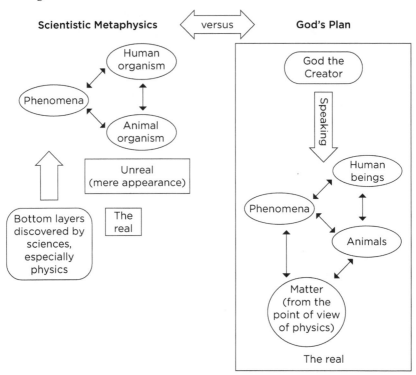

This metaphysics has no real warrant based on details of scientific investigation, but is a groundless assumption that is imposed on the investigation as an interpretation of its metaphysical significance. In other words, we have here an instance of credulity, faith without grounds. The metaphysical claim has credibility partly because it is socially transmitted from one person to another, and the modern atmosphere is such that few people question the key assumption.

Interestingly, a similar lesson was relevant to generations before the rise of modern science. The Ptolemaic system of ancient Greek astronomy and its popularized forms tempted people to interpret the system as a metaphysical statement about the ultimate foundation of the cosmos rather than a specialized framework for astronomical calculations. Jews, Christians, and pagans alike sometimes fell into this trap, and then projected parts of that metaphysics into Genesis 1.

The period during which Copernicus and Galileo Galilei lived was influenced by Aristotelianism, which also seemed to provide answers about the ultimate metaphysical character of the world. If people viewed the Copernican theory as a metaphysical claim, it contradicted Aristotle. The fight was then between two metaphysical systems, each claiming to reveal the ultimate structure of the world.

Of course, it was natural for biblical interpreters to explore how Genesis 1 might have correlations with the astronomical claims of their times. But to explore *possible* correlations is distinct from locking in a particular metaphysical analysis or overestimating the quality of knowledge contained in premodern astronomy.

Relief from fights of this kind comes partly from seeing that more than one perspective can offer a true but not exhaustive account of the world.[22]

We have brought in some rather heavy discussion of mythic influences in order to assure people that the sun rises. But actually all of the heavy apparatus ought not to have been necessary. Ordinary people in virtually any culture tacitly understand that if someone describes events without overtly indicating an observational standpoint, he is describing the events from his own standpoint. Hence, it is correct and true to say that the sun rises. We have introduced the apparatus only because we need to become aware of the myths in the background so that we might be able to see straight and admit to ourselves and to others that the sun rises (really!).

The Myth of Progress

The second myth is the myth of *progress*.[23] The popular myth of progress says that since science gives us more knowledge and more gadgets, we are getting better and better scientifically, religiously, morally, and in our understanding of ourselves and God. We are

---

22. Vern S. Poythress, *Symphonic Theology: The Validity of Multiple Perspectives in Theology* (repr.; Phillipsburg, NJ: P&R, 2001).
23. There are affinities between this section and Noel Weeks's discussion of "progressivism." Weeks, "Cosmology in Historical Context," 283–84.

superior to the "primitive" cultures of Amazonian tribes and the ancient Near East. (See Fig. 5.3.)

Fig. 5.3: The Myth of Progress

That is what we think. But more sensitive people avoid saying it out loud. If we say it out loud, it is hard to conceal from ourselves questions about cultural paternalism, prejudice, and overreaching generalizations. So we may draw back a bit and say only that we are superior in our knowledge of the universe. But even that is not fully true. As we have seen, superiority in details is compatible with bad metaphysics.

Consider another modern myth. This myth says that demons do not exist, but are a product of primitive superstition. (See Fig. 5.4.)

Fig. 5.4: The View that Demons Are Mythical

The myth says that we know this due to specialized scientific investigation. But actually we do not. Natural science investigates empirically, while demons are spiritual beings, and therefore outside the focus of most natural science. Moreover, the average secularized Westerner thinks he "knows" that demons do not exist, not because he has extensively investigated the question or demanded extensive evidence from those who have, but because the people around him believe the same thing. And they believe it because demons are incompatible with the reigning materialism. The nonexistence of demons is an atmospheric assumption—a myth.[24] (See Fig. 5.5.)

---

24. In the West, the myth is being challenged by certain kinds of modern mysticism, spiritism, and monism, but right now it seems to me still to be the default belief in circles of power. The myth has to marginalize non-Western cultures, where people believe in a spirit world.

Fig. 5.5: Why Western People Believe Demons Are Mythical

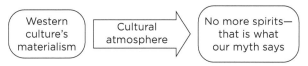

Many modern people think that science supports scientistic metaphysics, and this metaphysics says that the world is mechanistic, and therefore, at root, impersonal. By contrast, many ancient people, as well as some tribal and non-Western cultures, populate the world with personal beings—spirits and gods. Religiously, they are deeply wrong when they give themselves over to worship these spirits and gods. But in one sense, they are close to the truth, because God is personal, and his personal activity is present in all the world. Moreover, God created angels as personal beings. Some of the angels rebelled, so there are now both good and evil angels (the demons). These angels may be involved in the world, including the world of nature (Job 1:12, 19; Dan. 6:22; Acts 12:7–10, 23). In affirming the presence of personal intentions in the world of nature, non-Western cultures are closer to the truth than the modern mechanistic worldview, which declares that the world and the laws of the world are completely impersonal. In this respect, then, mainstream modern Western thinking has regressed rather than progressed. (See Fig. 5.6.)

Fig. 5.6: Western Regression in Metaphysics

Nevertheless, for the sake of argument, let us suppose that our knowledge is overwhelmingly superior. The assumption that it is may still have unfortunate effects. It may close down serious attempts to understand other cultures with an insider's sympathy, because they have nothing interesting from which we could learn. The myth of progress applied to Genesis 1 says that it is an ancient document from an ancient culture, and so can have little to say except perhaps for some core religious message about God, if indeed that message can rise above the limitations of its cultural trappings. This attitude under-mines empathy, and lack of empathy hinders genuine understanding.

The Myth of Understanding Cultures from Facts

Our observations about cross-cultural understanding lead to consid-eration of a third myth, a popular myth about understanding other cultures. It is less powerful than the first two, but still influential. The heart of the myth is the idea that we can study and understand a culture effectively with a dose of armchair learning about the facts. "After all," says popular thinking, "everyone else is like us, except that variant customs and beliefs are plugged in at appropriate places here or there."

The difficulty here is that other cultures can be startlingly different, in ways not easily anticipated by an inhabitant of a modern culture. Moreover, in analyzing another culture, people can give multiple inter-pretations to the same facts, each interpretation having some plausibil-ity. The feeling of understanding can be illusory.

In fact, deep understanding of a radically different culture is a chal-lenging business. Asian cultures are radically different in some ways from Western cultures, and subtly but irritatingly and surprisingly different in others. It is not easy for just anyone to progress beyond a tourist's impression. With the ancient Near East, these difficulties go together with the absence of direct contact. We cannot function like a well-trained field worker in social anthropology, actually immersing ourselves within an ancient culture and learning it seriously and empa-thetically "from inside." In addition, the ancient Near East consists of many interacting subcultures that changed over a period of millennia. The extant documentary and archaeological evidence is fragmentary. People who are richly informed by evidence, who have skills in cross-cultural thinking and adaptation, and who have innate empathy may often make good inferences up to a point. But knowledge of such a culture *as an interlocking whole* remains partial and tentative.[25]

---

25. Wayne Horowitz indicates the difficulties: "This approach poses certain dangers, not the least of which are our distance in time and space from the ancient writers, as well as the vagaries of archaeological discovery. . . . The current evidence simply does not allow us to know, for in-stance, if ancient readers of Gilgamesh really believed that they too could have visited Utnapištim by sailing across the cosmic sea . . . or if a few, many, most, or all ancient readers understood the topographical material in Gilg. IX–X in metaphysical or mystical terms." Horowitz, *Mesopota-mian Cosmic Geography* (Winona Lake, IN: Eisenbrauns, 1998), xiii–xiv.

There are further worries. It is eminently feasible for an intelligent modern person to read ancient Near Eastern myths while constantly recognizing that they come from a different culture. Indeed, it is easy, because the evidence is there constantly in the form of references to ancient gods and goddesses. What is not so easy is for this same intelligent modern person to read ancient material without fitting the mythical references to items in "nature" into the scheme of nature that he himself knows to be "true." In other words, he carries around with him the baggage of modern popularized science.

For example, a reference to the sky in ancient literature is automatically a reference to the blue sky overhead, which the modern student knows is the atmosphere, and in which the blue color comes from diffracted sunlight. The modern student thinks in terms of a scientific account of the sky rather than a poet's view, a painter's view, a farmer's view, a priest's view, or a description in terms of appearances, because the scientific analysis provides us with what is "real" according to the myth of scientistic metaphysics.

The modern student also knows that the ancient writer did not have this modern scientific information. The ancient writer must be referring to something, namely, to the sky. He must be referring to it as a *physical* object (because, remember, scientistic metaphysics has told us that the physical aspect of things is ultimate). The modern student then proceeds to infer that the ancient people, who did not have modern knowledge of the atmosphere, must have had faulty ideas about the physical structure and composition of the sky.[26] For instance, it may be alleged that they thought that the sky was a solid dome. In other words, they must have had a kind of faulty substitute for the "right" account given by modern science. The faulty substitute may even be labeled as "ancient science."

All of this is eminently plausible, given the starting point of the modern student. But it may involve a misreading. Into his reading, the modern student can easily inject the assumption that questions about physical structure and physical causes are ultimate, not merely in the eyes of modern culture but for all mankind. Hence, the ancients must

---

26. Weeks makes the same point about false inferences: "It follows that we need to ask whether the similar attempt to read a physical and geometrical cosmology into the biblical text also faces the danger of substituting the primary concerns of the modern world for those of the biblical text." Weeks, "Cosmology in Historical Context," 290.

have had views on the subject that they expressed in their favorite cosmologies and myths. Modern cosmology is a physical-structural account, what we might call a *physicalistic* account. It focuses on matter, motion, and energy, and its explanations rely on physical causes and effects. Hence, ancient cosmology would have included that too. The ancients wrote poetry, but that too must somehow reveal what they thought about the "real thing"—physical structure.[27]

I do not know everything that the ancients believed. It looks to me as if beliefs in the ancient Near East varied from one subculture to another, and that one belief sometimes contradicted another, though also showing affinities.[28] But when a modern student postulates the presence in the ancient world of a detailed mistaken physicalistic account of what the world is like, I might still venture to suggest that we should be cautious. The actual interests of the ancient peoples in the Near East may have been wide-ranging. But (except for the Bible) the most noteworthy writings about the cosmos as a global whole, so far as we can recover them from fragmentary remnants of the cultures, appear to me to be found mostly in poetic accounts that explained how the gods were involved in both the origins and the present patterns in what people observed around them.

In Egypt, it appears that gods were confusedly identified with sun, sky, Pharaoh, the Nile, and the earth. The interaction of gods accounted for what an Egyptian saw around him, and above all what he could expect in the underworld:

> The universe was for them [the ancient Egyptians] an awesome system of living divine beings. The earth, the sky, and the Nile were all entities that had a distinct life-force and personality and drew

---

27. I believe that the Bible gives us truth, not relativism. But human notions about the ultimate structure of the world need to be critically inspected.

28. Weeks, "Cosmology in Historical Context," 283–93. Consider an example: E. A. Wallis Budge, in analyzing the Egyptian *Book of the Dead*, claims that the "ceiling [of the sky]" was "either flat or vaulted." If flat, it "was rectangular, and was supported at each corner by a pillar"; the pillars were identified with the gods "Amset, Hapi, Tuamautef, and Qebhsennuf," who "were supposed to preside over the four quarters of the world, and subsequently were acknowledged to be the gods of the cardinal points." E. A. Wallis Budge, *The Book of the Dead: The Papyrus of Ani in the British Museum: The Egyptian Text with Interlinear Transliteration and Translation, a Running Translation, Introduction, etc.* (London: Longmans, 1895), ci, http://www.sacred-texts.com /egy/ebod/. This description is technically inconsistent with a physicalistic interpretation of the pictures of Nut (for sky) and Shu (for air), which Budge mentions a few lines later. Inasmuch as both pictures involve gods, one may doubt whether a physicalistic interpretation captures the point in either case. Both pictures may perhaps be artistic representations, not quasiscientific models of physical structure.

their life from the original creative power, no matter what name that power may have borne.[29]

The Egyptians lived in a universe composed not of *things*, but of *beings*. Each element is not merely a physical component, but a distinct individual with a unique personality and will. The sky is not an inanimate vault, but a goddess who conceives the sun each night and gives birth to him in the morning.[30]

This kind of description is antimaterialistic and antithetical to science, not at all akin to the interest in secondary physical causes and physical structure characteristic of modern science. It is so different that it is challenging to imagine what it would be like actually to live in a culture of that kind. Egyptologist Vincent Tobin observes:

Creation myths in any culture are not intended as scientific explications of the way in which the universe came into being; rather, they are symbolic articulations of the meaning and significance of the realm of created being.[31]

Note how Tobin contrasts creation myths with "scientific explications." According to Tobin's view, creation myths are not crude substitutes that attempt to give the same *kind* of information as modern science. Rather, they are "symbolic articulations." They focally address religious depth and the meaning of the world relevant to human living.

Over against Tobin's view, a student may of course find other modern interpretations of ancient myths that move in physicalistic directions; these interpretations may see in the myths a direct analogue to "scientific explications." My point is not to decide between various interpretations, but to point out that the existence of variant interpretations constitutes a difficulty. Typical semipopular accounts of the ancient Near East may pass over these difficulties. Such accounts

---

29. Vincent Arieh Tobin, "Myths: Creation Myths," in *The Oxford Encyclopedia of Ancient Egypt*, ed. Donald B. Redford (New York: Oxford University Press, 2001), 2.471; also 2.469.

30. James P. Allen, *Genesis in Egypt: The Philosophy of Ancient Egyptian Creation Accounts* (New Haven, CT: Yale Egyptological Seminar, Department of Near Eastern Language and Civilizations, The Graduate School, Yale University, 1988), 8. See also p. 62.

31. Tobin, "Myths: Creation Myths," 2.469. See also Allen: "The Egyptian explanations are more *meta*physical than physical. They are concerned with what lies beyond physical reality." *Genesis in Egypt*, 56.

are written not for specialists in Egyptology or in the study of ancient Mesopotamia, but for a broader audience. Understandably, simplifications take place. Semipopular accounts may then end up with physicalistic interpretations of some of the pieces from ancient myths. These physicalistic interpretations may look plausible to beginning readers, because such physicalistic interpretations can cite both primary and secondary literature in their favor. Nonspecialist readers remain unaware of the possibility of different interpretations.

The vehicle-cargo approach has a difficulty here. This approach is appealing only if it is correct in making the claim that Genesis 1 contains some erroneous views with respect to the physical structure of the cosmos. But does such a claim hold up?

Actually, the vehicle-cargo approach can be tempted to want to have it both ways. At one time, it may tell us that Genesis 1 is only about theology and the functions of things for human benefit, not about events that change the appearance of the world. It says that God is the sole Creator. God exhibits his power in the world; he made a world suitable for human habitation; and he made things that would give us human benefits. But according to this view, Genesis 1 is not at all about particular events that happened in space and time, such as the appearing of the dry land (Gen. 1:9). The vehicle-cargo approach tells us that this is so because Genesis is correcting the false theology of the surrounding polytheistic myths, which were also theological in essence.

At another time the vehicle-cargo approach may tell us that Genesis 1 includes and does not correct a false cosmology of ancient times. Common examples would include the earth-centered description and the theory of the solid dome of sky with a heavenly sea above it. But, it is said, Genesis includes such things innocently, because it does not intend to teach this cosmology. The vehicle-cargo approach tells us that this is so because Genesis 1 exhibits some parallels with the surrounding polytheistic myths, which (it alleges) contain a false cosmological view of the physical composition and physical structure of the universe.

But we need to make up our minds. Are the cosmological myths in the surrounding cultures interested only in religious explanations for natural phenomena, together with the practical functions and benefits for mankind, or are they also interested in issues of physical composition, structure, and secondary physical causation in a manner similar to modern scientific interests? If the former, then they do not really address physical composition and structure. For example, according to a narrowly religious, poetic interpretation, the ancient Near Eastern myths did not say that the sky is literally a solid dome. Rather, they merely used a stock of poetic or symbolic pictures to communicate what they considered to be religious truths about the gods and their relation to the visible sky (its appearance). Therefore, Genesis 1 cannot be using or including false physicalistic cosmology borrowed from the myths because such cosmology did not exist.[32]

Suppose, on the other hand, that cosmological myths *do* include an interest in physical structure. Suppose that they say, among other things, that the sky is a materially solid dome. According to the vehicle-cargo principle that says that Genesis 1 is analogous, Genesis 1 addresses the same concerns. In that case, the vehicle-cargo claim that Genesis 1 is restricted narrowly to theological concerns collapses.

I believe, then, that the vehicle-cargo case borders on incoherence. I suspect that behind this lack of coherence lies the difficulty of understanding cultures that not only lacked modern scientific knowledge, but did not really have anything like a global framework of complex interlocking theories of physical structure and secondary causation to serve as a plausible substitute. Instead, they had a spiritistic, antimaterialistic vision that saw gods in the forces and phenomena (appearances) of nature. Such a vision is not a twin to science but merely a

---

32. One possible reply from the vehicle-cargo approach might be to say that information about material composition, material structure, and physical causation has a kind of indirect presence in the myths. Allegedly, such information is—more or less—presupposed but not discussed. But this should be recognized for what it is, a tenuous inference, given our cultural distance from the ancient Near East and given the partial character of our knowledge. Tenuous inferences become more problematic when they are influenced by the myth of modern scientistic metaphysics, which generates a confident expectation that "of course" the ancients would have had physicalistic theories in the background on which their myths would have built.

The question also rises on whether the vehicle-cargo approach is distinguishing adequately between what the myths actually say and the total corpus of what the surrounding cultures believed. Likewise with Genesis 1: Israelite cultures through the centuries may have included a variety of mistaken beliefs and assumptions, and these would have varied somewhat from one individual to another, from one group to another, and from one time to another. (In particular, intellectuals and ancient experts would have had opinions beyond what would have been typical of an ordinary farmer.) The totality of what was in the cultures is different from what Genesis says. On a fair reading, Genesis simply does not address all the detailed beliefs of individuals. We are back to Ramm's discussion of "nonpostulational" language (Ramm, *Christian View of Science*, 69) and to Calvin's point that Scripture addresses ordinary people in ordinary ways (appearances). See also Poythress, *Redeeming Science*, 96n8; Poythress, *Inerrancy and Worldview*, chaps. 3–4, 8–13.

counterfeit spiritual analogue to the biblical teaching about angels, demons, and the rule of God over nature.

Theoretically, such antimaterialistic visions could of course be combined with speculations of a physicalistic sort. Once a culture enters the darkness and confusion of false gods, confusions can multiply. But one may still ask questions about relative likelihood. Within the theistic worldview of the Bible, we may distinguish between God as the primary cause and secondary, physical causes within the world (e.g., Ex. 22:6; Neh. 4:3; Job 1:19; Eccles. 11:3; Matt. 7:27), because God as Creator is distinct from his creatures.[33] Within a polytheistic worldview, there is no such distinction. The lack of distinction may lead to single-level thinking in which the gods are identified with natural forces, and so there is only one kind of cause. Interest in a second, subordinate level of physical causation may collapse into interest in the activities of the gods. Within a worldview of this kind, it is not clear that it would make sense to seek for a physicalistic explanation *in addition to* or *as background for* the personalistic explanations involving gods.[34]

It might also be the case that people in these cultures retained an interest in a separate level of secondary causes, but that the polytheistic mythic genre ignored this level. In this case also, it would be a mistake to try to infer theories of physical causation from the myths.

Finally, it might be the case that God in the Old Testament from time to time used the typical images and analogies used by the Israelites in discussing the world around them. We ourselves can use stock images and analogies without hardening them into a physicalistic *theory*. Today, we can talk about the mind without adopting a particular *theory* of cognition. We talk about a person with a big "ego" without committing ourselves to Sigmund Freud's *theory* of the ego. Likewise,

---

33. The technical expressions "primary cause" and "secondary cause" came into use subsequent to biblical times. But their use summarizes distinctions found within the Bible. In Job 1:19, the house falls because of "a great wind"—a secondary cause. In Job 1:21, Job acknowledges God as the primary cause. Similarly, Exodus 14:21 says that "the LORD drove the sea back by a strong east wind," thereby acknowledging the Lord as the primary cause and the strong east wind as the secondary cause. One could multiply such examples.

34. "Causation emanates from the divine [gods], not from within the material world itself." Walton, *Genesis 1 as Ancient Cosmology*, 39. There is also the issue of *magic*, which, according to Mesopotamian records, could be used by either gods or humans. Magic belongs to a larger system involving a delusive religious desire for control. But human beings in the ancient world were drawn to it. Does the human desire for magic presuppose an impersonal, abstract order on which the tricks of magic rely? John D. Currid, *Ancient Egypt and the Old Testament* (Grand Rapids, MI: Baker, 1997), 40.

might ancient discussion of the observable world—or modern discussion—creatively use the imagery of a house with pillars, windows, doors, or upper chambers; the image of a tent; or the image of an expanse?[35] Could such imagery appear without teaching a detailed physicalistic *theory*? Modern physicalistic readings run the danger of not recognizing analogy and metaphor in ancient texts. (See Fig. 5.7.)

Fig. 5.7: Using Imagery versus Postulating a Detailed Physicalistic Theory

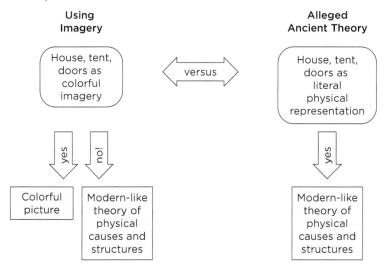

Example from Myth: Tiamat Becoming the Sky

For the sake of illustration, let us consider a small example. I would ask readers to bear with the example because it illustrates the possibility of *multiple* interpretations of ancient polytheistic thinking about the world. Reading a physical theory into an ancient text is not the only possibility, and not even the most attractive possibility.

Our example comes from the Babylonian creation myth *Enuma Elish*. Tablet IV describes how, after Marduk killed Tiamat,

> He split her in two, like a fish for drying,
> Half of her he set up and made as a cover, heaven.

---

35. A list of instances from the ancient Near East might be quite expansive. We could begin with Job 38:4–11, 22; Isa. 40:22; and Amos 9:6.

He stretched out the hide and assigned watchmen,
And ordered them not to let her waters escape.[36]

Consider now some possible interpretations, and how they are affected by the interpreter's assumptions. For each interpretation, I shall make a few critical observations.

Physicalistic Interpretation

Student A offers a physicalistic interpretation:

> The ancient people, having no knowledge of scientific explanations of physical structure and causal origin, produce stories of gods as a substitute explanation. The poem attributes the origin of the sky to Marduk, which is natural, given that Marduk was the patron god of Babylon. The physical stuff with which he begins is the slain body of Tiamat, the water goddess, which implies that the material composition of Tiamat is water. Marduk splits Tiamat in two. The sky consists of half the body of Tiamat. It is a body of water. It is held in by a physical barrier, formed from her hide. This picture coheres with other ancient Near Eastern texts, which have essentially the same picture of a heavenly sea held up by a solid barrier of sky.

Critique. This interpretation proposes that one of the purposes of the ancient myth is to explain the same *kinds* of things that are in focus in popularized modern science, namely, physical composition and causal origins. Given that assumption, the explanation is plausible. But there are a few flies in the ointment.

One fly is that earlier lines in the poem *Enuma Elish* depict Tiamat in bodily form (with references to legs, mouth, lips, belly, heart, and carcass). This depiction, if taken as referring to physical "composition," is at odds with the view that she is water (as suggested by her role as water goddess and by the line [line 140] that refers to "her waters" that must not be allowed to escape).

---

36. Benjamin R. Foster, trans., *Enuma Elish*, in *The Context of Scripture*, ed. William W. Hallo (New York: Brill, 1997), 1.398 [item 1.111], Tablet IV.137–40. See also Horowitz, *Mesopotamian Cosmic Geography*, 112. In my earlier published article "Three Modern Myths," I used the translation of E. A. Speiser in *Ancient Near Eastern Texts Relating to the Old Testament*, ed. James B. Pritchard (Princeton, NJ: Princeton University Press, 1969), 67, Tablet IV.137–40. But I am now persuaded that the key Akkadian cuneiform is better translated "skin" or "hide" (from mašku), not "bolt" or "bar" (from parku). See Oliver Hersey, "Hammering Out the Meaning of *Rāqîaʿ* and 'Waters Above' in Gen. 1:6–8 against Its Ancient Near Eastern and Biblical Context," unpublished manuscript, p. 4n7.

Fig. 5.8: Interpreting Description in a Physicalistic Way

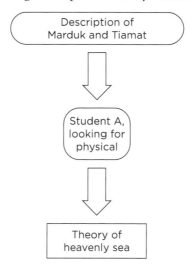

The key line 139 in *Enuma Elish* may indeed suggest that Tiamat furnishes two components. Her hide furnishes the solid barrier, while her internal waters make up the heavenly sea. But if Tiamat is the *water* goddess, with a focus on the theme of water, is this division into two components a colorful picture rather than a physical speculation?

Second, the solid barrier is Tiamat's hide, and in human experience, hides are typically flexible, in contrast to a solid hemispherical dome made of, let us say, stone or brick. What keeps the hide from simply falling down to earth? If Tiamat's hide offers us a physicalistic theory for what holds the waters up, it is not a good theory. It is not plausible, given ancient experience of the different properties of hides and stonework.

Third, Marduk posts "watchmen" and gives instructions. So the more fundamental feature that keeps in the waters is the personal activity of the watchmen. What are they guarding against? Presumably, against some other personal being or beings who would come and let the waters loose. The picture as a whole is really not physicalistic, but remains decidedly personalistic or, we might say, spiritistic. If so, one may raise the question of how much this myth is really intent on giving an explanation based on physical causation in the sense of modern science.

It is sometimes alleged that the division of Tiamat in two parts, like a fish (line 137), corresponds to the division in Genesis 1:6–8 between upper and lower waters. But it should be noted that later in the poem, Marduk divides the Anunnaki, a group of six hundred gods, into two companies, then assigns one company to carry out tasks in the heavens and the other on earth.[37] The whole picture of two realms focuses on works by spirits, not mechanisms.[38]

Finally, the description in *Enuma Elish* occurs in lines of poetry, which are part of a large epic poem about the gods. The genre encourages us to expect imaginative, metaphorical, symbolic, and evocative language rather than a focus on the physical composition or structure of the cosmos. There is, moreover, an obvious use of figurative language in a detail: the comparison with a fish laid out to dry (line 137).

Spiritistic Interpretation

Next, student B offers a spiritistic interpretation:

> The author of the text was a spiritist, who saw spirits everywhere. There is no "matter" in the modern sense. Tiamat, the water goddess, is, after all, a goddess, a spiritual being. The water is simply a phenomenal manifestation of her being and her activity. When Marduk kills her, he kills her chaotic fighting activity, but the resulting corpse is an inactive spirit. The language about her bodily parts is a pictorial representation, expressing the fact that she has powers to produce visible effects. The watchmen are spirits, subordinate gods under Marduk's orders. The breaking out of the waters would represent a breaking out of the spirit of Tiamat, which would imply the reintroduction of her chaos-creating effects. The hide is a pictorial representation of spiritual binding (which might, for example, take place through a spell).

Critique. This interpretation has the advantage of taking seriously the presence of gods and the personalistic character of the overall description. According to this interpretation, the purpose is not to offer

---

37. Pritchard, ed., *Ancient Near Eastern Texts* 68, VI.39–46.
38. See also Weeks's observations about the difficulty in harmonizing a physicalistic interpretation with the distinction between fresh water and salt water. Weeks, "Cosmology in Historical Context," 286–90.

an explanation of physical composition and physical causation that would ignorantly substitute for modern science (student A). Rather, the purpose is to supply the audience with a picture that in the long run will enable them to interact in wise and profitable ways with the world of spirits around them.

Fig. 5.9: Competing Interpretations of Marduk and Tiamat

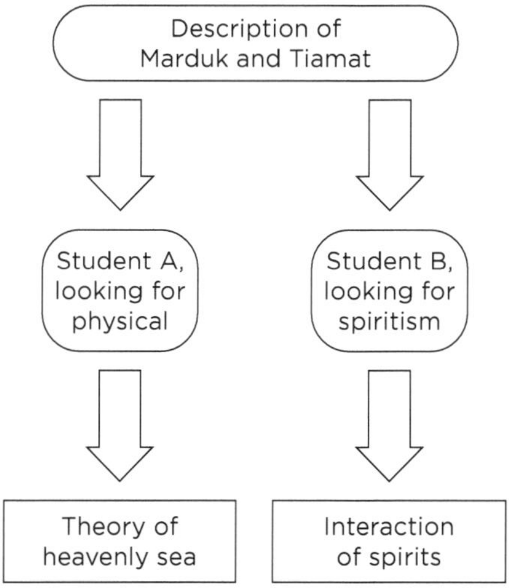

Dualistic Interpretation

Student C offers a dualistic interpretation:

> The author of the text was a dualist, who believed in body and spirit, and the interaction of the two. Gods as well as human beings have both body and spirit, the latter animating the former. Tiamat's body is water, while her spirit is the spirit of chaos. Marduk's triumph over chaos is depicted by the killing of the spirit of Tiamat. The water then becomes the sky. But it is still capable of being reanimated and breaking out to reintroduce chaos. So Marduk appoints subordinate gods ("watchmen") to make sure it does not happen.

According to this interpretation, the narrative makes suggestions about why things appear as they do, namely, because some kind of body has been fixed in a certain location. But there is little worry about whether the "body" is solid, liquid, or gaseous (to import modern terminology), or just how it is geometrically shaped. The principal purpose, as with the spiritistic interpretation, is to help orient people as to how to interact with the spirits of the gods, who are the principal power sources. It is important that a human being either has a god or goddess on his side or at least takes care that the gods not become antagonistic toward him. Information about the gods is supplied in the long run in order to guide humans about how to interact with the gods. For example, by worshiping Marduk, people guard against chaos entering their lives.

Critique. The principal weakness of the dualistic interpretation is that it may be anachronistically projecting onto the ancient Near East a later dualism, such as Plato's or Descartes's.

Monistic Interpretation

Student D offers a monistic interpretation:

> The author thought in terms of fluid wholes, rather than dualistic separation between body and soul. The water is both water and the water goddess Tiamat. And Tiamat is present when we speak about her manifestations through bodily parts, which show us the visible side of an integral whole. When Marduk splits Tiamat like a fish, he is splitting the water in two and splitting the goddess in two, because they are the same thing in the end—two different ways of describing the same thing. When Marduk makes the sky out of Tiamat, the sky is both the sky and the goddess Tiamat. The "watchmen" to whom Marduk gives orders are presumably both subordinate gods and processes that result in the water remaining up there.

Critique. This interpretation is similar to the spiritistic interpretation of student B. But it does not result in quite the same flavor of antimaterialism. That which is visible or "material," whether water, sky, earth, or sun, is not "matter" in the sense of an Aristotelian form-matter distinction. It is "matter" that is simultaneously "spirit," because spirits are in water, sky, and so forth, to the point of identification.

In addition to these interpretations, we can contemplate others that are somewhat minimizing.

Sociological-Functional Interpretation

Student E offers a sociological-functional interpretation:

> Myths serve to unify a social group by explaining its origin and nature, and by giving it common foundational guiding beliefs. A myth need not be literally true to accomplish these goals of social stability and unity. So it is with the myth concerning Tiamat. The victory of Marduk and the utter defeat of Tiamat provides the society with a functional basis for religious unity in worshiping Marduk, and that in turn leads to social unity in serving the Babylonian kingdom, for whom Marduk is the patron god.

Critique. This kind of interpretation shows the influence of reductionistic assumptions that crop up within some modern forms of social anthropology. It is weak partly because it does not distinguish clearly between the modern view by the anthropological observer and the view of those who lived within the ancient culture. The ancient people could have successful results in social unity only if they actually believed the myth to be true. For all we know, there may have been skeptics here and there, analogous to the skepticism about gods that cropped up among Greek philosophers. But the myths would have ceased to produce social allegiance if the majority of people had ceased to believe them.

Allegorical Interpretation

Student F offers an allegorical interpretation:

> The myth of Marduk and Tiamat is an allegory about the conflicts and harmonies among natural forces, such as those of water and sky.

Critique. The allegorical interpretation still allows for the myth to have some social effectiveness, because people still believe it to be "about" something other than social effectiveness. It is about natural forces, and social unity results from unified views about these natural forces and how people should interact with them. But this allegorical interpretation is implausible as a general explanation for the ancient Near East, because there is widespread evidence—including child sacrifice—that many people of the time took seriously the actual existence of gods.

There may be still other interpretations. But this list should be enough to illustrate the difficulty of interpreting the full significance of a text coming from an ancient culture. The background assumptions that we bring to the text, whether physicalistic, sociological, or dualistic, contribute to the shape of the interpretation that comes out. All but the physicalistic interpretation (student A above) lead to doubts about whether the ancient texts testify to a detailed theory about the composition, physical and spatial structure, and secondary physical causes of "nature" and of the sky in particular. We do not know for sure how to interpret these texts. (See Fig. 5.10.)

Fig. 5.10: Multiple Competing Interpretations

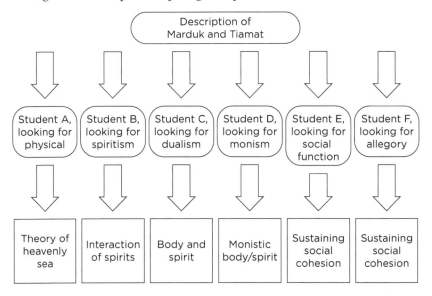

For readers who are interested, I have included two more examples in Appendix D. These examples show that interpreting ancient texts and their cultures is more difficult than it might first appear. They undermine the easy confidence in the third modern myth, the idea that we can understand a culture effectively with a dose of armchair learning about the facts.

The Sacred in Modern Thinking

I call the three mistaken modern notions *myths* for four reasons. First, they are not true, but distortions of truths. Second, they function at a popular level and are seldom challenged at that level. Rather, they underlie and guide the global directions of people's thinking. They have coherent social functions, and that is one reason why they endure and propagate from one person to another. Third, though not all the myths have a prominent narrative structure, they all interlock with and depend on the second myth, the myth of progress, which definitely employs a narrative. The myth of progress is the story of enlightenment triumphing over darkness.

Fourth, the myths are sacred, particularly the first myth (scientistic metaphysics) and to some extent the second. People are tempted to respond to critical questions about the myths not with careful analysis, but with mere dismissal, or with astonishment that anyone would be so obtuse as to entertain doubts. Because the myths have an important role in guiding people's thinking, to question or abandon them threatens to leave people spiritually and intellectually "naked," disoriented and frightened by the loss of familiar landmarks. People's stake in them is deep. People give their allegiance. They live their lives based on them. In practice, the myths are treated in the same way that we treat what is sacred.

Misreading of Genesis 1?

My concern, then, is that a vehicle-cargo approach to Genesis 1 may still allow the unwitting propagation of modern myths. These myths interfere with understanding Genesis 1 and may result in projecting modern ideas onto the interpretive process. Interpretation may include negative projection that detects alleged primitive mistakes, such as the rising of the sun or the idea of a heavenly sea, or positive projection that sees in the ancient world a direct but primitive analogue to modern science.

The irony is that a vehicle-cargo approach arises directly from a desire to hear Genesis 1 on its own terms rather than in terms of modern science. The vehicle-cargo approach is reacting to a real need; in fact, two needs. On one side, dismissive critics reject Genesis 1 completely because they allege it is contradicted by science. On the other side, some young-earth creationists endeavor to find detailed harmonies with technical science, with the hope of showing that the Bible holds up under such scrutiny. The vehicle-cargo approach tries to rise to the challenge by telling people on both sides that they are misreading the text.

I agree that the two sides are both misreading the text.[39] But I differ from the vehicle-cargo approach by raising the question of whether it too unwittingly propagates more misreading, albeit of a different kind.

There is a further irony in the vehicle-cargo approach. It criticizes naive modern readings of Genesis 1 for artificially projecting onto Genesis ideas from modern science. It also criticizes the philosophers and theologians who resisted Copernicus, because they projected Aristotelian and Ptolemaic theories of ultimate structure—metaphysics— into Genesis 1. But is the vehicle-cargo approach doing something analogous? It also projects its own brand of "metaphysics" into Genesis 1, namely, the metaphysics that it has found from reading ancient Near Eastern myths. As a result, instead of being captive to modern science or to Ptolemaic metaphysics, Genesis 1 is made captive to a hypothesized ancient Near Eastern metaphysics—a view of ultimate material structure.

The vehicle-cargo approach would, of course, reply that its projection is legitimate because such projection originates from the environment in which Genesis was originally written. Yes, an environment helps us to understand a text. But an environment is not a text. If one moves too easily from environment to text, one makes the mistake of assuming that, when God writes, his writing is captive to the culture at the time. An additional subordinate mistake can arise if we fail to make a careful distinction between what the Bible says and the full complex of beliefs held by people to whom it comes. Despite its appeal to Copernicus, the vehicle-cargo approach has not learned the lesson that it should have learned from Copernicus: do not read culturally derived physicalistic metaphysics into the Bible. Ramm's principle needs attention: the Bible lacks *"theorizing."*[40]

Misinterpretation as a Minor or Major Problem

Is my disagreement with the vehicle-cargo approach major or minor? In a way, it might seem to be a small matter, because adherents of

---

39. Readers who want to know what I think a good reading would look like may see Poythress, *Redeeming Science*, chap. 6, and more broadly, chaps. 4–10; Collins, *Genesis 1–4*; and subsequent chapters in the present book.

40. Ramm, *Christian View of Science*, 69 (emphasis original).

some forms of the vehicle-cargo approach assure us that they believe in the divine authority and the inerrancy of the Bible. They work within that framework, but they want to say that Genesis 1 simply does not mean what many modern readers think it does. The naive modern reader thinks that Genesis 1 is about science, or at least that it is about particular events in space and time in which science has a stake. Some forms of the vehicle-cargo approach say that Genesis 1 is only about theology and about functions of created things for human benefit, but not about events. It teaches that God is the only God and sole Creator, and emphasizes how various aspects of creation serve human interests (for example, that plants provide food for man and animals, as is indicated in Gen 1:29–30).

I agree that Genesis 1 is centrally about theology and about human benefit, but I also think that it sets forth particular events that illustrate and express the theology by exhibiting God's rule over the world. The events are described not in a technical, scientific manner, but in ordinary language. In sum, the vehicle-cargo approach and the approach in this book differ about details, but we agree (and the young-earth creationist student also agrees) about the core of the theological teaching.

Nevertheless, hermeneutical questions make the disagreement of larger consequence. The vehicle-cargo approach invokes principles about the nature of Scripture in its interpretation of Genesis 1. A reader can follow these principles and run further than more cautious interpreters would approve. For instance, suppose that a modern interpreter says that Genesis 1 is about theology and *not* specific events in time and space. This dichotomy is problematic. Theology is expressed precisely through God's actions in events in time and space. This principle holds especially when we deal with narratives that show theology by events rather than tell it by direct exposition of theological truths. If we make a false dichotomy in Genesis 1, this same dichotomy can spread to other parts of the Bible. A principle of this kind easily becomes a wedge by which people pull away from the reality that God acts in history and speaks about history. God *shows* himself through events that the Bible narrates. God does not merely teach general truths about himself.[41]

---

41. Weeks, "Cosmology in Historical Context," 293.

As a second step, people may also find themselves pulling away from New Testament teaching that refers to Old Testament events. One difficulty with the vehicle-cargo approach is that the New Testament sometimes refers to Old Testament events in ways that presuppose that the Old Testament is actually giving us nonfiction, not parable. So if a vehicle-cargo approach reconfigures Old Testament history as parable (or folklore with a small historical core, or theology dressed out to imitate historical narrative), the next step is to reconfigure the New Testament by saying that its writers were men of their time who mistakenly believed that the Old Testament gave them history, and that this feature in the New Testament is a form of vehicle-cargo communication. At this point, the idea of the "vehicle" expands to remove not only history but pieces of New Testament teaching. Of course, an advocate of this approach may say, as his mantra, that the pieces in question are not the teaching (the "cargo") but merely the "vehicle" for the actual core of real teaching. By a series of such concessions, vehicle-cargo thinking may arrive at a point where the actual teaching of the Bible shrinks to a smaller and smaller core.

It gets worse. Given the propensity of sinful human nature not to submit to any teaching whatsoever that it does not find pleasing to the flesh, readers armed with a sufficiently expansive view of the vehicle can simply excise anything they want by labeling it in their minds as merely a vehicle. By such a process, one may, for example, arrive at the conclusion that the real teaching of the Bible is the fatherhood of God, the brotherhood of man, and the principle of love—old-fashioned liberalism.

The advocates of a more conservative form of the vehicle-cargo approach disagree with these conclusions. I am glad they do. But I would point out that an alleged distinction between vehicle and cargo needs critical inspection.

Further Alternatives in Biblical Interpretation

There remain many other approaches to explaining Genesis 1. We touched on some of them just now by reflecting on ways in which people might travel well beyond the starting position of the vehicle-cargo approach. We cannot explore these alternatives fully within the scope of this chapter, but it is worthwhile to mention a few, if only to compare them with their more conservative alternatives.

Some people adopt a full-blown critical stance. They say that the Bible is a human document, not a divine document at all. As a human document, it is subject to all the foibles of humanity and of the cultures within which it arose. In principle, these foibles may include mistaken ideas not only about the cosmos but about God or gods. People with such a critical stance may still admire the Bible after a fashion. They may say that the Bible includes some of the best of the world's religious literature, and we can learn a lot from it. But they also draw a clear conclusion: there is no particular reason for anyone to trust its theological explorations any more than he trusts what it says concerning the cosmos.

Another alternative is found in neoorthodox theology. Neoorthodoxy takes various complex forms, which we cannot catalog here. If we are allowed to simplify, we might say that it wants to allow a full scope to historical criticism at the level of propositional content, but still wants to ascribe to the Bible a role in divine encounter. Since, however, the "encounter" does not have stable propositional content, in practice the Bible does not function as a divinely authoritative text in any sphere. As a result, neoorthodox theology itself does not have any authoritative basis.[42]

Other people might draw the line between theology on the one hand and science on the other. According to this view, the Bible is right in everything it teaches about God and religious ideas, but it may fall into error in statements that impinge on science or cosmology. This position is akin to what we have described above as the vehicle-cargo approach, because it draws similar conclusions about what we can trust in the Bible. But it differs by directly and openly allowing for errors in matters of science. It does not hesitate to call them errors, and so it does not find it necessary to give elaborate explanations that appeal to genres in the ancient Near East. Traditionally, this position has been labeled "limited inerrancy"—that is, inerrancy limited to the sphere of theology. According to this view, any verse that does

---

42. John M. Frame, "God and Biblical Language: Transcendence and Immanence," in *God's Inerrant Word: An International Symposium on the Trustworthiness of Scripture*, ed. John W. Montgomery (Minneapolis: Bethany Fellowship, 1974), 159–77. http://www.frame-poythress.org /god-and-biblical-language-transcendence-and-immanence/.

not offer us theology may be dismissed as possibly a cultural error. By contrast, a more cautious form of the vehicle-cargo approach insists that the Bible is without error in whatever it teaches, but that modern readers have largely misunderstood the actual teaching of Genesis 1.

The theory of limited inerrancy at least has the advantage of being able to talk in a simple, coherent way about the message of Genesis 1 in comparison to the surrounding myths. In principle, it leaves open what is the exact relationship between Genesis 1 and the myths. The myths may or may not be making physicalistic claims. And Genesis 1 may or may not be making similar claims. Whatever may be the truth about such things, the theory of limited inerrancy says that the separation of truth and error in Genesis 1 does not depend on answering such detailed questions. Rather, the separation of truth and error takes place by a clear-cut criterion, namely, the criterion of *content*. Theological content is true, while scientific content or content touching on issues of science need not be true.

Some writings that adopt a form of the vehicle-cargo approach travel beyond Genesis 1. They use New Testament as well as Old Testament examples, taken from various genres of literature. This broader selection of examples raises a broader question. Are these vehicle-cargo writings merely making a claim about Genesis 1 (or Genesis 1–11) as a unique text? Or do they address the larger issue of whether we have to accept as true certain kinds of content whenever this content occurs *anywhere* in the Bible? Some forms of the vehicle-cargo approach might answer that only Genesis 1 or Genesis 1–11 is affected; in that case, the dispute appears to limit itself to the meaning of a single text. If, on the other hand, a form of the vehicle-cargo approach makes a claim about a whole list of other texts, a general principle may be at work: certain kinds of content are judged to be outside the scope of divine truth-telling. Inerrancy is limited to contents *inside* the scope of truth-telling—primarily "theological" content. This position is a form of limited inerrancy. Such a form of the vehicle-cargo approach may be dressed up with appeals to the ancient Near East and to questions of genre, and may gain plausibility by expanding its arguments. But at heart, it is just a variation on the doctrine of limited inerrancy.

Limited inerrancy may sound simple on paper, but it is not as simple as it sounds: it has liabilities.

1. Science, particularly science that researches the past, cannot be rigidly isolated from history, and history cannot be rigidly isolated from the theological teaching found in the Bible. God works in history; the work of Christ took place in history; and the Bible indicates that it is important to maintain that this is so (1 Cor. 15:1–28). The entanglement of the three spheres means that other forms of limited inerrancy can easily develop, in which the scope of divine truth telling is further narrowed. Not only science, but also history, and if history, also theology entangled in history, are moved outside the scope of inerrancy. Only a theological core may remain as the guaranteed center. And what belongs to the core is ultimately determined by human choice.

2. The Bible in its teaching about the Word of God makes no distinction as to when it can be trusted and does not indicate that its trustworthiness is confined to one sphere. The theory of limited inerrancy disagrees with the Bible's teaching concerning its authority.[43]

3. Following Christ involves submitting to him as Master, which in turn involves submitting to his teaching, which includes affirmations of the divine authority of the Old Testament. So where are we? Are we disciples of Christ or not? Does the theory of limited inerrancy have the practical effect of redefining Christian discipleship? I fear that it truncates Christian discipleship of a genuinely biblical kind, because it releases would-be disciples from a submissive attitude to the Old Testament in selected spheres where modern people now experience desires to escape. It imitates the attitude of the Serpent: "Did God actually say . . . ?" (Gen. 3:1).

By contrast with limited inerrancy, a more modest form of the vehicle-cargo approach has the advantage of trying to preserve Christian discipleship in a recognizable form. It says that we should accept whatever the Bible teaches on any subject, but that we need to be thoughtful in trying to interpret the Bible. Fair enough.

Consequences of Failure to Dispel Myths

But we need to be equally thoughtful about modern myths. Otherwise, we may swallow the myths by unconscious osmosis. Having swallowed the myths, we will find ourselves with no reasonable alternative *except*

---

43. It would be nice if some of the advocates of new theories of inspiration and divine truthfulness would wrestle directly with major defenses of the "old" theory, such as John M. Frame, *The Doctrine of the Word of God* (Phillipsburg, NJ: P&R, 2010), rather than just ignore them.

to follow interpretive practices that conform to the patterns dictated by the modern myths. In practice, we will end up dismissing anything and everything in the Bible, from whatever genre and in whatever context, that does not fit comfortably within the confines of the alleged assured verities projected by the modern myths. That is, we will dismiss material on the basis of content, prior to detailed interpretation, rather than receiving it positively on the basis of sound interpretation.[44]

The myths dictate, for example, that modern people know that the sun does not rise. Thus, any statement to the contrary within the Bible is already an infallible signal to modern people. They "know" that they are reading a genre that does not really intend to say what it says, but only uses an accommodated, erroneous expression as a vehicle for some theological truth. As a result, modern mythic "truths" become unchallengeable. The myths tell people beforehand the limits of what the Bible must actually be communicating.

Consider another illustration of how the process works. Let us say that popularized modern science tells us that mankind evolved by purely gradualistic means from simian ancestors. Rather than ask critical questions, the person who accepts the myth of progress just accepts this pronouncement as the fruit of superior knowledge. Then, without lifting a finger to reengage the interpretation of Genesis 2–3, Romans 5:12–21, and 1 Corinthians 15:21–22, 44–49, he instantly "knows" that any apparent claim about a historical Adam must be part of the vehicle whereby the Bible uses a historically erroneous picture to teach theological truth.

This approach is different from merely using modern knowledge claims as an occasion to reexamine both sides together: we examine (1) whether we have properly understood what the Bible is saying and (2) whether the modern knowledge claims are as solid as they are commonly assumed to be. We should critically analyze not only simple, popularized summaries from the scientific establishment but simple summaries of the worldview of the ancient Near East and summaries of critical and traditional claims about what Genesis 1 or any other key text allegedly means.[45]

---

44. Noel Weeks, "Problems in Interpreting Genesis: Part 1," *Creation* 2, no. 3 (June 1979): 27–32, http://creation.com/problems-in-interpreting-genesis-part-1.

45. My own encounters with a sample of modern arguments and explanations suggest to me that in discussions about the ancient Near Eastern environment, uncertainties in interpreting

Positive Understanding of Genesis 1

We have a further reason for criticizing vehicle-cargo alternatives, both of the more extreme and modest kinds. As Christians, we should love Genesis 1 and what God says through it. We should expect that, if God is gracious to us and if we take Genesis 1 with the utmost seriousness, including its cultural alienness, we may be progressively freed from bondage to modern cultural myths, including, preeminently, the myth of scientistic metaphysics. This freedom is important for spiritual health. We should be disappointed with the vehicle-cargo approach because it unwittingly conceals the meaning of Genesis 1 and reinforces rather than challenges the myths that stand in the way of understanding it. As we understand it, we may more and more receive the full benefit of its spiritual nourishment.

In subsequent chapters, we will take up the positive teaching of Genesis 1.

---

details, uncertainties about a focus on physicality, and incompatibilities between different ancient Near Eastern texts often disappear from view as one moves from the texts themselves to further stages of interpretation: translations, specialists' analyses, surveys for pastors and seminarians, and finally, semipopular accounts directed to the general public. The result is that scholarly uncertainties get transformed at the popular level into confident assertions.

6

The Genre of Genesis

Before dealing in greater detail with Genesis 1–3, we need to discuss the issue of genre. To what genre does Genesis 1–3 belong? This question makes a difference because a decision about genre affects how we assess details within Genesis 1–3. For example, if someone decides—wrongly, I believe—that Genesis 1–3 belongs to a genre of "edifying fiction," he would consider all the details also as fiction.

The structure of Genesis unfolds according to genealogical lines. After the initial section, Genesis 1:1–2:3,[1] each subsequent section begins with the words "These are the generations of . . ." or a similar expression. The section beginning in Genesis 2:4 comes to a conclusion at 4:26, since the next section opens with the words "This is the book of the generations of Adam" (5:1). Accordingly, Genesis 1:1–2:3 is a distinct piece, belonging to a particular genre. So is Genesis 2:4–4:26. Both of these sections belong to a larger discourse, the book of Genesis, with its own genre. Since the genre of the whole influences our assessment of the genre of the pieces within it, we start by asking about the genre of Genesis as a complete book.[2]

By and large, the scholarly world does not seem to devote much disciplined attention to the genre of Genesis as a whole.[3] There are

---

1. On the division between 2:3 and 2:4, see C. John Collins, *Genesis 1–4: A Linguistic, Literary, and Theological Commentary* (Phillipsburg, NJ: P&R, 2006), 40–42.

2. From this point onward, the chapter reproduces a good deal of Vern S. Poythress, "Dealing with the Genre of Genesis and Its Opening Chapters," *Westminster Theological Journal* 78, no. 2 (2016): 217–30. Used with permission.

3. There are plenty of scholarly articles on the genre of *smaller pieces* within Genesis, but less discussion of the genre of the whole of Genesis. Just as a check, I decided to choose five major

106 Basic Interpretive Principles

some exceptions, of course. This lack of attention is odd, because scholars routinely affirm the importance of genre. So what happens when we do pay attention?

What Is Genre?

First, let us clear away some underbrush. What do we mean by *genre*?

A genre is a natural grouping for pieces of discourse. Within the Bible, proverbs, sermons, letters, and poetic songs are all genres. Each individual proverb belongs naturally together with all other proverbs in the genre "proverbs." Each sermon belongs naturally together with all other sermons in the genre "sermons."

However, the word *genre* can have a range of meanings, and that is at least part of the problem. The *Merriam-Webster's Collegiate Dictionary* gives as meaning number one "a category of artistic, musical, or literary composition characterized by a particular style, form, or content."[4] A definition like that one can be a reasonable starting point. But there are ambiguities. Are we supposed to be focusing on style, on form, on content, on all three equally, or on any one of the three that we choose? To some extent, style and form may overlap in meaning, but what about content? A focus on content seems different.

Suppose we say that, whenever two pieces of discourse have similar content, they belong to the same genre. That choice does not lead to expected results. For example, Exodus 14:15–31 and 15:1–18 are both about the crossing of the Red Sea and the defeat of Pharaoh's army in the sea. They both have the same content, loosely speaking. But do we normally say on that basis that they belong to the same genre? No. The first is prose narrative, while the second is a poetic

---

commentaries from the historical-critical tradition and five written by broadly evangelical scholars. The historical-critical commentaries all failed to devote significant attention to the genre of the *whole* of Genesis. They were dominated by concerns about sources and smaller discourse units; on this tendency, see V. Philips Long, *The Art of Biblical History* (Grand Rapids, MI: Zondervan, 1994), reprinted in *Foundations of Contemporary Interpretation, Six Volumes in One*, ed. Moisés Silva (Grand Rapids, MI: Zondervan, 1996), 311 (my citations from this work always give the pagination of the 1996 edition). Among the five evangelical commentaries, three had significant attention to "structure," focusing on the unique way in which Genesis 1 divides itself into sections of genealogical history. But structure does not equate to genre (see discussion later in this chapter). Only one commentary actually discussed genre in the sense given here. And even then, there was no attention to comparing Genesis to other ancient works of the same or similar genre.

4. *Merriam-Webster's Collegiate Dictionary*, 11th ed. (Springfield, MA: Merriam-Webster, 2003), 522.

song. What people normally have in mind when they mention genre is a category like "prose narrative" or "poetic song." They do not have in mind the idea of "all discourses dealing with the episode of the crossing of the Red Sea." Similarly, Judges 4:12–22 and 5:2–31 both have the same content, namely, the defeat of Sisera and his forces by the Israelites under Barak (and, of course, Jael). But the first is prose narrative and the second is a poetic song. The Gospel of Matthew and Acts 10:37–41 both have as their content the life, death, and resurrection of Christ. But the first is a Gospel and the second is part of a sermon.

Suppose we ask about the genre of Genesis 1. The closest match in terms of content is Psalm 104. Both have as their content God's acts of creating the world. The first is a prose narrative, while the second is a poetic song. Psalm 8 is also related, because it reflects on creation. Somewhat more distant are other pieces that speak about creation, such as Nehemiah 9:6; Psalms 19:1–6; 74:12–17; 95:3–5; 136:1–9; 148; and Proverbs 8:22–31. Of course, we can have an illuminating discussion by comparing all these passages. But do we really want to say that Genesis 1 belongs to the same genre as the other passages? Or do we want to say that Genesis 1 belongs to the same genre as Acts 17:24–26 because both are about God creating the world? That is not the way that most people use the word *genre*.

It is certainly useful to compare passages based on overlapping content. But such comparison is a different *kind* of thing than what we do when we look at style and form. In fact, style and form are not perfectly separable from content.[5] In actual acts of communication, they are all woven together. So it can be useful to add content as an additional secondary guiding factor along with style and form. But to include content as the most prominent principle for guiding classification is just to introduce another kind of classification, one radically at variance from normal classification by genre. Thus, for our purposes, let us stipulate that the word *genre* involves focus on style and form, as primary aspects, and on content only as a possible

---

5. Note Kenneth L. Pike's insightful discussion of form-meaning composites: Kenneth L. Pike, *Language in Relation to a Unified Theory of the Structure of Human Behavior*, 2nd ed. (The Hague/Paris: Mouton, 1967), 62–63; Kenneth L. Pike, *Linguistic Concepts: An Introduction to Tagmemics* (Lincoln, NE/London: University of Nebraska Press, 1982), 111–17.

supplemental or secondary contributor. I think that, for the most part, that is also what biblical interpreters have had in mind when they talked about genre.[6] (See Fig. 6.1.)

Fig. 6.1: Genre, Involving Style and Form

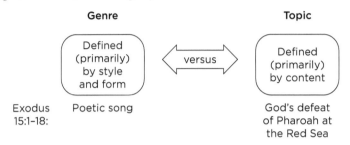

Genre Belonging to Smaller Pieces

As a second step in clarification, let me stipulate that I will use the word *genre* to cover all sizes of discourse, big and small. Some biblical interpreters prefer to use the word *genre* only for whole books of the Bible. They use the word *form* for smaller unified pieces, such as narrative episodes, songs, and individual proverbs. This choice is merely a difference in vocabulary.

Genre as Emic

Next, genre is an emic category,[7] having to do with an insider's perception rather than an outsider's or a theorist's analysis using universal "types" that are postulated to organize all literature in every culture. To take one example: apocalyptic literature, such as in Daniel 7, is one kind of genre in the Old Testament, but does not correspond in a strict way with a familiar genre in modern English. Thus, what counts as a single genre depends on the language, the culture, and the context. (See Fig. 6.2.)

---

6. For a further distinction between literary form (which is close to my meaning), register, and style, see C. John Collins, *Reading Genesis Well: Navigating History, Poetry, Science, and Truth in Genesis 1–11* (Grand Rapids, MI: Zondervan, 2018), 48–50.

7. On the contrast between an insider and an outsider with respect to culture or language, see Pike, *Language*, 37–72; Thomas Headland, Kenneth Pike, and Marvin Harris, eds., *Emics and Etics: The Insider/Outsider Debate* (Newbury Park, CA: Sage, 1990); Vern S. Poythress, *In the Beginning Was the Word: Language—A God-Centered Approach* (Wheaton, IL: Crossway, 2009), 150–54.

Fig. 6.2: Genre versus Universal Cross-Cultural Classification

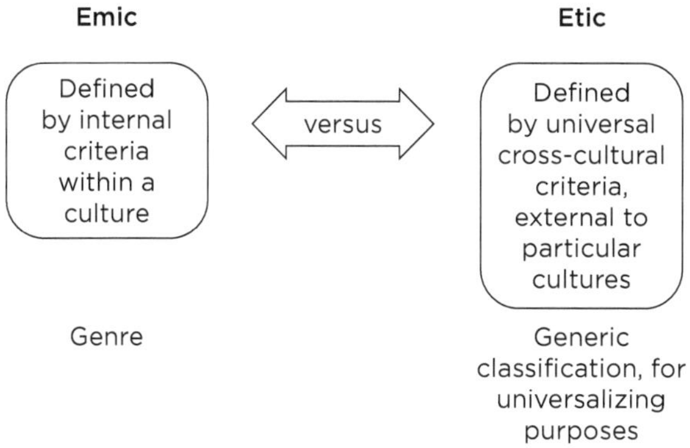

Emic   **Etic**

Defined by internal criteria within a culture

versus

Defined by universal cross-cultural criteria, external to particular cultures

Genre

Generic classification, for universalizing purposes

Nevertheless, there are some universal tendencies, because of universal human nature. The commonalities of human nature enable us gradually to come to understand communication in other cultures. Robert E. Longacre, on the basis of experience with discourses in many languages, sets forth a tentative universal typology that classifies discourses at a high level of generality by two intersecting axes, namely, "succession" and "projection."[8] The first axis, that of succession, classifies discourses according to whether they focus on succession in time or not. Is a discourse organized with a focus on the passage of time? Narratives (such as Jesus's parables or a story of a miracle by Elisha) are characterized by succession in time, while expository discourses (such as Ephesians 1) are not. The second axis, that of projection, classifies discourses according to whether they focus on "projected" time rather than time that has already taken place (realized time). Narrative focuses on realized time, while procedural discourse focuses on projected time by specifying what is to be done. For example, a procedural discourse may describe how to cook a chicken whenever and wherever it is done. The specification for the peace offering in Leviticus 5:1–6 is a procedural discourse. It

---

8. Robert E. Longacre, *An Anatomy of Speech Notions* (Lisse, Netherlands: Peter de Ridder, 1976), 199–201. To appreciate the scope of Longacre's experience, note, for instance, his book on Philippine languages: *Discourse, Paragraph, and Sentence Structure in Selected Philippine Languages: Volume 1: Discourse and Paragraph Structure* (Santa Ana, CA: Summer Institute of Linguistics, 1968). For a list of publications, see "SIL Language & Culture Archives," http://www .sil.org/resources/search/contributor/longacre-robert-e. From the standpoint of Old Testament studies, it may be worth noting that Longacre also has analyzed Old Testament Hebrew discourse: Robert E. Longacre, *Joseph: A Story of Divine Providence: A Text Theoretical and Textlinguistic Analysis of Genesis 37 and 39–48* (Winona Lake, IN: Eisenbrauns, 1989).

is intended to give direction for many future instances of peace offerings. It differs in this respect from Leviticus 8–9, which describes a single, unrepeatable set of events in which Moses consecrated Aaron and his sons. Leviticus 5:1–6 is procedural (focusing on projected time), while Leviticus 8–9 is narrative (focusing on realized time). (See Fig. 6.3.)

Fig. 6.3: Two Kinds of Classification for Verbal Discourses

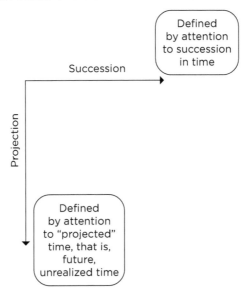

The intersection of the two axes gives us four types of discourse:

1. *Narrative,* with a focus on succession but not on projection (for example, Luke and Acts).
2. *Expository discourse,* without a focus on either succession or projection (i.e., no focus on time) (for example, Romans 1–3).
3. *Procedural discourse,* with a focus on succession and projection—it is typically dealing with a succession of steps to be undertaken in a projected future or a general time (for example, Lev. 14:1–9, concerning the procedure for cleansing from leprosy).
4. *Hortatory discourse,* with a focus on projection but not on succession: "You should do this (in the future)" (for example, Ephesians 5). (See Fig. 6.4.)

Fig. 6.4: Four Classes of Discourse

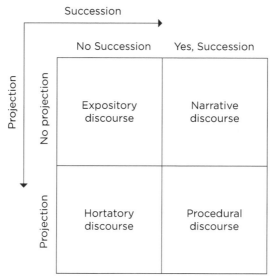

Longacre further divides narrative according to the location of the events: "It recounts events supposed to have happened somewhere, whether in *the real or in an imaginary world*."[9] Jesus's parables take place in an imaginary world, while the narratives in the Gospels that *describe* Jesus as teaching in parables are set in the real world. (See Fig. 6.5.)

In many languages, each of these categories may be further subdivided into prose and poetry. And there are further divisions beyond that, according to the unique emic expectations of a particular language and culture.[10]

According to this classification, Genesis as a whole is clearly prose narrative, with some embedded pieces that are poetic and sometimes future-oriented (Genesis 49). Prose narrative is the broad genre to which Genesis belongs. We may also consider the genre of Genesis 1. It, too, is prose narrative, with one short poetic or semipoetic embedded piece at verse 27. In an obvious way, it is in a separate category from the poetic songs in Psalms 8 and 104.

The principle of emicity also implies that we must be careful not naively to carry genre classifications from one culture to another or from one language to another. In a situation of multiple cultures and

---

9. Longacre, *Anatomy of Speech Notions*, 199 (emphasis added).
10. Longacre, *Anatomy of Speech Notions*, 202, 205.

languages (such as the ancient Near East), where people from different cultures and languages interact, we may naturally expect a certain degree of borrowing and influencing across cultures. But we cannot take it for granted. Each language has its own genius, and while some features may be borrowed, others will not be. There is likely to be common *content* to some extent because all of the cultures involve human beings and all have agriculture and/or herding as their economic base. But as we have seen, content is not the major determiner of what most people have in mind when they speak about genre.

Fig. 6.5: Real and Imaginary World

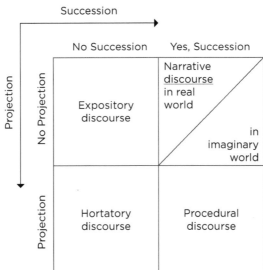

Genre as Synchronic

Next, genre is a *synchronic* rather than a diachronic category. That is to say, a genre describes what is true at one particular time in a particular language and culture. By contrast, *diachronic* analysis focuses on changes through time and on comparisons between earlier and later stages in historical development. (See Fig. 6.6.)

Of course, genres can evolve over time. We can talk about the *development* of the genre of the modern novel, the detective story, or the blog post. But people happily read detective stories and understand them without any knowledge of the history of the development of the genre. Once in place, a genre is what it is. The history of its development gives various insights to scholars. But in the end, it is virtually irrelevant for understanding the way in which common people customarily interpret a genre that they know. They know and recognize the genre without any reference to a multigenerational history behind it. That is what is meant when we say that it is a synchronic category. Readers do not need to know the diachronic story—whether, generations ago, the genre came from something else or owed its origin to a confluence of several factors.

Fig 6.6: Synchronic versus Diachronic Analysis

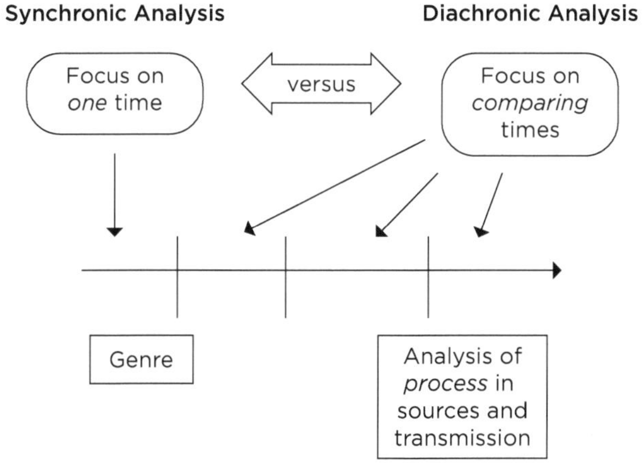

Consider how this understanding of genre interfaces with the historical-critical tradition. For a considerable time, the historical-critical tradition was oriented primarily to the discovery of *sources*, whether written or oral. The JEDP documentary hypothesis is the classic case. This kind of discussion is essentially diachronic. According to this kind of thinking, the "J" document is one of the sources behind the Pentateuch (see the discussion in chap. 3, p. 53). It is to be compared both with the later composition represented by the finished books of the Pentateuch and with earlier sources in either written or oral form. Within this scenario, each individual written or oral production—whether Genesis, postulated sources such as J, or oral sources behind it—naturally has its own synchronic genre at the time of its composition. If a later redactor integrates a number of sources in a jumbled fashion or just sews together disparate pieces, the resulting composition may show unevenness. Yet as a completed composition, it still has its own genre.

A composition may also have some archaizing features, if the composition is deliberately imitating the past or if an editor does not recognize the tension between the present and a genre belonging to an earlier epoch. But because genres tend to change slowly, this problem is not especially troublesome.

Though each layer of source has its own genre, the historical-critical tradition nevertheless focuses primarily on diachronic study. It compares and contrasts sources at various layers in the time up until the final composition.

In contrast to the predominantly diachronic approach to sources, we find other approaches that are synchronic. In the late twentieth and early twenty-first centuries, so-called "literary" approaches characteristically have had a synchronic focus. They take each discourse as a whole and aspire to treat it according to the genre that it represented at the time when it arrived at its finished form.[11]

Fig. 6.7: Literary versus Historical-Critical Analysis

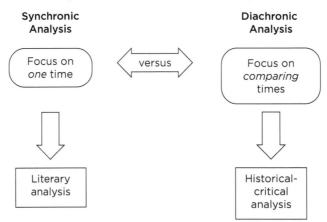

My contribution here is to claim that if we focus on the practical use of verbal communication within a cultural setting, the meaning of a discourse is best sought by attending to what it says, given its

---

11. On the interaction of diachronic and synchronic approaches, see Noel K. Weeks, *Sources and Authors: Assumptions in the Study of Hebrew Bible Narrative* (Piscataway, NJ: Gorgias, 2011), chap. 2.

context of authorship and circumstances. In this sense, the meaning is essentially synchronic. The history of putative sources behind the author and the circumstances is virtually irrelevant. The meaning of a text is found in what it says (in context), not in the history of its origins. We find the meaning of Genesis 1 or Genesis as a whole by reading Genesis, not by trying to reconstruct its sources.

If we believe, as I do, that in the case of the Bible we have divine speech and divine meanings, not merely human meanings in isolation from the divine, the point holds even more strongly. God is creative. He can say new things. So even if there is a background of earlier things that he said or that human beings said, and even if he uses some of the same words as before, the speech is new and must be accorded attention. Because meaning is communicated by a textual expression in *context*, a different context at a later time may lead to a different assessment of meaning. Memory of earlier speeches counts as part of the *synchronic* context, because *memory* of the past is still memory *in the present*. At the same time, the synchronic social *context* for a discourse is still not to be confused with the discourse that God in his creativity actually expresses at a particular point in time and space.

The upshot is that source criticism has very limited value when it comes to actually interpreting the texts that we have.[12] In other words, with respect to the book of Genesis or to a piece within it, such as Genesis 1 or Genesis 1–3, we must attend to the piece as divine speech. Speculation about the sources, whether a supposed P document for Genesis 1 or a J document for Genesis 2–3, is a deflection from the right focus when it comes to understanding the meaning of a text.

Genre Concerned with Shared Features

Next, a genre is a unified class, exemplified by multiple discourses that share common features. In this sense, genre and structure are not the same. Scholarly discussions of structure often focus on the unique structure of a *single* discourse and undertake to produce a structural outline that is unique to the discourse in question. That which is unique is *not* a feature of genre. Genre is a classification according to what is *common* or shared among a number of discourses.

---

12. Vern S. Poythress, *Inerrancy and the Gospels: A God-Centered Approach to the Challenges of Harmonization* (Wheaton, IL: Crossway, 2012), chap. 16.

"Prose narrative" and "proverb" are genres. A structured outline that is unique to a single book is not a genre and does not contribute in and of itself to an identification of genre. It becomes relevant, of course, if we discern a *common* structure belonging to a number of distinct discourses.

Genres in Written and Oral Communication

Next, written communication has a set of genres distinct from (though influenced by) oral communication. Wycliffe Bible Translators has almost certainly had more experience than any other organization in the world with the process of introducing written communication for the first time into cultures that previously were completely oral. Members of Wycliffe analyze a new language, develop an alphabet for it, and then start a literacy program. They also encourage newly literate native speakers to start recording and composing in written form stories and other pieces of communication in their own language. Within a short period of time, the written forms begin to deviate from the oral forms in subtle ways. There may be many reasons for this tendency, but one is that the written form is suitable for communication over gaps in time and space, whereas oral communication is necessarily face to face (apart from such technology as the telephone, radio, and audio recording devices). The absence of face-to-face contact leads writers to put into written communication signals that make up for the lack not only of facial expressions and gestures, but of intonation, timbre, volume, speed of delivery, and other features of oral communication. In addition, extended analysis of oral communication by a recipient has to rely completely on memory, while analysis of written communication can use backtracking to check and recheck the wording of any part of the total discourse. This difference also has its effect in encouraging distinctions between written and oral genres.

The consequence is that in any culture that already has a history of writing, the written genres differ from oral genres, though the two still show affinities. This principle is likely to be reinforced in cultures where literacy exists but is confined mainly to a scribal class. The scribes may easily take more steps in making innovations in a written genre because they have a subculture of their own with specialized interests and goals.

Within a predominantly oral culture, the written compositions that are narratives may be recorded with a view primarily to oral recitation. The same may be the case for songs, prophetic discourses, proverbs, and other genres. This oral purpose will, of course, influence the character of the written genres. But in the end, what is written must still be seen as belonging to a written as opposed to an oral genre.

The upshot of all this is that the book of Genesis and the embedded discourses within it (such as Genesis 1) must be considered as exemplifying *written* genres, not to be confused with the oral genres that statistically would have been used more often in a predominantly oral culture. In a sense, this observation makes little difference, because we have no direct examples from the ancient Near East of oral communication—there are no audio recordings. Rather, there are instances of oral speech cited in the written documents. The citations of oral speech may show genre differences from the matrix of written discourse around them. But technically, both are instances of written genres. The scholarly world rightly wants to discuss the social environment, which includes much oral communication. But in the process, it is easy to overlook the principle that written genres may show differences.

Genres with Fuzzy Boundaries

Next, genres may have fuzzy boundaries. They are not airtight boxes into which every discourse fits with perfect snugness. Human beings and their acts of communication have flexibility.[13] So any of Longacre's four discourse types and emic subclasses within them remain rough-and-ready classifications that allow room for exploration and stretching out in new directions. It would be convenient for some of the purposes of scholarship if genres were neat boxes with sharp boundaries and rigorous rules for what happens inside each box. But life is more complicated than that.

Genres Embedded within Genres

The final principle is that a genre may be embedded within a larger piece of discourse that has its own genre. This embedding is a common feature in long discourses. So, for example, the Gospels include

---

13. Poythress, *In the Beginning Was the Word*, chaps. 19 and 23.

miracle stories, exorcisms, teaching blocks, and stories of conflict between Jesus and his opponents (sometimes combined with miracles or
other incidents). Genesis 1:1–2:3 is embedded as an opening section
in the book of Genesis as a whole. Genesis as a whole also includes
genealogical records (Genesis 5, 10, 11:10–26) and poetic prophecies
(9:25–27; 25:23; 49:2–27). In such cases, as literary analysts would
emphasize, interpreters must take into account the genres character-
izing all the levels of embedding. So, for example, the poetic prophecy
concerning Issachar constitutes Genesis 49:14–15. It is embedded in
a larger structure of prophecies concerning each of the twelve sons of
Jacob, found in 49:3–27. This whole prophecy is in turn embedded
in a last speech of Jacob, 49:1b–27. That in turn is embedded in the
narrative episode in which Jacob gives the speech, namely, 49:1–33.
And that in turn is embedded in the narrative of the last days of Jacob
in 48:1–49:33, and that in turn in the narrative of the time after Jacob
and his family arrived in Egypt, 47:1–50:26, which is the final portion
of the section on "the generations of Jacob," 37:2–50:26. This section
is embedded as one subdivision within the book of Genesis as a whole.
(See Fig. 6.8.)

Fig. 6.8: Genres Embedded

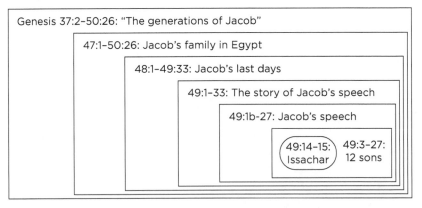

In view of the more or less continuous historical line represented
by the books of the Pentateuch, we may also ask whether Genesis
is to be treated as embedded in the larger unity of the Pentateuch—
separated into a distinct "book" mainly because there are practi-

cal limits to the physical size of a single book. Or do we go even further out and see Genesis as embedded in the continuous story that extends not only through the Pentateuch but through Joshua, Judges, 1–2 Samuel, and 1–2 Kings? We could extend the story into the New Testament and the anticipation of the new heavens and the new earth, since God as the divine Author gives us a historical line that extends that far.

Treating Genesis according to Its Genre

Many biblical scholars and literary scholars tell us to treat a document according to its genre. So we need to discuss this question: "What is the genre of Genesis?" It is prose narrative in ancient Hebrew. People may debate the fine-tuning of ancient historiographic practices. But such debates can easily become speculative in the absence of extant ancient Israelite discussions on the subject of historiography. So it is safer to start with basics.

What are the basics in the case of Genesis? The most obvious thing about the genre of Genesis is that it is prose narrative (with some embedded poetry of various kinds, as we have observed). Genesis is not only prose narrative, but a giant-sized instance of it, in comparison to almost any of the documents that we have recovered in other languages of the ancient Near East.[14] In terms of contents (which, remember, are not the primary focus), it covers generations of descendants. It contains many distinct individual episodes, held together primarily by the promises of God, perceived obstacles to the promises, and the thread of genealogical connection through the line of descendants of Adam through Abraham, Isaac, and Jacob.

What is the nearest match to Genesis in terms of genre (not, mind you, in terms of content, which would lead us to 1 Chron. 1:1–2:4)? The nearest matches are other instances of prose narratives in ancient Hebrew, particularly the ones that carry on an

---

14. Long, *Art of Biblical History*, in *Foundations of Contemporary Interpretation*, 312, citing J. B. Porter, "Old Testament Historiography," in *Tradition and Interpretation: Essays by Members of the Society for Old Testament Study*, ed. G. W. Anderson (Oxford: Clarendon Press, 1979), 130–31; Derek Kidner, *Genesis: An Introduction and Commentary* (Leicester, England: Inter-Varsity; Downers Grove, IL: InterVarsity Press, 1967), 13. Outside of other books in the Bible, the closest in genre may be the Sumerian king list; see Thorkild Jacobsen, *The Sumerian King List* (Chicago: University of Chicago Press, 1939). But it is little more than a list of the names of kings and the length of their kingships. It is far from the stylistic complexity of Genesis.

extended, connected story through many individual episodes. The closest matches in this respect might be Numbers, 1–2 Samuel, and Ezra-Nehemiah. But all of these books cover time periods much shorter than the time spanned by Genesis. There are quite a few other narrative books, but they too show special features. For example, Exodus has a large section on the tabernacle. Leviticus has a large amount of material that is procedural or hortatory. Deuteronomy is hortatory (within a narrative framework). Joshua has a large section about dividing the land into tribal portions. Judges has the repeated cycle of deliverance and bondage summarized in Judges 2:16–19. Ruth is a smaller book that involves only a few main characters and a limited amount of time. Jonah is similar, and to some extent also Esther. First Chronicles has an elaborate genealogical record in chapters 1–9. First and 2 Kings and 2 Chronicles have unique features belonging to the regularities in the way that they treat the reign of individual kings. The second half of Daniel is dominated by visionary experiences and communications. Yet all of these are still recognizably prose narratives. Job has an outer framework of narrative, but inside this framework we find almost nothing except poetic speeches.

As a prose narrative, Genesis shows some general similarities with these other narrative books. But it is also distinct in its form because of the way it is organized into a genealogical history. It has distinct sections that begin (with slight variations), "These are the generations of . . ." As far as I can see, there is nothing quite like this anywhere else among the extant literature in biblical Hebrew or in the extant documents we have recovered from elsewhere in the ancient Near East. And here, I propose, is one reason why there is less discussion of the genre of Genesis than there might otherwise be. The reason is that there is, in one sense, nothing much to discuss. Genesis is unlike any other document. The lesson we can draw is that we must, accordingly, to a large extent treat it on its own terms and not be enamored by appeals to formal parallels.

Though Genesis is unique in the details of its form, it *does* still belong to the broad genre composed of prose narratives in ancient Hebrew. The closest parallels, as we observed, are to be found in other narrative books in the Old Testament canon.

Claims to Real Events

So far, we have not put in the foreground one other major distinction that Longacre introduces when discussing narrative: the distinction between recounting events "in the real world and in an imaginary world."[15] This is the distinction, if you will, between nonfiction and fiction. Though *nonfiction* and *fiction* are modern English terms, the reality is culturally more extensive. At a principal level, this distinction is culturally universal, because all human cultures have creativity, and one aspect of creativity is the ability to make up stories.

We need to be clear about our terminology at this point. Among biblical scholars, the word *fiction* is sometimes used to describe literary artistry. This use seems to me to be unfortunate in its potential to confuse. For our purposes, let us use *fiction* as a descriptive label for nonfactual narrative, or, in Longacre's terms, a narrative that claims to recount events "in an imaginary world."[16]

Given the potential for lying and deceit, we need also to distinguish between an author's claims and the truth of the matter. A human author may want to claim that some event happened in the real world when it did not. *Fiction* and *nonfiction*, as labels for genres, are more suited to describing the *claims* made by an author by means of his discourse. That is, a nonfictional narrative is a narrative that *claims* to be about the real world, whether or not the author is lying. (See Fig. 6.9.)

In other contexts, of course, people may use the same terms to evaluate the *truth* of an author's claims.

We must not oversimplify by assuming that there can be no mixture of fiction and nonfiction, or that there can be no discourse that temporarily pretends to be nonfiction but is later revealed to be fiction. Neither do the broad categories of fiction and nonfiction settle the question of the detailed choices people make in different *kinds* of nonfictional narrative and fictional narrative.[17]

We can see instances of fictional narrative in the Bible, such as Jotham's parable (Judg. 9:8–15) and Jesus's parables. We can also see occasions when the effectiveness of a parable depends partly on

---

15. Longacre, *Anatomy of Speech Notions*, 199.
16. See also Long, *Art of Biblical History*, in *Foundations of Contemporary Interpretation*, 319–22.
17. See Long, *Art of Biblical History*, in *Foundations of Contemporary Interpretation*; Poythress, *Inerrancy and the Gospels*, chaps. 4, 5, and 10.

temporarily concealing the fact that it is fictional. We have Nathan's parable to David in 2 Samuel 12:1b–4 and the parable by the woman of Tekoa in 2 Samuel 14:5b–7. In 1 Kings 20:39b–40a, we have a made-up story from "a certain man of the sons of the prophets" (v. 35). Ahab, the king of Israel, renders a judgment based on the assumption that the man is telling a nonfictional story. Then the man reveals that it is actually a parable about Ahab himself (vv. 41–42).

Fig. 6.9: Fiction and Nonfiction as Genres

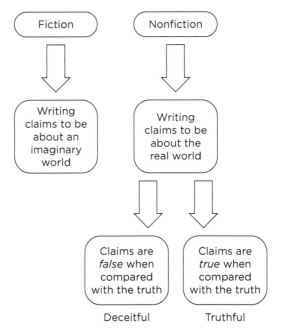

We also have cases of out-and-out deceit, where a story offers itself in the genre of nonfiction, but where some of the events described did not actually happen. For example, in 1 Kings 13:18, the old prophet in Bethel deceived the man of God from Judah using a short made-up story about what he had heard from "an angel."

These instances confirm that people in ancient Israel knew the difference between reality and make-believe. The instances also confirm that sometimes the recognition of an instance of reality or make-believe makes a big difference in human responses. In 1 Kings 13:19, the man of God from Judah clearly would not have stayed for a meal if he had not believed that the old prophet was telling the truth. And the narrative itself gives a blunt evaluation: "But he lied to him" (v. 18). In the cases involving Nathan, the woman from Tekoa, and one of the sons of the prophets, the plan from the beginning was that at a crucial point the fictional nature of the story would be revealed. In all three cases, the communication as a whole depends for its effectiveness on a principial distinction between fiction and nonfiction. This distinction is recognized and familiar not only to Nathan, the woman, and the son of the prophets, but to the people whom they address. In other words, the distinction is emic to Israelite culture of the time.

We can also see that fictional prose can use more than one style. Jotham's parable not only sets the story in an imaginary world where trees talk, but addresses pointedly the treachery of Abimelech. A number of converging features let Jotham's audience know that his story is fiction. On the other hand, according to their plans, the parables uttered by Nathan, by the woman of Tekoa, and by the son of the prophets have realistic settings within the time and culture of the addressees because they are deliberately intended to sound like nonfiction. These examples also show that ancient people understood the possibility of deception when the narrative setting was realistic. A storyteller could deceive, either temporarily, as a parabolic stratagem, or permanently, if he lied about the events. (Still another option is that a storyteller could mistakenly think he was telling the truth.)

Consider, for example, 2 Samuel 1:6–10. The Amalekite tells David an account according to which he killed Saul. In terms of genre, the account has the marks of nonfiction. It includes a dialogue between two nonfictional characters, namely, the Amalekite and King Saul. It has a realistic setting and realistic events within the setting. It occurs in answer to David's question about facts in the real world. It coheres with the fact, which David will later be able to confirm from other sources, that Saul has died in the battle. But it does not easily cohere with 1 Samuel 31:4–5. It looks as though, in 2 Samuel 1:7–9, the Amalekite invents a dialogue between two nonfictional persons, himself and King Saul. He lies in hopes of ingratiating himself with David. According to our terminology, the narrative from the Amalekite belongs to the genre of nonfictional narrative. It needs to belong to that genre precisely in order to accomplish its deception. It *claims* to refer to events in the "real world." But in some of its parts, it does not—it is deceiving.

This incident illustrates a broader principle. If a storyteller wants to deceive, he has to pay attention to making his story plausible. It has to sound like nonfiction. In terms of *genre*, it has to be a nonfictional narrative. So it has to cohere within itself and with the situation. If, on the other hand, a storyteller is speaking in good faith, he should give some signal when he is giving out fiction or when he is giving out a combination (as with a fictional story set in a realistic cultural setting of the time or a made-up dialogue between identifiably nonfictional persons).

Now let us apply this emic distinction between fiction and nonfiction to the books of narrative prose. What may we conclude? The books of 1–2 Kings and 1–2 Chronicles both mention earlier records, "books" about events in the period of the monarchy. The mention of earlier written records underlines the fact that, at face value, 1–2 Kings and 1–2 Chronicles are asking readers to regard the narratives as describing real events in the past, not fiction. The events are such as could be recorded by observers and recordkeepers at the time. The records in 1–2 Kings and 1–2 Chronicles are selective and have theological and literary interests. But that does not destroy the fact that they claim to refer to events in the real world and that they expect the hearers to regard the events as happening in the real world rather than an imaginary world.

Genesis belongs to the same broad genre of narrative prose as does 1–2 Samuel and 1–2 Kings. Since there is no literary signal to tell us that it is fiction, and since, indeed, it belongs to a continuous temporal development leading from creation to the exile, we conclude that it is nonfiction.[18]

And so it was treated, by both Jewish and Christian audiences, almost uniformly until the Enlightenment. The Enlightenment and the

---

18. Some scholars within the historical-critical tradition have endeavored to reply to this reasoning by appealing to categories like "legend." A genre label like "legend" may supposedly characterize some earlier sources behind Genesis. At an early point, a scholar may suppose, those who passed on legends may not have cared particularly about whether they were fiction, nonfiction, or mixed. This approach relies on speculative reconstruction of sources, and in so doing, it neglects the issue of the synchronic genre of Genesis. Moreover, most of these same scholars would say that Genesis as a finished whole belongs to a later period. But if that were so, it would only strengthen the argument that it belongs to the same genre of nonfiction prose narrative as 1–2 Samuel or 1–2 Kings. The modern scholar may choose to judge that the claims by Genesis about events in the world are false. But that is different from claiming that Genesis presents itself emically on its own terms as something other than a nonfictional genre. In fact, it does not. It is nonfiction.

post-Enlightenment period changed things. But that was not because scholars discovered something new about genre. Rather, they became skeptical of claims to religious authority made by various church figures. That skepticism then extended to the Bible itself. Along with such skepticism came changes in worldview, which made the Bible's claims have less sociological plausibility among intellectuals. The genres of biblical literature remain what they have always been. The difference is that some modern critics do not accept the claims made through the genre about events in the past.

It is possible, of course, to refine our sense of what ancient Hebrew nonfictional prose narratives are doing and to grow in our ability not to impose artificial expectations drawn from our own modern culture. That is all to the good. Such adjustments are quite different, however, from a large-scale attempt to avoid dealing with the commonalities between Genesis and other narratives in the Old Testament, and the fact that some of these narratives present themselves as nonfiction.

Joint Function of Historical, Theological, and Literary Aspects

It is useful at this juncture to say a bit about the intersection of historical, theological, and literary concerns.[19] One temptation in modern critical analysis of texts is to separate the three kinds of concern. If a text promotes a certain theology, those elements promoting the theology must not be historical. Or if the text shows literary artistry, that shows that it is artistic and therefore to that degree *not* historical. That kind of reasoning takes place because of a conception of "bare" history, one event after another in isolation from theology and literary artistry. It is understandable that such an approach should grow up in the ideological context of the Enlightenment. But it tends to falsify the emic structure of ancient genres, which did not make this separation. For example, if you believe, as many of the Jews of the Second Temple period believed, that God rules history according to his comprehensive plan, the theology of God's purposes in events is intrinsically built into history. The artistry of God's crafting is also built into it, because he is the final origin for beauty, adornment, and symmetry.

---

19. See also Long, *Art of Biblical History*, in *Foundations of Contemporary Interpretation*, 309, 315, 318, 327, 329.

In effect, the purpose of many ancient texts in the Bible is to give us all three aspects.[20] We would be doubtful about that claim only if we were also doubtful about the worldview and the view of God that are therein presupposed.

The Genre of Genesis 1

Having dealt with the genre of the book of Genesis as a whole, we may ask briefly about the genre of Genesis 1. Literarily, the proper unit of text is Genesis 1:1–2:3, because Genesis 2:4 begins a distinct new section of genealogical history.[21]

To what genre does Genesis 1:1–2:3 belong? Like Genesis as a whole, it is prose narrative. Nothing in the immediate literary context marks it out as a dream or as mere speculation. Since it is embedded in a normal way in the book of Genesis, it offers us, like the book as a whole, a nonfiction account, that is, an account of what it claims to be real events.

Genesis 1:1–2:3 does show some distinctive features in comparison to the rest of Genesis. We should briefly take note of them. First, 1:1–2:3 is not a part of the genealogical histories that begin with the expression "These are the generations of . . ." It functions as a kind of prologue for them. Second, it is "exalted prose," as Jack Collins has said.[22] It has literary artistry, as shown by the inclusion of poetic parallelism within the climax at Genesis 1:27. It has repetitions, such as "And there was evening and there was morning" and "God said." But it is possible to misconstrue the way in which such repetition makes a passage "special." Consider some other passages with repetitions. Genesis 5 has repetitions and artistic structure in the way that it organizes its genealogy. But what the passage offers us is still a genealogy. Similarly, Numbers 7 has a lot of repetition and careful structure, but its extra structure does not remove it from the category of nonfiction prose narrative.

So what about Genesis 1? What makes it "exalted"? Yes, there is literary artistry. But once we distinguish formal features from content, we can see that what is most exalted about Genesis 1 is not the literary

---

20. Poythress, *Inerrancy and the Gospels*, chap. 4.
21. For an argument that the proper point of division is at the end of 2:3, not midway through 2:4, see Collins, *Genesis 1–4*, 40–42.
22. Collins, *Genesis 1–4*, 36, 44; Collins, *Reading Genesis Well*, 157, 157n77.

artistry but the content. God speaks and acts in majesty to create the world and everything in it. The exaltedness of God and his activity imparts exaltedness to the passage. But that is a matter of content, not genre.

Similarly, what is most special about Genesis 2–3 is not a special formal feature about its Hebrew prose, but the content—these chapters describe the beginning of mankind and the beginning of human sin and death. These chapters have universal implications because the beginning is intrinsically universal in its scope and, according to God's determination, has effects on all of subsequent history.

Some scholars distinguish Genesis 1–11 from the rest of Genesis. This distinction makes some sense. Genesis 12–50 is focused primarily on one family, that of Abraham, and on a few generations within his line—Abraham, Isaac, Jacob, and his sons. By contrast, Genesis 1–11 covers many generations and encompasses the whole human race. In addition, Genesis 1–11 covers events from long ago. To modern historical reflection, it is not clear how accurate information about such distant times could have been retrieved by merely human agencies. Divine agency would have been necessary. And that leads us back to the crucial question of God's involvement in writing the text of Genesis. These features about Genesis 1–11 do indeed distinguish it from Genesis 12–50 *in certain respects*. But these respects primarily concern the type of content found in the chapters, not their genre. In terms of genre, Genesis 1–11 clearly links itself to Genesis 12–50 as part of one overall narrative development. Together with Genesis 12–50, it is nonfiction prose narrative, structured by the refrains "These are the generations of . . ."

It is useful here to look at another principle about genre and about the embedding of one discourse into a larger context. As a general rule, the "control" of meaning moves from the top down rather than from the bottom up. The meaning of an embedded piece can be radically altered, depending on the larger context in which it is embedded.[23] For example, individual speeches within narrative episodes in Genesis make sense only because of who makes them and in what context. The affirmation "There is no God" in Psalm 14:1 has a

---

23. Long, *Art of Biblical History*, in *Foundations of Contemporary Interpretation*, 312, citing Robert Bergen, "Text as a Guide to Authorial Intention: An Introduction to Discourse Criticism," *Journal of the Evangelical Theological Society* 30, no. 3 (1987): 330.

distinct meaning because it is embedded in the context: "The fool says in his heart, 'There is no God.'" This principle of top-down control confirms the idea that Genesis 1:1–2:3 and the larger block of Genesis 1–11 fit comfortably into the whole book of Genesis. These passages tell us about events in time and space. They do so, of course, with a theological purpose in mind, and with reinforcing elements of literary artistry. But we have already talked about that.

What we must be careful about, in dealing with Genesis 1:1–2:3, is running away from attention to genre into speculative reasonings about content. It is easy in comparative study of ancient Near Eastern texts to treat content as if it were more or less a free-floating piece in the general environment of the ancient Near East. Content apart from the genre of an embedding text can have multiple meanings, depending on the imagination of the interpreter. And the generation of multiple meanings is indeed what has happened with people who pay attention primarily to parallels in content when they interpret Genesis 1. It is only what one would expect, because the embedding context of Genesis, as designed by the author, has been shoved aside. Moreover, scholars often are interested in comparing Genesis 1 not with the closest parallels in content, namely, Psalms 8 and 104, but with various accounts of development of cosmic structure ("cosmogonies") in the ancient Near East. Even in terms of content, these are more remote, because they are polytheistic—they involve the interaction of multiple gods. But in terms of genre, they are even further away. They are poetry, not prose.

I do not mean to say that the ancient Near Eastern documents throw no light on the cultural surroundings of ancient Israel. Of course they do. They present fascinating detailed contrasts and similarities with Genesis 1 and with other pieces of Genesis, such as the flood story. Some degree of parallel is to be expected, because the false polytheistic religions of the ancient Near East present *counterfeits* of true religion. And the counterfeiting may extend to accounts concerning origins. But both genre and content link Genesis 1 more directly with other parts of the Old Testament canon.

Showing versus Telling

It is also helpful to observe that Old Testament Hebrew narratives are customarily sparse and selective in character. They usually focus on core events. They usually narrate what the key characters do and say rather than include extensive comments by the narrator explaining the significance of the events or morally evaluating them. They present characters by *showing* the characters in action rather than by directly *telling* us what sort of people the characters are.[24] For example, Genesis does not spend a lot of time telling us in purely general terms about Abraham's personality or the kind of husband and father he was. It does not give us a long exposition to tell us directly that Abraham was a kind and loving father, but that he still put his loyalty to God above his affection for his son Isaac. Rather, it tells us stories of what Abraham said and did. It *shows* us Abraham in action rather than *telling* us about him.

The same principle holds in Genesis 1, where God is the chief character or actor. Genesis 1 shows us what God is like by narrating his actions, not by giving us an explicit list of his attributes. We can contrast this approach to Exodus 34:6–7, which, to be sure, appears in the middle of a longer narrative and contains pieces that suggest a narrative ("visiting the iniquity"), but in which the speech of God expounds who he is and what he is like.

This narrative technique of "showing" relies on the narration of *events* to carry the load. And they can carry this load only if the events actually belong to the same world as the character. This principle holds with respect to both fictional and nonfictional narrative. In a fictional narrative, the events must belong to the same imaginary world as the narrative characters in order for the events genuinely to contribute to portraying the characters. Likewise, in a nonfictional narrative, the events must belong to the same world as the characters, namely, the real world. It will not do for a nonfictional narrative to show us a character through events that do not really show anything because the character did not actually participate in the events described. Showing does not work well if the narrative has nothing substantive that

---

24. V. Philips Long, *The Reign and Rejection of King Saul: A Case for Literary and Theological Coherence* (Atlanta: Scholars Press, 1989), 31–34; Collins, *Genesis 1–4*, 11–12, citing Long, *The Reign and Rejection of King Saul*, and other works on narrative poetics; C. John Collins, *Did Adam and Eve Really Exist? Who They Were and Why You Should Care* (Wheaton, IL: Crossway, 2011), 60–64, 164–65; C. John Collins, "The Evolution of Adam," The Gospel Coalition, April 26, 2012, a review of Peter Enns, *The Evolution of Adam: What the Bible Does and Doesn't Say about Human Origins* (Grand Rapids, MI: Brazos, 2012), https://www.thegospelcoalition.org/reviews/the_evolution_of_adam. The predominance of "showing" makes it all the more notable when the narrator in his own voice finally provides a comment (such as 2 Kings 24:3–4; 1 Chron. 10:13–14).

is capable of being shown. This observation further confirms that Genesis 1 purports to narrate acts that God did in time and space. It is nonfictional narrative.

What Is "Literal"?

The key word *literal* sometimes comes into the picture. Is Genesis 1 a literal description? One difficulty is that the word *literal* can be used in more than one way.[25] It can be used merely as an equivalent to *nonfictional*. Yes, Genesis is nonfictional. But using the word *literal* this way invites misunderstanding, since "nonfictional" is not its most common meaning. The word *literal* can mean that a text is completely free of figurative language and is "flat," with no literary depth or artistry, or with no theological depth. It can also be used to exclude what Genesis 1 does when it uses analogies between God's action and human action. God speaks in Genesis 1:3: "Let there be light." His speech is analogous to human speech, but clearly on a different level, because he is God.

Since all of Genesis is God's speech, we should take it with utmost seriousness and respect. Respecting what God is saying includes respecting his mastery of literary artistry, analogy, and poetry (as in Genesis 49). We should avoid reading Genesis in a flat way that ignores its depth dimensions. Rather, we should read it as the Word of God, who is Master of language in all its richness, and who wisely addressed the Israelites before we came along. We will return to the word *literal* at a later point (chap. 15).

---

25. Vern S. Poythress, *Understanding Dispensationalists*, 2nd ed. (Phillipsburg, NJ: P&R, 1994), chap. 8.

7

Summary of Hermeneutical Principles

Having come this far, it is useful to summarize the hermeneutical principles that we have covered. I will also add a few more that we will not discuss in detail in this book.[1]

God as Sovereign Author

1. There is one true God who does as he pleases, who is able to work miracles, and whose faithfulness is the foundation for scientific research.

2. Genesis has God as the divine Author, who guided the human author. As a result, Genesis is the written word of God, God's own speech in written form.

3. Genesis is completely true, as a whole and in its details, because God is true and trustworthy.

4. God had Genesis written as one book of a growing canon, which serves as the official covenant document in God's relationship to his people. Consequently, in Genesis, God also addresses subsequent

---

1. Most of these principles are taken, with some revision, from Vern S. Poythress, "Correlations with Providence in Genesis 1," *Westminster Theological Journal* 77, no. 1 (2015): 71–99 [72–74]. Used with permission. Further discussion of hermeneutic principles can be found in Poythress, *God-Centered Biblical Interpretation* (Phillipsburg, NJ: P&R, 1999); and Poythress, *Reading the Word of God in the Presence of God: A Handbook for Biblical Interpretation* (Wheaton, IL: Crossway, 2016). See also Poythress, "Dispensing with Merely Human Meaning: Gains and Losses from Focusing on the Human Author, Illustrated by Zephaniah 1:2–3," *Journal of the Evangelical Theological Society* 57, no. 3 (2014): 481–99.

generations of his people, including us who live today. His communication to us includes later canonical books, which throw more light on Genesis. What he says to *us* through Genesis builds on what he said to the ancient Israelites.

Human Author and Historical Background

5. The human author desired to convey the word of God, so he intended to say what God intended. As a result, we can focus on God's intention; we do not need to know a lot of personal detail about the human author. Of course, we know that he was a human being like ourselves. But he was also the recipient of divine revelation. So we cannot assume that it was impossible for him to know anything more than what was common to his culture.

6. Genesis comes substantially from the time of Moses, with a few possible editorial notes and explanations added later under divine inspiration.[2] God addressed the ancient Israelites of that time. (However, it turns out in practice that the exact time at which Genesis was written does not affect interpretation much, due partly to the fact that it is a part of the canon and was also intended to address subsequent generations, not merely the generation in which it was written down.)

Implications of Genre and Structure

7. Genesis and other canonical books teach about God partly through recounting God's deeds in history. Consequently, historical accounts are both history and theology, according to God's design. Noah, Abraham, Isaac, Jacob, and Joseph were real people who lived long ago and to whom God showed his grace in time and space. At the same time, God wrote about what happened to them in a way that instructs us (Rom. 15:4; 1 Cor. 10:6, 11).

8. Genesis as a whole has the structure of a "genealogical history," with sections characteristically introduced by the expression "These are the generations of . . ." This structure shows that the early chapters of Genesis, like the later chapters, describe events that happened in space and time.

---

2. Edward J. Young, *An Introduction to the Old Testament*, rev. ed. (Grand Rapids, MI: Eerdmans, 1960), 45.

9. Close examination of the sections of genealogical history shows chronological "backtracking" at points. Not everything was written in chronological order. This observation opens the possibility of considering whether Genesis 1:1–2:3 or 2:4–25 has some back-and-forth movement in chronology.

10. The language of Genesis is sparse.[3] It is more like a sketch than a minutely detailed photograph. Everything it says is true, but it is not pedantically precise. We have many questions about the past that it simply does not answer. In particular, lack of *mention* of means (secondary causes) that God may have used does not imply that there were no means. God was working whether or not he was pleased to use means. We can provide examples outside of Genesis. Exodus 15 mentions no secondary causes when God divided the Red Sea, but the parallel passage in Exodus 14 mentions "a strong east wind" (v. 21). Psalm 105:40 says only that God "brought quail." Numbers 11:31 offers the detail: "Then a *wind* from the LORD sprang up, and it brought quail from the sea . . ." In God's works in Genesis 1, he may or may not have used means that are not mentioned in the sparse account.

11. The language of Genesis describing the world of nature is characteristically "phenomenal language," that is, language describing how things appear to ordinary people.

12. The language of Genesis is *"non-postulational with reference to natural things."*[4] That is, it does not postulate any particular scientific cosmology. It lacks *"theorizing."*[5] For example, the Bible does not "theorize" about what the sun is made of or how far away it is. It describes the sun as "the greater light" (Gen. 1:16), which gives light and functions to mark out "days and years" (v. 14). This description does not go beyond what a human being in any culture could observe for himself.

13. Genesis 1 proclaims that God is the only sovereign Lord and the Creator of all. By so doing, it polemicizes against all forms of polytheism and pantheistic confusion, which identify or mix gods with nature. But its polemic is *indirect*. Other passages in the Bible directly

3. See Vern S. Poythress, *Inerrancy and the Gospels: A God-Centered Approach to the Challenges of Harmonization* (Wheaton, IL: Crossway, 2012), chaps. 7–10.
4. Bernard Ramm, *The Christian View of Science and Scripture* (Grand Rapids, MI: Eerdmans, 1954), 69 (emphasis original).
5. Ramm, *Christian View of Science*, 69 (emphasis original).

criticize polytheism and idolatry (for example, Deut. 4:15–39; Isa. 44:9–20). Genesis 1 sets forth positive teaching about God; it does not directly criticize false religion, but it nevertheless implies such a criticism. The ancient Near East offers examples of polytheistic accounts of the origin of the cosmos, while Genesis 1 gives us the monotheistic foundation.

14. As a result of point 13, comparisons between Genesis 1 and ancient Near Eastern polytheistic myths have value, but it is limited. At times, Genesis 1 discusses the same subjects as some of the myths. But the contrasts are strong between the sole sovereignty of God in Genesis and the gross polytheism of the extrabiblical literature. The contrasts underline the uniqueness of Genesis 1. At the same time, the lack of direct polemics in Genesis 1 invites us not to focus on the contrasts as such, but on what Genesis 1 is saying positively.

15. Genesis 1 shows how God's acts of creation have a relation to humanity. God creates a suitable home for mankind, and his acts should evoke our praise. (The same goes for Genesis 2.)

PART 2

EXEGETICAL CONCERNS

8

Correlations with
Providence in Genesis 1

Now that we have considered some of the main hermeneutical issues, we are ready to focus more on the detailed interpretation of Genesis 1. But we retain a primary interest in hermeneutics. We will not look at every interpretive question or every verse in equal detail. Instead, I propose an overall strategy for interpreting Genesis 1. The strategy is to pay attention to correlations between (1) God's present-day governance of nature and (2) the descriptions of God's acts of creation in Genesis 1. Why this focus? God's present-day governance provides a key framework for interpretation, because God knows that readers' familiarity with his providential governance of nature offers the natural starting point for understanding what he did in Genesis 1.

Basic Features of Analogy in God's Work of Creation

It may help if we summarize beforehand the main result. The descriptions in Genesis 1 regularly use analogies connected to the natural processes in the present-day world in order to provide a simple, easily understood, nontechnical description of what God did. Genesis 1 offers us a true description, but it does not delve into technical details that are of most interest to modern science.

Poetic passages in the Old Testament compare God's acts of creation to the human work of building a house or erecting a tent:

He *built* his sanctuary like the high heavens,
  like the earth, which he has *founded* forever. (Ps. 78:69)

[He] *builds* his upper *chambers* in the heavens
  and *founds* his *vault* upon the earth. (Amos 9:6a)

[He] *stretches out* the heavens like a curtain,
  and *spreads* them like a *tent* to dwell in. (Isa. 40:22b)

My hand *laid* the *foundation* of the earth,
  and my right hand *spread out* the heavens. (Isa. 48:13a)

  [He] *stretched out* the heavens
  and *laid* the *foundations* of the earth. (Isa. 51:13b)

(See Fig. 8.1.)

Fig. 8.1: God Building the World, Analogous to Man Building a House

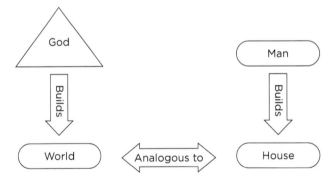

Interestingly, even the experience of living in one's own body can be compared to dwelling in a house:

  . . . how much more those who dwell in houses of clay,
  whose foundation is in the dust. (Job 4:19a)

How did people experience things in an ancient environment? One of the more common, prominent human crafting activities would have been building houses. This building involved human planning, wisdom, purpose, effort, and engagement with the world of things—stone, wood, and clay. For nomads, it would have involved producing material for tent curtains and poles, and setting up the tent. People also built walls and cities, and crafted furniture. But the building of a house or tent would have been a common and accessible reference point. Because human building is analogous to God's purposeful action, it lies close at hand to think of God as "building" the whole world. In fact, this analogy itself is built into the reality that man is made in the image of God. It is not surprising that this analogy should be taken up in poetry. We must be suspicious of the idea that such an analogy would necessarily imply a detailed physicalistic theory about how God's cosmic house holds together after it is built. The point in the comparison is the personal planning, activity, and wisdom of God, not a physicalistic theory.

Indeed, we can see features of a kind of building process in Genesis 1. God crafts the world in a manner analogous to what Moses will do later in building the tabernacle. The world has specific spaces, such as the heavens, the sea, and the dry land, which are analogous to rooms (like the two rooms in the tabernacle, plus the space of the outer court). God sets up the spaces and then fills them with creatures: the sun, moon, stars, and birds, which are creatures of the heavens; fish, which are creatures of the sea; and plants, land animals, and man, which are creatures of the dry land. These creatures are like furnishings that are put in the rooms of a house.

To prepare for comparing Genesis 1 with the later experience of the world by the Israelites and ourselves, we need some terminology. *Providence* is the usual theological term used to describe God's supervision of all the events in nature and history. He controls events big and small for his own purposes: "The LORD has established his throne in the heavens, and his kingdom rules over *all*" (Ps. 103:19; cf. Eph. 1:11).[1] More specifically, we will use the word *providence* to designate God's rule in the *present* world, subsequent to the completion of his creative acts at the end of the sixth day of creation (Gen. 1:31). Providence as the *present-day* activity of God is thus distinguished from the various works that he accomplished in Genesis 1, which he completed in the *past* (by the end of the sixth day).

In contrast to providence, we will use the word *creation* to designate the acts of God during the six days of Genesis 1. The word *creation*

---

1. For further discussion and a more comprehensive survey of the biblical teaching, see Vern S. Poythress, *Chance and the Sovereignty of God: A God-Centered Approach to Probability and Random Events* (Wheaton, IL: Crossway, 2014), chaps. 1–7; John M. Frame, *The Doctrine of God* (Phillipsburg, NJ: P&R, 2002), chap. 14. The Westminster Confession of Faith (1647) summarizes: "God the great Creator of all things doth uphold, direct, dispose, and govern all creatures, actions, and things, from the greatest even to the least, by His most wise and holy providence . . ." (5.1).

in ordinary English can sometimes be used to refer to the present-day created order, as when we say that the "creation" around us is beautiful and testifies to its Creator. But now we are using the word *creation* more narrowly, to refer to the acts of God during the first six days, but to exclude the subsequent acts of God, in which he *sustains* by providence the world that he made at an earlier point in time. With this sense of the words, creation and providence are distinct. They occur at two distinct times. Acts of creation bring into existence the world itself, new kinds of creatures, and a new structural organization. Acts of providence begin subsequently, once the world is "finished" (Gen. 2:1) at the end of the sixth day. But providence and creation are also closely related conceptually.[2] The correlations between creation and providence help us to understand the meaning of details in Genesis 1.

Attention to Providence

We may sum up the importance of the relation of providence to creation in two principles.

1. Genesis 1 shows interest not only in the events of creation but in their later effects. (See Fig. 8.2.)

Fig. 8.2: Connection between Creation and Providence

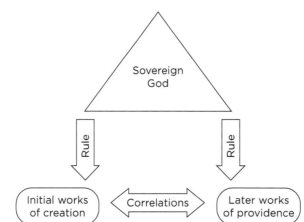

---

2. From here onward, this chapter is a revision of part of Vern S. Poythress, "Correlations with Providence in Genesis 1," *Westminster Theological Journal* 77, no. 1 (2015): 71–99. The article also contained a summary of hermeneutical principles, which are presented in revised form in the previous chapter. Used with permission.

For example, Genesis 1:11–12 describes the origin of vegetation, but also talks about a general pattern of growth, in which seeds play a part. Apple trees produce apples that have apple seeds, and the apple seeds can produce more apple trees in the next generation. Verses 11–12 indicate that God has ordained this general pattern: "trees bearing fruit in which is their seed, each according to its kind" (v. 12).

Genesis 1:14 indicates that the lights of heaven will "be for signs and for seasons, and for days and years," indicating their permanent function. This function continues from the time of creation onward until today. Genesis 1:28 sets forth the human task of fruitfulness, multiplication, and dominion, which continues during this present age (see 9:1–3, 7). (See Table 8.1.)

Table 8.1: Creation and Providence Illustrated

Creation	Providence
God separates the seas and the dry land (Gen. 1:9).	Seas and dry land continue to be separate.
God creates kinds of plants, and establishes a pattern according to which the plants produce seeds (vv. 11–12).	Plants continue to produce seeds, which produce plants of the same kind in the next generation.
God creates heavenly lights, and establishes a pattern for their movements in order to mark periods of time (vv. 14–18).	The heavenly lights continue to move according to God's pattern.
God creates sea creatures and birds, and tells them to multiply (vv. 20–22).	Sea creatures and birds continue to multiply.
God creates mankind, tells them to multiply, and gives them dominion (vv. 26–30).	Mankind continues to exist, to multiply, and to exercise dominion.

These connections between creation and later effects contribute to showing how God cares for mankind (principle 15 of the previous chapter). The lights in the heavens enable mankind to enjoy cycles of days, months, seasons, and years. The productivity of seeds and fruits leads to food for mankind (Gen. 1:29) and lies behind the creation of the garden of Eden (2:9). Psalm 104 further elaborates on the benefits. (See Table 8.2.)

Table 8.2: Creation, Providence, and Human Benefit

Days of Creation	New Order	Providential Continuation	Human Benefit
Day 1	light and darkness	cycle of light and darkness	light for beauty, for seeing, and for work; dark for sleep
Day 2	expanse, heavenly water	sky, clouds, rain, water	beauty of the sky; rain
Day 3	dry land; plants	dry land; plants reproduce	dry land for living on; plants for beauty and for food
Day 4	heavenly lights	heavenly lights keep time	human cycles of work and rest, seedtime and harvest
Day 5	sea creatures; birds	sea creatures and birds reproduce	animals for beauty and for food
Day 6	land creatures	land creatures reproduce	animals for beauty, for food, and (domestic animals) for work and other benefits (milk, wool, hides)

The language of finishing and rest in Genesis 2:1–3 indicates that the six days of creation are set off and are distinguished from God's subsequent activities in providentially governing the world. Such providential governance is described in many passages, such as Hebrews 1:3, "He upholds the universe by the word of his power," and Psalm 103:19, "His kingdom rules over all."

Providence is distinct from the work of creation, but the two are closely related. The one leads to the other. God's works of creation establish patterns that he maintains by providence. We can see this point illustrated at some length in Psalm 104. This psalm reflects on creation, but contains a good deal of material that meditates on the providential governance of God subsequent to the completion of the six days of creation. One verse, verse 30, even uses the word *created* in a context that refers to the fact that God brings to life the next generation of animals: "When you send forth your Spirit, they [animals] are created, and you renew the face of the ground."

Genesis 1 has as its climax the creation of man, and Genesis 2:4–25 also focuses on the creation of man and woman. It is clear from Genesis 1–2 that God's works of creation have produced a home suitable for mankind, and that God had such a purpose in mind from the beginning (principle 15 of chap. 7).[3] The resulting creation order *continues* to be a suitable home for mankind, by providing light, dry land, fruits, seasons, and animals for human use in subsequent generations (though the suitability is marred by the fall, 3:17–19).

2. God's description of his creative works in Genesis 1 instructs the Israelites through analogies with providence.[4]

Analogies between the acts of creation and works in providence have a key role in the meanings communicated in Genesis 1. We can illustrate the use of analogy by considering Psalm 104:30. God providentially brings new animals into existence, and the psalmist describes this work of God by saying that animals are created (the same Hebrew word, *bara'* ברא, as in Gen. 1:1). They are created by analogy with the original creation of new things in Genesis 1. But the relationship between the passages involves an analogy, not an identity, since Genesis 1 discusses the *origins* of the different kinds of animals, while Psalm 104:30 discusses the *continuation* of the kinds that already exist.

The use of analogies between creation and providence also makes sense because the ordinary experiences of the Israelites and other people involve interaction with God's providential activities in the world around them. Therefore, their experience of providence offers a natural starting point for virtually any ordinary human understanding of creation.

The Bible also provides theological reasons for expecting that God may have set in place many analogies between creation and providence: (1) the works of creation and the works of providence come from the hand of the same God, who exercises the same wisdom in both cases (Ps. 104:24; Prov. 8:27–31); (2) God plans that creation should form the foundation for later providential developments; (3) God's plan for the whole of history has inner unity, and this unity

---

3. C. John Collins, *Genesis 1–4: A Linguistic, Literary, and Theological Commentary* (Phillipsburg, NJ: P&R, 2006), 78–80.

4. Richard Averbeck comes close to this view when he says that "both the Bible and the Baal myth [are] reflecting the same underlying cosmological pattern common to both *the observable world* and the cultural world in which both were written" (emphasis added). Richard Averbeck, "A Literary Day, Inter-Textual, and Contextual Reading of Genesis 1–2," in *Reading Genesis 1–2: An Evangelical Conversation*, ed. J. Daryl Charles (Peabody, MA: Hendrickson, 2013), 15. Interested readers can fruitfully compare my approach here with the five interpretations offered in the volume *Reading Genesis 1–2*.

includes a fundamental unity of purpose with respect to creation and providence together; and (4) God reflects his character in the works within the created world, and this reflection includes a pattern in which God displays some specific aspects of his character in the things that he has made.[5] This pattern of reflecting God's character extends to both creation and providence.

Interpretation of Genesis 1:1–2:3

With these principles in place, we are ready to begin reading Genesis 1. For the sake of brevity, we will not cover all the aspects of interpretation normally addressed in commentaries,[6] and neither will we pursue biblical-theological reflections on major themes such as light and darkness or multiplication and fruitfulness,[7] because this would greater expand the discussion. Instead, we will concentrate narrowly on how the passage builds on analogies between creation and providence.

Genesis 1:1–2 (Introduction)

In the beginning, God created the heavens and the earth. (Gen. 1:1)

"In the beginning" denotes an absolute beginning point in time, by analogy with small beginnings that take place when God brings to life new creatures and brings about new events in providence.[8] The word *God* denotes the same God who rules in providence (Ps. 103:19). In Genesis 1:1, the word *created* indicates an absolute newness, by

---

5. See especially Rom. 1:19–20; Meredith G. Kline, *Images of the Spirit* (Grand Rapids, MI: Baker, 1980); Vern S. Poythress, *Redeeming Science: A God-Centered Approach* (Wheaton, IL: Crossway, 2006), chaps. 18 and 20; Vern S. Poythress, *Theophany: A Biblical Theology of God's Appearing* (Wheaton, IL: Crossway, 2018), chap. 11.

6. Collins, *Genesis 1–4*, may serve as a primary resource. Collins has now supplemented this book with another: C. John Collins, *Reading Genesis Well: Navigating History, Poetry, Science, and Truth in Genesis 1–11* (Grand Rapids, MI: Zondervan, 2018), chap. 7.

7. For example, see G. K. Beale, *The Temple and the Church's Mission: A Biblical Theology of the Dwelling Place of God* (Downers Grove, IL: InterVarsity Press, 2004), 31–45, 60–66. In the larger context of the Bible, creation and re-creation belong together, as many have observed. So there are many biblical themes that link the creation account in Genesis 1–2 to redemptive re-creation. We may also point to the theological theme of chaos and order, and the relation between the creation of light in Gen. 1:3 and the theme of light in the Gospel of John. Many such relations exist; we leave them aside in order to focus on the relation between creation and providence.

8. The exact implications of Gen. 1:1 are disputed. Some interpreters do not think that it describes a creation out of nothing. But see Collins, *Genesis 1–4*, 50–55; Collins, *Reading Genesis Well*, chap. 8; Appendix A in the present book, p. 291. Col. 1:16 and other verses of the Bible contribute to an overall picture of creation in which God is completely sovereign. There is no matter or other stuff that is coeternal with him.

analogy with the relative newness that arises when God creates a new generation of animals, as in Psalm 104:30. (See Table 8.3.)

Table 8.3: A New Beginning

Creation	Providence
1:1—new world	new generation of animals

"The heavens and the earth" is a compound expression that denotes the entirety of what God created.[9] It functions by analogy with present providential experience, wherein people experience what is below and around them (earth) and what is above them (heaven). Together, these constitute the whole. The sparse language leaves in the background those aspects that are invisible, but such aspects are included by implication.

Since the expression "the heavens and the earth" operates by analogy, it can denote an initial, early situation rather than the completed heavens and earth mentioned in Genesis 2:1 and experienced now providentially. (See Appendix A, p. 291.)

I agree with those interpreters who think that verse 1 is not merely a title for the rest of Genesis 1, but describes the initial act of creation.[10] The result of the initial act is that there are "heavens," whose condition is not further described, and "earth," whose condition is described in verse 2. If, on the other hand, verse 1 is a title,[11] it makes little difference in interpreting the rest of Genesis 1.

> The earth was without form and void, and darkness was over the face of the deep. And the Spirit of God was hovering over the face of the waters. (Gen. 1:2)

The earth was unstructured and empty, by analogy with a desert place with no inhabitants (compare Isa. 34:10; Jer. 4:23–26). This situation contrasts with the structure introduced in the rest of the chapter. By the

---

9. Gordon J. Wenham, *Genesis 1–15*, Word Biblical Commentary 1 (Waco, TX: Word, 1987), 15; Collins, *Genesis 1–4*, 55; Appendix A in the present book, p. 291.

10. Wenham, *Genesis 1–15*, 11–16, especially 13; Collins, *Genesis 1–4*, 50–55; Appendix A in the present book, p. 291.

11. E.g., Bruce K. Waltke, with Cathi J. Fredricks, *Genesis: A Commentary* (Grand Rapids, MI: Zondervan, 2001), 58; Bruce K. Waltke, "The Creation Account in Genesis 1:1–3: Part III: The Initial Chaos Theory and the Precreation Chaos Theory," *Bibliotheca Sacra* 132 (1975): 216–28. However, the idea that God did not create the initial unformed earth needs to be repudiated (see Appendix A, p. 291).

time we come to Genesis 2:1, the earth is formed ("finished") and filled ("all the host of them"). The transition from early formlessness to the completed creation in Genesis 2:1 is analogous to a providential situation in which human beings come into a desolate place and begin to grow crops, herd animals, and erect tents or permanent houses. (See Table 8.4.)

Table 8.4: From Formlessness to Completed Structure

Creation	Providence
1:2—formless world	empty, deserted regions
1:3–31—structuring the world	human filling and structuring a region

The transition from emptiness to fullness implies practical benefits for human beings (principle 15). Human beings cannot live in a completely unformed place. We should praise God for his provision, which he gives us in the structured, filled world in which we now live.

The darkness in Genesis 1:2 is analogous to a dark night, a dark cave, or a dark house. Within God's providential order, darkness makes it impossible to see structures or furnishings, so that in darkness, human visual experience is that of emptiness, analogous to the emptiness of the early situation on earth.

The deep in verse 2 is a large mass analogous to the seas that we experience providentially. The end of verse 2 mentions "waters," indicating that the deep has a watery surface. The sparse, nonpostulational account does not say whether this material is H_2O, according to a modern chemical analysis.[12] It is *analogous* to a sea, but the account does not go into details as to all the points of analogy. The obvious prominent point of analogy between creation and providential experience is that water in general and lakes and seas in particular are somewhat "formless."

The Spirit of God is present and active ("hovering"), by analogy with his presence in creating the animals in Psalm 104:30 and creating human life in Job 33:4.[13]

---

12. Strictly speaking, the Pacific Ocean is not wholly H_2O either. It contains dissolved salts—sodium ions, chloride ions, potassium ions, iodide ions, etc.—as well as algae, plankton, and discarded plastic bottles, to name a few. The complicated analysis illustrates again the difference between being sparse ("waters") and being detailed and precise.

13. On the understanding of "Spirit" (or "wind"), see Poythress, *Theophany*, chap. 11; Appendix B.

Day One

And God said, "Let there be light," and there was light. (Gen. 1:3)

God speaks commands. Providentially, human beings made in the image of God issue their own commands in imitation of God. Human beings understand what it means for God to issue commands by analogy with human commands. (See Table 8.5.)

Table 8.5: God's Command and Human Commands

Creation	Providence
1:3—God commands	human commands; God continues to command

In this connection, and elsewhere in Genesis 1 as well, we should reckon with two complementary principles. First, God has designed analogies between himself and man. The analogies are real, and they are one aspect of the nature of the created order in its relation to God. Second, an asymmetric relation exists between the two parties. God is the originator and the archetype, while man is the imitator. Human actions are derivative. Man imitates not only in his actions, but in his very constitution. Theologians say that the Bible describes God "anthropomorphically," that is, by analogy with human nature and human activities. That is true. But the analogy works because God made man "theomorphically," in the image of God.[14]

The analogies between God and man are not an afterthought, and neither are they merely invented by human beings, as if to "patch up" a glaring deficiency in language. God designed the analogies from the beginning and intended that they would serve as one means by which we come to know him and think about his character. At the same time, God, not man, is the standard for knowledge. Our knowledge of God is derivative and incomplete in comparison with his knowledge of himself. The analogies give us real knowledge of God, but not exhaustive knowledge.

These principles hold when we consider God's commands, as in Genesis 1:3. God's commands are the original commands, while human commands are imitative of God's authority and his speaking ability.

---

14. I remember hearing this point orally from J. I. Packer.

The appearance of light in creation is analogous to the providential experience of seeing light beginning to dawn after the night. Thus, we might translate "light" as "daylight." Genesis 1:3 is not discussing light in a technical, scientific way—for example, as electromagnetic radiation. It is saying that the coming of light on the first day is like the coming of daylight that we experience within God's providential order at the beginning of a new day.

Within the larger context of the Bible as a whole, Genesis 1:3 implies that God is the Creator who has brought about all the aspects of light that we can experience. For example, on the fourth day, God created "the two great *lights*" and "the stars" (v. 16), which are also classified as "lights" (v. 14). In the tabernacle, the lampstand with seven lamps was made "so as to give *light* on the space in front of it" (Ex. 25:37). So we can say that the artificial light from lamps is imitative of the original creation of light by God. Artificial light is possible only because God has ordained a complex order within which human beings can make lamps, harvest olives, and make olive oil to burn in the lamps (Lev. 24:1–4). God also governs the processes involved in fire and burning, so that the Israelites can depend on the process by which olive oil produces light as it burns.

So as a further implication within a modern social context with scientific interests, we can say that God ordains all the technical scientific aspects of light. But Genesis 1:3 is not directly speaking about such aspects. It is speaking in ordinary ways, in order to address people in ancient Israel and in all cultures. God's original creation of daylight now serves as a blessing to mankind and a stimulus for praising him, because light continues to exist and to serve God's purposes in providence. (See Table 8.6.)

Table 8.6: God's Provision of Light

Creation	Providence
1:3—God creates daylight	God continues to provide daylight

And God saw that the light was good. And God separated the light from the darkness. (Gen. 1:4)

The text says that God saw that the light was good. He evaluated it. God, as the Sovereign, has the divine authority to evaluate everything. Man, as a creature made in the image of God, makes derivative evaluations. When the morning begins to dawn, human beings may experience the goodness of God and respond by thinking or saying that the light is good. Their experience within the context of God's providential control is analogous to what it means for God to evaluate the light as good.

God "separated the light." This original act of separation, on the first day of creation, is analogous to a providential process of separation. In providence, light gradually separates from darkness as morning keeps coming. When dawn begins to break in the early morning, human surroundings include both light and darkness, and the two are not cleanly "separated." There is relative darkness on one side of the sky, a little light on the other side, and a gradation in between. Gradually, the light that originally was only dimly present at the horizon comes to fill the sky. Once it has done so, it is "separated" from the darkness, which remains only in caves and other dark holes.

By analogy, God accomplished the original, archetypal division in his sovereign distinguishing between light and darkness, and in his determination of the distinct roles that the two would play throughout history. By implication, God ordains the conceptual differentiation between light and darkness, as opposites. The text illustrates this more abstract idea by the physical process of separation. God also ordains the temporal succession of light and darkness that we see in the cycle of daytime and nighttime. The daytime is temporally "separate" from the nighttime. These "separations" are a blessing for human life. (See Table 8.7.)

Table 8.7: Separation of Daylight and Nighttime

Creation	Providence
1:4—God separates day and night	day and night continue to be separate

God called the light Day, and the darkness he called Night. And there was evening and there was morning, the first day. (Gen. 1:5)

God gives verbal names to the two distinct things. By analogy, human beings use names already given to day and night by the languages God has given. And sometimes they invent new names, by imitation of God (Gen. 2:19–20). God exhibits his authority and control through naming, and by analogy, human beings also exercise a kind of derivative control as they engage in naming and conceptualizing in their providential actions.

The evening and morning are obviously analogous to the evening and morning of one human day. We will discuss the structure of the days later on, after going through Genesis 1 as a whole.

The Second Day

> And God said, "Let there be an expanse in the midst of the waters, and let it separate the waters from the waters." (Gen. 1:6)

God's command shows analogies once again with human commands.

> And God made the expanse and separated the waters that were under the expanse from the waters that were above the expanse. And it was so. (Gen. 1:7)

When we take into account the picture of waters in Genesis 1:2, the description as a whole, up until this point, has been analogous to a situation within God's providential order wherein a human being observes the sea or a large body of water. Looking out over the sea, a human being may sometimes see clouds traveling toward the land. In phenomenal terms—appearance—a cloud starts a long way off, not clearly separated from the sea. It rises (1 Kings 18:44; Luke 12:54) as it approaches, and there is an increasing separation between the cloud above and the sea beneath. In between the cloud and the sea is a horizontal line that grows into a space.

This visual experience is analogous to what God did in an original act of separation when he made the expanse. Once again, we have a correlation between providential experience and the original acts of creation during the six days. (See Table 8.8.)

Table 8.8: Separating the Waters

Creation	Providence
1:6-7—God separates waters above and below	waters above and below continue to be separate (as in rising clouds)

The "waters that were under the expanse" in Genesis 1:7 correspond to the sea, which we observe today within God's providential order. The "waters that were above the expanse" correspond to waters above us in the sky, wherever they may be located and whatever form they might take in detail. The waters in the clouds are naturally included. The term for "the expanse" is sparse. It denotes what separates the sea and the waters above. This general principle of separation is illustrated concretely in the particular case when a cloud rises from the sea.[15]

The expanse is designated "Heaven" (Gen. 1:8, שָׁמַיִם). This term is flexible. It can denote the sky, in which are the heavenly lights (vv. 14, 15). It can be used to include the bottom side of clouds: "And in a little while the *heavens* grew *black* with clouds and wind, and there was a great rain" (1 Kings 18:45). In fact, the term can denote, in a general way, the whole area above: rain comes from "heaven" (Deut. 11:11; 2 Chron. 7:13; Ps. 68:8; Isa. 55:10; James 5:18; etc.).

We must also reckon with the providential experience of mist. On the one hand, God makes mist rise (Jer. 10:13; 51:16). On the other hand, rainwater comes down:

> For he [God] draws up the drops of water;
>   they distill his mist in *rain*,
> which the skies pour down
>   and *drop* on mankind abundantly. (Job 36:27–28)

The rising of mist represents a providential analogue to the original separation of waters from waters. The down-pouring of rain from the skies presupposes that the water was up in the skies first. The water that comes down as rain derives from the "waters that were above the expanse."

> And God called the expanse Heaven. And there was evening and there was morning, the second day. (Gen. 1:8)

When there are no clouds, the most obvious visible denotation for "Heaven" is the visible sky, in which are the sun and the moon, as well

---

15. After the publication of my article "Correlations with Providence in Genesis 1" (2015), in the light of Oliver Hersey's work ("Hammering Out the Meaning of *Rāqîaʿ* and 'Waters Above' in Gen. 1:6–8 against Its Ancient Near Eastern and Biblical Context," unpublished manuscript, pp. 33–37), I realized that I had focused too exclusively on the illustration provided by water rising from the sea. Gen. 1:6–8 is sparse and does not say that the waters above take only one form—water in clouds. The verses specify neither the form of the water nor its precise location (only that it is above the "expanse"). In principle, invisible water (what we now call water vapor) would also be included. There is mystery (Job 36:26–29). See also Poythress, *Redeeming Science*, 94.

as blue areas in the day and black areas at night. Because appearances are a concern in Genesis 1, we must expect that there will be less focus on the space separating the earth from clouds, sun, and moon. The birds "fly above the earth across the expanse of the heavens" (v. 20), and the Hebrew underlying the English word "across" (עַל־פְּנֵי) might be woodenly rendered "upon the face of." In this context, the "expanse" is the background appearance (typically blue sky or clouds), and birds fly against this background. In addition, the birds are called "the birds of the heavens" (v. 28; compare v. 30). In its loose use, the term "heaven(s)" is flexible, and can designate the heavenly sphere, everything above us, or, more narrowly, the visible background.

(In the next chapter, we will discuss the modern theory of a "heavenly sea.")

The Third Day

> And God said, "Let the waters under the heavens be gathered together into one place, and let the dry land appear." And it was so. (Gen. 1:9)

Providentially, human experience includes heavy rains (1 Kings 18:45) and floods. After a rain or a flood, the water drains off the land. That is, it "gathers together into one place"—a sea, a lake, or a river. The dry land appears as the water disappears off it. This providential experience, given by God, offers an analogue to his original act of making dry land appear. (See Table 8.9.)

Table 8.9: Sea Separate from Dry Land

Creation	Providence
1:9—God makes dry land appear	sea and dry land continue

God's provisions for water serve mankind. Dry land functions as a basis for human habitation. The waters above provide rain for crops. There must be enough water, but not too much, and not everywhere at once (Gen. 1:2).

> God called the dry land Earth, and the waters that were gathered together he called Seas. And God saw that it was good. (Gen. 1:10)

God's naming and evaluation are similar to Genesis 1:5. We commented earlier on how mankind imitates God's acts in these respects.

> And God said, "Let the earth sprout vegetation, plants yielding seed, and fruit trees bearing fruit in which is their seed, each according to its kind, on the earth." And it was so. (Gen. 1:11)

As we saw earlier, verses 11 and 12 describe God's original creation of vegetation on land, but also indicate that he establishes a general pattern of reproducing "according to their kinds." Ordinary observers can see the providential continuation of reproduction in plants today. Plants are obviously a blessing to mankind, which implies that we should bless God both for his providential provision and for the initial creative acts that brought plants into being. (See Table 8.10.)

Table 8.10: God Produces Plants

Creation	Providence
1:11—God produces plants	God continues to provide for plant growth and reproduction

> The earth brought forth vegetation, plants yielding seed according to their own kinds, and trees bearing fruit in which is their seed, each according to its kind. And God saw that it was good. (Gen. 1:12)

The earth brings forth vegetation providentially when new grass, bushes, and trees spring up, beginning with shoots coming out of the ground ("the earth"). This providential growth is analogous to the original growth described in verse 12. The plants spring up, "each according to its kind." Barley seeds give rise to barley plants. Pomegranate seeds give rise to pomegranate trees. And so on. Farmers rely on the reproduction of plants according to their kinds. God established this general pattern when he created plants.

> And there was evening and there was morning, the third day. (Gen. 1:13)

I will comment on the structure of the days later.

The Fourth Day

> And God said, "Let there be lights in the expanse of the heavens to separate the day from the night. And let them be for signs and for seasons, and for days and years . . ." (Gen. 1:14)

God specifies the location of the lights—"in the expanse of the heavens." Providentially, they are still in the sky today. God also specifies some of their functions. They "separate the day from the night." In agreement with my interpretation of verse 4, this separation has a temporal aspect. With respect to time, the day is separate from the night. The day is present when the sun is in the sky, but the night comes when the sun sinks below the horizon. The position of the sun functions to separate the two phenomena, day and night.

God also specifies that the lights will be "for signs and for seasons, and for days and years." This specification constitutes a sparse reference to the fact that the relative positions of the sun, moon, and stars keep track of months (which are related to the position of the moon relative to the sun) and years (which are related to the points on the horizon where the sun rises and sets, and to the position of the stars during the night). The year also has within it a cycle of seasons. The specifications from God in Genesis 1:14 put in place a general pattern that is here today according to the providential rule of God.

> ". . . and let them be lights in the expanse of the heavens to give light upon the earth." And it was so. (Gen. 1:15)

Providentially, the lights still shine "light upon the earth." (See Table 8.11.)

Table 8.11: God Provides Heavenly Lights

Creation	Providence
1:14–15—God makes the lights (first appearance)	the heavenly lights are still there

> And God made the two great lights—the greater light to rule the day and the lesser light to rule the night—and the stars. (Gen. 1:16)

"The greater light" is the bright disk in the sky. God's act of making the disk in the sky is analogous to its continuation in the sky by

God's sustaining power. It "rules" the day in the sense that it is the source of light that makes the daytime what it is in appearance.

"The lesser light" is the pale white disk that appears at some times of the month in the night. It is not always a complete disk, but sometimes a crescent or a gibbous shape, depending on the time of the month. It supplies some dim light by which one can see the nighttime appearance of the earth.

The stars are the small pricks of light in the night sky.

All three kinds of heavenly lights are designated according to phenomenal description, as they appear to the human eye. The descriptions confirm the principle that biblical language is "nonpostulational." There is no "theorizing" about whether these lights are just lights, whether the light originates in material objects, or how far away and how big these material objects might "really" be.

> And God set them in the expanse of the heavens to give light on the earth . . . (Gen. 1:17)

God put the lights in the heavens initially by analogy to the fact that by his providential rule he puts the sun in the sky each morning and the moon and stars in the sky each night (Ps. 104:20; cf. 19:4–6).

> . . . to rule over the day and over the night, and to separate the light from the darkness. And God saw that it was good. (Gen. 1:18)

This language repeats the functions that God intended the lights to have, as given in verses 14–16. The events in time and space fulfill the purpose that God specifies in his words of command.

> And there was evening and there was morning, the fourth day. (Gen. 1:19)

We will consider these refrains later.

The Fifth Day

> And God said, "Let the waters swarm with swarms of living creatures, and let birds fly above the earth across the expanse of the heavens." (Gen. 1:20)

God issues his command, in analogy with human commands by his image bearers.

> So God created the great sea creatures and every living creature that moves, with which the waters swarm, according to their kinds, and every winged bird according to its kind. And God saw that it was good. (Gen. 1:21)

God's initial acts in creating sea creatures and birds are analogous to his creating new generations of sea creatures and birds through his providential rule (Ps. 104:12, 25). (See Table 8.12.)

Table 8.12: God Provides for Sea Creatures and Birds

Creation	Providence
1:20-21—God makes the first sea creatures and birds	sea creatures and birds continue

> And God blessed them, saying, "Be fruitful and multiply and fill the waters in the seas, and let birds multiply on the earth." (Gen. 1:22)

God's blessing continues to produce providential effects. By his providential governance, sea creatures multiply and fill the seas, and birds multiply on the earth in producing the next generation.

> And there was evening and there was morning, the fifth day. (Gen. 1:23)

We will consider these refrains later.

The Sixth Day

> And God said, "Let the earth bring forth living creatures according to their kinds—livestock and creeping things and beasts of the earth according to their kinds." And it was so. (Gen. 1:24)

God issues his command in a way analogous to human commands. The earth "brings forth" the living creatures. The expression "the earth" may be sparse usage referring inclusively to the surface of the earth and everything on the surface. So the text describes the fact that living creatures appear within this region. Or, more narrowly, the text could be suggesting an analogy with the providential observation that animals come out of the earth when they come out of their holes and dens.

> And God made the beasts of the earth according to their kinds and the livestock according to their kinds, and everything that creeps on the ground according to its kind. And God saw that it was good. (Gen. 1:25)

God originally created the kinds of animals. By analogy, he providentially continues to create new generations of animals, according to Ps. 104:30. (See Table 8.13.)

Table 8.13: God Provides for Land Animals

Creation	Providence
1:24–25—God makes the first land animals	land animals continue

> Then God said, "Let us make man in our image, after our likeness. And let them have dominion over the fish of the sea and over the birds of the heavens and over the livestock and over all the earth and over every creeping thing that creeps on the earth." (Gen. 1:26)

God speaks his plan in a way analogous to human discussion of human plans. In this case, the plural pronoun "us" is special. Its exact significance is debated. Without entering into the full debate, we may suggest that it represents self-consultation. This "consultation" has partial parallels: (1) God's use of wisdom in Proverbs 8:30, (2) the reflection on God's not having need of counsel outside his Spirit (Isa. 40:13–14), and (3) the picture of a king consulting his counselors, as in 1 Kings 22:5–22 (but God has no need of counselors outside himself). This self-consultation adumbrates the New Testament doctrine of the Trinity.[16]

> So God created man in his own image,
>   in the image of God he created him;
>   male and female he created them. (Gen. 1:27)

The poetic parallelism in verse 27 sets this verse apart as the climax of the narrative. Mankind is indeed central in God's plan for

---

16. Collins, *Genesis 1–4*, 59–61.

creation, and then in the providential order that later follows. God's original creation of man is analogous to his providential creation of each human individual, who is created in the image of God (Job 33:4; Ps. 139:13–16; 1 Cor. 11:7; James 3:9). (See Table 8.14.)

Table 8.14: God Makes Human Beings

Creation	Providence
1:26–27—God makes the first human beings	God continues to make new human beings (Ps. 139:13–16)

> And God blessed them. And God said to them, "Be fruitful and multiply and fill the earth and subdue it, and have dominion over the fish of the sea and over the birds of the heavens and over every living thing that moves on the earth." (Gen. 1:28)

God's instructions in the original situation of creation extend in their implications to all mankind today. Mankind continues to be fruitful and multiply, through God's providential rule in human reproduction. Mankind continues to exercise dominion (Gen. 9:1–3).

Unfortunately, the entrance of sin means that dominion can be twisted into cruelty and exploitation. So it is worthwhile to say that the original dominion is a delegated authority, under God's rule. Man is a steward of God's property rather than an absolute owner, and in this respect the mandate from creation is analogous to a situation in which a manager or chief servant works under the direction of a human owner for the benefit of the owner and his property. Human dominion according to God's intention should be thoughtful and caring rather than exploitive or selfish.

> And God said, "Behold, I have given you every plant yielding seed that is on the face of all the earth, and every tree with seed in its fruit. You shall have them for food." (Gen. 1:29)

Human beings eat plant food today in a providential continuation of God's original gift.

> "And to every beast of the earth and to every bird of the heavens and to everything that creeps on the earth, everything that has the breath of life, I have given every green plant for food." And it was so. (Gen. 1:30)

In accord with God's original specification in creation, the pattern continues in providence. According to God's providential order, animals eat plants for food.[17] (See Table 8.15.)

Table 8.15: God Provides Food

Creation	Providence
1:29–30—God makes provision for food	God's provision continues

And God saw everything that he had made, and behold, it was very good. And there was evening and there was morning, the sixth day. (Gen. 1:31)

The expression, "behold, it was very good," obviously forms a culmination and capstone for the previous evaluations, where God "saw that it was good." We will discuss these refrains after considering Genesis 2:1–3.

The Seventh Day

Thus the heavens and the earth were finished, and all the host of them. (Gen. 2:1)

Genesis 2:1 marks the end of the narrative of the works of creation. God has finished the works by which he created various regions and various creatures filling them. God continues his providential work of ruling over the creation that he has made, and he moves it forward to its destiny according to his plan. The difference between initiation and continuation means that, though the relations between the two are sometimes close, they are at many points analogous rather than merely identical.

And on the seventh day God finished his work that he had done, and he rested on the seventh day from all his work that he had done. (Gen. 2:2)

---

17. In accord with the sparseness of the account, nothing is said about animals eating other animals as prey. Some people have postulated that all animals were vegetarian before the fall, but the text does not say so. Its silence should not be used to draw a confident conclusion. See Ps. 104:21; Poythress, *Redeeming Science*, 120–22; Robert R. Gonzales, Jr., "Predation & Creation: Animal Death before the Fall?" ETS paper, March 23, 2013; Kenneth D. Keathley and Mark F. Rooker, *40 Questions about Creation and Evolution* (Grand Rapids, MI: Kregel, 2014), chap. 26, 255–62. I am here distinguishing animal death from human death. The latter was a result of the fall (Rom. 5:12).

As part of the book of Genesis, this verse is addressed to Israel and to subsequent generations as well. The Sabbath institution is explained in Exodus 20:8–11. God commands the Israelites not to work on the Sabbath. All their work is to be done on six days. Their pattern of work and rest obviously imitates God's pattern:

> Six days you shall labor, and do all your work, but the seventh day is a Sabbath to the LORD your God. On it you shall not do any work. . . . *For* in six days the LORD made heaven and earth, the sea, and all that is in them, and rested on the seventh day. (Ex. 20:9–11)

God's pattern of work and rest is clearly analogous to Israel's pattern. (See Fig. 8.3.)

Fig. 8.3: God's Work and Rest, Compared to Human

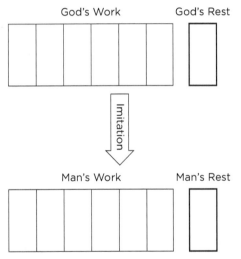

However, while God's pattern is analogous to Israel's pattern, it is not identical, because God does not grow physically tired like a human being. Genesis 2:2 says he rested, which means that he ceased to work. More specifically, verse 3 says that he "rested from all his work that he had done *in creation.*" Reflection on providence shows that God continues to accomplish his works of providence, while he continues to rest from his works of creation, which have analogies to providence but are not identical to it.

So God blessed the seventh day and made it holy, because on it God rested from all his work that he had done in creation. (Gen. 2:3)

Making the seventh day holy celebrates God's rest and his completion of his work. In response, we should honor and praise God for his completed work, and for the greatness and beneficence that he displays in his work. The text does not specifically say whether the blessing rests on the Sabbath day celebrated by human beings or on the original day when God rests. It takes its start with God's rest, which offers the pattern after which man's rest is supposed to be modeled. So the text probably implies both notions: blessing starts with the time of God's rest, and then by implication extends to the Sabbath days on earth, when man is enjoined not to work.

Mankind has a temporary rest on the seventh day of the week. But then he goes back to work. By contrast, God's work of creation is permanently finished. He does not go back to work and do more works of creation, because the work of creation is "finished" (Gen. 2:1). Using other, later Scripture as a supplement, we can confirm the hint in Genesis 1:28 that man's work of multiplying and subduing will eventually be finished, and mankind will enter into a consummation, in which he will rest from his former work of multiplying and subduing. The weekly Sabbath is an emblem and a foretaste of that final rest (Heb. 4:1–11).

Thus, Genesis 1:1–2:3 invites us to see analogies between the six-one pattern in God's work and rest, which is the original pattern, and the six-one pattern in man's work and rest, which is imitative, and which issues finally in consummate rest for mankind.

We will discuss further the issues about the days of creation in chapters 11–14.

Surveying the Whole

All in all, the narrative in Genesis 1:1–2:3 makes good sense when we read it with attention to the analogies between creation and providence. Everything is simple for ordinary people to understand. God designed this simplicity so that, even outside the original historical context, people in all cultures and all times could grasp the basic meaning of God's acts of creation. We know from other passages in the Bible that God created what is *invisible* as well as what is visible (John 1:3; Col. 1:16). But Genesis 1 focuses on the visible world, for simplicity.

There is no sign of speculation or "theorizing" in a manner similar to modern science. Genesis 1 is not in principle antagonistic to the practice of science, but neither does it put forth any piece of technical science. In particular, it does not contain any faulty piece from an alleged ancient physicalistic cosmology.[18] It remains on a level of simplicity in order to address the Israelites and peoples from all cultures concerning what God did when he created the world.

"Functional" Orientation

Readers familiar with competing interpretations may wonder about the relation of my interpretation to an interpretation that emphasizes the practical "functions" of what God made and the "functional" character of the description of God's creative acts.[19] It depends on what the word *functional* means. In a broad sense, every object and every action that has a purpose is functional by serving that purpose. Principle 15 (given in chap. 7) expresses the idea of functionality: God has purposes in creation. Everything that God made, he made with a purpose in view. In fact, he had multiple purposes. God has a unified plan, but within this unity everything he created has multiple purposes. The plants, for instance, serve as food for animals and for mankind. In addition, some are beautiful, and they exemplify God's care (Matt. 6:28–30). God also cares for them when no one sees them (Job 38:26–27).

Since God addresses human beings in Genesis 1, he displays prominently some aspects of creation that are of interest to and have benefits for human beings. By describing these aspects, God also leads human beings to praise him, and his name is therefore glorified. These results come about in accord with God's purposes, and so they too are among

---

18. Israelite readers may or may not have had some false ideas in their minds about the composition and structure of the cosmos. Genesis 1 does not endorse such ideas merely by referring to what anyone can observe. See the caution about a mental-picture theory of truth in chap. 5, note 18, p. 74.

19. E.g., John H. Walton, *Genesis 1 as Ancient Cosmology* (Winona Lake, IN: Eisenbrauns, 2011), 24; Walton, "Reading Genesis 1 as Ancient Cosmology," in *Reading Genesis 1–2: An Evangelical Conversation*, ed. J. Daryl Charles (Peabody, MA: Hendrickson, 2013), 141–69. For a detailed response to Walton, see Collins, *Reading Genesis Well*, 168.

the functions of creation. In a broad sense of the word, the whole description in Genesis 1 is functionally oriented; that is, it is oriented to show functions of the creation order for the benefit and enjoyment of mankind, and for the glory of God.

These principles are fully consistent with the inclusion within Genesis 1 of observational descriptions of visible changes in the environment. In verse 3, light came where it was not before. In verse 7, God made an expanse where there was not an expanse before. In verse 9, the dry land appeared where it had not appeared before. And so on. The orientation to functionality in Genesis 1 includes attention to those changes that lead to the final functions being in place. Genesis 1 invites us to praise God not only that we live in an environment suitable for human living, but that he had a plan to produce a world of that kind. God brought his plan progressively into action to bring the earth from an uninhabitable state (v. 2) to a habitable state (v. 31) so that we can now enjoy the resulting blessings. God's purposes include plans for the far future as well, when the creation will be made new (the new heaven and the new earth of Rev. 21:1). The goal of consummation is among the purposes of the original creation.

An Analogy with the Making of the Tabernacle

As usual, we can illustrate by use of an analogy with human experience in providence. Consider the making of the tabernacle. God's instructions to Israel start out with overall direction:

> "And let them *make* me a sanctuary, that I may dwell in their midst. Exactly as I show you concerning the pattern of the tabernacle, and of all its furniture, so you shall *make* it." (Ex. 25:8–9)

Once the tabernacle is made, it functions as the dwelling place of God, according to Exodus 25:8, as confirmed in 40:34–35. Technically, in a narrow sense of the word *functional*, the tabernacle as a whole is not functional until God's presence comes and the cloud of glory settles on it. God's presence is the culminating act, which makes the completed structure not merely a physical tent, but a sanctuary where God dwells. But the final act of God's presence is not the only act of "making."

Bezalel is filled with "the Spirit of God," and his associates are given ability (Ex. 31:3, 6). They are supposed to "make [Hebrew עשׂה] all that I [God] have commanded you" (v. 6). The narrative in Exodus 36–39 then continues in detail, describing the making of the tabernacle curtains, the loops, the clasps, the frames, and so on. These things are made and then put together, which involves physical restructuring. In a broad sense, all the actions performed by Bezalel and the workmen are functional. They all have purpose, and they all function to lead forward to the final assembling of the tabernacle as a complete whole, followed by the coming of the cloud of glory. The word *make* (עשׂה) is used to describe the earlier stages. It is *not* used to describe the final consecration in 40:34–35 (though presumably it could have been).

After the tabernacle is completed and consecrated, God has still further purposes. The tabernacle as a symbolic dwelling of God points forward to the final dwelling of God described in Revelation 21:3.

Now consider how the providential acts of "making" in Exodus 36–39 have correlations with God's original acts of making in Genesis 1. In Genesis 1:1–2:3, the end product of the acts of making is the completed heavens and earth in 1:31–2:1. In an indirect sense, God "consecrates" the completed whole by celebrating the Sabbath and declaring it "holy" in 2:3—though what is declared "holy" is not the world but the seventh day, the Sabbath.

In some respects, the world as a whole is like a cosmic temple, filled with the presence of God.[20] Genesis 1 describes the acts of making and restructuring that lead up to the end point. Genesis proclaims the end point, but it *also* teaches us about the acts of God leading to the end point. In this way, it is analogous to Exodus 36–40, which joins the end point (a completed tabernacle) to the earlier acts of human beings—and the acts of God empowering those human beings—all the way through the process. In both Genesis 1 and Exodus 36–40, God's purposes include both the particular acts of making and the completed whole. His purposes also extend beyond the initial achievement; that is, they extend beyond the completed heavens and earth in Genesis 2:1 and beyond the completed tabernacle in Exodus 40:33.

---

20. See Beale, *The Temple and the Church's Mission*, 60–66; C. John Collins, "Reading Genesis 1–2 with the Grain: Analogical Days," in *Reading Genesis 1–2*, 91; cf. 180–81.

The tabernacle has distinct spaces: the court, the Holy Place, and the Most Holy Place. In these distinct spaces, Moses places distinct furnishings, such as the bronze altar, the laver or bronze basin, the table of the bread of the presence, the lampstand, and the ark (Ex. 40:16–33). In an analogous manner, when God makes the heavens and the earth, he creates distinct spaces, namely, heaven, sea, and dry land, and makes furnishings (specific creatures) for each of them.

The parallel between creation and the tabernacle is strengthened by the fact that the tabernacle is a kind of image of God's dwelling place in heaven. God's presence fills all things (Jer. 23:24; see Isa. 66:1), but he is especially, intensively present in heaven (1 Kings 8:27, 30, 34, 36, 39). It therefore makes sense that the tabernacle and later the temple of Solomon would have images of heaven and of the world as a whole as the dwelling place of God.[21] The functions as well as the correlations that are found in creation and in the tabernacle all take place according to God's design. (See Table 8.16.)

Table 8.16: God Crafts Functions

Creation	Providence
1:1–31—God makes things for his purposes (functions)	God instructs Bezalel to make things for his purposes in the tabernacle (functions)

By contrast, modern readers influenced by materialism are not used to thinking in terms of purpose. Materialism understands scientific laws as impersonal. Within such a framework, Genesis 1 either does not make sense or has to be interpreted as adding an additional layer of purpose *on top of* a purposeless structure of scientific law. But such a picture misconstrues both the nature of God's purposes and the nature of scientific law. The real law is God's personal word, which is personal and therefore also full of purposes.[22]

Correlations with Ancient Near Eastern Myths

Modern students of the ancient Near East have raised questions about Genesis 1 because some of its details have fascinating similarities to points in ancient Near Eastern mythic material. Since some of the

---

21. Beale, *The Temple and the Church's Mission*, 60–66; Kline, *Images of the Spirit*, 35–42.
22. Poythress, *Redeeming Science*, chap. 1.

ancient Near Eastern material has a date of origin earlier than the book of Genesis, do we infer that Genesis 1 borrowed ideas? Did it thereby incorporate some elements of a false cosmology? (We addressed some aspects of this question in chapter 5).

Students who are struck by similarities in detail might read (if they can stomach the blasphemies) some of the major mythic accounts in the ancient Near East, such as *Enuma Elish*, the Atrahasis Epic, and "Enki and Ninmah." The amount of polytheistic wildness in these documents completely overwhelms the occasional details that suggest similarities.

On this basis, one might wonder whether the parallels between Genesis and the myths are purely accidental, the product of a hit-or-miss relationship. Most of the time, we get misses. But by perusing enough material, we can gradually accumulate random "hits." Does such a hit-and-miss accumulation explain the similarities?

I do not think this is the most plausible explanation. Rather, the similarities arise for three main reasons.

First, Genesis 1 is providing for the Israelites an alternative to the myths within their environment. It is natural that it should address at least some of the same subjects.

Second, the thinking of the ancient Near East tended to correlate present-day patterns with origins.[23] That is, it correlated providence with creation. (We still do so today). When people wondered about present-day patterns, they sometimes went on to speculate about how the patterns must have come into existence through originating events. But polytheism distorted and confused the understanding of both providence and creation. In particular, it distorted the truth about the wise relationship that God had ordained between providence and creation. It offered what were in effect counterfeit versions of the narrative of creation.

---

23. For example, Vincent Arieh Tobin hypothesizes that the Egyptian symbol of Nun for the primeval waters "derived at an early (probably prehistoric) date from the flooding of the Nile; the primeval mound reflects the emergence of the isolated hillocks that appeared as the waters subsided." Vincent Arieh Tobin, "Myths: An Overview," in *The Oxford Encyclopedia of Ancient Egypt*, ed. Donald B. Redford (New York: Oxford University Press, 2001), 2.464. See also the discussion of the annual and daily cycles in J. Gwyn Griffiths, "Myths: Solar Cycle," in *The Oxford Encyclopedia of Ancient Egypt*, 2.476–80. In general, myths have their sources in "the natural world, which humans perceived and interpreted by personalizing the natural forces so as to relate to them," and "historical individuals and incidents, which were idealized." Tobin, "Myths: An Overview," 2.464; see also 2.467. "Each natural principle has a specific function in the creation analogous to that of daily life." James P. Allen, *Genesis in Egypt: The Philosophy of Ancient Egyptian Creation Accounts* (New Haven, CT: Yale Egyptological Seminar, Department of Near Eastern Language and Civilizations, The Graduate School, Yale University, 1988), 12. Also Averbeck, "A Literary Day," 15.

Third, because of cross-cultural communication in the ancient Near East, distinct cultures and subcultures may have shared some stock images, analogies, and themes, such as analogies between the cosmos and a house or between the cosmos and a tent, or the thematic contrast between chaos and order or between darkness and light.

How, then, do we conceptualize the derivation of ancient Near Eastern myths and their relation to Genesis 1? The actual order of derivation would be as follows: (1) from all eternity, God had a plan for creation and providence involving unity and analogies between the two; (2) God brought his plan into execution by the actual events of creation and providence; (3) ancient Near Eastern polytheists observed providence and inferred analogues in their mythic accounts of origins; and (4) God spoke in Genesis 1 to instruct the Israelites on creation. Genesis 1 draws on analogical correlations between creation and providence. It offers a true account in contrast to polytheistic accounts. Both the mythic accounts and Genesis 1 have ties with providential patterns. Similarities should be expected between Genesis 1 and creation myths all over the world, because both have analogical ties to providence.

In fact, we might be surprised that we do not find *more* similarities in detail between Genesis 1 and the ancient Near Eastern mythic accounts. The only way I can find to account for the meagerness of similarities is that the darkness of polytheism has suppressed appreciation for the patterns evident in providence. These patterns testify unambiguously to the Creator (Rom. 1:18–23) and provide numerous analogies for understanding God's work of creation.

In short, the similarities that do appear in the two kinds of literature (Genesis 1 and myths) come about for several reasons: (1) God offers in Genesis 1 a true alternative to the counterfeit polytheistic stories of the ancient Near East, and more broadly to the myths in cultures throughout the world; (2) all people have common access to providential patterns;[24] (3) God has permanently established correlations between creation and providence; and (4) God highlights these correlations as he calls people out of darkness into light. (See Fig. 8.4.)

---

24. Some conservative scholars have suggested that creation myths arose from garbling authentic traditions about creation that go back to the time of Noah. This is possible. But in view of the connections that arise through God's general revelation in providence, such access to special revelation is not necessary to account for the similarities.

Fig. 8.4: The Origin of Genesis 1 and Myths

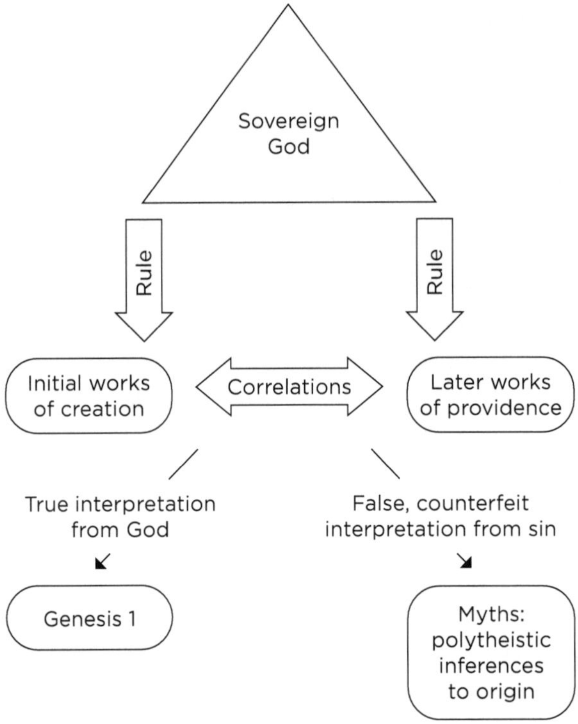

Summary of Correlations

All in all, Genesis 1 uses a large number of correlations between creation and providence. There are more than what we have mentioned. (See Table 8.17.)

Table 8.17: Some of the Correlations between Creation and Providence

Creation	Providence
1:1—absolute beginning	new events; new animals
1:2—formless world	empty, deserted regions
1:3–31—structuring the world	human filling and structuring a region
1:3—God commands	human commands; God continues to command
1:3—God creates daylight	God continues to provide daylight

Creation	Providence
1:4—God separates day and night	day and night continue to be separate
1:6-7—God separates waters above and below	waters above and below continue to be separate (as in rising clouds)
1:9—God makes dry land appear	sea and dry land continue
1:11—God produces plants	God continues to provide for plant growth and reproduction
1:14-15—God makes the lights (first appearance)	the heavenly lights are still there
1:20-21—God makes the first sea creatures and birds	sea creatures and birds continue
1:24-25—God makes the first land animals	land animals continue
1:26-27—God makes the first human beings	God continues to make new human beings (Ps. 139:13-16)
1:29-30—God makes provision for food	God's provision continues
2:1-3—God rests after six days	man rests after six days; God continues his rest from creating
1:1-31—God makes things for his purposes (functions)	God instructs Bezalel to make things for his purposes in the tabernacle (functions)

9

The Water Above (Gen. 1:6–8)

Let us now consider a particular dispute related to Genesis 1:6–8.[1]

It has become commonplace among some scholars to say that ancient Near Eastern people believed that the sky was a strong, solid dome, holding up heavenly waters above it.[2] (See Fig. 9.1 for a sketch of what some modern scholars think that the ancients believed.)

---

1. From this point on, this chapter is a revision of Vern S. Poythress, "Rain Water versus a Heavenly Sea in Genesis 1:6–8," *Westminster Theological Journal* 77, no. 2 (2015): 181–91. Used with permission.

2. E.g., Paul Seely, "The Firmament and the Water Above: Part I: The Meaning of *raqia'* in Gen 1:6–8," *Westminster Theological Journal* 53, no. 2 (1991): 227–40; Seely, "The Firmament and the Water Above: Part II: The Meaning of 'The Water above the Firmament' in Gen 1:6–8," *Westminster Theological Journal* 54, no. 1 (1992): 31–46. The theory is so well established that it has made its way into standard lexicons. Thus, Francis Brown, S. R. Driver, and Charles A. Briggs, *A Hebrew and English Lexicon of the Old Testament* (Oxford: Oxford University Press, 1953), 956, in the entry on רָקִיעַ , sense 2, say, "the vault of heaven, or 'firmament,' regarded by Hebrews as solid, and supporting 'waters' above it." But the same entry also offers the glosses "extended surface" and "expanse" (sense 1), neither of which meanings includes within it the idea of solidity. Cf. Walther Eichrodt, *Theology of the Old Testament* (Philadelphia: Westminster, 1967), 2.93–94. John H. Walton offers a variation, according to which רָקִיעַ designates the air and שַׁחַק designates the solid sky. John H. Walton, *Genesis 1 as Ancient Cosmology* (Winona Lake, IN: Eisenbrauns, 2011), 155–61. Inevitably, we can also find pictorial diagrams of the "OT conception of the world" that show both the heavenly sea and the solid firmament holding it up; e.g., T. H. Gaster, "Cosmogony," in *Interpreter's Dictionary of the Bible*, ed. George Arthur Buttrick (New York: Abingdon, 1962), 1:703.

Note also critical interaction with this idea: R. Laird Harris, Gleason L. Archer, Jr., and Bruce K. Waltke, eds., *Theological Wordbook of the Old Testament* (Chicago: Moody Press, 1981), 2.862 (with appended bibliography); James Orr, ed., *International Standard Bible Encyclopedia* (Grand Rapids, MI: Eerdmans, 1955), 1.314–15; R. K. Harrison, "Firmament," *International Standard Bible Encyclopedia*, ed. Geoffrey W. Bromiley, et al., rev. ed. (Grand Rapids, MI: Eerdmans, 1979), 2.306–7; Vern S. Poythress, *Redeeming Science: A God-Centered Approach* (Wheaton, IL: Crossway, 2006), 96n8; C. John Collins, *Genesis 1–4: A Linguistic, Literary, and Theological Commentary* (Phillipsburg, NJ: P&R, 2006), 260–65; Robert C. Newman, "The Biblical Teaching on the Firmament," ThM thesis, Biblical Theological Seminary, 1972; Noel Weeks, "Cosmology in Historical Context," *Westminster Theological Journal* 68, no. 2 (2006): 283–93.

Fig. 9.1: Modern Theory concerning Ancient Beliefs

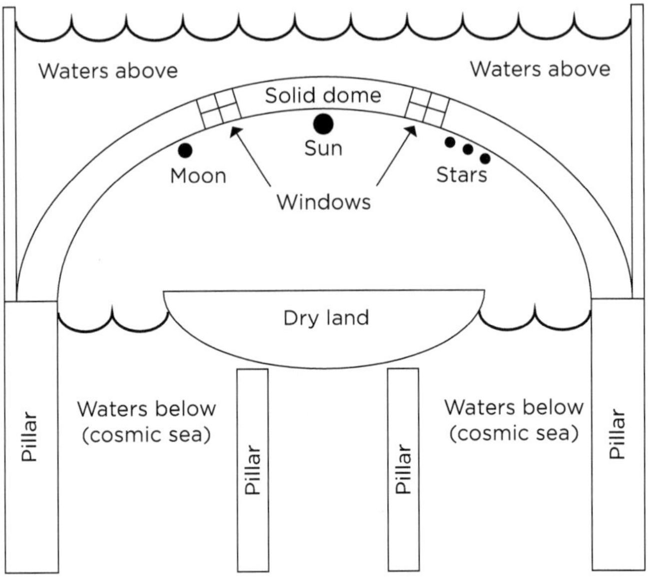

James P. Allen, in analyzing the Egyptian material, offers several comments. On the one hand, he says that Gen. 1:6–7 has "the same image" as Egyptian texts where the "vault is what keeps the waters from the world." On the other hand, he says, "In the Egyptian conception, the sky is not so much a solid 'ceiling' as a kind of interface between the surface of the Waters and the dry atmosphere. The sun sails on these waters just as people can sail on the Nile: 'The bark of the Sun courses through the Waters.'" James P. Allen, *Genesis in Egypt: The Philosophy of Ancient Egyptian Creation Accounts* (New Haven, CT: Yale Egyptological Seminar, Department of Near Eastern Language and Civilizations, The Graduate School, Yale University, 1988), 4, 5. If the sun is in the sky, which Allen says is the "interface" *between* the waters and the atmosphere, the analogy of sailing means that the sun must sit on the waters with no intervening solid barrier vault. So the idea of the solid dome has disappeared. Moreover, the fact that Allen describes the whole thing as an "image" means that, in spite of his use of physicalistic-sounding language, he may be acknowledging the imagistic and symbolic character of the ancient texts. The language about "the bark [sailing vessel] of the Sun" would constitute one example of imagistic language, since no physical or visible bark is in view. If this reading is correct, Allen is not advocating a physicalistic interpretation of these Egyptian descriptions, but is saying that the representations are symbolic in nature. On the other hand, even if he *is* advocating such a physicalistic interpretation, the texts themselves are still debatable.

On the key verse Job 37:18, see Collins, *Genesis 1–4*, 264n25; Newman, "The Biblical Teaching on the Firmament," 18–22. Newman observes that in Job 37:18, the word רְאִי, usually translated as "mirror," occurs only once in the Old Testament. Its meaning is uncertain. With a slight repointing (רֳאִי), it means "appearance" (Brown, Driver, and Briggs, *A Hebrew and English Lexicon*, 909, sense 2), which finds additional support in the LXX translation "appearance" (ὅρασις). Newman offers the translation:

Can you, with him,
spread out the mighty clouds,
like an appearance of being poured out?
(Newman, "The Biblical Teaching on the Firmament," 21)

Newman's proposal may not be right, but it shows the difficulty of relying on a single poetic verse.

In support of the theory of a heavenly sea, scholars cite texts, not only from ancient Near Eastern myths,[3] but from the Bible itself. Genesis 1:6–8 is one such text.

How should we evaluate this view? It is not true. Instead of a heavenly sea, we should be thinking about water in clouds, as well as the possibility of invisible water.[4]

Positive Understanding of Genesis 1:6–8 as Phenomenal Language

We cannot undertake a full analysis of every text that has entered the argument. But we may at least sketch out the directions in which an analysis might proceed. Recall that in chapter 8 I offered an interpretation in which the word translated as "expanse" (רְקִיעַ) in Genesis 1:6–8 is the same as "Heaven" (שָׁמַיִם, v. 8).[5] Both words refer flexibly to what is above us. (The word *heaven* can also refer to the invisible dwelling of God with his angels.) Depending on the context, the weather, and the time of day or night, we might see clouds (by day), the sun in a blue sky, stars and sometimes the moon in a black night sky, and a black sky when there is cloud cover at night. In many biblical contexts, the word *heaven* is roughly equivalent to our modern English word *sky*. We can comfortably speak of a cloudy sky, a blue sky, a fiery sky (at sunset), and a night sky. Likewise, the Hebrew term for heaven (שָׁמַיִם) covers the same spectrum (1 Kings 18:45; Gen. 1:14–15). The expression "waters that were above the expanse" primarily designates water above a cloudy sky, that is, water inside clouds, whose lower side is the sky. (But it is left open whether there is also invisible water.)

All this would have made sense to an ancient Israelite, just as it does to a modern reader with appropriate understanding of the point of view and *kind* of description that Genesis 1:6–8 offers. Genesis 1:6–8 gives us an ordinary description, a phenomenal description, a description of appearances, and does not offer any detailed "theory"

---

3. See the discussion of the division of Tiamat in chap. 5, p. 87.

4. So John Calvin, *Commentaries on the First Book of Moses Called Genesis* (Grand Rapids, MI: Baker, 1979), 1.80; H. C. Leupold, *Exposition of Genesis* (Grand Rapids, MI: Baker, 1965), 1.60; and others. On invisible water, see Oliver Hersey, "Hammering Out the Meaning of *Rāqîaʿ* and 'Waters Above' in Gen. 1:6–8 against Its Ancient Near Eastern and Biblical Context," unpublished manuscript, pp. 33–37; and Poythress, Redeeming Science, 94.

5. On whether the "expanse/firmament" is distinguishable from the "heavens," see Seely, "The Firmament and the Water Above: Part I," 237; with a reply in Weeks, "Cosmology in Historical Context," 292.

about the expanse ("Heaven") or the water above it.[6] Genesis 1:6–8 be-comes intelligible when we realize that it works with analogies between creation and our present experience of God's providence in bringing rain.

But this interpretation is vigorously disputed. Why?

Physicalistic Interpretation

One factor that comes into play is the difference between physicalistic and nonphysicalistic interpretations of ancient Near Eastern texts, as discussed in chapter 5. If a person *expects* physicalistic information in ancient mythic texts or in the Bible, he can "find" what he expects.[7] Consider the account of Noah's flood. When Noah's flood begins,

> The windows of the heavens were opened. And rain fell upon the earth forty days and forty nights . . . (Gen. 7:11b–12)

Afterward,

> The windows of the heavens were closed, the rain from the heavens was restrained . . . (Gen. 8:2b)

The water comes from above the windows. In a physicalistic and woodenly literalistic interpretation, this means that it comes from the heavenly sea, which lies above the barrier, which is "heaven." The

---

6. "For, to my mind, this is a certain principle, that nothing is here [in Genesis 1] treated of but the visible form of the world. He who would learn astronomy, and other recondite arts, let him go elsewhere." Calvin, *First Book of Moses*, 1.79. Seely's central interpretive mistake lies in trying to pry out of the word רָקִיעַ a physicalistic theory. Seely, "The Firmament and the Water Above," Parts I and II). Such a move pays insufficient attention to the word-concept distinction. James Barr, *The Semantics of Biblical Language* (London: Oxford University Press, 1961).

7. Seely accumulates an impressive number of witnesses from church history in favor of a heavenly sea. Seely, "The Firmament and the Water Above: Part II," 37–40. Only in modern times (Calvin onward) do people start moving toward other interpretations. The pattern that Seely detects from history suggests to him that Bible-believing interpreters in modern times may be prejudicially influenced by modern science, and so fail to interpret the text of Genesis with complete fairness. Ironically, the same may be true of the ancient church. Greek astronomy developed a theory of heavenly spheres from the fourth century BC onward. Over time, educated people in the Alexandrian Empire and later the Roman Empire were influenced by this theory. Moreover, the translations of the Hebrew רָקִיעַ ("expanse") with στερέωμα ("solid body," in Henry George Liddell, Robert Scott, and Henry Stuart Jones, *A Greek-English Lexicon*, 9th ed., with supplement [Oxford: Oxford University Press, 1968]) in Greek and *firmamentum* in Latin might encourage the idea of identifying the "firmament" as a solid sphere, corresponding to one of the Greek astronomical spheres. Ancient church interpreters could also be biased if they wanted Genesis 1 to "measure up" to the more technical knowledge represented by Greek astronomy, and so the temptation would arise to interpret Genesis 1 with a more technical and physicalistic slant than what the original Hebrew called for. I would suggest that the early church may already have been struggling with an analogue to the "myth of scientistic metaphysics" (chap. 5 above) and the tendency to interpret Genesis 1 in terms of "known" Greek science.

opening of the windows allows the water to come down. In addition, the language of "windows" may be interpreted as implying that the windows are attached to a solid barrier. There is a difficulty in that the literal opening of physical windows, like sluice gates, would produce a river from the sky, not forty days of "rain." But a modern interpreter can brush aside such a difficulty by saying that it is due to the inconsistencies arising from ancient ignorance and a primitive mentality.

But if we are not expecting an explanation in terms of physical mechanisms, we can approach the same passages in a different way: as imagistic, colorful pictures. They are part of a larger pattern, according to which the Old Testament uses analogies between the cosmos and a house or a tent.

Principles Guiding Understanding of the Waters Above

Which interpretation is correct? We will approach the question through a series of principles.

1. *The Israelites could be expected to have some knowledge about rain.* Many of the people of ancient Israel were farmers or herdsmen who were familiar with the outdoors, and in the land of Palestine, they depended on rain for crops and for pasturage. It was natural for them to develop some experience and elementary knowledge about rain.[8]

2. *Old Testament passages show that the Israelites knew that rain came from clouds.* Any number of passages show this:

> The heavens dropped,
> yes, the *clouds dropped water.* (Judg. 5:4b)

> He [God] made darkness around him his canopy,
> thick clouds, a gathering of water. (2 Sam. 22:12)

> He [God] binds up the *waters in his thick clouds.* (Job 26:8a)

> He [God] loads the thick *cloud with moisture;*
> the clouds scatter his lightning. (Job 37:11)

> . . . thick clouds dark with water. (Ps. 18:11)

---

8. During their stay in Egypt, the Israelites would have seen much less rain. Today (and presumably also three thousand to four thousand years ago) Egypt has a desert climate, but there is still a small amount of rain in the north (reported as about 8 inches per year on the coast at Alexandria, but more like ½ to 1 inch in Cairo, and even less south of Cairo). Exodus 9:18–19 suggests that the Egyptians knew the meaning of hail, even though the particular storm of hail in the seventh plague was miraculous.

The clouds poured out water;
> the skies gave forth thunder. (Ps. 77:17a)

> His [the king's] favor is like the *clouds that bring the spring rain*. (Prov. 16:15b)

If the clouds are full of rain,
> they empty themselves on the earth. (Eccles. 11:3a)

I [God] will also command the *clouds*
> that they *rain no rain* upon it. (Isa. 5:6b)[9]

In addition, 1 Kings 18:44–45 contains a more extended description of a cloud rising from the sea and then the coming of rain:

> And in a little while the heavens grew black with *clouds* and wind, and there was a great *rain*. (v. 45a)

In fact, taken as a whole, the information has some complexity. Clouds can bring rain (Prov. 16:15b), but they can also disappear (Job 7:9; Isa. 44:22; Hos. 6:4) or blow over without yielding rain (Prov. 25:14). The people of the time were familiar with what could happen.

3. *Other materials from the ancient Near East confirm that people of that time were familiar with the idea of rain coming from clouds*. In Ugaritic poems, Baal, the god of storm and rain, is repeatedly referred to as "Rider on the Clouds."[10] He supposedly brings clouds with rain:

> Now, too, the *seasons* of his rains will Baal *observe*,
> The *seasons* of . . . with *snow*;
> And <he will> peal his thunder in the clouds,
> Flashing his lightnings to the earth.[11]

> But thou, take thy cloud, thy wind,
> Thy . . . , thy rains.[12]

---

9. See also Ps. 147:8; Jer. 10:13; 51:16; Zech. 10:1.

10. James B. Pritchard, ed., *Ancient Near Eastern Texts Relating to the Old Testament* (Princeton, NJ: Princeton University Press, 1969), 130, III.ABA.8; 131, III.ABA.29; 132, II.AB.(iii).11, 18; etc.

11. Pritchard, ed., *Ancient Near Eastern Texts*, 133, II.AB.(v).68–71 (in this source, italics indicate that the translation is uncertain). Further references to clouds appear in 135, II.AB. (vii).19, 28, 57.

12. Pritchard, ed., *Ancient Near Eastern Texts*, 139, I.AB.(v).6–7.

Other passages from the ancient Near East confirm the association of rain with clouds.[13]

4. *The Bible sometimes describes rain as coming from "heaven."*

But the land that you are going over to possess is a land of hills and valleys, which drinks water by *the rain from heaven.* (Deut. 11:11)

For he [God] draws up the drops of water;
    they distill his mist in *rain,*
which the skies pour down
    and *drop* on mankind abundantly.
Can anyone understand the spreading of the *clouds,*
    the thunderings of his pavilion? (Job 36:27–29)

The *heavens* poured down *rain.* (Ps. 68:8b)

For as the *rain* and the snow come *down from heaven . . .*
    (Isa. 55:10a)

---

13. From Pritchard, ed., *Ancient Near Eastern Texts*, 153, AZHT C.(i).39–48:

Straightway Daniel the Rapha-man,
. . . s a cloud in the heat of the *season;*
. . . s a cloud raining upon the figs,
Dew distilling upon the grapes.
Seven years shall Baal fail,
Eight the Rider of the Clouds.
No dew,
No rain;
No welling-up of the deep,
No sweetness of Baal's voice.

The Epic of Gilgamesh mentions a black cloud briefly in connection with the coming of the south-storm:

With the first glow of dawn,
A black cloud rose up from the horizon.
Inside it Adad thunders . . . (Pritchard, ed., *Ancient Near Eastern Texts*, 94, XI.96–98; William W. Hallo, ed., *The Context of Scripture* [New York: Brill, 1997–2002] 1.459).

Afterward the south-storm brings the deluge. Pritchard, ed., *Ancient Near Eastern Texts*, 94, XI.108, 113, 129; cf. Hallo, ed., *The Context of Scripture*, 1.459.

Hersey's analysis ("Hammering Out," 37) has suggested to me that ancient Near Eastern peoples may have *combined* a heavenly sea with a role for clouds. The idea is that there were four distinct stages in the production of rain: (1) the heavenly sea functioned as a permanent reservoir of water; (2) water descended from time to time from the sea to fill the clouds; (3) the clouds had water in them; and (4) the clouds emptied water onto the earth in the form of rain. But there are difficulties. (1) Ancient Near Eastern texts do not actually exhibit four stages. Rather, discussion of rain from clouds occurs in *parallel* with discussion of rain from heaven (Judg. 5:4; Job 36:27–29). (2) The theory of four stages does not help to explain why the water would sometimes remain in clouds rather than descending from the sea to the earth in one stage. In this theory, the clouds seem not to matter, which is in tension with the texts that we have examined. (3) The movement of water *down* from the sea to the clouds is opposite to what we see in the clear-cut description in 1 Kings 18:44. At the level of phenomena, human beings see water *rising* in a cloud from the level of the sea (see also Job 36:27; the Epic of Gilgamesh, XI.96–98).

He did good by giving you *rains from heaven* . . . (Acts 14:17b)

Heaven gave rain . . . (James 5:18b)

A stubbornly physicalistic, literalistic account could insist that this language about rain from heaven is inconsistent with the language about rain from clouds. But such arguments are foolish. Judges 5:4b puts "heavens" in a parallel line with "clouds":

> The *heavens* dropped,
> yes, the *clouds* dropped water.

In addition, Job 36:27–29 mentions clouds in close association with rain from the skies. The clouds are in the heavens, so we have here two ways of describing the same phenomena of rain, not two competing sources for rain. The reference to heaven reminds people indirectly that rain comes from God's provision. It is completely consistent with saying that rain comes from clouds.

5. The Bible uses language about the heavens being "shut" to describe a lack of rain.

> He [God] will *shut up the heavens*, so that there will be no *rain*. (Deut. 11:17b)

> When heaven is *shut up* and there is no *rain* . . . (1 Kings 8:35a; 2 Chron. 6:26a)

> When I [God] *shut up* the heavens so that there is no *rain* . . . (2 Chron. 7:13a)

> They [the two witnesses] have the power to *shut the sky*, that no *rain* may fall. (Rev. 11:6a)[14]

Given Israelite knowledge that rain comes from clouds (principle 2), language about the heavens being "shut" should be interpreted as a vivid image, not an expression of an alleged physicalistic "ancient scientific" theory about how rain is kept from falling. But we can imagine how a physicalistic interpretation might approach this

---

14. See also Lev. 26:19b, "I will make your heavens like iron and your earth like bronze" (also Deut. 28:23).

language. It would say that ancient people were naive about rain. They thought it came from the heavenly sea. God shut or opened the solid barrier holding up the sea in order to control the rain. When the barrier was shut, there was no rain. But this kind of interpretation respects neither ancient knowledge of clouds nor ancient ability to use colorful images.

Or should we conclude that the ancients thought that the clouds were the lower side of a heavenly sea, and that a solid barrier formed the lower edge of the clouds? Job 26:8 says,

> He [God] binds up the waters in his thick clouds,
>   and the cloud is not split open under them.

This imagistic, poetic language, if taken literally, might suggest a solid barrier. But a cloud "fades and vanishes" (Job 7:9) and is comparable to a mist (Isa. 44:22). By observing the disappearance of a cloud, ancient people could learn that there is no solid stuff defining the lower sides of the clouds.

In connection with theophanies, the Bible contains accounts of entering a cloud: Exodus 24:18; Ezekiel 1:4; Luke 9:34; possibly also Exodus 19:16, 20. The clouds of theophanies, of course, are not ordinary clouds, but they are analogous, so these descriptions are still suggestive about the Israelites' experiences with ordinary clouds. The theophany at Mount Sinai is described as a time when God came down and "descended" (Ex. 19:11, 18). The clouds are symbolic of God's presence in heaven, and thus confirm the association of clouds with heaven (confirmed also by Job 22:14; Dan. 7:13; Matt. 26:64; Mark 14:62).

Moreover, for an ordinary observer, ancient or modern, a single experience of entering a low-lying cloud and encountering fog or mist might suffice to show that clouds can contain moisture and that the lower surface of a cloud is not literally a solid barrier that is shut until the time when it is opened for the rain to be dumped. A physicalistic interpreter could of course still escape by claiming that there is a conceptual incompatibility between rain from clouds on the one hand and the idea of "shut" or open heavens on the other hand, and that this tension only shows the inconsistencies that remain within a primitive mentality. If an interpreter chooses to go this way, he cannot of course be dissuaded. He has made himself deaf to evidence.

6. *In a manner analogous to the heavens being "shut," the Old Testament sometimes describes rain as coming when the heavens are "opened."*

> *The windows of heaven were opened.* And rain fell upon the earth forty days and forty nights. (Gen. 7:11b–12)

Afterward,

> . . . the *windows of the heavens were closed,* the rain from the heavens was restrained . . . (Gen. 8:2)

In conformity with the earlier principles, this language about the windows is imagistic. That is, it provides a colorful image for God bringing voluminous rain from clouds.

Similar imagistic language is used about heaven being opened when God supplies other goods:

> "If the Lord himself should *make windows in heaven,* could this thing [abundance of flour and barley] be?" (2 Kings 7:2b; cf. v. 19)

> Yet he commanded the skies above
> and opened the doors of heaven,
> and he rained down on them manna to eat
> and gave them the grain of heaven. (Ps. 78:23–24)

> And thereby put me to the test, says the Lord of hosts, if I will not *open the windows of heaven* for you and pour down for you a blessing until there is no more need. (Mal. 3:10b)

A physicalistic account for these passages could perhaps say that they indicate an ancient belief in a heavenly granary and a heavenly storehouse for blessing. The interpretation would perhaps then postulate that the heavenly granary is in a separate chamber from the heavenly sea, lest the grain get wet and spoil. And, of course, there would have to be a system of channels so that the grain or the water could be distributed suitably anywhere on earth. Moreover, this interpretation would have to deal with an apparent inconsistency, as to whether "windows" or "doors" let out the contents of the chambers. There is no doubt that a person could produce a physicalistic interpretation if he came to the Old Testament with that in mind. This mode of interpretation illustrates the danger of importing assumptions.

7. *The Israelites thought of dew as another form of provision of moisture "from heaven," more or less parallel to rain.* A number of passages express this idea (e.g., Deut. 32:2; 2 Sam. 1:21; 1 Kings 17:1; Job 38:28; Mic. 5:7).[15] Some passages make no comment about the source of dew. Others indicate that it comes from "heaven" (Gen. 27:28, 39; Deut. 33:28; Dan. 4:15, 23, 25, 33; 5:21; Hag. 1:10; Zech. 8:12). What do these passages tell us?

Modern observation of providence shows that dew can appear on a clear night as well as at a time when there are clouds. So in terms of technical detail, clouds cannot be the only physical source for dew. If we were to read the biblical passages expecting technical detail, we could reason that "heaven," from which dew comes, must designate a source quite distinct from clouds. But the focus of the passages is not on providing technical details (some of the passages are poetic); it is on indicating the relation of human beings to the general providential order. Heaven as the source of dew symbolizes the more ultimate truth that God is the source. Moreover, some passages associate dew with clouds:

> The *clouds* drop down the dew. (Prov. 3:20b)

> Your love is like a morning *cloud*,
>   like the *dew* that goes early away. (Hos. 6:4b)

Hosea 6:4 might not be significant, because the point of comparison might be simply that dew, like clouds, can disappear. Proverbs 3:20 is more significant, because, if taken literally, it indicates that clouds are a main source for dew. As usual, the verse does not offer a technical discussion. But it appears that clouds can be a source for both rain and dew.

If we asked an Israelite how dew could appear after a cloudless night, it is not clear what the answer might have been. There remains mystery, not only for us, but maybe for the Israelites. Perhaps the appearance of dew might have suggested that sometimes the heavenly

---

15. I am grateful to Hersey for pointing out the significance of dew ("Hammering Out," 35–36).

water was invisible before it came down. But we do not find any explicit discussion of this possibility in the Bible. It is best to leave the matter at that level and understand that the biblical texts are presenting us with a general pattern, one that was relevant to the Israelites' practical need for water for crops and herds. Dew is a source—but it is minor. It fits into the main picture, which involves rain from clouds—clouds that, it should be said, are the clouds of heaven, symbolizing God's providential provision from heaven, his dwelling place. The terminology of "clouds" and "heaven" offers two alternative ways of describing water coming from above.

8. *In general, the Old Testament instructs the Israelites about things that affect their lives.* The individual observations about the various texts fit into a larger picture. The Israelites had to depend on rain (Deut. 11:11–17). They lived in a land that "drinks water by the rain from heaven" (v. 11). It is reasonable to credit them not only with some familiarity with rain and clouds, but a practical interest. They could live well only if they had neither too much rain nor too little. The flood of Noah was an instance of having too much. If the heavens were "shut," they had too little. The Israelites knew that these situations could come about by means of rain or lack of rain from clouds.

By contrast, an alleged heavenly sea closed in by a solid barrier would have no relation to clouds that allegedly floated underneath the solid barrier. Such a sea could have no practical interest to the Israelites, because *clouds*—and not the alleged heavenly sea—were their source for rain. An alleged heavenly sea is, however, exceedingly relevant to a modern student who is looking for "ancient science" in the form of physicalistic explanations.

The physicalistic interpreter could still allege that the flood of Noah was an exception that illustrates the relevance of the heavenly sea. But our examination of the language about Noah's flood shows that, even though the volume of water was greater than normal, there is no indication that the water came by other than the normal ways involving rain "from heaven."

In fact, the same principle about relevance to the Israelites applies when we interpret the account of the flood in Genesis 7–8. The Israelites who heard Genesis 7–8 recited in their presence did not experience Noah's flood themselves. They had to picture it with the help of the textual description in Genesis. Genesis 7–8 invited them to understand the flood by analogy with their own providential situation, wherein they had experiences with smaller rains and smaller floods. Hence, when they interpreted Genesis 7–8, they understood it as involving processes analogous to those that they observed providentially: rain from clouds and floods from overflowing rivers.

The connection between Noah's flood and clouds is confirmed after the flood. Though the narrative in Genesis 7–8 does not mention clouds, the later covenant with Noah in Genesis 9:8–17 does:

> And God said, "This is the sign of the covenant that I make between me and you and every living creature that is with you, for all future generations: I have set my bow in the *cloud*, and it shall be a sign of the covenant between me and the earth. When I bring *clouds* over the earth and the bow is seen in the *clouds*, I will remember my covenant that is between me and you and every living creature of all flesh. And the waters shall never again become a flood to destroy all flesh. When the bow is in the *clouds*, I will see it and remember the everlasting covenant between God and every living creature of all flesh that is on the earth." (vv. 12–16)

Verse 14 in particular, with the expression "When I bring *clouds* over the earth," hints at the prospect that the clouds may bring rain. If they bring too much, there will be another flood. God puts his bow specifically "in the *clouds*." Its location strengthens the guarantee that the clouds, which might signify to the Israelites the threat of a flood, will not bring such an intense deluge again.

Finally, let us suppose for the sake of argument that we allow that Noah's flood involved the opening of the heavenly sea, which had nothing to do with clouds. God's promise to Noah (Gen. 9:8–17) guarantees that the Israelites will not have to worry about a recurrence. Hence, the alleged heavenly sea is irrelevant in practice.

9. Genesis 1 speaks about things relevant to the Israelites. In Genesis 1 as a whole and in Genesis 1:6–8 in particular, God speaks about acts of creation that not only evoke praise but have practical interest to human beings. Thus, Genesis 1:6–8 is speaking about water above, such as the Israelites received from clouds. The alleged heavenly sea is irrelevant, and so it must be rejected as not pertinent to interpreting 1:6–8.

In fact, introducing a heavenly sea creates interpretive problems rather than solving them. Once we acknowledge that the Israelites knew that rain comes from clouds, a modern theory about the heavenly sea has to postulate not two bodies of water, but three: the sea on earth, the water inside the clouds, and the heavenly sea. It has to say, in effect, that Genesis 1:6–8 mentions the first and the third, even though the third is irrelevant, while leaving out the second, which is continually relevant for crops and for herds. May we ask whether this interpretation is plausible?

Finally, we may observe that an interpretation of Genesis 1:6–8 as a reference to a heavenly sea violates the key principle that Genesis 1 teaches about creation using analogies from providential experience. There is no providential experience of a heavenly sea, whereas there is a providential experience of rain descending from clouds. The implausibility of the heavenly-sea interpretation increases because of its lack of contact with ordinary experience. In reality, the heavenly-sea interpretation imposes an alleged ancient quasiscientific physicalistic theory of the heavenly sea on the text, which is just as bad as imposing on the text the expectation for modern scientific-technical precision.

Some Objections

Let us consider two possible objections[16] that might be lodged against our interpretation.

The first objection concerns a rabbinical text. Paul Seely cites the Talmudic tractate Ta'anith 9b in favor of the idea that the clouds receive water from the firmament, toward which they rise in order to be filled.[17] In fact, the passage in Ta'anith 9b is discussing two views. (1) Rabbi Eliezer says that the water all comes from the ocean, and speaks of mist that "went up." (2) Rabbi Joshua maintains that the water comes from the "upper waters," which he associates with the firmament, and that clouds "catch the rain water" from that source. Both rabbinical reasonings are, of course, later than the biblical texts themselves; both exhibit the tendency to overread the Bible under the assumption that it is speaking in more technical detail. The main positive point is this: the existence of two interpretations shows that there

---

16. Hersey, "Hammering Out," 37.
17. Seely, "The Firmament and the Water Above: Part II," 37.

was no overwhelming consensus at the time. It was *not* simply taken for granted that a heavenly sea was the source of rain.

The second objection appeals to evidence from Psalm 148. The text is clearly divided thematically into praise for heavenly things (vv. 1–6) and for earthly things (vv. 7–12, perhaps extending to later verses as well). The "waters above the heavens" belong with the heavenly things (v. 4), while "hail, snow and mist" belong with the earthly things (v. 8). Does that division imply that clouds belong with the earthly things, and must be distinguished from the "waters above the heavens"? No. Hail, snow, and rain come down from clouds to the earth. Human beings experience them when they arrive in the earthly sphere. But the clouds as the higher *source* of water belong to the heavenly sphere, broadly speaking. They are called "clouds of heaven" (Dan. 7:13; Matt. 24:30; cf. Deut. 4:11; Rev. 11:12). Judges 5:4b says it well:

> The *heavens* dropped,
> yes, the *clouds* dropped water.

Conclusion

Since we cannot go back and interview ancient Israelites, modern interpreters can always postulate that the Israelites had strange beliefs about a heavenly sea. Such postulates are likely to be around for a long time. The postulates have become embedded in the tradition of Old Testament scholarship. They seem at first glance to be supported by various ancient Near Eastern texts, at least if the texts are read physicalistically. The postulates are further sustained by the modern myths that make us complacent about our superiority to the ancients and patronizing toward their alleged primitive naivete. But if we are alert, we may entertain doubts. Whether or not the Israelites had strange beliefs, God does not address such beliefs directly, and neither does he presuppose them. He teaches that there is water above, separated from water beneath by an expanse. The language is sparse. If any ancient Israelites or modern interpreters do not realize that rain does indeed come from water above, that is their problem.

10

Correlations with Providence in Genesis 2–3

In chapter 8, we saw that we could coherently understand Genesis 1 by using correlations between creation and providence. Let us explore the same principle with Genesis 2 and sketch the implications for Genesis 3.[1]

Interpreting Correlations in Genesis 2:4–25

1. *Genesis 2:4.*

> These are the generations
> of the heavens and the earth when they were created,
> in the day that the LORD God made the earth and the heavens.

The expression "these are the generations" introduces the first of a number of sections of genealogical history in the book of Genesis.[2] It is succeeded by analogous headings, such as "This is the book of the generations of Adam" (Gen. 5:1) and "These are the generations of Noah" (6:9). In 2:4, it is clearly an expression that uses analogy, since

---

1. This chapter is a revision of Vern S. Poythress, "Correlations with Providence in Genesis 2," *Westminster Theological Journal* 78, no. 1 (2016): 29–48. Used with permission.
2. The unity and function of Gen. 2:4 are disputed. See C. John Collins, *Genesis 1–4: A Linguistic, Literary, and Theological Commentary* (Phillipsburg, NJ: P&R, 2006), 40–42; Derek Kidner, *Genesis: An Introduction and Commentary* (Leicester, England: Inter-Varsity; Downers Grove, IL: InterVarsity Press, 1967), 23–25; Victor P. Hamilton, *The Book of Genesis, Chapters 1–17* (Grand Rapids, MI: Eerdmans, 1990), 150–53; Gordon J. Wenham, *Genesis 1–15*, Word Biblical Commentary 1 (Waco, TX: Word, 1987), 49. On the structure of genealogical history, see Wenham, *Genesis 1–15*, xxi–xxii; Hamilton, *Genesis, Chapters 1–17*, 2–11.

the heavens and the earth do not father ("beget," "generate") children in the same way that human beings do.

The first section of generations, extending from Genesis 2:4 to 4:26, includes elements belonging to the original acts of creation, such as the creation of Adam (2:7) and Eve (v. 22),[3] and elements belonging to the subsequent providential history (3:1–4:26). Technically, we might expect that the "generations" would include only events after the completion of the heavens and earth in 1:31. But 5:2 shows that a genealogical section can include some recapitulation of earlier events. Using the word *generations*, Genesis 2:4 makes the point that the heavens and earth bring forth events leading to an unfolding history, in a manner analogous to the unfolding of generations that an Israelite could observe in his own time.

2. *Genesis 2:5–6.*

> When no bush of the field was yet in the land and no small plant of the field had yet sprung up—for the LORD God had not caused it to rain on the land, and there was no man to work the ground, and a mist was going up from the land and was watering the whole face of the ground.

The English Standard Version of the Bible uses the word *land* twice to translate the Hebrew word אֶרֶץ, the same word used in Genesis 1:1 and 2:4 for the whole earth. It is possible that 2:5 is returning us to the unformed situation of 1:2 in order to recommence a narrative of the acts of creation.[4] But this interpretation is less likely because 2:4 has promised us a new section, and because the terminology for the plants in 2:5 does not correspond directly to the terminology in 1:11–12. The trees go unmentioned in 2:5. Verse 5 may be describing a dry place before the rainy season starts. The "land" is then not the whole "earth" but a smaller region, where the garden of Eden will later be planted. If so,

---

3. Some interpreters have suggested that the events in Gen. 2:5–25 take place in a time period subsequent to the sixth day of 1:24–31; see, for example, John H. Walton, "A Historical Adam: Archetypal Creation View," in *Four Views on the Historical Adam*, ed. Matthew Barrett and Ardel B. Caneday (Grand Rapids, MI: Zondervan, 2013), 109. But this suggestion fails to consider all the evidence. (1) Gen. 2:1 shows that God's acts of creation were finished by the end of the sixth day. When taken together with 2:5–25, it implies that the creation of Adam and Eve, a creation of new creatures, belongs within the sixth day. (2) Moving 2:5–25 to a subsequent time creates tension between the "very good" of 1:31 and the "not good" of 2:18. From the standpoint of literary craft, "not good" in 2:18 is clearly meant to allude to and contrast with the repeated refrain in Genesis 1, "And God saw that it was good" (vv. 10, 12, 18, 21, 25). Thus, man being alone represents a situation prior to the "very good" endpoint in v. 31. (3) Man being alone in 2:18 implies that there are not yet any women. So the time in view is prior to the completion of 1:27, which explicitly includes female humanity.

4. So Derek Kidner, "Gen 2:5–6, Wet or Dry?" *Tyndale Bulletin* 17 (1966): 109–14.

God's work in verses 5–6 enjoys an analogy with his later acts of providence, when he makes a land green after a dry spell. (See Table 10.1.)

Table 10.1: Barren Land and Rain

Creation	Providence
2:5—barren land in Eden, before rainy season	dry land before rainy season

In verse 6, the Hebrew word אֵד, translated "mist" (ESV), is rare. It occurs elsewhere in the Old Testament only at Job 36:27. The ESV provides an alternative marginal reading, "spring." It is some kind of source of water.[5] The verse may be describing the beginning of the rainy season.

3. *Genesis 2:7.*

> Then the LORD God formed the man of dust from the ground and breathed into his nostrils the breath of life, and the man became a living creature.

God's provides the "breath of life" in a unique way with the creation of Adam. But by analogy, God also acts providentially in giving the "breath" of life to each individual human being:

> The *Spirit* of God has *made* me,
>   and the *breath* of the Almighty gives me *life*. (Job 33:4)

Table 10.2: God's Original Forming of Adam and Later Forming of Human Beings

Creation	Providence
2:7—God forms Adam	God forms each of us in the womb

The language about "forming" and "dust" in Genesis 2:7 also occurs in the context of God's providence. It describes the fact that God forms each new individual human being:

---

5. See Collins, *Genesis 1–4*, 104n6. Job 36:27–28 seems to use אֵד in a context where it designates water coming down from above ("mist [אֵד] in *rain*, which the skies *pour down* and *drop* on mankind abundantly"). In view of Job 36:27 and the uncertainties in etymology, "mist" or "rain cloud" seems better as a translation in Gen. 2:6 than "stream" or "spring." Mark Futato, "Because It Had Rained: A Study of Gen 2:5–7 with Implications for Gen 2:4–25 and Gen 1:1–2:3," *Westminster Theological Journal* 60, no. 1 (1998): 1–21 (5–9); but see Edward J. Young, *Studies in Genesis One* (Philadelphia: Presbyterian and Reformed, 1964), 62n50.

Your hands *fashioned* and made me,
> and now you have destroyed me altogether.
Remember that you have made me like *clay*;
> and will you return me to the *dust*? (Job 10:8–9)

For he knows how we are *formed*;
> he remembers that we are *dust*. (Ps. 103:14 ESV mg.)

For you *formed* my inward parts;
> you knitted me together in my mother's womb. (Ps. 139:13)

God's acts of creation also have analogies with human acts of formation. The mention of "dust" as the starting material suggests an analogy with a potter who forms clay (Jer. 18:1–6; Rom. 9:21).

Further verses indicate that both man and animals come from dust and return to dust:

For you are *dust*,
> and to *dust* you shall return. (Gen. 3:19b)

When you take away their breath, they [animals] die
> and return to their *dust*. (Ps. 104:29)

All [man and beast] go to one place. All are from the *dust*, and to *dust* all return. (Eccles. 3:20)

The *dust* [of man's body] returns to the earth as it was, and the spirit returns to God who gave it. (Eccles. 12:7)

Within God's providential order, the Israelites could observe that the bodies of dead animals and dead human beings gradually disintegrate. If not torn apart by scavengers, they gradually lose their distinctive shape and structure, and become less and less distinguishable from the ground on which they lie or in which they are buried. So after death, the body ends up becoming dust.

As usual, the language is not technical. Genesis 2:7 is not making a theoretically precise statement about the chemical constituents of the human body or about the molecular structures present in the body or in soil, but is making a statement that makes sense against the background of ordinary observations about what happens to bodies after they die.

What about the beginning of human life? Within the order of providence, God makes new human beings in the womb. But the way in which he does it is mysterious (Ps. 139:13–15; Eccles. 11:5). Instances of miscarriage and observations of gestation and birth among animals would provide some further information for the Israelites.

The description of God making the first man invites the Israelites to see analogies between the original creation and later providence. But not everything is analogous. The fact that Adam is made of dust and will return to dust is clearly analogous. But Adam is the first man ever made. This prime role for Adam is implied not only by the context of Genesis 1–2, which intends to tell us about origins, but by later theological reflections (Rom. 5:12–21; 1 Cor. 15:45–49; see Acts 17:26).[6] It is confirmed by Genesis 2:18: "It is not good that the man should be alone." This statement implies that the man was alone until God did something to remedy the lack.[7] We may infer that there were no other human beings until the creation of Eve. If Adam is first, he cannot have a human mother who gave birth to him. So at this point, the text invites the Israelites to see *discontinuity* rather than a positive analogy with later human conception and birth. (We will discuss this discontinuity and others more thoroughly later in the chapter.)

The biblical texts outside Genesis that talk about "forming" and "dust" echo Genesis 2:7. But none of them *combines* terms for *form* and *dust* in order to say that God forms a human individual from dust (Ps. 103:14 does have both terms, but not in the key combination). Some texts use the language of forming or fashioning, as is appropriate to indicate God's involvement as primary cause along with the secondary causes involved in the growth of babies in the womb. Some texts say that human beings *are* dust or are "from dust." That language echoes Genesis 3:19 and is confirmed by what happens to corpses. But the later biblical texts do not say that God *makes* or *forms* a human being from dust. In a sense, that would be true, but it would be odd to

---

6. See J. P. Versteeg, *Adam in the New Testament: Mere Teaching Model or First Historical Man?*, trans. and with foreword by Richard B. Gaffin Jr. (Phillipsburg, NJ: P&R, 2012); Hans Madueme and Michael Reeves, eds., *Adam, the Fall, and Original Sin: Theological, Biblical, and Scientific Perspectives* (Grand Rapids, MI: Baker, 2014); Philip G. Ryken, "Pastoral Reflection 2: We Cannot Understand the World or Our Faith without a Real, Historical Adam," in *Four Views on the Historical Adam*, 267–79.

7. William D. Barrick, "A Historical Adam: Young-Earth Creation View," in *Four Views on the Historical Adam*, 210.

say it that way, because doing so would overlook the key role of the mother and the very indirect way in which dust gets involved.

In sum, Genesis 2:7 has a distinctive message. It stands out notably from the verses around it precisely because it does not have a complete analogue within providence. This lack of analogue serves to underline the unique character of the original creation of man.

We may nevertheless include a note of caution: we must be careful when dealing with analogies. Genesis 2:7 does have a relation of analogy to later instances when God brings human beings into existence. In every case of analogy, we have to respect the fact that there are both similarities and dissimilarities. Where do the similarities end? My view is that the context of Genesis 2:7, with its concern for the once-for-all *origin* of man, together with the indications in Genesis as a whole that Adam stands at the head of the whole human race, encourage us to see the act of creation in Genesis 2:7 as unique and as not involving the use of living ape ancestors. But this issue is highly disputed in our day, and we must refer readers to other books for a fuller discussion.[8]

Granted the desirability of fuller discussion, we may nevertheless mention a few other issues that affect our understanding of the creation of Adam.

Let us briefly consider an alternative. Those who want biological gradualism in human origins picture for themselves in the dim past a tribe, a larger group, or a race instead of Adam as the first man.[9] If they are theorists with atheistic or deistic inclinations, they may imagine a random or purposeless evolution toward humanity. If they are robust theists, they may imagine that God worked within and on a tribe such that he gradually or suddenly switched on defining religious

---

8. Versteeg, *Adam in the New Testament*; Madueme and Reeves, eds., *Adam*. For multiple views, see *Four Views on the Historical Adam*. On the scientific issues, see Ann Gauger, Douglas Axe, and Casey Luskin, *Science and Human Origins* (Seattle: Discovery Institute, 2012); Vern S. Poythress, "Adam versus Claims from Genetics," *Westminster Theological Journal* 75, no. 1 (2013): 65–82, http://www.frame-poythress.org/adam-versus-claims-from-genetics/; John Sanford, Wesley Brewer, Franzine Smith, and John Baumgardner, "The Waiting Time Problem in a Model Hominin Population," *Theoretical Biology and Medical Modelling* 12, no. 18 (2015), https://tbiomed.biomedcentral.com/articles/10.1186/s12976-015-0016-z.

The last of these publications is particularly interesting because it shows up a genetic problem with gradualism. We hear claims that genetics conclusively shows that there never was a single pair who were the exclusive biological ancestors for all human beings. But the article in question poses a problem for gradualism that looks insuperable. There is not enough time to establish gradualistically, by known random processes in population genetics, the unique DNA pool of the human race.

The research on genetics is blossoming, so we may continue to see new discussion.

9. Though not endorsing the tribal view as superior, C. John Collins discusses it in *Did Adam and Eve Really Exist? Who They Were and Why You Should Care* (Wheaton, IL: Crossway, 2011).

characteristics of humanity within them. In other words, a whole tribe or race somehow traveled from a prehuman to a human state.

But if that were indeed the way it happened, a text is capable of saying so. (I have just showed how in the previous paragraph.) It should be noted that, even apart from the special character of divine inspiration, ancient people were just as capable as we are of telling a story that involves a group, a tribe, or an animal ancestry rather than a single man from whom came a single woman. For example, the Atrahasis Epic has humanity originate with seven human pairs, not one.[10] In addition, according to Atrahasis, the creation of humanity was an extended process, involving multiple stages and multiple gods. The poem could easily have included an animal stage if the author had so desired. The story of Enki and Ninmaḫ involves the creation of several human beings, some of whom are handicapped.[11] The *Hymn to E'engura* has human beings break through the earth like plants springing up.[12]

We can find various stories in other parts of the world. The Korean legend of Dangun contains a part in which a bear becomes a woman. The woman then mates with the god Hwanung to produce a son, Dangun, who "founded the first Korean kingdom."[13] A Tibetan myth says that Tibetan people originated from the union of a spirit/ogress with a monkey or ape.[14] A Samoan myth of the creator god Tangaloa says that he "took maggots and shaped them into humans. When he gave them a heart and soul, they came to life."[15] A Chinese myth says that the goddess Nu Wa created *many* humans by molding yellow earth.[16] We could multiply examples.

The story of the origin of humanity in Genesis 2:4–25 is not merely a general assertion that God created humanity. In its details, by its

---

10. W. G. Lambert and A. R. Millard, *Atra-ḫasīs: The Babylonian Story of the Flood* (Winona Lake, IN: Eisenbrauns, 1999), 60–63; Tablet I.255–60; S iii 5–14.

11. Jacob Klein, "Enki and Ninmaḫ," in *The Context of Scripture*, ed. William Hallo (Leiden/New York/Köln: Brill, 1997), 1.517–18.

12. Richard J. Clifford, *Creation Accounts in the Ancient Near East and in the Bible* (Washington, DC: Catholic Biblical Association of America, 1994), 30, from line 3 of the *Hymn to E'engura*.

13. "The Myth of Gojoseon's Founding-King Dan-gun," http://www.san-shin.org/Dan-gun_Myth.html.

14. "The Descent of the Tibetan People from a Monkey and a Rock-Ogress," Tibet, http://www.presscluboftibet.org/china-tibet-23/the-descent-of-the-tibetan-people-from-a-monkey-and-a-rock-ogress.htm.

15. "Polynesian Mythology," Myths and Legends, http://www.mythencyclopedia.com/Pa-Pr/Polynesian-Mythology.html.

16. "Tag Archives: Nu Wa: On the Origin of Species," Heathen Chinese, http://heathenchinese.wordpress.com/tag/nu-wa/.

focus on Adam as a single human being, it *contrasts* pointedly with other possible stories involving groups. And by starting with dust rather than an animal ancestor, it appears to imply that Adam was a fresh creation, not a transformation from an animal.

4. *Genesis 2:8.*

> And the LORD God planted a garden in Eden, in the east, and there he put the man whom he had formed.

God planted a garden in a manner analogous to later work by human beings, in which they plant gardens and grow crops (Ps. 104:14). (See Table 10.3.)

Table 10.3: The Garden of Eden and Later Gardens

Creation	Providence
2:8—God plants the garden of Eden	Human beings plant and cultivate gardens

In this verse, we observe the first of a whole series of events in Genesis 2 that are not completely in chronological order. Rather, they are in *teleological* order. They show how God's works in creating various things suit human needs. The garden of Eden is planted in order to provide a suitable environment in which man may live. By analogy, human beings plant gardens and do other types of work to suit their own needs and those of their families and neighbors.

5. *Genesis 2:9.*

> And out of the ground the LORD God made to spring up every tree that is pleasant to the sight and good for food. The tree of life was in the midst of the garden, and the tree of the knowledge of good and evil.

The verse says that trees sprang up. In his providence, God continues to cause trees to grow (Ps. 104:16). Trees are still pleasant to the sight, and many are good for food. So the act of creation in Genesis 2:9 has analogies with later acts of providence. (See Table 10.4.)

Table 10.4: God Provides for Trees to Grow

Creation	Providence
2:9—God causes trees to grow in the garden of Eden	trees grow in gardens

The tree of life and the tree of the knowledge of good and evil are both special trees, no longer encountered in providence. Part of the point of the narrative is that these two trees are *not* like all the rest. They play special roles with respect to the relation between God and man, and they may become an intense source of blessing or curse.

When Adam and Eve are cast out of the garden of Eden, the cherubim bar the way to the tree of life (Gen. 3:23–24). Thus, God explicitly indicates that this tree is no longer accessible to mankind. The lampstand within the Holy Place of the tabernacle probably symbolizes a tree of life, as does Aaron's staff that budded (Num. 17:8). Both are inaccessible to ordinary Israelites (v. 10).

In several places, the Bible provides symbolic references to a tree of life: wisdom "is a tree of life to those who lay hold of her" (Prov. 3:18a); "the fruit of the righteous is a tree of life" (11:30a; cf. 13:12; 15:4). So is the tree of life in the garden of Eden merely a figurative representation of wisdom, righteousness, or some other blessing? In view of its close connection with "every tree" (Gen. 2:9) and the geographical markers used in describing the garden of Eden (vv. 8, 10–14), the text of Genesis 2 represents Eden as an actual garden, and the trees as physical trees. The later symbolic references build figurative usages on top of the original use in verse 9.

6. Genesis 2:10.

> A river flowed out of Eden to water the garden, and there it divided and became four rivers.

The presence of a river is analogous to God's present providential order, which includes rivers. Commentaries debate whether the division from one river into four means that one water source splits into four downstream rivers, or that four rivers come together into one downstream river. Since in providence the latter is far more typical, the latter is probably being communicated at this point, by analogy with present-day providence.

7. *Genesis 2:11–14.*

> The name of the first is the Pishon. It is the one that flowed around the whole land of Havilah, where there is gold. And the gold of that land is good; bdellium and onyx stone are there. The name of the second river is the Gihon. It is the one that flowed around the whole land of Cush. And the name of the third river is the Tigris, which flows east of Assyria. And the fourth river is the Euphrates.

The rivers Tigris and Euphrates, as well as the place-name Assyria, are identifiable. These names show continuities with the present providential order. Commentaries discuss the identification of the rest.[17] (See Table 10.5.)

Table 10.5: God Provides Rivers

Creation	Providence
2:10–14—God provides rivers in Eden	God provides rivers now
2:14—Tigris and Euphrates then	Tigris and Euphrates now

8. *Genesis 2:15.*

> The LORD God took the man and put him in the garden of Eden to work it and keep it.

The task of working and keeping the garden is analogous to gardening and agricultural tasks that continue within God's providential order. (See Table 10.6.)

Table 10.6: God Appoints Man to Garden

Creation	Providence
2:15—God appoints Adam to garden	God appoints people for work in various forms, including gardening

17. See, e.g., Kidner, *Genesis*, 63–64; Collins, *Genesis 1–4*, 119–20. Given the information about the Tigris and the Euphrates, it seems probable that the two other rivers once flowed into the area near the Persian Gulf where the Tigris and the Euphrates join. The joining of the four rivers at a downstream location would confirm our interpretation that Gen. 2:10 describes four tributaries joining into one downstream river.

9. *Genesis 2:16–17.*

> And the LORD God commanded the man, saying, "You may surely eat of every tree of the garden, but of the tree of the knowledge of good and evil you shall not eat, for in the day that you eat of it you shall surely die."

The first of this pair of verses contains the permission: "You may surely eat of every tree . . ." Within God's providential order, mankind continues to enjoy the privilege of eating fruits (Acts 14:17). The effects of the fall mean that it is now harder to get them (Gen. 3:17–19). (See Table 10.7.)

Table 10.7: God Gives Mankind Trees and Their Fruits

Creation	Providence
2:16—God gives Adam fruits	God gives us fruits

In verse 17 comes the prohibition: "you shall not eat." As we observed, the tree of knowledge is unique, and does not correspond directly to any tree in God's present providential order. The significance of the tree lies in the fact that it is used as a test of obedience or disobedience. This test is analogous to the ones that later confront the patriarchs and the nation of Israel, as to whether they will serve God faithfully or turn to false gods and their own devices. Thus, we find analogies both in the test and in the fact that this tree is similar in some ways to other trees. (See Table 10.8.)

Table 10.8: God Tests Human Beings concerning Obedience

Creation	Providence
2:17—God tests Adam and Eve	God tests our obedience

10. *Genesis 2:18.*

> Then the LORD God said, "It is not good that the man should be alone; I will make him a helper fit for him."

At this point, the text shows explicitly the theme of God's purpose and the theme that God's work establishes a home suitable for mankind. By analogy, within the subsequent providential order, the Lord continues to bless mankind in his mercy. One of the blessings is marriage and children. (See Table 10.9.)

Table 10.9: God Provides Marriage and Children

Creation	Providence
2:18—God provides Eve	God provides marriage and family

11. *Genesis 2:19.*

> Now out of the ground the LORD God formed every beast of the field and every bird of the heavens and brought them to the man to see what he would call them. And whatever the man called every living creature, that was its name.

The man names the animals, in imitation of God's earlier naming (Gen. 1:5, 8, 10). Within God's providential order, mankind continues to use and invent names, and this use of language is one expression of human dominion. (See Table 10.10.)

Table 10.10: God Empowers Human Naming and Dominion

Creation	Providence
2:19—God empowers human naming and dominion	we give names and exercise dominion

12. *Genesis 2:20.*

> The man gave names to all livestock and to the birds of the heavens and to every beast of the field. But for Adam there was not found a helper fit for him.

The lack of a fitting helper has an analogy with human experience in providence. Human beings continue to experience the fact that a man can have children only in cooperation with a woman. In a broader way, other human beings serve as companions, coworkers, conversation partners, and fellow worshipers in ways that no animal can. The intimacy in marriage is a particularly strong expression of this companionship and cooperation. A good wife complements her husband in a unique way.

13. *Genesis 2:21.*

> So the Lord God caused a deep sleep to fall upon the man, and
> while he slept took one of his ribs and closed up its place with flesh.

The "deep sleep" described here is obviously uniquely designed by
God to provide a context for a unique work. At the same time, it is
analogous to everyday sleep that human beings experience in providence. (See Table 10.11.)

Table 10.11: God Gives Deep Sleep

Creation	Providence
2:21—God gives Adam deep sleep	God gives sleep.

When a person is asleep, he does not notice what is going on
around him. If his sleep is deep, he may not be awakened even when
he is touched, softly spoken to, or lightly shaken. By extrapolation
from such ordinary experiences, the Israelites could understand what
it would mean for a person to be so deeply asleep that God could
remove a rib. Would they have worried about pain being inflicted on
Adam? Modern anesthetics were not known in the time of ancient
Israel, but people could have observed cases in which neurological
malfunction dulled or eliminated the experience of pain in some parts
of the body. God's power gives him the ability to eliminate pain in the
case of Adam.

What about the "rib"? Elsewhere I have argued that the text designates a rib, and does not just offer a vague metaphorical picture
for Eve's social and spiritual status in relation to Adam.[18] This and
the following verse are the only places in the Old Testament where
the Hebrew word צֵלָע designates a rib, but the same meaning is at-
tested in rabbinic Hebrew with reference to the ribs of animals.[19] The
Israelites would have been familiar with ribs, from experience with
cutting up the meat of slaughtered animals, from experience with
human bones (cf., e.g., 2 Kings 13:21; 23:16), and from the experience

---

18. Vern S. Poythress, *Redeeming Science: A God-Centered Approach* (Wheaton, IL: Crossway, 2006), 249–51.
19. Marcus Jastrow, *A Dictionary of the Targumim, the Talmud Babli and Yerushalmi, and the Midrashic Literature* (New York: Pardes, 1950), 2.1285.

of feeling one's own ribs underneath the skin. All these experiences offered providential analogues for understanding Adam's rib.

14. *Genesis 2:22.*

> And the rib that the LORD God had taken from the man he made into a woman and brought her to the man.

Providence offers no complete analogue for the miraculous construction of a whole body from a rib. God's way of making Eve is unique, as is fitting for the creation of the first woman. Nevertheless, the text does invoke an analogy between God's work and man's work. It says, "he *made* [the rib] into a woman." The key word *made* (from בנה) is not the most common word for making (עשׂה), but a word often translated as "build." God made the woman in a manner analogous to a man building a house. (See Table 10.12.)

Table 10.12: God Builds Eve

Creation	Providence
2:22—God builds Eve	we build houses

15. *Genesis 2:23.*

> Then the man said,
>
> > "This at last is bone of my bones
> > and flesh of my flesh;
> > she shall be called Woman,
> > because she was taken out of Man."

The unique way in which God makes Eve has analogies to the providential experience of the spiritual, social, and familial bond between man and woman, especially expressed in the intimacy of marriage. The unique, once-for-all creation of Eve forms the foundation for a permanent providential order.

16. *Genesis 2:24.*

> Therefore a man shall leave his father and his mother and hold fast to his wife, and they shall become one flesh.

Marriage as an institution within God's providential order has its foundation in the original act when God created Eve. The first marriage, between Adam and Eve, offers the paradigm case that subsequent marriages imitate.

17. *Genesis 2:25.*

And the man and his wife were both naked and were not ashamed.

Nakedness in this verse has a correlation with the nakedness experienced providentially in sexual intercourse. The lack of shame expresses Adam and Eve's innocence, which is *unlike* the present postfall situation, in which we feel shame (Gen. 3:8–11). However, shame is partially overcome in the expression of intimacy in marriage. So people in the postfall situation have some analogy with which to work in order to understand the prefall situation.

The Meaning of Correlations

The pattern of correlations between Genesis 2:4–25 and later providential events should now be evident. Nearly everything in Genesis 2 has obvious suitable analogues within the present-day providential order. Even the points that stand out as different employ *some* degree of analogy with the providential order. Just as with Genesis 1, the resonances between creation and later providential events occur by God's design and in accord with his unified plan. (See Table 10.13.)

Table 10.13: Some Analogies between Creation and Providence from Genesis 2

Creation	Providence
2:5—barren land in Eden, before rainy season	dry land before rainy season
2:7—God forms Adam	God forms each of us in the womb
2:8—God plants the garden of Eden	human beings plant and cultivate gardens
2:9—God causes trees to grow in the garden of Eden	trees grow in gardens
2:10-14—God provides rivers in Eden	God provides rivers now
2:14—Tigris and Euphrates then	Tigris and Euphrates now

Creation	Providence
2:15—God appoints Adam to garden	God appoints people for work in various forms, including gardening
2:16—God gives Adam fruits	God gives us fruits
2:17—God tests Adam and Eve	God tests our obedience
2:18—God provides Eve	God provides marriage and family
2:19—God empowers human naming and dominion	we give names and exercise dominion
2:21—God gives Adam deep sleep	God gives sleep
2:22—God builds Eve	we build houses
2:23—Adam bonds with Eve	we have social bonds, especially intimate in marriage
2:24—Adam is married to Eve	we marry
2:25—original nakedness without shame	nakedness associated with shame, except in the marriage bond

The entire description remains at a level of simplicity. It uses ordinary language. It uses analogies from ordinary life that were familiar to the Israelites and many other cultures. It offers only a comparatively sparse description of events. The formation of the garden of Eden, the formation of Adam, Adam's naming of the animals, and the formation of Eve all involved many details about which the narrative is silent. It sticks to the main points.

The correlations between creation and providence are real. But these correlations include a distinction between the two poles involved in the correlation. Creation is *distinct* from providence, as well as *analogous* to it. The events in Genesis 2:4–25 are real events in time and space, not a mere metaphor for providence. (See Fig. 10.1.)

Fig. 10.1: Correlations between Creation and Providence as Two Poles

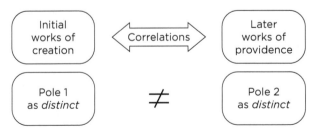

The correlations thus actually count *against* rather than in favor of the modern view that Genesis 2:4–25 is not really about creation, but *only* and *wholly* concerned to articulate God's providential care for humanity. This modern view basically wipes out the doctrine of creation and reductionistically collapses it into providence. This view has a superficial plausibility because it invokes the meaning of *correlations*. But it does not really work because all the correlations presuppose two distinct poles that are being correlated.

For example, the creation of Eve is one pole. It correlates with a second pole, namely, the meanings of later analogous events and cultural settings within God's providential control. Among these providential meanings are the meaning of the creation of each individual woman, the meaning of womanhood, the meaning of the providential relationship between man and woman, and the meaning of marriage as an institution within God's providential order. This correlation between creation (Gen. 2:4–25) and providence (all later history) presupposes the reality of two poles, with creation distinct from the later providence.

The same holds for Genesis 1. Some modern interpreters might say that Genesis 1 does nothing more than articulate a theology of God's wisdom and care for the world. Creation gets collapsed into present-day significance, namely, God's providential rule over the world. This interpretation has the same superficial plausibility as does the providentialistic interpretation of Genesis 2. It plausibly appeals to correlations, but in reality the correlations make sense only with two poles (creation and providence), not merely one (providence). Creation ought not to be collapsed conceptually into providence.

Some interpreters try to back up their attempt to collapse two poles into one by appealing to analogies from the ancient Near East. As discussed in chapter 5, the ancient Near East did have its cosmogonic myths. Scholars can interpret these myths in a variety of competing ways, depending on the modern assumptions that they presuppose. In particular, an approach using a reductionistic form of social anthropology can reduce the "meaning" of myths to their functions in maintaining social order.

According to this anthropological view, the work of myths is to provide common social reference points: they offer stories that generate divine significance for the culture and offer explanations for various social customs and structures. When myths are interpreted this way, their meanings all belong to the present providential order. A mythic story about the past is interpreted as "really" being about the present.[20] (See Fig. 10.2.)

Fig. 10.2: Modern Views concerning Stories of Gods

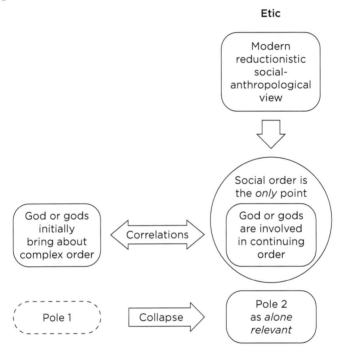

No doubt myths have *implications* for the present. But to collapse the past into the present is a form of reductionism. It looks suspiciously like a product of modern assumptions rather than ancient consciousness. Ancient consciousness understood a correlation between two distinct poles rather than collapsing them (see Fig. 10.3).

In ancient times, myths could indeed contribute to social stability, and their perceived social importance was presumably one reason why they were recited and shared. They also had attraction because they seemed to promise a higher and deeper knowledge about the

---

20. Some myths, of course, may focus only on a repeated pattern (e.g., the dawn as rebirth of the sun god), not on a founding event. The general principle is that each myth must be interpreted by respecting the correlations it evokes, not by abolishing one pole of the correlations.

world, including the world of spirits. This feeling of shared knowledge also contributed to religious and social cohesion. But the myths effectively strengthened social stability and fulfilled the promise of knowledge only if, at some level, people believed them.[21] The myths depended on correlations between beginnings at one pole and the present order at the other. Both poles were needed if the myths were to offer an effective social *foundation* and a deeper knowledge, in contrast to mere commentary on social life. Commentary on present-day social life does not in itself offer a *foundation* for that life.

Fig. 10.3: Ancient Views concerning Stories of Gods

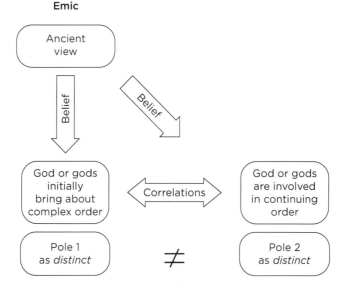

In reply, the reductionistically inclined student of social anthropology might admit that ancient peoples mostly believed in their myths. "But," he says, "we, with our superior knowledge, know that the spirits and gods postulated in these ancient myths were not real. So the *real* function of the myths can be found only in their social function of promoting social cohesion."

That reply misses the point in two ways.

---

21. Thus, Socrates was tried and condemned to death on two charges, not one: allegedly he did not properly respect the Greek gods, and he was corrupting the youths of Athens by his skepticism. Belief or lack of belief has social consequences.

First, it depends on a modern metaphysical commitment to the nonexistence of the spirit world. This modern view is false, according to biblical testimony about angels and demons. Such a view undermines a sympathetic understanding of the ancient myths.

Second, even if the modern view were right in its assumptions, it should analyze the myths according to their *meanings* and in their own contexts, not just inject its own opinions about whether they are actually true. Analysis does not take place merely to find the social truths that modern people think they can extract. Within their own cultural context, the meanings in myths support both social cohesion and belief in the gods whose past actions have brought things into their present shape. It is a distortion to eliminate one pole. It amounts to an imposition of modern dogma by a reductionistic form of anthropology.

Similarly, it is a distortion—a form of reductionism—to eliminate one pole of the correlations involved in Genesis 1–2. The communicative power of Genesis 1–2 depends on retaining the function of both poles. Genesis 1–2 is unlike the ancient Near Eastern cosmogonic myths because of its consistent monotheism and its simplicity in description. And it is prose, not poetry (chap. 6). But if, for the sake of argument, we were to grant that it belongs to the same genre as the myths, the same arguments would hold for both the myths and for Genesis 1–2: they both use two poles that are correlated.

In sum, Genesis 1–2 and the ancient Near Eastern myths about origins both rely on the distinction between *founding* events in the past and *providential* continuation in the present. The difference is that Genesis 1–2 offers a true account concerning the work of the true God, in contrast to the corrupt, counterfeit accounts that depict the interaction of many gods.

Genesis 3 and the Fall

We can apply to Genesis 3 similar reasoning to what we have used with Genesis 1 and 2. We could go through Genesis 3 verse by verse and consider in detail correlations between the events recorded there and later providential events. But by this time, the pattern should be evident. So we may pass on to summarize the results for Genesis 3.

The narrative in Genesis 3 as a whole obviously resonates with all subsequent temptations to rebellion and sin, such as human beings experience daily. It also resonates with Jesus's temptation in the wilderness in Matthew 4:1–11 and Luke 4:1–13. Jesus successfully resisted the Devil's temptations, whereas Adam did not. Modern theorists may therefore propose that Genesis 3, along with Genesis 2, is really about the temptations of "everyman" rather than Adam as an actual historical individual. Though superficially plausible, this argument ignores the presence of two poles to the correlation: (1) Adam and Eve are real historical individuals and (2) their temptation follows a pattern analogous to subsequent instances of temptation and sin, as Genesis 5:1–5, Luke 3:38, Romans 5:12–21, and 1 Corinthians 15:45–49 indicate.

Points without Full Analogy

It is also worthwhile noting which points in Genesis 1–3 have *less* strong analogies with the present providential order. All the analogies that we have discussed involve both similarity and dissimilarity. So analogy is a matter of degree. In which cases do dissimilarities stand out more prominently? We can point to seven examples:

1. *The beginning in Genesis 1:1.* In Genesis 1:1, God's original act of creation is an absolute beginning. It tacitly implies that God uses no preexisting, eternal material.[22] This absolute beginning is unlike any later "relatively new" beginning. It is such by necessity, of course, and this uniqueness can be appreciated by ordinary readers who in normal circumstances are looking for analogies with their present providential experience.

2. *The creation of man in Genesis 2:7.* By necessity, the creation of the first human being cannot involve the present providential process of gestation and birth from a human mother. Accordingly, the description of Adam's creation in Genesis 2:7 has only limited parallels with passages elsewhere in Scripture about God's subsequent providential work of creating new human beings, such as Psalm 139:13–18.

---

22. See Collins, *Genesis 1–4*, 50–55; C. John Collins, *Reading Genesis Well: Navigating History, Poetry, Science, and Truth in Genesis 1–11* (Grand Rapids, MI: Zondervan, 2018), chap. 8B. Collins and I maintain that Gen. 1:1 describes the initial act of creation rather than being a title covering what happens in detail in 1:2–31 (see Appendix A, p. 291). But even if it is a title, the phrase "in the beginning" has a unique function. Even if it does not directly denote an absolute beginning, it implies it. Otherwise, we have eternal matter, and eternal matter plays a godlike role in addition to the true God. Religiously, such a view about eternal matter undermines the thrust of Gen. 1:2–31 as well as the whole rest of the Bible. And it directly contradicts the claims of 1 Cor. 8:6 and Col. 1:16.

Language about "forming," "breathing," and "dust" occurs later, but later passages do not bring everything together into a single event: "Then the LORD God formed the man *of* dust from the ground." In providence, God forms individuals in the womb (Ps. 139:13). God "forms" man in a manner analogous to a potter "forming" clay, but no human potter actually creates a living being.

3. *The two special trees in Genesis 2:9.* The tree of life and the tree of the knowledge of good and evil (Gen. 2:9) both function as special symbols for God's blessing and curse. The trees exercise their distinct functions within the unique initial situation of testing that Adam and Eve confront in Genesis 3. Accordingly, they have no direct parallels today.

4. *The creation of woman in Genesis 2:21–22.* In a manner parallel to the creation of Adam, the creation of the first human woman cannot involve the present process of gestation and birth from a human mother. God's use of Adam's rib to create Eve is a truly extraordinary, miraculous process.

5. *The appearance of the talking Serpent in Genesis 3:1.* The snake in 3:1 is special. As any number of skeptical interpreters have pointed out, snakes do not talk. Of course, we have providential experiences of encountering snakes. But the description in 3:1 is utterly without parallel in normal providence. (The closest we can come is Balaam's donkey in Num. 22:28–30. In Numbers, the text itself clearly recognizes the extraordinary, miraculous character of the event by explaining, "Then the LORD opened the mouth of the donkey," recognizing that donkeys do not normally speak.)[23]

Within Genesis 3, skeptics have taken the presence of a talking snake to be a sign of its fabulous or allegorical character. But the extraordinary character of the Serpent's action actually fits the context. It takes a supernatural, demonic source boldly to attack the truthfulness of God within the original situation of fellowship and peace with God. The Serpent is not merely a serpent, as later scriptural reflection explicitly recognizes (Rev. 12:9).

The extraordinary character of the talking Serpent is meant to shock readers into deeper reflection. Through reflection, they understand that the Serpent does not merely represent one animal among

---

23. Collins, *Did Adam and Eve Really Exist?* 63; Collins, *Genesis 1–4,* 171–72.

many within the original created order, which is "very good" (Gen. 1:31). Rather, this animal has become a mouthpiece for a deep, super-natural evil. The function of rhetorical shock has its full effect only if the text *is* presenting us with a real talking Serpent and not an allegory or a fable.

6. *The judgment by the Lord God in Genesis 3:8–19.* In 3:8–19, God confronts Adam, Eve, and the Serpent, and pronounces judg-ments on each, together with a promise of redemption for the man and woman (v. 15). God's speech involves supernatural action—any time that God speaks, it is a special event. In many ways, God's speeches in Genesis 3 are like his speeches in Genesis 1. There are so many in-stances of God speaking in Genesis 1–3 that it could be debated how much any particular speech stands out. But in 3:8, a visible appearance in some form may have accompanied his speeches. There is also an analogy: God "walking" in the garden is like a human being walking.

7. *The cherubim guard the way to the tree of life in Genesis 3:24.* The cherubim appear as supernatural creatures (angels) who prevent human access to the tree of life. They function in a manner analogous to human guards used in kings' courts and in prisons.

PART 3

INTERPRETING GENESIS 1–3 AS A LARGER WHOLE

11

Time in Genesis 1

Having looked at the many analogies that connect the verses of Genesis 1–3 with our present providential order, I now propose to stand back and assess some larger issues.

The first such issue concerns time.[1] How do we relate time in Genesis 1 to time in mainstream scientific claims? Genesis 1 speaks of six days, while mainstream science speaks of billions of years. What do we do about that? The question has several dimensions and continues to elicit voluminous discussion.[2] Several different approaches claim to do justice to Genesis 1 and scientific evidence.[3] In this chapter, I explore one dimension only, namely, the *measurement* of time.[4] That issue is important because it affects what we think is the *meaning* of passing time. And that, in turn, affects how we interpret both Genesis 1 and modern science.

We have to be patient with this aspect of our discussion. The issue is not as simple as it may appear because the period when God was creating the world, in Genesis 1, is distinct from the subsequent

---

1. From this point onward, this chapter is a revision of Vern S. Poythress, "Time in Genesis 1," *Westminster Theological Journal* 79, no. 2 (2017): 213–41. Used with permission.

2. Vern S. Poythress, *Redeeming Science: A God-Centered Approach* (Wheaton, IL: Crossway, 2006), especially chaps. 7–10, 16, where ten distinct approaches are discussed; J. Daryl Charles, ed., *Reading Genesis 1–2: An Evangelical Conversation* (Peabody, MA: Hendrickson, 2013); David G. Hagopian, ed., *The Genesis Debate: Three Views on the Days of Creation* (Mission Viejo, CA: Crux, 2001). These works, in turn, build on earlier voluminous discussion about the days of creation.

3. For a survey, see Poythress, *Redeeming Science*, chap. 5.

4. Poythress, *Redeeming Science*, chaps. 10 and 16, touches on the question in a more summary fashion.

period of providence, within which scientists can now observe regular rhythms in time. Did these rhythms extend back into the creation period described in Genesis 1? It is a good question.

In the next chapter, we will consider implications for a number of theories that deal with the relation of Genesis 1 to modern scientific claims.

Measuring Time

Let us begin by thinking about time measurement within the present order of God's providential rule. Time measurement has a complexity to which we seldom pay attention in ordinary life. We can talk meaningfully about the *length* of a segment in time only by reference to a standard with which the segment can be compared. For example, if we say that we spent fifty minutes eating dinner, the *minute* serves as our standard. In principle, we have a choice among several possible standards, such as the second, the minute, the hour, the day, the month, the year, or the century. Most of the time, we do not worry about the standard itself because we live in a world with chronological regularities that are maintained by the providence of God in his faithfulness. Nevertheless, as we shall see, the issue of the standard can affect the interpretation of Genesis 1 and modern scientific claims about the far past.

So let us briefly consider ways of measuring time. To be useful, standards for time must involve recurring events in the world. We measure the time length of an event by counting the rhythmic recurrences of *another* phenomenon that we consider regular. For example, the sun completes a circuit in the sky once a day. On this basis, we can choose the *day* as our standard. An event is said to last for four days if its span encompasses four circuits of the sun. More precisely, the standard for a day would be a *solar* day, since the word *day* (and the underlying Hebrew word *yôm*, יוֹם) can also designate the period of daylight *within* a solar day (e.g., Gen. 7:12). Once we understand what we mean by *day*, we can talk meaningfully about how many days old Isaac was when Abraham circumcised him (eight days, 21:4). Or for longer periods of time, we may use the *year* as our standard for measurement. For example, we may say, "Abram was seventy-five *years* old when he departed from Haran" (12:4). This statement has a clear meaning because the word *year* already has a meaning. This meaning is tied in with the rhythm of the seasons and the yearly cycle of the sun and the stars.

In the details, there can be some complexities when we try to mesh more than one of these standards. Our calendar months are not all the same number of days long. Our calendar year is 365 days, except on leap years, which have 366 days. The sidereal year and the tropical year are standards of measurement that differ slightly from each other and from the calendar year.[5]

One effect of having multiple standards is that we need ways of transferring from one standard to another. So, for example, we say that a year is 365 days and a day is twenty-four hours long. The latter statement specifies how we transfer back and forth between a measurement using hours as the standard and a measurement using days as the standard.

But what do we mean by an *hour*? For some centuries, an hour was defined as 1/24 of a day. So if a day is twenty-four hours long, and an hour is 1/24 of a day, which of the two is our starting point? (See Fig. 11.1.)

Fig. 11.1: Correlations between Days and Hours

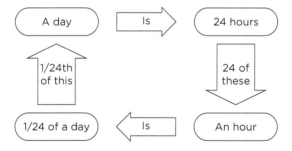

If we say that either one can be the starting point, it can become unclear what we are actually claiming.

Here we already have our first minor difficulty with interpretations of Genesis 1. Some Bible interpreters claim that each of the six days mentioned in Genesis 1 is a twenty-four-hour day. This theory is

---

5. *The New Encyclopaedia Britannica: Micropaedia*, 15th ed. (Chicago/London/Geneva/Sydney/Tokyo/Manila/Seoul/Johannesburg: Helen Hemingway Benton, 1974), 10:808.

216 Interpreting Genesis 1–3 as a Larger Whole

sometimes called "the twenty-four-hour-day theory." But if we stipulate that an "hour" is actually *defined* as 1/24 of a day, a day is *by definition* composed of twenty-four hours. That in itself is just telling us what we want the word *hour* to mean.[6] By itself, it gives us no information that separates one interpretation of Genesis 1 from another. Other theories, such as the day-age theory and the analogical-day theory, are also twenty-four-hour-day theories if we use this definition of the word *hour*. For instance, if, according to the day-age theory, the sixth day is two hundred million years long by sun time, an hour is 1/24 of this, or about 8.3 million years.

This difficulty may appear to be a mere quibble. We may imagine a representative figure, named Bob, who articulates a commonsense point of view. "Surely," Bob replies, "the meaning is clear. Whatever might be the labels, the twenty-four-hour-day theory is talking about days that have more or less the same length as our days have now, while the day-age theory and the analogical-day theory are talking about 'days' in some metaphorical sense, because these so-called 'days' are actually very long periods of time."

This reply is commonsensical. It is the natural reply as long as we think we are on firm ground with respect to our notions of time. But what is this "firm ground"? In fact, there are mysteries down below. Despite its commonsense appeal, Bob's reply skirts a difficulty. We can see the limited viewpoint of Bob's reply if we observe that, in his description of alternative theories, Bob uses the expression "very long periods of time." But the expression "very long" implies some standard for measurement. Suppose we were to choose one hundred billion years as our base unit of time. According to mainstream cosmologists, the universe has not existed very long at all *in comparison to this standard unit.*

But Bob still has a reply, namely, that a unit of one hundred billion years is completely artificial. For human beings, units such as days, months, and years are what we must keep in mind.

Yes, this is so. So let us consider these more human-sized units. Bob uses the expression "the same length" to compare the six days in Genesis 1 to days in our present experience. "The same length" implies that

---

6. An additional difficulty arises because ancient systems for hours sometimes divided the daytime into twelve subdivisions and the nighttime into twelve subdivisions, even though the daytime is longer in the summer than in the winter, when measured by modern clocks.

we have some stable standard for measuring the length. Indeed, a suitable standard is at hand: the day. Using this standard, each day among the first six days is one day long, and each day in our present experience is one day long. But this is a tautology. If the "day" is our unit of measurement, and we measure a day, surely we find that it is a day. According to this definition of length, the day-age theory and the analogical-day theory also involve six days, each of which is one day long.

To separate between the viewpoints, we must have some standard for measuring time that is not the same as what is measured. Indeed, we supplied this standard earlier in talking about the *solar day*. A solar day is the length of time in which the sun completes one circuit in the sky.[7] In more detailed terms, the rhythmic recurrence in the movement of the sun offers us a standard for time; the standard unit is one cycle of the sun. We then proceed to measure *other* time segments by seeing how many circuits or fractions of a circuit the sun completes during the segments in which we are interested. (See Fig. 11.2.)

Fig. 11.2: Definition Using a Solar Day

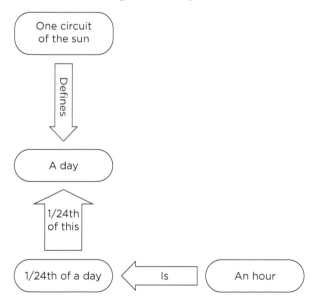

___

7. Scientists now talk about the "mean solar day," that is, the *average* length of a solar day, because there are tiny variations when measured by precise instruments such as atomic clocks. *The New Encyclopaedia Britannica: Macropaedia*, 18:414.

But then, by this definition, the first three days in Genesis 1 cannot be solar days. The sun completed no circuits at all, not even a fraction of a circuit, during these earlier time segments. That is why, lacking the existence of the sun, an interpreter such as E. J. Young writes, "The length of the days is not stated."[8]

But again, a commonsense reply is at hand. "No," Bob says, "I did not mean that. I did not mean that the sun was literally there during the first three days, but only that the length of one of the early days was the same as the length of a later solar day." To this statement, the reply may be to inquire again as to what Bob proposes as a way of understanding the meaning of his expression "the length." That expression *seems* to promise that we are using some standard unit of time. Such a unit would be based on a periodic rhythm within the created world. And—here is the important point—to be usable in practice, the rhythm in question must already be in place *during* the first three days, not merely afterward.

Different Standards for Measurement

There *are* such rhythms—many of them. But if we are going to have clear meanings, we must begin to specify what these rhythms are, in order that one or more of them may serve as a standard. So let us hear Bob again. He says, "I mean that it would be the same length as measured by a stopwatch." (See Fig. 11.3.)

Very well. But now he has introduced another standard for measurement, namely, the stopwatch. The stopwatch has its own rhythms in its internal mechanisms. In addition, it has rhythms that are observable to human users when they watch a second hand or a digital readout that changes over time. The point is that there is no avoiding an appeal to a standard.

Stopwatches did not exist during the six days of creation. But the principle is still useful. The kind of physical rhythms that are encapsulated in the stopwatch (or some of the rhythms) did exist during the six days. Any rhythm that existed back then could *potentially* be used as a standard for measuring the length of other events during those

---

8. Edward J. Young, *Studies in Genesis One* (Philadelphia: Presbyterian and Reformed, 1964), 104. Augustine also notices the challenge of the first three days. Robert Letham, "'In the Space of Six Days': The Days of Creation from Origen to the Westminster Assembly," *Westminster Theological Journal* 61 (1999): 149–74 (154–57).

times. We could talk about the rhythm of pendulums swinging, of springs coiling and uncoiling, of quartz crystals vibrating, or of electric current oscillating in a circuit. We could ask, "How does this rhythm correlate with one of the six days? In particular, how many vibrations of the pendulum take place during the course of the first day, then the second day, and so on?"

Fig. 11.3: Definition Using a Stopwatch

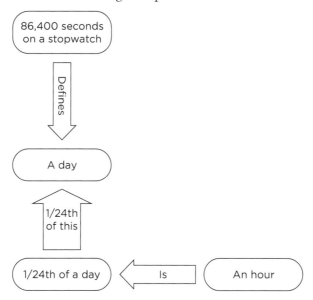

Bob may not appeal to a stopwatch. He may be uncomfortable doing so because the stopwatch is a comparatively modern invention. Pendulums are older, but still not old enough. So Bob may go back to the old, faithful resource, the sun. He says, "I mean that, if the sun *had* been there, it would have completed one circuit." If this is Bob's answer, we are dealing with a counterfactual claim.

It is not always clear how we can check a counterfactual, but let us consider the possibility. Suppose that God decided to bring the sun into the created world on the first day or the second day. He can do as he pleases. He can make the sun travel on its circuit at whatever rate he chooses. But it would seem reasonable to many people that he would have it go at the *same* rate on the first three days as on the later days. But what do we mean by "the same rate"? We can tell what counts as the same rate if we use some measuring apparatus to do it. We can use a stopwatch to time the rate of movement of the sun across the sky. But if we do that, our stopwatch has become a standard for measuring time. We are back to where we were before.

Or Bob could try to avoid appealing to another timekeeping device *within* the created world by appealing to God. "God knows what it is for the sun to go at the same rate." But this divine knowledge does *us* human beings no practical good unless *we* know something about what might count as being "at the same rate." And to know that, we would have to have some standard for measuring time. Without some standard that human beings can potentially access, anyone anywhere could claim that a specific rate is "the same rate."

Human intuition is strong, and some participants might wish that we could leave the discussion with human intuition. Bob, for one, might say, "But we just *know* when the rates are the same." The trouble is that different people's intuitions do not always agree. If just "knowing" at an intuitive level is the last thing back in the discussion, we run the danger of making human intuition an unchallengeable fixed point. "Knowing" is treated as if it were virtually equivalent to divine certainty. And then there is no way to settle quarrels between different intuitive viewpoints. Moreover, the strong intuition that we "know" may still have underneath it, buried in the depths, some unconscious sense of a standard. And, as we have seen, there is more than one possible choice of a standard. So the appeal to intuition can have the effect of concealing the difficulty and then denying that there is a difficulty—because the difficulty exists only at an unconscious level, which has not been analyzed.

We can further illustrate by imagining a hypothetical situation in which Bob actually asks God whether two periods of time are the same length or whether two rhythms that are not contemporaneous are going at the same rate. Because God knows everything, Bob expects that God will provide a clear-cut answer: yes or no. But God might not choose to answer. Or if he does, it is possible that he might answer, "The answer to your question depends on what rhythm you propose to use as a standard." God, who knows everything, knows all about standards for human time measurement. Not only that, it was he who ordained every aspect of the complexity and the relations between different possible standards. Bob's question represents an attempt to move beyond the systems for time measurement that God has supplied for human beings. In doing so, Bob projects onto God's mind his own idea of an absolute measurement not based on any created rhythm. But there is no guarantee that this projection actually represents God's mind. Since it is at odds with what God has actually supplied to us, it seems rather doubtful whether Bob's question is on the right track. It may *not* represent God's mind.

My purpose here is not to settle the questions immediately or to dismiss the concerns that Bob has, but to point out that there is a difficulty that could use reflection. Ordinarily, we know what we mean when we talk about the length of some time segment. We know because we have a background of stable rhythms, including the rhythm represented by the circuit of the sun. But the rhythm of the sun or the rhythm of a stopwatch is only *one* of many rhythms that we could use.

Comparing Rhythms

We can cross-check the regularity of one rhythm using another. For example, we can check the regularity of the movement of the sun by timing it using a stopwatch. Or, vice versa, we can check the regularity of a stopwatch by using the sun as a standard. But all the rhythms are inside the world. We understand them by correlating between two rhythms. The meaning of each rhythm is understood by its correlations with other rhythms. To measure any one rhythm, we have to specify another rhythm as the standard by which we measure it.

Let us do a thought experiment. Imagine that one day God suddenly doubles the rate of every rhythm in the universe. Everything is going twice as fast. All the physical laws are adjusted, so light travels twice as fast, our hearts beat twice as fast, our minds work twice as fast, and so on. What is the difference? There is no discernible difference. The rate of one rhythm within the universe can be measured only with reference to another rhythm. To speak of "doubling the rate" of every rhythm is to talk nonsense, because such hypothetical doubling cannot be understood except by reference to something *else* that is left undoubled. Changing equally all the standards for measuring time changes nothing at all.[9]

---

9. Could we use angels or God himself as a standard outside the universe? Since angels are created beings, to be thorough we would have to stipulate that their sense of time would be

The upshot is that discussing the length of a time segment makes sense only in terms of a standard for measuring it. And that is so even if the time segment is itself one of the possible standards.

The Challenge of Beginning the World

Genesis 1 presents a special challenge, because its tells about the beginnings of things—not only the absolute beginning of the created world, but the beginning of light, the beginning of dry land, the beginning of plants and animals, and the beginning of the heavenly lights. God gives the narrative in a way that is accessible to ordinary people. He speaks of things that happened once and for all, and that the addressees did not themselves directly experience. They can nevertheless understand what God means, because the originating events are analogous to things that happen within God's providential order, within which we now live (see chaps. 8, 9, and 10, pp. 137, 171, and 187).

We can understand. But we cannot understand exhaustively. It should be evident that God's present providential order is not in all respects the same as what is described in Genesis 1. If we as human beings simply extrapolate backward from our everyday experience, which is intertwined with the rhythms of everyday life, we can imagine a past in which things were going on in more or less the same way indefinitely, for innumerable millennia. But God tells us that it was not always so. Not all days had an earlier day before them. The ancestry of sheep or the ancestry of human beings does not go back forever into previous generations of sheep or human beings, respectively.

So we cannot just extrapolate. During the six days of creation, some things were different. And God does not give us all the details of the *ways* in which they may have been different. The narrative in Genesis 1 is sparse. It does not fill in all the details. We can guess about the details. Some of the guesses might be relatively good, because we are made in the image of God and we think "like him." But we are not God. We are still guessing.

So what were the six days like? How do we picture one of the days?[10] In particular, what were they like with respect to rhythms

---

made twice as fast along with the doubling of all other rates. Since "with the Lord one day is as a thousand years" (2 Pet. 3:8), it is not clear how we would compare God himself to rhythms inside the created world.

10. We shall have occasion later to touch on the difficulties associated with mental pictures.

in time? Within God's providential order, there are many wonderful rhythmic correlations between ten or a hundred various kinds of timekeeping devices, and there are correlations between these and the rhythms of the sun, the stars, and our own bodies and minds. There are clocks based on pendulum swings, clocks based on spring motions, and clocks based on vibrations of quartz crystals. There are clocks with digital readouts and clocks with hands. God's providential order gives us an incredibly rich variety of regularities in rhythms in time, including specialized, hidden rhythms that scientists have discovered only within the past century.

In addition to the rhythms that we associate with technical devices, there are more "homely" rhythms: the psychological feeling that time is passing; the rhythms of eating, working, resting, and sleeping within human societies; and the rhythms of breathing, chewing, swinging our legs when we are walking, swinging an ax to chop wood, or feeling our heart beating. There are the rhythms of a cow chewing her cud, a seagull beating its wings, waves of the sea crashing on rocks, or water flowing down a slope. There is the rhythm according to which some kinds of animals have a time of sleep once a day; the rhythm in which flowers open to the sun in the day and close up at night; the rhythm of the seasonal growth of plants and trees; and the rhythm in which some kinds of animals bear young at a particular time of the year. The list goes on.

Within God's providential order, a good many of these rhythms keep in time with each other remarkably well. For example, each solar day is about 86,400 seconds, as measured by a pendulum clock. So did all of these rhythms extend back into the six days of Genesis 1? And did they all keep in time with each other in the same way as they do now? Perhaps they did. But we have to be cautious because of the uniqueness of the six days of creation in Genesis 1. Maybe many rhythms did keep in time, but maybe some of them did not.

When we look at the details, the question begins to look complicated. Some rhythms cannot be traced back to the very beginning. The rhythms of work, rest, and sleep for human beings did not begin before the sixth day, when human beings were created. The rhythm of a cow chewing her cud did not begin before the sixth day, the day when cows were created. The rhythm of the movements of the sun may not have begun before the fourth day.[11] The rhythm in some plants, which differ in activity in daytime and nighttime, did not appear in the time before the plants were created on the third day. Some other rhythms, such as the rhythm of the vibrations of light emitted by a specific spectral line from a specific kind of atom,[12] may have commenced with the creation of light on day one.

We may also ask whether the various rhythms always keep in time with each other. For instance, the rhythm of a stopwatch, measuring seconds or even hundredths of a second, correlates with the sun, in the sense that every solar day is almost exactly 60 seconds x 60 minutes x 24 hours, as measured by a stopwatch. Did correlations in timing like these extend back into the period of the first six days?

Maybe many of them did. But there are questions in some cases. When God planted the trees in the garden of Eden, he "made to spring up every tree that is pleasant to the sight" (Gen. 2:9). Genesis does not say merely that he created the trees, but that he made them "spring up." That description is analogous to the way in which man, in imitation of God, is instrumental in causing trees and other plants to spring up in a garden that he plants. If God planted the garden of Eden during a period of one circuit of the sun, we can compare the rhythm of the circuit of the sun with the rhythm of the growth of the trees in the garden. It appears that the relation between the two rhythms was different in the garden of Eden than what it is now.

One suggestion might be that God miraculously accelerated the growth of trees, so that during the period of one day they grew from seeds or small sprouts into mature trees. But with the word *accelerated* we again confront the question of a standard for measurement. The growth of the trees was speedy as measured by the day as a standard. What would have taken years within our present providential order took only one day. Equally, we could say that the passing of the day was slower when measured by the standard of the growth of the trees. Within providence, a day passes within only a tiny fraction of the period marked by the maturing of trees. But on the sixth day of creation, it took the whole time of maturing or longer for the day to pass.

---

11. I say "may not" rather than "did not" in order not to exclude views that propose that the sun as a ball of plasma existed earlier, but that on the fourth day it was made to function as a timekeeper.

12. *The New Encyclopaedia Britannica: Macropaedia*, 18:416.

The point here is not to figure out precisely what methods and means God may have used during the sixth day. We might guess, but the text of Genesis 1–2 does not tell us. What does seem to be the case is that the two rhythms, the rhythm of the growth of trees and the rhythm of a solar day, may not have had the same correlation to each other that they now enjoy within the stable order of providence.

Similarly, we may look at Genesis 1:12a: "The earth brought forth vegetation, plants yielding seed according to their own kinds, and trees bearing fruit in which is their seed, each according to its kind." The rhythm of plants growing during day three can be compared to the rhythm marked by the third day itself. It seems that the relation between the two was different then than now. The plant growth was accelerated or the day slowed down, depending on our point of view. We could mitigate the difficulty by suggesting that the expression "yielding seed" anticipates what the plants *will* do during an entire growing season, not what they had already done by the end of the third day. Maybe so.

Still, it sounds as though, by the end of the third day, the earth had brought forth vegetation, plants, and trees. This activity of bringing forth took place during the course of one day. If we think that we need to pre-serve the timing of all the rhythms in phase, we might picture the trees as being only tiny sprouts, virtually indistinguishable from the other vegeta-tion. Maybe all the vegetation was still in this form at the end of the third day. The language in Genesis 1:12 does not give us great detail. But what it does give invites us to think by comparison with plants today, whose growth encompasses not only an initial event of sprouting but continu-ing growth to maturity. So we may wonder whether the rhythm of plant growth during day three was in step with the rhythm of day three itself in exactly the same way that we see it now. Or maybe the growth was miraculously accelerated. But how do we measure the pace of growth? We have the same difficulty as we did with the growth of trees in the garden of Eden.

I conclude that God has not provided a firm guarantee that all of the familiar rhythms of the providential order were in place all the time during the first six days. Neither has he provided a firm guarantee that these rhythms were in time with each other exactly as they nor-mally are today. (Later we will also look at the seventh day described in Gen. 2:1–3; it, too, raises some issues.)

Two Other Rhythms

Two other rhythms have been noteworthy candidates for explaining the meaning of the first three days. One is the rhythm of work and rest for *God*. This rhythm makes sense as a reference point, because the rhythm of work and rest for God is the archetype for the rhythm of work and rest for man, as Exodus 20:8–11 reminds us.

The other is the rhythm of oscillation of day and night. It is easy to guess that such a rhythm was set in motion by God with the conclusion of the first day, partly because such a rhythm characterizes days within our experience of the providential order. In addition, the text mentions evening and morning (Gen. 1:5). But a lot depends on our focus. In our setting within God's providential order, if our focus is on the cosmic surroundings, we pay attention to the oscillation of light and darkness in the sky. If our focus is on personal activity, we pay attention to work and rest. In our experience within providence, morning is not only the time when light begins (cosmically), but the time when work begins (personally). Evening is not only the time when darkness comes, but the time when rest begins.[13]

It is worthwhile drawing attention to the particular phraseology in Genesis 1:5 and the parallel verses. Genesis 1:5b says, "And there was evening and there was morning, the first day." The Hebrew corresponding to "there was" uses the normal tense (waw-consecutive imperfect) for narrative continuation. We might translate it, "And evening came, and morning came." Evening follows the time during which God created light. The sequence given in Genesis 1:3–5 is one of work followed by rest.

Genesis 1:3–5 tells us about God's pattern of work. It does not tell us directly about the *oscillation* of light and darkness. It just says that God called the light day and the darkness night. It does not say that there immediately began an oscillation between the two. Neither does it say that the rate of oscillation, measured by a modern timekeeping device, would exactly match what we now measure by such a device within our stable providential order.

So did an oscillation between daytime and nighttime begin in Genesis 1:3–5, and is that oscillation what God designates by "the first

---

13. C. John Collins, *Genesis 1–4: A Linguistic, Literary, and Theological Commentary* (Phillipsburg, NJ: P&R, 2006), 77, articulates the correlation of evening and morning with the end and beginning of work. He appeals especially to Ps. 104:23, which indicates how man works from morning until evening.

day"? Or does he designate by "the first day" the cycle of work and rest? Or is it both?

Human curiosity includes extrapolating and guessing about issues for which we do not always have clear answers. At a certain level, it seems reasonable to postulate that the six days of Genesis 1 were exactly like days in our providential experience, and exactly like such days in every way we can think of. But, of course, no two of our experiential days are exactly alike. They may be nearly alike with respect to the narrow issue of how many seconds (measured by a stopwatch) compose them. But certainly on the level of ordinary experience, each day contains both similarities and dissimilarities to all the days before and after it. Each day is filled with its own host of human activities, both individual and social. God certainly assures us that the six days of creation were like ours in salient ways. But what counts as most important? Is it the seconds on a clock, or is it our activities and our interactions with other people and with the world of plants and animals? It depends on our point of view.

Suppose we hypothesize that the evenings and mornings in Genesis 1 designate transitions from light to darkness and from darkness to light. But that does not imply that they were exactly like the experience of light and darkness in an evening or morning in our day. In our time, during an evening, the sun may show itself going down on the western horizon. There may be red in the clouds on that horizon. The light in the sky gradually dims. For a time, there is more light in the west than in the east. And in the morning, we may see the reverse pattern. Did all the complexities in this pattern characterize the evenings and mornings in Genesis 1, in the first three days? Did the pattern exactly correspond to what the sun produces today, except that there was no sun? Genesis 1 does not tell us how much or in exactly what way the phenomena of light and darkness on days one to three was like what we are accustomed to see during evenings and mornings in our own time.

In like manner, Genesis 1 does not tell us how long each day was, as would be measured by a modern technical timekeeping apparatus. Maybe the days were the same length (about 86,400 seconds, measured by a stopwatch) as a modern solar day, but maybe not. Because of this uncertainty, the *point* of the narrative cannot be to inform us about the length of each day in relation to a particular technical timekeeping apparatus. The point must be something else. That something else concerns the activity of God the Creator. His activity comes in cycles of work and rest. That is fundamental within the narrative in Genesis 1. Within the point of view used in Genesis 1, a day is *first of all*—in terms of prominence—a cycle of work and rest.

But Bob may be uneasy. He has an objection: "Granted that Genesis 1 does not give us details about the length of each day, isn't it still fair to *infer* that each day has the same length? After all, the six days are all called 'days,' and Exodus 20:8–11 correlates them with later days, the length of which we know." The answer is at hand: yes. But the practical result of Bob's inference depends on what standard one uses to measure the length. Twice in the quotation above, Bob used the word *length*, which is ambiguous until he specifies the standard for measurement. He might specify a stopwatch; that is one possibility. But it is equally possible not to be drawn at all into the concern for a more precise quantitative measurement according to some modern technical apparatus. The reply might be, "Yes, they are all the same length, measured by the standard offered to us by the rhythmic cycle of personal work and rest. Each of them has the same length—exactly *one* cycle of work and rest."

This appeal to the cycle of work and rest may seem odd if we live in a culture that has taught us to orient our lives by the clock. But not all cultures are that way. Many cultures do not have modern technology and modern clocks. They have an "interactive orientation," which focuses primarily on human action and social interaction.[14] (See Fig. 11.4.)

Fig. 11.4: Defining a Day by a Clock or by Personal Activity

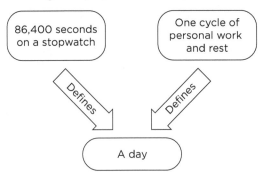

---

14. Poythress, *Redeeming Science*, 140–43.

The very word *length* can be a problem for us because, when we use it, it may already mean for us intuitively that we must focus on some *quantitative* approach to time. And we may feel in addition that our approach must mesh with modern scientific apparatus for measuring time with quantitative precision.

The difference between Bob's answer and an answer in terms of work and rest brings into view larger issues. What is more important in the long run? What is more "central"? And for what purposes? Is it measurements with modern technological equipment? Or is it personal activity? And if it is personal activity, the six days in Genesis 1 are not about *human* activity, as their main focus, but about the activities of a personal God, who plans, works, and achieves. He rests at the end of each day,[15] then celebrates a big rest on the seventh day. A day is a cycle of work and rest. And so it is for us. And we also have a longer cycle of a week, as Exodus 20:8–11 points out. A succession of six days in our experience is a succession of six cycles of work and rest. These cycles are really days. Likewise, the first six days were really *days*. It just takes an adjustment from our modern focus on quantitative, technologically enhanced precision to see that Genesis 1 might not involve stopwatch measurements. It may be focusing on the cycle of personal work followed by personal rest.

Theological Foundations

So why do we like stopwatches? To address the question, let us start with a brief review of the theological foundations that distinguish a Christian worldview from the materialist philosophy that influences the understanding of modern science. We can touch only on some basic features of this foundation.

The world had a beginning in time. God did not. He always exists. According to a plan he had from all eternity, he brought the world into existence at a particular time, "in the beginning" (Gen. 1:1).

God is *personal*. He created the world and sustains it by purposeful, personal action involving the three persons of the Trinity. The world of things includes subpersonal created things, such as animals, plants, and nonliving things. But God rules them personally. There is no *impersonal* mechanism holding things together. Rather, it is God

---

15. J. Ligon Duncan III and David W. Hall, "The 24-Hour View," in *The Genesis Debate*, 33.

in his faithfulness (Col. 1:17). He is so faithful and consistent that we can describe many regularities, such as the fact that grass grows for the livestock (Ps. 104:14). But for his personal purposes, God can also act in a surprising way, which we might call a "miracle." (See Fig. 11.5.)

Fig. 11.5: Impersonal Mechanism versus God's Personal Rule

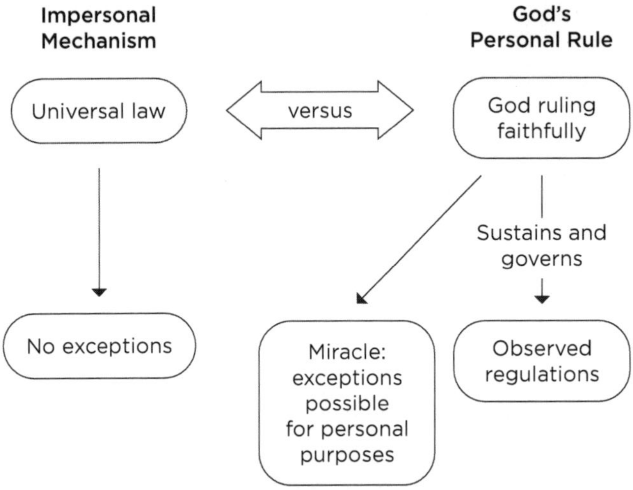

God made human beings in his image (Gen. 1:26–27). He gave us dominion (v. 28). Human beings, as created *persons*, were designed by God to have personal communion with him. We may have personal intimacy with God; we may know him; and we may worship him in awe. These are not possible for animals. We have a uniquely central role in God's plan for creation.

All of this belongs to the basics of a Christian worldview. It must be contrasted with the atmosphere in the modern West, which is deeply influenced by materialist philosophy. Materialist philosophy says that the basic constituent of the world is matter—or, more elaborately, matter, energy, and motion, and the physical interactions among these bits. Materialist philosophy is a worldview. (See Fig. 11.6.)

There is a widespread impression that modern science supports this worldview because science is widely interpreted as revealing to us the deepest structure of the world, what really *exists* at the deepest level. That deepest level is physical matter.

Fig. 11.6: Materialist Philosophy versus a Christian Worldview

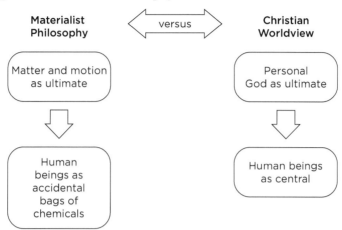

But if God is God and is personal, this materialist worldview is an illusion. God is the foundation for everything else. And we as persons have a central role. Science can exist because God rules the world with faithfulness and wisdom. Human thinking in science is one way of thinking God's thoughts after him, on a creaturely level.[16] But science, along with all other areas of academic life, ought to cohere with reality, and reality involves the centrality of persons. The molecules in our bodies exist, but persons are not reducible to bags of molecules.

The Centrality of Human Experience

So if God is God, we have to think through carefully what the world is like. We should do so in antithesis to materialist philosophy and its spokesmen, who claim to speak in the name of and with the prestige of science. We have to think about what is *real*, that is, metaphysics.[17]

For this purpose, let us first consider John Calvin, who in his time interacted with insights that were beginning to come to light with the dawn of modern astronomy:

Moses makes two great luminaries [sun and moon]; but astronomers prove, by conclusive reasons, that the star [i.e., planet] of Saturn, which, on account of its great distance, appears the

---

16. Poythress, *Redeeming Science*, chap. 11.
17. Vern S. Poythress, *Redeeming Philosophy: A God-Centered Approach to the Big Questions* (Wheaton, IL: Crossway, 2014), parts II–IV.

least of all, is greater than the moon. Here lies the difference; Moses wrote in a popular style things which, without instruction, all ordinary persons, endued with common sense, are able to understand; but astronomers investigate with great labour whatever the sagacity of the human mind can comprehend. . . . Nor did Moses truly wish to withdraw us from this pursuit [of modern astronomy] in omitting such things as are peculiar to the art; but because he was ordained a teacher as well of the unlearned and rude as of the learned, he could not otherwise fulfil his office than by descending to this grosser method of instruction. . . . If the astronomer inquires respecting the *actual dimensions* of the stars, he will find the moon to be less than Saturn; but this is something *abstruse*, for to the sight it appears differently. Moses, therefore, rather adapts his discourse to *common usage*.[18]

Calvin affirms the importance of two distinct points of view, an ordinary point of view, which sees Saturn as a point of light, and an astronomer's point of view, which inquires about "the actual dimensions of the stars." Or, if we may generalize, there is an *experiential* point of view, in ordinary human life, and an "abstruse" view, that is, a specialized, technical point of view, developed in various sciences. (See Table 11.1.)

Table 11.1: Views on Life

Specialized, Technical	Experiential
for scientific specialization	ordinary observation
astronomer's estimate of the size of Saturn	Saturn to the naked eye
"great labour"; "sagacity"	"common usage" (common sense)

Calvin implies that both points of view are legitimate. Moses legitimately "adapts his discourse to common usage," because his purpose (and God's purpose) is to address "all ordinary persons," while the astronomer has a different purpose: to explore "whatever the sagacity of the human mind can comprehend."

---

18. John Calvin, *Commentaries on the First Book of Moses Called Genesis* (Grand Rapids, MI: Baker, 1979), 1.86–87 [on Gen. 1:16] (emphasis added).

After making these remarks, Calvin does not dwell on the contrast between the experiential view and the specialized, technical view. He moves on quickly to address in more detail the purposes of Scripture and of Moses. That is his calling. Calvin is not an astronomer, but a teacher, pastor, and commentary writer. We might say in addition that he is not an epistemologist or a cognitive psychologist, who might want to explore with sagacity just how remarkable and how mysterious it is that human beings have the capability of employing two such different points of view.

It turns out that the contrast between the two views is significant for our understanding of *time*. In the twenty-first century, after further developments in the sciences, we have at least two views of time, namely, an experiential point of view and a specialized, technical point of view. (See Table 11.2.)

Table 11.2: Views of Time

Specialized, Technical	Experiential
for scientific specialization	ordinary observation
atomic clocks; theory of relativity; quantum theoretical treatment of time	a sense that time is passing

What Is Metaphysically Central? What Is Real?

Now we come to a major issue. Does one point of view give us reality, while the other gives us mere "appearance," or even an illusion? If the world were indeed the one imagined in materialist philosophy, it would be a world in which persons were an accident. The astronomer's description might seem to offer us reality, because in certain ways it aspires to be independent of how big Saturn looks to any particular observer's eye. By contrast, the world from the personal, experiential point of view would be merely an appearance. After all, given the assumptions of materialist philosophy, it is merely accidental that persons somehow have come into being in a materialist universe, and that those persons have a perceptual apparatus that includes vision. And vision has to be broken down into the effects that certain photons of certain wavelengths have on certain molecules and cells in the human retina, all of which might have been quite different if chance had gone otherwise.

On the other hand, if we live in a personalistic universe crafted by our personal God, ordinary experience becomes important. God has designed us and our perceptual apparatus as part of the gift of human life. Visual perception is real, and it confronts us with reality because God designed it to be just as it is. Yes, God designed the intricacies that the astronomer explores. But it is just as true that he rules over every instance of human perception throughout history. On a basic metaphysical level, each is just as real as the other, because God's design and God's speech governing the world specify every detail (on the reality of the ordinary, see chap. 5, p. 69).

In this respect, every created thing is metaphysically on the same level as every other created thing. They are all creatures. And every detail is specified by the speech of God governing the universe (Pss. 33:6, 9; 147:15, 18). In two important respects, however, ordinary personal human experience is *more basic* than specialized science.

First, without ordinary human experience, including basic visual and aural perception, science as a human project could not have arisen. We have to observe the world and learn the ways of God in it. To deny the metaphysical reality of human perceptual experience is also to undermine its epistemological reliability, and without that we have no possibility for the natural sciences to be forms of knowledge rather than playful dreams.

Even the person who believes in materialist philosophy cannot dispense with common sense. He knows that Saturn remains the size of a dot to his naked eye. That fact does not change just because he adds further knowledge about its size from an astronomical point of view. He knows that what he sees through the telescope is the same object that he sees with the naked eye, and that every new generation has to begin by tying scientific observations to eyesight.

Second, God made us in his image and cares for us. He makes himself known to us in verbal revelation in Scripture and in nonverbal revelation through the world he has made (Rom. 1:18–23). A rainbow is beautiful and testifies to the beauty of God. The stars are beautiful not only in their appearance but in their courses, which testify to the wisdom of God (Ps. 19:1–6). We are meant to respond to this testimony by acknowledging God, and by loving and worshiping him. For the purposes of personal communion with God, this testimony in ordinary experience is central—more central than the specialized findings in natural sciences, which are not so easily accessible to all people. The specialized findings have their own testimony, of course. But their testimony does not compete with or undermine the more obvious testimony that we receive in connection with our senses.

Therefore, I conclude, the appearance of the world to ordinary human beings is not *mere* appearance but also reality. It is a reality that is a means for worshiping God. It is a reality in God's sight, and therefore also should be in ours. It is one dimension, and a central one at that, to which scientific investigation can eventually add specialized layers.

Calvin does not yet worry about these issues concerning the metaphysics of reality. He does not need to, because for him the value and authenticity of human experience are not in question. But he uses terms that have the potential to create, in later historical developments, the growth of pride in the superiority of science and the claim that what is ordinary is not real. For example, Calvin says that astronomy comes from the use of "sagacity." No doubt it does. And Calvin can rightly stand in admiration of sagacity as a gift from God. But once it is detached from God, it can become a source of prideful superiority. What is "common usage" then becomes vulgar and inferior. Calvin also employs some other labels for the level of common experience: "unlearned and rude"; "descending to this grosser method of instruction." There is a fine line here between two attitudes: admiration for the gracious benefits that we receive from God in applying ourselves to learning, and contempt for anyone who is not as learned as the elite.

I do not think Calvin despises what is ordinary. In fact, as he continues on the same page, he calls for all of us to be roused in our spirits to magnify and praise God for his magnificence displayed in creation through ordinary means. Yet the door lies open for later generations, less humbled by the majesty of God than he was, to fall into an attitude of contempt.

What relevance might such things have for the interpretation of Genesis 1? They are relevant because a worldview that *privileges* the specialized, technical view and downgrades the reality of the experiential view changes our expectations about what we will find in Genesis 1. On the one hand, we might be tempted to try to find specialized, technical truths in Genesis 1 in order to show that the Bible measures up to the prestige of modern sciences. On the other hand, if we concede that the content belongs naturally to an experiential view, we might be tempted to despise the Bible as primitive or as trapped in primitive culture.

Experiential Space and Specialized Views of Space

We may illustrate using views of space and motion. The Copernican revolution is the main exhibit here. The Copernican revolution placed the sun at the center of the solar system, with the earth revolving around the sun and also rotating on its own north-south axis. This picture is specialized and technical. It is not as technical as some twentieth-century developments in science, but a person needs intellectual effort ("sagacity") to understand it, and even more effort to decide whether it is superior to the older model (the Ptolemaic system), and whether and in what sense it is true. The Copernican view contrasts with the experiential view, according to which the earth is fixed and the sun moves in an arc through the sky. (See Fig. 11.7.)

Fig. 11.7: Specialized versus Experiential View of Space and Motion

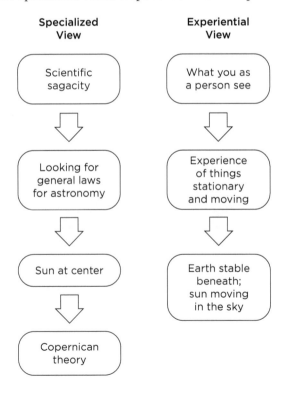

Historically, the conflicts concerning the Copernican theory had many dimensions. But at least one dimension had to do with the differences between the specialized, technical point of view, which the Copernican theory embodies, and the experiential point of view. An easy resolution lies at hand, namely, to say that *both* points of view address various dimensions of reality, but that the starting focus and purpose of each point of view is distinct (see chap. 5, p. 65). There are three powerful precedents for such a resolution.

The first precedent lies *within* the experiential view itself. Every individual human being has his own experience of space, distinct from that of other persons. For example, Emily and Samantha may observe the same rabbit in the backyard. Emily is in the yard and observes the rabbit from close up, while Samantha is inside the house and observes the rabbit from farther away. The rabbit is "bigger" to the eye of Emily. Likewise, Emily observes the rabbit from in front, and sees both its eyes. Samantha observes from the side, and sees one eye. A third person, Victoria, observes from the rear and sees no eyes. It is the same rabbit, and each person's view of the rabbit is real: it is exactly what God specifies. This illustration shows that there can be different views that are intrinsically compatible with each other. It also shows that the visual "size" of an object depends on one's point of view.

The second precedent lies in the nature of the specialized point of view. Even the specialized point of view involves the scientist as a personal participant. It is impossible to understand Copernican theory except as an explanation with regard to things that we see from an experiential point of view. Our starting point for understanding space is our experience of spatial orientation with respect to our own bodies. Moreover, the Copernican theory itself involves picturing the solar system, and any picture, mental or visual, uses a spatial point of view. For example, we picture the solar system as it would look from a point outside the plane of the planets so that we can imagine ourselves looking down on their circular (or, more accurately, elliptical) motions around the sun. (See Fig. 11.8.)

The third precedent lies in the nature of mankind: he is made in the image of God. If we reflect on the meaning of the image of God, it eventually leads us back to the unity and diversity in God, one God in three persons. The unity and diversity in human beings, and derivatively, the unity and diversity in distinct points of view or perspectives, have their ultimate foundation and archetype in the unity and diversity in God.[19] So there is a deep foundation, in God himself, for diversity among human beings. God created us and a world that includes spatial viewpoints. He created human beings with the capacity for diverse points of view, and he himself knows all about every point of view. We naturally experience these multiple viewpoints when we move from one location to another, or when we interact with other people who occupy distinct locations in space.

Fig. 11.8: View of the Copernican System

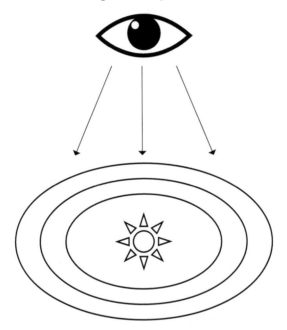

Unfortunately, this affirmation of several perspectives was not the main route chosen during the original debates over Copernican theory. Many people seemed to think that a person who chose to believe the ideas of Nicolaus Copernicus had to deny that the earth was fixed. Not that people would literally deny what they saw with their eyes, but perhaps they thought that either Copernican theory or some view

19. Vern S. Poythress, *Symphonic Theology: The Validity of Multiple Perspectives in Theology* (repr.; Phillipsburg, NJ: P&R, 2001), chap. 5.

with the earth as stationary must be the *one* metaphysically ultimate point of view. The affirmation of the one was therefore the denial of the other. But the problem was bad metaphysics—the assumption that there must be one perspective that is ultimate and that therefore degrades all other perspectives.

The Specter of One Perspective to Rule Them All

I do not know all of the reasons why people missed out on the possibility of affirming both the experiential view and the specialized, technical view. But I might suggest that one reason lay in the existence of a specialized, technical view that was already in place before the time of Copernicus, namely, the Ptolemaic system for understanding the motions of the heavenly bodies. This system was endorsed by Aristotle, and Aristotle was respected as "the Philosopher." Some of his views had been adopted and become entrenched in Roman Catholic tradition. Aristotle claimed to tell us what is metaphysically ultimate. But because Aristotle had suppressed his knowledge of the one, true, *personal* God, his metaphysical system is basically impersonalistic. You cannot have personal intimacy with his idea of the unmoved Mover. Therefore, human beings cannot have a central role in the metaphysics of the world.

Yes, human beings may aspire to understand that metaphysics. But they do so by *reason*, conceived of abstractly and therefore impersonally. To reach the bottom, Aristotelian metaphysics has to dispense with personal viewpoints. There is one ultimate metaphysics that is independent of personal perspectives. And, derivative from this, an Aristotelian thinker expects one ultimate astronomical system, which will be impersonalistic in that it dispenses with human observers. Within this impersonalistic framework, the specialized Copernican view, the specialized Ptolemaic view, and the ordinary experiential view must duke it out to see which is ultimate. But the experiential view has already lost the battle at a fundamental level. Centuries earlier than Copernicus, it was shoved aside in favor of the ultimacy of the Ptolemaic system.

All this is now history. But it continues to have an effect. Some scholars continue to bring up the story of Copernicus in order to convince us that, just as the church eventually accepted Copernican theory, so it must now accept the latest "assured results" of modern science, whether it be with respect to the age of the universe, to Darwinism, or to the nonexistence of a single Adam who was the progenitor of the whole race. Such arguments need to be examined at more than one level. What is fact, what is assumption, and what is interpretation within the latest claims from some scientists?

The arguments also need to be slowed down by refusing to concede that persons and the importance of persons have disappeared from the scene. In the first place, Copernican astronomy never should have been made into an ultimate metaphysics. It never should have competed with the experiential point of view. And it never should be conceded that Copernican theory or any other theory is independent of the persons who have developed it as a perspective. Theories are always embedded in a larger framework of personal understanding, a vast network that explains the meaning of the specialized point of view to the next generation of inductees, who are themselves persons, and whose starting point can only be with an experiential point of view.

And if persons are indispensable, so is the orientation of their hearts. As Abraham Kuyper and Cornelius Van Til loved to point out, people are either regenerate or unregenerate, either for God or against him. And that affects their worldview, and their worldview affects their scientific research and the metaphysical framework for that research.

One effect of a materialist worldview is to generate a feeling of human insignificance. People talk about how insignificant humanity is shown to be now that we know how vast is the universe. The universe is big beyond imagining. And, it is then said, we are merely tiny specks of dust. But note that the measurements for the extent of the universe and the number of stars are specialized and technical. The numbers are so big that no one can really "take them in" on a direct, personal level of ordinary human experience. Humanity is made to be insignificant because the specialized point of view swallows up the experiential view and destroys it. That is bad metaphysics, a bad worldview, at work. The worldview eats out the humanity of the very people whose humanity, including marvelous intellectual gifts from God, has made it possible to understand the vast technical edifice of modern cosmology. We need to pity such people, and also, in the name of God and for the cause of truth, to stand up for them and tell them that they are more central to the universe than all the big numbers that they can conjure, because of the very fact that they can conjure them. In other words, they are made in the image of God.

Experiential Time and Specialized Time

Now we turn to the topic of experiential time and specialized time. It should not be surprising that, with the development of modern sciences, more and more specialized treatments of time have arisen. It is not a bad thing. Man has a mandate to exercise dominion, and this includes the sagacity and the intellectual exploration that Calvin approved. In the exercise of sagacity, scientists have uncovered layers of specialized meanings with respect to time. Time can be measured by complex instruments, such as atomic clocks. According to the special theory of relativity and, even more, the general theory of relativity, specialized technical measurements of time and space are interlocked in beautiful ways, and the observer has an indispensable role. The observer! It turns out that echoes of the experiential perspective appear even in the midst of the most specialized theories. (See Fig. 11.9.)

Some of the lessons to be learned run parallel to what we have observed concerning space, motion, and the Copernican theory. For example, specialized discussions of time include big numbers: 4.5 billion years for the history of the earth and 14 billion years for the history of the universe. An ordinary experiential view cannot really "take in" such vast stretches of time any more than it can take in the vast stretches of space. Some people shrink in their own estimation. Humanity is a mere blip on the screen. But that is bad metaphysics, where the specialized point of view becomes an exclusive metaphysical claim, and the claim destroys persons.

Some of the results of specialized work with time are around us constantly. There are mechanical clocks, electric clocks, and clocks within computers and cell phones. These are, in a sense, familiar to us. But their inner workings are technical and hidden. Very few people have checked out the inner workings. Very few understand in depth the principles by which these clocks work. In one sense, there are as many views of measuring time as there are different kinds of clocks.

And then there are different theories in which time plays a role—Newtonian, relativistic, and quantum mechanical theories.

Fig. 11.9: Specialized versus Experiential View of Time

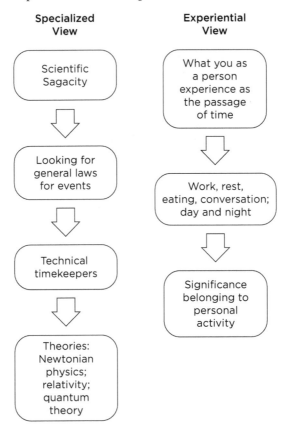

One lesson here is that the presence of these clocks, and the specialized, technical thinking about time that is behind their manufacture, does not displace or invalidate experiential time. And what is experiential time? It is time as we experience it in bodily and mental interaction with the world. Without the experiential view of time, none of the ways in which scientists and engineers work with specialized treatments of time would be possible. Specialized time is an additional layer of conceptual development, based on experiential time.

In addition, we need to reckon with the metaphysical question of what is real about time. The reasoning here is parallel to what we saw about experiential and specialized views of space and motion. Experiential time is just as metaphysically real as any of the specialized views. God planned them all; he ordains them all. They are all real. By contrast, if we adopt the view of materialist philosophy, it follows that people are an accident and their lived experience of time is an accident. Real time is the impersonal time belonging to physical events, and everything else is built on this fundamental impersonalism.

As with space, so with time. There are, in fact, multiple perspectives on experiential time: there is one perspective for each person. This multiplicity is obvious when we are asleep. If we fall into a deep sleep, we cannot tell afterward how long we slept. But another person who remains awake can tell, even without reference to modern, specialized technology. The awake person says, "It was only a short time, the time it took me to eat a cluster of grapes." Or, "It was a long time, and I went to the market and had several conversations before I returned." Each person's personal experience of time meshes with the personal experiences of other individuals in a larger society.

In two respects, the experiential view of time is in fact more metaphysically central than any form of specialized time. First, as we observed, people must have a sense of time as the starting point for developing specialized studies of time. Without a sense of time, we would not know what we are studying. Second, God cares for human beings and has appointed for them a central role in his plan. The death and resurrection of Christ are at the center of redemption and of the history of redemption. These events took place in the context of human interactions. The personal experience of time is their primary framework. Understanding their significance does not depend on our ability to understand microseconds or the interlocking of time and space within the special and general theories of relativity.

Genesis 1 as Involving an Experiential View of Space

Finally, we can turn to Genesis 1. As many have observed, Genesis 1 tells its narrative from the perspective of what a human observer would see from the earth. It does not start with the Milky Way Galaxy, but with earth. It is, in a certain respect, earth-centered. But that is a valid perspective. Because God is communicating to persons, about matters that are important to persons and are not technical, he shows his wisdom in using the experiential point of view of space and motion in his narration.

Genesis 1 as Involving an Experiential View of Time

Similarly, the development in time takes place in six days, including evenings and mornings. The narrative is undoubtedly using an experiential point of view rather than a modern, specialized point of view, which would involve appeals to various technological products, such as mechanical or electronic timekeepers.

Let us think for a moment about experiential time. Moving out from an intuitive, psychological sense of time and the passage of time, people gain familiarity with many temporal patterns and rhythms. They engage in activities of conversing, eating, working, walking, running, and resting. They also gain familiarity with the process of human reproduction and growth, from birth to old age to death. Because of people's ability to transcend a focus on the present moment, they are aware of longer-range action, typically consisting in planning, working, and achieving (or sometimes failing to achieve) the planned goal. Some plans and their goals extend over short periods: find your ax and pick it up or prepare a meal and then eat it. Others extend over days or years.

One fundamental pattern is that of a day. For human bodily existence, the daytime is typically composed of many smaller pieces of action, but conversation, eating, working, walking, and rest are among the main pieces. At night, we sleep (cf. Ps. 104:23). (And many cultures have a midday rest or nap of some kind; Gen. 18:1; 2 Sam. 4:5.) The daily rhythm of work and rest fits in well with the biological rhythm that makes us feel sleepy at night, as well as the rhythm of light and dark, and the rhythm of the daily cycle of the sun and the stars in the sky. The rhythms extend outward: many animals sleep in a daily cycle. Some flowers open to the sun in the day in a cycle. There are also longer cycles, such as the cycle of the seasons (Gen. 8:22) and the cycle of the year (1:14). These cycles may have many purposes according to the plan of God, which is a *personal* plan. But among these, and central to the purpose of human fellowship with God, is a purpose to bless mankind and glorify God's name. The cycles all touch on human existence, some more directly (the daily cycle of work, rest, and sleep), some less so (the seasons for planting and harvesting).

There is a correlation between (1) the human rhythm of work and rest, and (2) the sun's rhythm in the sky. Which is most important or most central? Both are important, each in its own way, but from different points of view. But in a certain respect, it seems that the sun and the heavenly bodies were created for man rather than man for them. They are "for signs and for seasons, and for days and years" (Gen. 1:14b) in *human* living. "The Sabbath was made for man, not man for the Sabbath" (Mark 2:27).

We can see one example in Scripture in which the rhythms are different from normal. According to Joshua 10:13b, "The sun stopped in the midst of heaven and did not hurry to set for about *a whole day.*" This was a miracle. Now consider the expression "a whole day." As usual, we may ask, "A 'whole day' measured by what standard?" Is it by the standard offered by the movement of the sun? The movement of the sun could not be the standard in this special case because the sun did not move. Rather, it stopped while other activities continued to go on for quite some time. The verse is talking about a whole day's worth of human activities, in accord with the rhythms associated with those activities—walking, running, swinging a sword, shooting an arrow, and so on. Joshua and his men carried out a considerable collection of such activities, and the number of them was such that, if they were mentally transposed to some *other* time during Joshua's conquest, they would have filled up the space of a day. The activities in the battle proceeded until about a day's worth of *activities* had passed.[20] In this special context, God preferentially chooses to narrate the episode using a sense of time based on the pace of human activities rather than on what the sun is doing at the time. The two rhythms, those of human activity and of the sun's movement, happen not to mesh with each other in the usual way because the stoppage of the sun is something exceptional.

---

20. The word *about* in Josh. 10:13 shows that there is some sense of doing an estimation—and an estimation takes place using a standard. What standard? Some modern readers may picture the standard as being a clock. But that is because we have clocks all around us in our culture. The obvious "standard" in the context of the verse, the thing that provides the sense of the passing of time, is the human pace involved in the human activity of fighting. A whole day's worth of opportunity for fighting activity opened up for the Israelite army in relation to their opponents.

The passage also affirms pointedly the importance of the personal relationship between God and his people: "There has been no day like it before or since, when the LORD heeded the voice of a *man*, for the LORD fought *for Israel*" (Josh. 10:14). God shows that the meanings tied to the personal relationship had a priority in comparison to the pattern set by the movement of the sun. (See Fig. 11.10.)

Fig. 11.10: The Meaning of "A Whole Day"

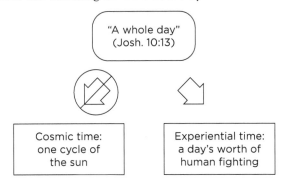

12

Implications for Modern
Views of Genesis 1

What are the implications for various modern views of the timing in Genesis 1? There are implications for evaluating the claims of modern science and for evaluating attempts at harmonizing science with Genesis 1.[1]

A Lesson for Modern Scientific Claims

Let us begin with the modern scientific claims. Modern mainstream scientific claims concerning the far past are all based on speculative extrapolation backward in time, using a framework of physical laws that have been inferred from the present providential order. The basic laws of physics and chemistry, and the basic regularities in biological development and reproduction, have been analyzed, worked out, and described by scientists who have worked within the providential order of God. They relied on that order. They assumed that it was stable from day to day, and that it would continue to be stable in the future.

How do they deal with the past? For the most part, they deal with it according to the same principle of stability and continuity in laws. The laws are assumed to be the same in the past as they are scientifically described in the present.

---

1. This chapter is a revision of the second half of Vern S. Poythress, "Time in Genesis 1," *Westminster Theological Journal* 79, no. 2 (2017): 213–41. Used with permission.

Hypothetically, extrapolations into the past might happen to be right. It may be that God in his faithfulness has maintained the same basic physical regularities since the first moment of creation. But what mainstream scientists *think* are the most basic regularities are specialized in character. And as we have seen, metaphysically they are on par with an experiential point of view. God is personal. He can work differently from what we now see. Hence, there is no guarantee that these extrapolations are actually correct, either with respect to time estimates (14 billion years for the age of the universe, estimated by specialized means) or with respect to the overall narrative in the far past that the extrapolations generate.

In the same way, there is no guarantee that the new heavens and the new earth will manifest the very same principles of basic physical law with which physicists now operate. What we are guaranteed is that there will be continuity in *persons*. That is exactly what we would expect given the centrality of persons in the plan of God.

Lessons for Attempts to Harmonize Science and Genesis 1

The Mature-Creation Theory

There may also be a lesson for the theory of mature creation, that is, the theory that by the end of the six days, God had brought the creation to a mature state that looked old.[2] More precisely, the mature state looks coherently old to a scientist who examines it on the basis of extrapolating the present into the past. For example, the trees in the garden of Eden might appear to be years or decades old when a scientist uses extrapolation. Adam might appear to be about twenty or thirty years old. But these scientific time estimates would be contrary to fact. They depend on the false assumption that the regularities of providence, on which the scientist relies, are unchanged when he projects a reconstruction into the far past.

One positive point concerning the theory of mature creation is that it is perceptive about the unique character of the first six days. The work of the first six days cannot be pinned down confidently merely by naive extrapolation. Since that is so, mature creation is a viable option.

But the theory also has a hidden weakness when it comes to measuring time within the six days of Genesis 1. One of the purposes

---

2. On the main theories, see Vern S. Poythress, *Redeeming Science: A God-Centered Approach* (Wheaton, IL: Crossway, 2006), chaps. 5–10.

of the theory is to reconcile the backward extrapolations of science with the six days of Genesis 1. The activities during the six days must have been radically different, it is reasoned, because by extrapolation, mainstream scientists claim that the universe is 14 billion years old.

But the scientific claim about age involves a specialized point of view. Once we adopt the experiential point of view in reading Genesis 1, we do not know how long the days were when measured by a modern, specialized scientific timekeeper. Indeed, the theory of mature creation agrees with this principle, because it affirms that once we enter the period of the six days, things are different. Thus, it cannot be assumed that modern timekeepers still operate during the six days in the way that they do within the mature world.

But if that assumption is invalid, adherents of the theory of mature creation have no means of measuring the length of the first three days using a technical timekeeper. (For the last three days, they have the sun, so then there is at least one *nontechnical* way of thinking about the length of the days.) And this lack seems at least partially to undermine the need for the theory in the first place. After all, the theory came into being partly to deal with an apparent discrepancy between an estimate of the length of days based on science-based backward extrapolations and a "length" based on Genesis 1. But the apparent discrepancy disappears if there is no clear technical standard for measuring the length of the days in Genesis 1.

The same principle also weakens the ability of the theory to specify the length of the last three days. To be sure, during the last three days, the sun is there. But the differences between the six days and the present providential order might mean that the sun was not cycling in tune with other possible means of measurement, such as modern clocks. If we cannot use scientific timekeepers to measure the length of the six days, it is not clear how the theory of mature creation makes anything more than a minimal negative claim that we cannot be dogmatic about processes during the six days. Would it then be compatible with other theories that also believe in a mature endpoint—virtually any of the other major theories for harmonizing Genesis 1–2 with modern scientific claims?

Actually, it is not that simple, because there are two experiential ways rather than one way of looking at the six days of creation. The first way is to view them as cycles of work and rest—God's work and temporary rest. The second way is to view them as cycles of work and rest and, *in addition*, as cycles of light and darkness. The mature creation view normally takes the second approach, not the first. At this point, it distinguishes itself from the analogical-day theory and the day-age theory.

The Analogical-Day Theory

The analogical-day theory may also have something to learn. This theory, in its most common form, says that the six days in Genesis 1 are analogous to human workdays within the present providential order—analogous, but not equal. Genesis 1 does not specify the length of each day, as measured by a modern technological timekeeper. The days might be short or long—Genesis 1 does not say. But part of the point of the analogical-day theory is often to suggest a harmonization with modern science. When we undertake harmonization, the claim is that the days in Genesis 1 were actually long periods of time, millions of years.

The problem here is with the language of description, and particularly the word *actually* in the preceding sentence. Whatever may have been the intent of the people who initially crafted the analogical-day theory, other people, when they hear it, may apply terms such as "*actually*" and "*long periods of time*." In using such expressions, they may move the language in the direction of acceding to the modern philosophical view that specialized scientific descriptions of time are metaphysically ultimate. The word *actually* can hint that the measurement of time with modern technical apparatus gives us the real thing; it gives us "actuality."

But we do not need to agree with this identification of "actuality" with a specialized scientific point of view. The specialized framework for time gives us a perspective that is no more ultimate than the perspective of the experiential point of view. Moreover, it gives us something technically specialized, something less integrally related to the central issues of human existence and struggle. So the six days were six *days*—really, actually, from a experiential point of view. The modern cosmological description offers a specialized picture that may be true, given its peculiar, specialized definitions of time measurement.

But they are peculiar, and they do not destroy the experiential point of view or the validity of its "measurement" of days using a cycle of personal activity and rest.

Let us put it another way. The problem is not with the underlying core intent of the analogical-day theory, but with some of the assumptions that may creep into explanations of it. Some of the language used in describing the analogical-day theory may unwittingly push us to accept the metaphysical claims of some modern scientists. These scientists imply that their system for time gets to the bottom—or nearer to the bottom—of the metaphysics of the universe. If we concede their point of view, Genesis 1 becomes merely an accommodation to unfortunate limitations in earlier human culture. We should reject this claim. It is the modern metaphysical claim that is limited by its reductionism. It overlooks the obvious, namely, the involvement in theory making of the sagacity of particular human beings, made in the image of God, who develop—in the form of modern cosmology—an insightful but *limited* perspective on time.

Lessons Concerning Basic Affirmations about Genesis 1

There may also be lessons for other readers of Genesis 1. Some people, particularly in the West but also in the rest of humanity, believe that God created the world in six days, and leave it at that. It might seem to many modern analysts that these people hold to a form of the twenty-four-hour-day theory. But if they do not choose to go beyond a simple affirmation, they are not necessarily committing themselves to any particular theory about the relation of Genesis 1 to mainstream scientific claims. Neither are they committing themselves to any particular theory about the *length* of the six days when measured by specialized technological apparatus. If they belong to cultures outside the West, they may not even be familiar with such apparatus. These people therefore may not manifest a clear commitment to *any* of the detailed modern theories for harmonization. Let us call this approach the *simple-affirmation view* of the days of Genesis 1.

In a way, some of these people may be closer to the analogical-day theory than to the twenty-four-hour-day theory, because they can recognize that one central point of Genesis 1 is to indicate the analogy between God's work and human work. The person who is content with the sparse description in Genesis 1 knows that the first six days were like our days within providence, but also unlike, because they were days of God's activity of initially creating instead of his activity of providential sustaining. That is, a person is content to know that the six days were like later days without insisting that the likeness had to extend to every detail that might be important for efforts in speculative scientific reconstruction of the past.[3]

Lessons for the Twenty-Four-Hour-Day Theory

Finally, there may be lessons for the twenty-four-hour-day theory. What is this theory? It has more than one form. In its most well-known forms within the last century, the twenty-four-hour-day theory seeks to address apparent tensions between its claims and the explanations of mainstream science. But in the *way* that it does so, it makes additional assumptions.

The central commitment for the twenty-four-hour-day theory is that the days of Genesis 1 had a twenty-four-hour length. And what does this mean? The claim has to be further defined by specifying the standard for measuring twenty-four hours. Does an hour mean 3,600 seconds measured by an appropriate technical apparatus? Representatives of the twenty-four-hour-day theory have a minor problem, because most of them do not directly address the issue of how they measure the lengths of the six days. If they do not define the length of a day with reference to some standard for measuring time, their view is not clearly distinguished from the analogical-day view. If they want to pick some specific way of measuring, they have to specify what it is.

---

3. What about scholars who interpret Genesis 1 and say that they hold the twenty-four-hour-day theory, but also say that they are not going to discuss how to harmonize their interpretation with mainstream science? Some of them may hold the simple-affirmation view. But many of them talk about twenty-four hours or ordinary days, normal days, or literal days. What do they mean? Often, it is not completely clear. Many of these people attempt to advocate a twenty-four-hour-day theory without specifying how to measure the length of hours or days. And as we have seen, that lack of specification leaves their work ambiguous. Despite their claim that their view differs from the analogical-day view or the day-age view, they have just given us ambiguities, not a theory at all. If, on the other hand, they told us how to measure the length of a twenty-four-hour day, an ordinary day, or a normal day within Genesis 1, they would by that commitment begin to wrestle with the issue of time measurement, and they could not altogether avoid dealing with the present providential order in time and the possibility of a difference between the providential order and the six days of Genesis 1.

The simplest disambiguation would be to specify that each day in Genesis 1 is a single cycle of light and darkness. That would not tell us the length of the cycles measured by technical apparatus, but it would disallow any simple harmonization with mainstream scientific descriptions of the far past.

With respect to this choice, people have several options. First, twenty-four-hour-day advocates may decide that they do not want to make a choice, but simply to specify that the six days were days, and leave it at that. Then they hold the simple-affirmation view described above.

Second, a twenty-four-hour-day advocate may choose to specify a particular standard for the length of the days. One such standard would be the cycle of light and darkness.[4] But as we have seen, the evening and morning may designate the times in which there is a gradual disappearance and appearance of light, or they may designate the end and the beginning of a workday. Moreover, if there is an oscillation of light and darkness during the first three days, it takes place without the sun "ruling" it, and so we do not know whether the oscillation had the "same length" as the last three days, when measured by some technical apparatus.

Third, a twenty-four-hour-day advocate may choose to specify a modern means of measurement, such as a stopwatch. But since there are many modern means, what motivates the choice of one means rather than another? Such a choice cannot be based just on the text of Genesis 1.

Fourth, an advocate may propose to measure the length of the six days in Genesis 1 not by any one timekeeping apparatus, but by using the assumption that all of the temporal rhythms were basically the same during the six days as they are today. This assumption may seem reasonable. Let us pursue it a little further. In doing so, we are trying to see what it might mean to make explicit in our thinking the intuitive idea of likeness between the six creation days and our days now.

If the six days are really days, they must be like our providential days. So it may seem reasonable to ask for a maximal amount of likeness, at least with respect to rhythms in time.

But can we be sure? The content of divine activities during the days is spectacular. The days are not altogether like our days. It would be

---

4. Similar, for example, to Josephus, *Jewish Antiquities*, trans. H. St. J. Thackeray (London: Heinemann; Cambridge: Harvard University Press, 1967), 1.28 (1.1.1), http://www.biblestudy tools.com/history/flavius-josephus/antiquities-jews/; Basil the Great of Caesarea, *Hexaemeron* 2.8, in *A Select Library of Nicene and Post-Nicene Fathers of the Christian Church*, 2nd series, ed. Philip Schaff (Grand Rapids: Eerdmans, 1978), vol. 8, Christian Classics Ethereal Library, http://www.ccel.org/ccel/schaff/npnf208.pdf; Ambrose, *Hexaemeron* (Washington, DC: Catholic University of America Press, 1961), 1.10.36–37, 41–43.

convenient if they were like our days with respect to all the rhythms. But has God guaranteed it?

An additional challenge arises because, as we have seen, some of the rhythms do not exist during the first few days. The rhythm of the human psychological sense of the passage of time does not exist until the creation of man. The rhythm of various aspects of plant and animal life does not exist until plants and animals exist. The garden of Eden apparently grew trees in one day.

An advocate can still try to hold to maximal likeness in rhythms, but allow for a number of exceptions. He could begin with the principle that all the rhythms that we see today extend back into the first six days, and also that the rhythms keep in time with each other in the same way in which they keep in time today. The first exception would be to allow that some rhythms did not exist until God created the things with which the rhythms are associated. In addition, the advocate could allow an exception for new rhythms. He could say that a newly created rhythm may not be in time with the rest of the rhythms until the end of the day during which it is established. But on the subsequent days, all the rhythms that are not newly established are assumed to be in time with each other, in a way exactly parallel to the way in which they are in time with each other in our own environment.

So, for instance, the act of creating plants on the third day would be miraculous. Immediately after the act of creation, the growth of these plants might be miraculous, and might involve something other than the normal rhythm for growth of plants. But after the third day, the plants would have rhythms that are in time with all the other rhythms, and these rhythms would remain in time with each other up until the present day. (Of course, we also have to make an exception for trees springing up in the garden of Eden.)

This proposal has three appealing aspects. First, it allows that God could act in special ways when he sets up a particular set of features of the created world, such as the plant kingdom, the heavenly bodies, the sea animals, the land animals, or the garden of Eden. Second, it tends to maximize the degree of continuity between the six days and the later days of providence, thus assuring us that we have a fairly detailed picture of what went on during each of the six days. Everything is "normal" about plants on all the days after the day on which they are created. And the same is true for light (day one), the expanse (day two), the dry land (day three), the heavenly bodies (day four), the birds and sea creatures (day five), and the land animals (day six). Third, this proposal provides a detailed set of assumptions for us to use when we are trying to extrapolate backward from the present state of the world. A scientist can reason with confidence concerning the six days because the proposal gives him clear guidelines as to what *kinds* of continuity he can expect with existing scientific laws, which describe God's providential order. A particular law or regularity can be extrapolated backward all the way until the day *after* the time when the pertinent element of order was first created during the six days. Let us call this proposal *the continuity hypothesis* with respect to the six days of creation. (See Fig. 12.1.)

Fig. 12.1: The Continuity Hypothesis

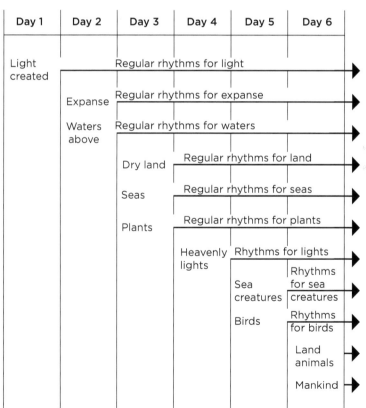

Difficulties with the Continuity Hypothesis

What should we think about the continuity hypothesis? It has a certain commonsense appeal because it seems plausible to postulate that the first six days were like our days *maximally*. However, we need to note three difficulties.

First, do twenty-four-hour day theorists actually hold to the continuity hypothesis? It is not clear that they do. Some of them seem at times to talk in ways that suggest that they may hold to it. But many times they simply do not become specific. If they are not specific, is it fair to classify them as holding to the simple-affirmation view? Probably not, because many representatives vigorously repudiate the alternative theories. Many twenty-four-hour-day theorists use labels such as "ordinary day" or "literal day," doing so apparently to distinguish their view from some of the other major views. But until they specify a standard for measurement, their labels do not resolve the ambiguities as to what kind of measurement they have in mind.

Second, the continuity hypothesis is, in the end, a hypothesis. It is one possible, plausible inference from the text of Genesis 1. But Genesis 1 does not clearly affirm it or deny it. Genesis 1 does not specify in exactly what ways the six days are like and unlike our days within the providential order. Therefore, advocates for this form of the twenty-four-hour-day theory might acknowledge its lack of certainty.[5]

Third, the continuity hypothesis provides only limited useful guidance with respect to modern scientific research. One of the strengths of this hypothesis is that it does appear to provide some guidelines, at least in a general way. It says that each of the regularities familiar to us in providence is in effect from a certain point onward. But when we go out and look at the world, some questions remain. In particular, how do we reconcile the continuity hypothesis with the proposed science-based explanations that young-earth creationists are currently providing?

For instance, if the rate of radioactive decay of certain elements is regular after the first day (which is presumably when the elements were created within the earth), how is that consistent with

---

5. Advocates who are not ready to commit themselves to the continuity hypothesis are admitting that they are not so certain as to what exactly might be the points of continuity and discontinuity between the six days and later days. If so, does that leave room for the kind of continuity and discontinuity proposed by the analogical-day theory or the mature-creation theory?

young-earth theorists' advocacy of large-scale changes in the rate at a later point in time (around the time of Noah's flood)? If the patterns for animal reproduction are fixed after the sixth day, how is that consistent with young-earth creationists' proposal that there was super-rapid speciation right after the flood of Noah? It looks as though twenty-four-hour-day theorists do not consistently hold to the continuity hypothesis. They introduce exceptions. But if they do not consistently hold to the continuity hypothesis, what do they hold to?

The twenty-four-hour-day theorists have the right to define their approach in a way that appears to them to be best. There are probably at least four main principles: (1) each of the six days of Genesis 1 is composed of exactly one cycle of light and darkness; (2) during the six days, God worked in exceptional, miraculous ways to create the new orders of things, but the details of his works are likely to remain mysterious; (3) Noah's flood was global in extent; and (4) Noah's flood was an exceptional, miraculous event, so it might involve changes in some of the normal rhythmic patterns in time. Together, these four principles separate twenty-four-hour-day theorists from advocates of most of the other theories, though not from all forms of the intermittent-day, mature-creation, or analogical-day theories. The twenty-four-hour-day theorists would affirm that there are analogies between the six days and later days, but hold firmly to the principle that one of the main points of analogy lies in each day being a single cycle of light and darkness.

The twenty-four-hour-day theory is motivated by an admirable impulse: to make sure that we believe that the Bible is true in all that it affirms and that we not compromise that truth with strange hermeneutics when it comes to Genesis 1. This impulse is indeed God honoring. But how do we work it out in detail? Some twenty-four-hour-day theorists might say that they want "literal" hermeneutics.[6] They want to say that the days of Genesis 1 are "literal" days. But this by itself does not tell us what *counts* as literal when it comes to picking out a standard for measuring the length of the days (especially the first three days). What is the standard?

---

6. On problems with the word *literal*, and alternative terms such as *plain* and *normal*, see Vern S. Poythress, *Understanding Dispensationalists*, 2nd ed. (Phillipsburg, NJ: P&R, 1994), chap. 8.

The word *literal* also has a way of pushing us toward *maximal* continuity with our days within providence (see chap. 15, p. 280). The tendency is to expect that one of the six days can be a truly "literal" day only if it matches our experience. And this kind of desire for literalness can easily push us toward the continuity hypothesis, even though a more measured reading of Genesis 1 would recognize that it does not teach maximal continuity. Maximal continuity is a *hypothesis*. A label such as "literal" seems to invite us to confuse loyalty to biblical teaching with loyalty to maximal continuity—loyalty to the continuity hypothesis.

This position still strives to produce Bible-affirming answers. But that desire can at times be combined with overconfidence about details. It would be better for people to say, "We believe that the Bible is true. But we don't really have a thorough explanation for how to put it all together with the claims of mainstream science. We have some tentative ideas, and we are working on it. *Part* of the explanation may just be that God, for his own purposes, did things differently than what we might expect."

We could also add, "And one of the things that we might not expect is that he describes the six days from an experiential point of view, not a specialized point of view. In doing so, he describes a day as a cycle of personal work and rest."[7]

Conclusion

In conclusion, most of the main proposals for harmonizing Genesis 1 with modern science have not sufficiently reckoned with the difficulty in time *measurement* and the possibility of more than one perspective on time. When we include this difficulty in our thinking, we can see that the proposals themselves are not always clear about what they mean in their pronouncements about time in Genesis 1. A simple affirmation of creation in six days by people unfamiliar with technical timekeepers is simpler than any of the detailed theories, and is compatible in principle with several of them, because it is less specific.

---

7. We have not dealt with some other views concerning the six days. See Poythress, *Redeeming Science*, chaps. 8–10.

13

Attitudes and Expectations

In trying to picture for ourselves the events during the six days of creation, corrupt attitudes may unfortunately influence us. What attitudes? Everyone is subject to sinful inclinations. But we have to be careful not to unjustly attribute bad motives to other people as individuals. Rather than speculate about individual motives, let us consider some of the temptations that arise for all of us, so that we may be on guard against them.

In previous chapters, we have discussed the difficult question of the extent to which the events during the first six days are like later events. This area presents us with temptations either to overestimate or underestimate the likeness between the six days and later events.

Pressure to Agree with Modern Scientific Claims

The first temptation is to minimize the claims of Genesis 1–2 in order to make it harmonize with modern scientific claims concerning the past. If Genesis 1–2 were a merely human document, the way forward would be easy: do not attempt harmonization. Say merely that Genesis 1–2 is wrong wherever it disagrees with modern scientific claims. If, on the other hand, Genesis 1–2 has divine authority (which it does; see chap. 3, p. 51), the easiest course for a quick peace is just to affirm whatever mainstream scientists affirm and reinterpret Genesis 1–2 so that it is not about anything that could be in tension with a scientific account of events that happened in space and time. According to this approach, Genesis 1–2 is merely a statement about God's providential governance, a theological affirmation, or a mythic expression of such an affirmation. We have already rejected such a course as out of line with a sound interpretation of Genesis.

If we reject both of these "easy" solutions, we have to do more work. That work includes the effort to interpret Genesis 1–2 faithfully as God's words, and also to interpret modern scientific claims with critical attention to their presuppositions, methods, and evidences.

Pressure to Maximize Detailed Similarity

A second temptation comes from pressure to maximize detailed similarity between Genesis 1–2 and later providence. This pressure can go together with what elsewhere is called a "mental-picture theory of truth."[1] Let us briefly consider this theory. It says that, in order to be true, an account must produce a mental picture within the reader in full accord with what actually happened. But this idea misconstrues what truthfulness means in verbal communication. Because a verbal account of an event does not include many details, it is natural for people who listen to such an account to form a mental picture that includes many *more* details as they imagine how the event would have taken place. These extra details do not necessarily match the event itself.

In the case of Genesis 1–2, in our imaginations, we might naturally fill in the details in harmony with what we now typically experience in God's providential order. But what our imaginations fill in goes beyond what the text actually says. Verbal truth does not involve a commitment to produce an exact, all-inclusive, photographically accurate mental picture, but a commitment to describe what happened in contrast to various alternatives that did not happen. A verbal account leaves out details. With Genesis 1–2, when we fill in details in our imagination, we move toward maximal continuity. And this move, though plausible, is not guaranteed by the text.

Pressure to Be as Impressive and Persuasive as Modern Science

Because science has obtained such prestige in our time, it is tempting for those who want to defend the claims of the Bible to wish that

---

1. Vern S. Poythress, *Inerrancy and the Gospels: A God-Centered Approach to the Challenges of Harmonization* (Wheaton, IL: Crossway, 2012), chaps. 7–9.

those claims could be effectively and persuasively defended within the territory prescribed by mainstream science. Mainstream science, not to mention popularizations of it and manipulations of it by vocal atheists, has frequently been a resource that people have used to attack the authority of the Bible and depreciate its trustworthiness. It would be very convenient if a hero could stand up and decisively refute these attacks by using science. So it is tempting to search for "scientific proofs" and then to hold to some such proof even though it is flawed. In the fervency of our desire to defend God and the Bible, we may overlook the flaws.

But such a move does not really honor God. He does not need this kind of defense.

There is no easy, quick answer to our cultural troubles. Elite Western culture despises the Bible. And that situation may not change soon. But notice that the apostle Paul does not look for a way to make the gospel measure up to the wisdom of the world. Rather, he rejects the wisdom of the world in favor of the wisdom of God (1 Corinthians 1). If people come to know the saving power of God in Christ, it will fundamentally be because of the power of the Holy Spirit, not human cleverness in argument and rhetoric. We should love God with heart, mind, and soul. We should use our minds and all their abilities. But that is different from conforming to the latest cultural trends.

Let us tell ourselves not to panic if we do not have all the answers and if orthodox Christianity looks as if it is on the cultural defensive. God does not need to prove himself to the world by spectacular details in the Bible that harmonize with science. God is God. He does not need to prove anything. Rather, the whole world is guilty because sinners suppress the obvious testimony that God has put in the natural world concerning himself (Rom. 1:18–23). The testimony of creation is obvious; it does not merely consist in specialized insights from science. And if we think that specialized, technical testimony would automatically be more powerful to change people's hearts, we do not know the darkness of the human heart in rebellion against God.

In particular, as we have seen, in Genesis 1–2, God addresses ordinary people, including prescientific cultures, concerning what is simple and obvious.

Pressure to Wish That Scientific Claims Would Go Away

We also may feel pressure to dismiss modern scientific claims too quickly. (See Fig. 13.1.)

Fig. 13.1: Pressures from Modern Context

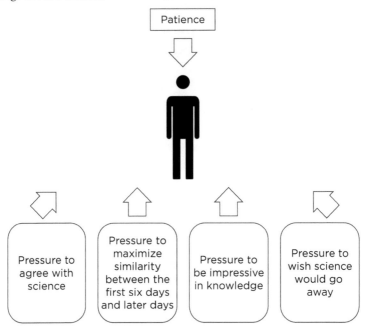

I observed earlier that the sciences are human projects, and that they are influenced by human biases in the form of precommitments, as well as by social influences toward conformity. In our day, materialistic philosophy has an undeniable influence, as does the dominance of Darwinism, understood as including two significant principles: (1) all life evolved *gradually*, and (2) this evolution took place without intelligent guidance or plan. So we may be tempted to appeal to these influences in order to dismiss scientific claims as a whole. But a quick dismissal is too simple. We must look carefully at evidences and arguments in detail. We must listen to minority voices that dispute mainstream claims, but we must not believe minority voices merely because they lead to conclusions that we like. We must be patient in evaluating the complex currents that go into scientific conclusions.

Obviously this is a major challenge. We cannot do it all in one book. Already, at earlier points, I have referred readers to other books that address in more detail the evaluation of mainstream science.

We must accept the fact that, however much we read, our human knowledge remains partial, and some of it may be seriously flawed. Scientific work is work in progress. Our limitations are an occasion to trust God, whose knowledge is unlimited.

14

The Days of Genesis 1

It now remains to ask ourselves again about the six days of creation. What kind of analogy exists between God's work and rest on the one hand, and man's work and rest on the other, as it pertains to understanding the days of creation? This is a vexed question about which there are several interpretive options. There are many arguments for and against the options.[1] We cannot consider them all. We must confine ourselves to a few highlights, leaving the details to other books.[2]

The Length of the Days of Creation

First, consider Genesis 2:1–3. It defines God's rest as a rest from his activities in *creating* (v. 3). He continues to govern the world in providence (Ps. 103:19). Since the fall, he also works in bringing salvation (John 5:17). But neither of these subsequent works involves creating new kinds of animals and plants, or creating the human race a second time. His work of *creation* is fundamentally "finished" (Gen. 2:1) and does not recommence after a temporary rest. Thus, God's rest mentioned in verses 1–3 goes on forever. It is analogous but not identical to the day of rest that the Israelites were supposed to observe in their Sabbath. The seventh day is consecrated because of God's rest (v. 3). The tight correlation between the rest and the day suggests that God's *day* of rest is everlasting.[3]

---

1. For an introduction to the arguments, see Vern S. Poythress, *Redeeming Science: A God-Centered Approach* (Wheaton, IL: Crossway, 2006), chaps. 4–10.
2. This chapter is a revision of part of Vern S. Poythress, "Correlations with Providence in Genesis 1," *Westminster Theological Journal* 77, no. 1 (2015): 71–99. Used with permission.
3. Poythress, *Redeeming Science*, 133.

Second, the narrative describing God's creation of the garden of Eden (Gen. 2:8–9) has analogies with the human work of planting and tending gardens. But the two kinds of works are analogous, not identical. God is the absolute Creator. Man is an imitator, and operates on the limited level that he enjoys as a creature. As measured by a modern timekeeper, the time periods for God's gardening and for man's gardening need not match one to one. If a man plants trees, it takes years for them to grow to maturity. God may do it, if he pleases, in a moment.

Third, Genesis 1 does not mention the sun until the fourth day. A simple reading of the first three days (vv. 3–13) reveals no obvious way for measuring lengths of time numerically by means of any obvious standard, such as the movement of the sun. Consequently, the text invites readers to consider the times with respect to the significant events that happen and the personal activities involved rather than in terms of a mechanistic measuring tool. Prior to the invention of mechanical clocks, most cultures of the world thought in terms of "social time" or "interactive time" rather than "clock time."[4] This kind of thinking fits the first three days of Genesis 1, as well as the cultures to which Genesis 1 was originally addressed.

The upshot is that Genesis 1, as a sparse account, does not give us information about the clock time for each individual day. We do know that the seventh day goes on forever. The six days may be interpreted as God's "workdays," the times of his personal activity. They are analogous to man's workdays. They are presented in terms of personal activity—interactive time—not in terms of clock time. Likewise, the seventh day is God's "rest day," which is analogous to man's rest day, the Sabbath.

This situation leaves open the question of how we harmonize Genesis 1 with technico-scientific measurements of time. That is to say, Genesis 1 leaves open the question of clock time. Suppose that we do a scientific investigation, using a time measurement determined by modern scientific clocks and extrapolating backward in time toward the origin. Would the days described in Genesis 1 turn out to be twenty-four hours or some other length? Genesis 1 does not say, because it is sparse. It sets forth periods of personal work ("interactive time"), not ticking clocks ("clock time").

---

4. Poythress, *Redeeming Science*, 140–43.

What about the refrain "And there was evening and there was morning"? C. John Collins has pointed out that within God's providential order, the period between evening and the next morning is the period when human beings rest for the night:[5]

> Man goes out to his work
> and to his labor *until the evening.* (Ps. 104:23)

By analogy, God's workdays in creation have times of initiation and times of completion, with rest before and after. The movement from rest to activity to rest constitutes an analogy between God's workdays and man's.

The Question of Chronological Order

Does Genesis 1 indicate that the activities on the six days occur completely in chronological order? Or is the order merely topical? As we observed earlier, later parts of Genesis are not all arranged in strict chronological order, though there is a gradual progression in time, with some backtracking, as we proceed through the book. Moreover, the order in Genesis 2:4–25 appears to be largely an order of narration that focuses on *purpose.* The creation of man is mentioned early in the narrative, and then other events are brought in to show how God arranges a suitable environment for the man whom he has created.

So what about Genesis 1? The "framework hypothesis" concerning Genesis 1 argues that the organization into six days is a literary framework and does not necessarily imply a chronological order.[6] In support of its view, the framework hypothesis observes that in the first three days God creates the major regions of the world, and in the next three days creates their "rulers" or inhabitants. (See Table 14.1.)

Table 14.1: Regions of the World and Inhabitants

Regions	Inhabitants
Day 1: light	Day 4: heavenly lights
Day 2: heaven	Day 5: birds of heaven
Day 3: dry land	Day 6: land animals

---

5. C. John Collins, *Genesis 1–4: A Linguistic, Literary, and Theological Commentary* (Phillipsburg, NJ: P&R, 2006), 77.
6. Poythress, *Redeeming Science*, chap. 10 and Appendix 1.

This structural correspondence seems to be real. The light is created on day one, while the rulers over the light are created on day four. The heavens are created on day two, while the birds of the heavens are created on day five. But the pattern is not uniform: the sea creatures created on day five correspond to the sea of day three. Moreover, the presence of some literary structure does not show that there is not *also* a chronological structure. The two need not compete with each other.

An ordinary ancient reader of Genesis 1 can observe a natural order in quite a few of the events:

1. Each region has to be there before the point at which the inhabitants of the region are created.

2. The narrative introduces the earth at an early point. If Genesis 1:1 describes early events and is not merely a title (see Appendix A, p. 291), the earth in verse 2 is not necessarily the very first thing to be created in chronological order. The narrative starts there at an early point because it intends to provide an explanation for ordinary people, and this explanation will use analogies from providence. In providence, human beings must have a place from which to observe. The story of creation, as analogous to providence, provides for the earth at an early point. As a sparse account, it leaves out details concerning events that may have occurred prior to the creation of the earth.

3. Light comes next. In providence, light is fundamental for most human activity. Likewise, in creation, as analogous to providence, it is fitting that light is introduced early. As a sparse account, the narrative passes over any details about events that occurred in darkness, before the first light appeared.

4. Next comes the division of waters, vertically (day two) and horizontally (day three). Both of the two divisions into major regions offer an important framework for the more specific forms of order that will come to exist within the regions. The analogies with providence include the annual flooding of the Nile and the occasional flooding elsewhere from strong rainstorms.

Logically, which might we expect to come first, the vertical division between waters above and below, or the horizontal division between sea and dry land? In one way, the presence of water in the heavens has a more fundamental function in the providential order, since it is possible in principle for such water to be present all through an annual cycle of floods, rains, and dry spells. Moreover, heavenly water is presupposed as the source of flooding in lands where rainstorms can bring floods.

According to our normal principle, we look for analogies between creation and providence. In this case, the more fundamental providential role for the waters in the heavens suggests a similar fundamental role that they might play in the creation. If so, the vertical separation of waters above from waters below could be expected to occur earlier in the order of creation. The separation of sea from dry land would come later. Moreover, in God's providential order, the separation between heaven and earth holds true over both the dry land and the sea. This broad scope for the vertical separation again suggests that the vertical separation might suitably come earlier in the works of creation.[7] (Of course, God is free to have chosen a different order; but the order he did choose makes sense.)

5. Plants appear on land (last part of day three) only after there is land (first part of day three).

6. Lights appear in the expanse (day four) only after there is an expanse (day two).

7. Creatures appear in the sea (day five) only after there is a sea (day three). Creatures (birds) appear in the heavens (day five) only after there are heavens (day two). Animals appear on the land (day six) only after there is land (day three) and plants for the animals to eat (day three; see Gen. 1:30).

The sense of progress through the events narrated on successive days weighs against a "pure" framework approach that says that the order of days is only a literary device.[8] In reply, the framework approach might point to the relationship between the appearing of light on day one and the appearing of the heavenly lights on day four. It is sometimes claimed that the descriptions on these two days are really

---

7. Cf. Edward J. Young, *Studies in Genesis One* (Philadelphia: Presbyterian and Reformed, 1964), 91.

8. For further discussion of the "framework hypothesis," see Young, *Studies in Genesis One*, 43–76; Poythress, *Redeeming Science*, 143–47, 341–45; Derek Kidner, *Genesis: An Introduction and Commentary* (Leicester, England: Inter-Varsity; Downers Grove, IL: Inter-Varsity Press, 1967), 54–55.

describing the same events from two points of view. But our reading in chapter 8 undermines this kind of argument. Ordinary analogies from providence show that we can have a consistent interpretation of day one and day four such that the two do not collapse into one another. Light can appear without the disks of heavenly light, in the form of diffuse light, such as the light of dawn before the bright sun disk comes above the horizon, and the light from the clouds on an overcast day. The assumption that light *must* come from light-bearing *bodies* comes from modern scientific knowledge, not from ordinary observation of providence. That assumption interferes with a perceptive reading of Genesis 1, days one and four.

Another interfering assumption can arise from a modern reader thinking that "the greater light" is the sun and "the lesser light" is the moon, where the terms *sun* and *moon* mean the sun and moon according to our modern scientific conceptions. The language in Genesis 1:14–16 is, as usual, phenomenal. The phenomena do not exist, are not "made" by God, until they actually *appear* in the sky with essentially the same kind of appearance as they have today. Of course, Genesis 1, as a theological document, implies that God created whatever unknown and invisible "things" are behind the appearances. But the focus is on God's making of the appearances. To think otherwise may involve partially falling victim to the myth of scientistic metaphysics and treating the language of the Bible in violation of its "nonpostulational" character.

Thus, Genesis 1 does include a sense of progression and a chronological order. The use of successive numbers for each day confirms this order. But that does not mean that it cannot also, as a sparse account, stick to the main points and group together created objects of one kind for topical simplicity.

Building on earlier work, Bruce Waltke points to the specific wording for the days in the Hebrew text. A more literal translation would have: "one day," "a second day," "a third day," "a fourth day," "a fifth day," and "*the* sixth day," the last with the definite article. Waltke and others suggest that this terminology allows a shuffling of chronology.[9] The evidence here is subtle, and it is a

---

9. Bruce K. Waltke, with Cathi J. Fredricks, *Genesis: A Commentary* (Grand Rapids, MI: Zondervan, 2001), 62, citing D. A. Sterchi, "Does Genesis 1 Provide a Chronological Sequence?" *Journal of the Evangelical Theological Society* 39 (1996): 529–36; and M. Throntveit,

matter of some subtlety to assess its meaning. Uncertainty about the significance of this variation should make us cautious about putting a lot of weight on it. And even if these details theoretically *allow* a shuffling of chronology, they do not positively indicate any such shuffling.[10]

Thus, there are grounds for thinking that the events come basically in chronological order. But the account sticks to high points rather than pretending to be exhaustive. Accordingly, all kinds of plants could be included in the creative activities of day 3, in order to include them under a single comprehensive heading, even though the creation of some kinds of plants might be spread over a large amount of clock time.

After considering an approach that treats the days as a literary device, Derek Kidner sums up his view of the message of Genesis 1:

> Yet to the present writer the march of the days is too majestic a progress to carry no implication of ordered sequence; it also seems over-subtle to adopt a view of the passage which discounts one of the primary impressions it makes on the ordinary reader. It is a story, not only a statement. As with all narrating, it demanded a choice of standpoint, of material to include, and of method in the telling. In each of these, simplicity has been a dominant concern. The language is that of every day, describing things by their appearance; the outlines of the story are bold, free of distracting exceptions and qualifications, free also to group together matters that belong together (so that trees, for example, anticipate their chronological place in order to be classified with vegetation), to achieve a grand design in which the demands now of time-sequence, now of subject-matter, control the presentation, and the whole reveals the Creator and His preparing a place for us.

"Are the Events in the Genesis Account Set Forth in Chronological Order? No," in *The Genesis Debate*, ed. R. F. Youngblood (Nashville, TN: Thomas Nelson, 1986), 53. The latter source is now available in a later edition: Mark A. Throntveit, "Are the Events in the Genesis Creation Account Set Forth in Chronological Order? No," in *The Genesis Debate: Persistent Questions about Creation and the Flood*, ed. Ronald Youngblood (repr., Grand Rapids, MI: Baker, 1990), 36–55. Throntveit also discusses the absence of the definite article in days one through five: "Are the Events in the Genesis Creation Account Set Forth in Chronological Order? No," 50–51. In addition, Sterchi's article cites R. Youngblood, *The Book of Genesis* (Grand Rapids, MI: Baker, 1991), 26.

10. As is admitted by Sterchi, "Does Genesis 1 Provide a Chronological Sequence?" 533, 536.

The view that the chapter is intended to reveal the general sequence of creation as it affected this earth, is based on the apparent character of the writing. But it is reinforced, one may think, by the remarkable degree of correspondence that can be found between this sequence and the one implied by current science. This has often been pointed out, and not always by those who set any store on the factual accuracy of Scripture . . . [11]

Kidner correctly observes that the account gives us a narrative progression, not just a list of topics. But it is sparse in order to stress "a grand design."

Doing a Correlation with Scientific Accounts

Genesis 1 needs to be interpreted first in a manner independent of modern scientific knowledge, lest we fall victim to the myth of scientistic metaphysics in our interpretation. If we were to fall victim to this myth, we might arrive at an approach that artificially imports misinterpretations because of prior expectations influenced by science. We should first attempt to interpret Genesis 1 with careful attention to its own terms.[12]

But afterward, we may raise other kinds of questions. We may ask how a reasonable interpretation of Genesis 1 could go together or fail to go together with a modern scientific account. When we approach this question, we should acknowledge that we are no longer simply interpreting the text of Genesis 1 on its own terms. We are no longer focusing on the primary purpose of Genesis 1, that of instructing the ancient Israelites and peoples of every culture. Rather, we are asking about its relation to modern scientific descriptions. In doing so, we are using one perspective, and it has fallibilities and liabilities. As I observed earlier, in interacting with scientific claims concerning the past, we should acknowledge that these claims depend on assumptions concerning the continuities of physical laws. These assumptions may or may not be true.

When we explore the relationships, we may find correlations between Genesis 1 and science ("concordisms"). If we do find correla-

---

11. Kidner, *Genesis*, 55.

12. "Though historical and scientific questions may be uppermost in our minds as we approach the text, it is doubtful whether they were in the writer's mind, and we should therefore be cautious about looking for answers to questions he was not concerned with." Gordon J. Wenham, *Genesis 1–15*, Word Biblical Commentary 1 (Waco, TX: Word, 1987), liii.

tions, we are not saying that Genesis 1 by itself directly and obviously "means" everything that we find in the correlations. We are only seeking to understand Genesis 1 in relation to other things that people have discovered in our own day. In all this, we must understand the tentative character and fallibility of science, as well as the fallibility of our interpretation of Genesis 1. On the other hand, because God reveals to us in the Bible that he is the author of nature as well as the author of the Bible, it is legitimate for us to explore how the two might fit together within his comprehensive plan.

Granted all these qualifications, it is not that difficult to form a tentative correlation between a mainstream scientific account and Genesis 1 once we allow each side to tell its story in its own way. Here is one scenario that attempts to do a combination.

The whole scientific account of the history of the universe up until the creation of the earth corresponds to Genesis 1:1. Light in day one could correspond to the time when the sun begins to give off light because of heating through gravitational contraction. Or more likely, it could correspond to the initial penetration of light to the surface of the new earth after a period in which the planet was covered with an opaque atmosphere and was encircled by interplanetary debris.[13] (The standard picture from mainstream science is that the present-day planets in the solar system condensed gradually from dust and smaller pieces that were part of the general environment of the sun, which itself condensed from a cloud of interstellar dust.)

The separation in day two could correspond to the first establishment of a weather cycle involving the rising of clouds and the coming of rain. Day three corresponds to the origins of continents and earlier forms of life. Day four corresponds to the oxygenization and clearing of the atmosphere (oxygenization presupposes plant life), so that from earth the heavenly bodies are visible and take on the appearance that they have at present. Day five corresponds to the origin of larger sea animals (fish), and day six corresponds to the origin of land animals and mankind. These events are in the same order in Genesis 1 and in a current scientific chronology concerning the far past. (See Table 14.2.)

---

13. I owe this insight to Hugh Ross.

Table 14.2: Days of Genesis 1 and a Scientific Account

Days	Phenomena in Genesis 1	Scientific Events
Day 1	light	light reaches the surface of the earth after a period when it was blocked by debris
Day 2	atmospheric water	beginning of the weather cycle
Day 3	dry land	first continents
	plants	first plants
Day 4	heavenly lights	sun, moon, and stars take on their present appearance as the atmosphere becomes oxygenated and transparent
Day 5	fish, birds	fish, birds appear (fossil record)
Day 6	large land animals	large mammals appear
	man	man appears

(Note that it is possible to have an order, corresponding to the order of fossils in the scientific column, and still believe in special acts of God by which he created different kinds of plants and animals. This idea is set forth by old-earth creationists who do not endorse macroevolution.)

Modern science is, of course, tentative and subject to correction. But the suggestive correlations with science show the problematic character of modern critical attacks based on alleged similarities between Genesis 1 and ancient myths. For example, critics may allege that the mention of waters in verse 2 shows that Genesis is simply borrowing from ancient Near Eastern mythic material that depicts order emerging out of primeval waters of chaos.[14] To the modern mind, such depictions show a false, primitive substitute for a modern scientific account. But the pattern of order from chaos actually took place with the annual flooding of the Nile, which began the Egyptian agricultural cycle. When the waters subsided, plants began to grow up, and the animals flourished by feeding on the plants. This series of events is providence, not myth. (But ancient Near Eastern myths could take such observations from providence and "mythologize" them into a polytheistic account.)[15] Similar works of God took place

---

14. E.g., Vincent Arieh Tobin, "Myths: Creation Myths," in *The Oxford Encyclopedia of Ancient Egypt*, ed. Donald B. Redford (New York: Oxford University Press, 2001), 2.469.

15. Tobin, "Myths: Creation Myths," 2.464 (see also chap. 8, note 23); Richard J. Clifford, *Creation Accounts in the Ancient Near East and in the Bible* (Washington, DC: Catholic Biblical Association of America, 1994), 102, 103, 105, 129.

in the creation of the earth, which, according to current science, was in a desolate and unformed state when it condensed from the disk of debris encircling the condensing body of the sun.

Similarity with a myth does not make Genesis 1:2 untrue. Confronted with the possibility that verse 2 represents truth, the skeptic may reply that it is true only by accident. But that response shows that he thinks that verse 2 is merely a product of human beings who could not know about the actual origins of the earth. If, on the other hand, verse 2 is divine discourse as well as human, God is free in his description to use the analogies that he himself has providentially put in place, such as the analogy between the flooding of the Nile and his work of creation.

Meanings in Analogies

Consider another example. Within God's providential order, the dry land appears after a heavy rainstorm or a flood. In creation, the continents appeared after an earlier period when water covered earth. God uses the providential events of flooding as an analogy to help ordinary people understand his work of creation.

The modern, scientifically educated person may not be impressed. He may point out that continent building depends on complex geophysical processes in the earth's mantle and crust, while flooding depends on the movement of water. Physically, the two are very different. "So," he says, "the analogy is superficial."

How we view the analogy depends on how we assess what is "superficial" versus what is "basic" and "real." Scientistic metaphysics says that physical causation by geophysical processes and the movement of water is basic. By contrast, visible appearances are "superficial." But God ordained the one kind of structure just as much as he ordained the other. God planned beforehand every analogy that we later discover, as well as every physical law that we detect.

Moreover, the world of appearances, including the world of more literary and poetic analogies, is in some respects closer to human living and personal concerns for human significance. In relation to highly personal meanings, we might even reverse the order and say that the analogy between continents and receding floodwaters is weighty, while the details of physical causation are superficial. The former analogy affects human nature at the level of existential concern, since human beings cannot live in a watery environment, such as a flood or a watery surface covering the earth. The pictures of water also contain symbolic dimensions concerning the distinction between chaos and order, and the transition from one to the other. Under God's control, the earth makes a transition from watery formlessness to separate regions of sea and dry land. The dry land has the capability for sustaining plant and animal life, and for being useful for human living.

In his sovereign plan, God has ordained not only the structure of physicalistic regularities that we see in geophysics, but the structure of analogies, including poetic analogies. Included among the analogies is one between continent building and recovery from a flood. Both processes involve a movement from spread-out water to bounded (separated) water, from formlessness to form, and from a situation inhospitable to humanity to one that is hospitable. By these and other analogies, God has linked creation and providence. And some of the links are very meaningful for the human appreciation of life. The scientistically oriented person may dismiss such an idea. But the problem is his. Through the apparent simplicity and "naivete" of the account in Genesis 1:9, God "catches the wise in their craftiness" (1 Cor. 3:19b).

15

Factuality and Literalism

We may now focus on two final issues concerning Genesis 1–3, the issue of factuality and the issue of literalism.[1]

The Exceptional and the Normal

Chapters 8–10 showed that Genesis 1–3 uses many analogies between God's acts of creation and his later acts of providence. But we also see some details in Genesis 1–3 that stand out as more unusual. In particular, the absolute beginning (Gen. 1:1); the creation of man (2:7), the two trees (v. 9), and woman (vv. 21–22); the talking serpent (3:1, 4–5); and the cherubim (v. 24) stand out as exceptional (see the end of chap. 10, p. 207). The descriptions of these events call for special attention precisely because they are different from the surrounding verses.

Since the events of providence occur in time and space today, the many analogies with providence in the early chapters of Genesis confirm that Genesis 1:1–3:24 is likewise giving us real events in space and time. In other words, Genesis 1–3 is providing us with a nonfictional, factual account. The cumulative force of the many analogies increases the confirmation. If we are going to deny the reality of the originating events in Genesis 1–3, we might as well go the whole way and deny the reality of present-day providence—which is what modern materialism virtually does.

---

1. The contents of this chapter are a revision of Vern S. Poythress, "Correlations with Providence in Genesis 2," *Westminster Theological Journal* 78, no. 1 (2016): 29–48. Used with permission.

The suspicion arises that modern agendas, modern myths, and pressures from a materialistic worldview are exerting influence on how people go about interpreting the first three chapters of Genesis. In opposition to these trends, a firm belief in God's providence, as well as a firm belief in supernatural salvation accomplished in Christ, aid us in recovering a godly view of the world in our own thinking. In such a view, we believe in the robust involvement of God in the world and the reality of the supernatural. Ultimately, our beliefs find their foundation in the nature of God. Not only Genesis 1 but also the rest of the Bible tells us that he is sovereign in creation and providence. A firm conviction about the true nature of God leads to a sound interpretation of Genesis 1–3.

Nonfiction Narrative versus Fable and Legend

We may also reflect more generally about the difference between a fable and a narrative such as Genesis 1–3 that purports to be about events in space and time (see chap. 6, p. 121). In Judges 9:8–15, Jotham tells a fable that involves talking trees. We know that it is a fable through several kinds of reinforcing information in the context. (1) In verses 16–20, Jotham interprets his fable as referring to Abimelech and the inhabitants of Shechem. (2) The fable has a clean literary boundary within Judges, with sharp shifts in subject matter at its beginning and end. (3) The larger interest of Judges 9 concerns Abimelech and his ambitions, with no direct relation to trees. (4) The fable has a relation to the surrounding context only when it is perceived as having allegorical meaning. We may make similar observations about many of Jesus's parables.

Both Jotham's fable and Jesus's parables set forth their meaning by providing us with two distinct levels of action. One level concerns actions within the story. The other concerns actions outside the story, to which the story intentionally points. In Jotham's fable, the actions of trees within the story correspond to the actions of individuals and groups outside the story.

These cases involving two-level fictional stories contrast with the account of Balaam's donkey, which fits solidly into the one-level historical narrative about Balaam's visit to Balak, or the account of the snake beginning in Genesis 3:1, which fits solidly into the fall narrative of verses 1–24. And if we are tempted to think that Adam and Eve are fictional figures, we should observe how they fit solidly into a one-level genealogical history going from Adam to Abraham and beyond. This history leads to the nation of descendants prophesied in Genesis (12:2; 13:16; 15:5; etc.), a nation that arrives in its multitudinous form in Exodus 1:7.

Scholars may reject the idea that Genesis 3 is fable or mythic invention and still downgrade the material in Genesis by classifying it as "legend." But such judgments have no real basis in the literary form of the text as we have it in the canon. The text connects itself forward to later history, with no indications of hesitancy about the relation of its narrative to actual events. Later Jewish and New Testament comments on Genesis confirm that Genesis is nonfiction; they show that the reference to real events is not a modern misreading. There is nothing in the literary contents of Genesis that qualifies it: comments such as "Our ancestors told us that . . . ," "People say that . . . ," "Our tradition says that . . . ," or the like. So when a scholar uses the label "legend" (or similar labels), the use of the label is not based on an emic assessment of the literary genre of Genesis (see chap. 6, p. 108). Rather, it is based on a broader historical skepticism or rejection of the divine authority of the product.

The issue of divine authority is key. Without that, Genesis reduces to a book that skeptical scholars imagine to be the endpoint of a long process of accretion. This accretion is alleged to have taken place by repeated retelling and rewriting without special divine superintendence, and therefore it is presumed to be of mixed value. But that skeptical view is something that is brought to the text and imposed on it. It is at odds with what Genesis actually claims.

We can conclude that, according to its genre, Genesis 1–3 purports to describe actual events that took place long ago in time and space. Its divine inspiration guarantees that what it purports to do is what it actually succeeds in doing—it does describe actual events. This understanding of Genesis 1–3 as referring to actual events is sometimes described as a *literal* interpretation, while an interpretation that treats the text as a fable, allegory, or myth is *figurative*. But we need to consider whether these labels are illuminating.

Literal and Figurative

The terms *literal* and *figurative* can be used in a range of ways.[2] In some contexts, the two terms are used in opposition. A literal use of a word is one that is close to the main dictionary meaning of the word. Figurative language is what is not literal, and literal language is what is not figurative. For example, when we speak about the door of a house, we are using the word *door* literally, but when we speak of a "door to understanding art," we are using the word *door* figuratively.

But there are some other uses of the term *literal*. For example, in popular discussion, people can say that they take the Bible "literally" when what they really mean is that they take it to be completely true. They are not denying that the Bible contains figures of speech. Neither are they saying that they have no sensitivity to figures of speech. For example, in John 10:7b, Jesus says, "I am the door of the sheep." People easily recognize that the words *door* and *sheep* are both used figuratively. The word *sheep* refers to people, not animals.

The word *literal* can also be used to describe a *preference* for non-figurative interpretation. Obvious figures of speech, such as "I am the door of the sheep," are recognized as figures, but anything not obviously figurative is treated using the most common dictionary meanings of the words. This approach is close to the principle "literal if possible." This principle may seem attractive, but it risks missing all but the most obvious figures of speech.

The word *literal* can be used to indicate that there are no extra symbolic dimensions of meaning in addition to an obvious, more prosaic meaning. For example, the tabernacle of Moses is a physical structure, but it *also* has symbolic meanings, because it is designed to symbolize God dwelling among his people during their wilderness journey. The animal sacrifices involve physical animals, but they also symbolize the need for a perfect substitute in order for people to be cleansed from sin and reconciled to God. Saying that the descriptions of the tabernacle and of the sacrifices are *literal* could be taken to mean that they have no symbolic dimensions.

---

2. See Vern S. Poythress, *Understanding Dispensationalists*, 2nd ed. (Phillipsburg, NJ: P&R, 1994), chap. 8.

There is still another use of the word *literal*. It is sometimes loosely used to describe all nonfiction. Someone might say a story is "literal" to distinguish it from a fable. (See Fig. 15.1.)

Fig. 15.1: Meanings of Literal

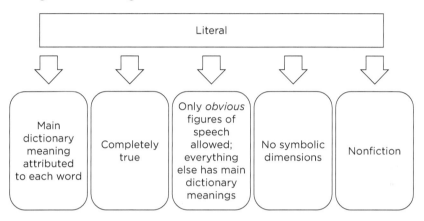

This plurality of uses is potentially confusing. Let me illustrate the difficulty. A poetic passage such as Exodus 15:1–18 uses figures of speech to describe how God brought the people of Israel out of Egypt and through the Red Sea. The same events are described in more prosaic fashion in Exodus 14. Similarly, Judges 5 poetically refers to the events that are described in prose in Judges 4; they both recount the defeat of Sisera and his army. Are the two poetic passages (Exodus 15 and Judges 5) literal or figurative? The poetry is "figurative" in the sense that it uses figures of speech, but at the same time, it is "literal" in the sense that it refers to events in the real world, unlike fables and allegories.

Thus, the polarity between *literal* and *figurative* does not prove to be helpful in discussing Exodus 15. In like manner, it is not helpful in discussing passages that use *analogies*. Analogies occur all the way through Genesis 1–3 (chaps. 8–10). Neither the word *literal* nor the word *figurative* gives us a well-rounded and clear description of the way that analogy functions.[3]

---

3. Analogy is sometimes classified as a figure of speech (see Michael Gladkoff, "Writing Speeches Using Similes, Metaphors, and Analogies for Greater Impact," Word Nerds, https:// www.word-nerds.com.au/writing-speeches-using-similes-metaphors-and-analogies/) and has been compared to simile: "Analogy: A resemblance between two different things, sometimes expressed

Consider: the word *literal* can be taken to mean that there is no use of analogy at all, anywhere in the text. If this is so with respect to Genesis 1–3, we have only a pure identity between descriptions of creation and descriptions of providence. But that route leads to identifying creation and providence, in tension with Genesis 2:2b: "God finished his work." Shall we then say that Genesis 1 is *figurative?* The word *figurative* might imply that Genesis 1–3 contains allegories whose whole point is to describe truths about providence, or perhaps to describe spiritual truths about the relation of God to the soul. Then God's works of creation are simply eliminated from the text.

As an example, let us consider Genesis 1:9, where God commands the dry land to appear. This is the *first* appearance of dry land after an earlier time when water covered everything. It is analogous to but not identical with later events in providence when waters recede off temporarily flooded land within a limited region.

We can ask whether the description in Genesis 1:9 is "literal" or "figurative." Neither label is apt. The word *figurative* is inappropriate because the verse is describing an event in the real world when the dry land first appeared. This event involved a physical change in the relative positions of water and the dry land. But the word *literal* can easily imply the rejection of analogy. It implies that analogies are irrelevant to understanding what the text describes. How, then, do we understand Genesis 1:9 at all? The ideas of "dry land" and of water being gathered together have to be somewhat like dry land, water, and gathering in our time if we are going to understand them.

So we are in a quandary. The first appearance of dry land comes after an earlier point when water covered the whole earth. It is not completely like later, providential appearances of land after a flood that comes to a limited area (e.g., the flooding of the Nile). The later reappearances of land within God's providential order are partly analogous to the first appearance. But if we reject analogy, we have to say that the later events have nothing to do with the first. That conclusion ignores the way in which God repeatedly communicates using analogies between creation and providence.

---

as a simile." Karl Beckson and Arthur Ganz, *Literary Terms: A Dictionary* (New York: Farrar, Straus and Giroux, 1975), 12; compare "What Is Analogy?" ThoughtCo, https://grammar.about .com/od/ab/g/analogy.htm. But just saying that analogy is "figurative" gives a one-sided impression about its functions.

Moreover, the word *literal* might imply that the verse has no dimensions of meaning beyond a minimal physical description. This inference creates tension with Genesis 1 as a whole, because in Genesis 1, the appearance of dry land involves not merely physical change but divine purpose. It prepares a space for plants, land animals, and man. The separation of sea from dry land also coheres with other acts of God in separating distinct regions and in bringing about a structured and ordered world. It is not an event that has its entire meaning in complete isolation from the other acts of God in creation.

In sum, the use of the word *literal* in the context of Genesis 1 can create difficulties. It can push interpretation in the direction of pure identity between creation and later providence, or between any two events that have similar verbal descriptions. If we assume a pure identity in the case of verse 9, the entire *nature* and the entire *process* of the appearance of dry land must be exactly the same in the details of the two cases. That is, creation and providence must involve exactly the same detailed physical processes. As a result, we cannot have mountain building in one case (creation) and water running back into the Nile in the other case (providence).

If the modern reader of Genesis 1:9 wants exact correspondence, he thinks not about waters receding after a flood, but modern developments in geophysics and the theory of plate tectonics, which have given us some understanding of the physical processes involved in mountain building. Geophysics presents us with specialized processes that are at work today. The modern reader seizes on a modern scientific description as the appropriate match for what happened in Genesis 1:9, rather than noticing the analogy with a flood, an analogy that would be relevant to an ancient reader or to contemporary readers in prescientific cultures.

The banner of "literalism" can unwittingly lead to reading Genesis 1 as if it were a precisionistic description, where everything must correspond exactly and precisely to later providential workings of God and to our expectations about how God does things, particularly in the light of specialized descriptions from science.

Does the word *figurative* function any better? No, it pushes interpretation in a minimalistic direction. If we use the word *figurative* to describe Genesis 1:9, it may seem to imply that there was no physical event in which the dry land appeared. Rather, it tells us to treat Genesis 1:9 as merely a symbol—perhaps a symbol for God's providential commitment to maintaining the dry land for the sake of human life (cf. 9:11, 15). People might say that the point is *only* that God is responsible in some principial way for the continued providential separation between water and dry land. The fact that the dry land appeared at a particular point in time is ignored. It is allegedly "not the point."

More controversially, the same polarity between *literal* and *figurative* interferes with a discussion of the nature of the six days of creation. The word *literal* easily encourages a mentality that there must be an exact match between the six days of creation and later days in providence. But clearly there cannot actually be an exact match for any of the days, precisely because they are days of creation rather than later days of providential action. Creation and providential action cannot simply be equated.

The General Problem with the Literal-Figurative Polarity

In such discussion, the words *literal* and *figurative* are not helpful. By themselves, they are too "thin" in meaning to robustly convey the meaning of what God is saying in Genesis 1–3. But the difficulty becomes even more complex because human beings and their actions have meaning in the context of analogies. For example, human beings are not purely "literal" beings, in the strictest sense, because they are made in the image of God, in analogy with God. A human father fathers sons. But the meaning of fathering is not self-contained. Human fathers are imitating God the Father's eternal relation to his Son. Neither are human beings purely "figurative" beings. They are real, not *just* symbols pointing to something else—perhaps to God, whose image they reflect. The meaning of humanity includes both aspects—symbolic and material/literal.

Symbolically a human being points to God, and simultaneously he is there as a created being distinct from God. Precisely as created beings, humans point back to God, who made them. Human personhood is intelligible only by reflecting on God, who is the origin of persons.

Similarly, human work is neither "literal" nor "figurative." It is real work in distinction from God's work in creation; simultaneously, it is analogous to God's work. It is empowered by God's presence. Neither are human days purely "literal," because they are analogous to the six original days of God's work and his final day of rest. Meaning throughout the universe is meaning in relationship to God, and so it cannot rightly be flattened into a purely prosaic, purely earthly, minimizing core. Neither can be it flattened into mere "symbol" for truths about ideas or ethereal realms.

Thus, the words *literal* and *figurative* easily contribute to an unhelpful polarization.

Overinterpretation or Underinterpretation?

Because any analogy involves both similarity and dissimilarity, it may not provide us with detailed technical information unless we artificially force such detail into our interpretation. For example, God "breathed into his [Adam's] nostrils the breath of life" (Gen. 2:7b). We should not deduce that God has a body that produced the "breath," and we do not know exactly what volume of air was used. We do not conclude that God used mouth-to-mouth resuscitation in exactly the same way as in modern human rescue operations.

God made the rib into a woman (Gen. 2:22b). But we cannot infer an exact relationship between Adam's DNA and Eve's. We do not know the technical details. We do not infer that God used physical fingers in the process of making Eve.

The tree of life was a physical tree. But we do not know whether it was an apple tree, a pear tree, or a tree with special fruit such as we never see today.

Genesis 1:6–8 provides no scientific "theory" about the physical structure of the expanse.

In short, it is easy to err by trying to supply extra details and imagining that they are actually there in Genesis 1–2. When we try to make correlations between Genesis 1–2 and modern science, we inevitably do fill in details, using information gathered from science. But we must not become confused and insist on reading those details directly back into Genesis 1–2. If we do, we are setting ourselves up for a clash if scientific opinion changes in the future.

It is also possible to err by denying phenomenal information that is actually provided by the text and claiming that the text has *only* the intention of supplying a very general picture—that God created the world and mankind. If we move in that direction, we lose details—for example, the indication that there was a special tree, called the tree of life. Under a minimizing interpretation, the tree of life becomes *only a symbol* for the general principle of life in the presence of God. We should take into account all the details that the text supplies, but still not *add* extra details.

Using analogy involves affirming both the physicality of the tree of life and its unique covenantal role, which includes symbolic dimensions. Though this one tree is unique, its significance also resonates with the significance of all fruit trees whatsoever. God gives us fruit trees for food (Deut. 6:11; Acts 14:17), and they symbolize the life of God that they reflect on a creaturely level, a level of lower intensity. No tree is merely prosaically a technical biological structure and "nothing more." All of creation testifies to the Creator (Rom. 1:20).

Similarly, in a minimizing symbolic interpretation of Genesis 1:9–10, the appearing of the dry land becomes *only a symbol* for the general principle that God sustains the distinction between the sea and the dry land, or *only a symbol* for God's power to triumph over chaos. By contrast, using analogy involves affirming the physical (i.e., phenomenal) reality of God's initial act in separating the sea and the dry land. Moreover, when Scripture chooses primarily to *show* God in action rather than merely to *tell* about who God is, that choice must be respected. What the narration of verses 9–10 shows, namely, God separating the sea from the dry land, carries its proper weight only if it is showing what God did actually do, not making up a fiction in order to tell who he always is. At the same time, we affirm the importance of this act as a manifestation of God's care and his faithfulness, which we now see in his commitment to preserve the separation. Through the continued separation of sea and dry land, God still provides today a suitable habitat for the land animals and mankind, and displays his goodness.

Consequently, we should acknowledge both a physical side to the descriptions in Genesis 1–3 and a theological side. Far from being in tension, the two reinforce each other.

Conclusion

What do we conclude? In interpreting Genesis 1–3, it is important to keep in mind several broader hermeneutical principles. Among the most significant are four, which we may highlight as we draw our reflections to a conclusion.

Four Significant Interpretive Principles

First, pronouncements made by modern scientists must be received critically. Science has made some wonderful achievements and has wonderful potential. But we need to note the widespread influence of bad presuppositions, bad metaphysics, and covert idolatry on the atmosphere of scientific research, as well as the simple fact that science is fallible. We must avoid twisting Genesis due to the assumption that it has to be made compatible with the "assured truths" of scientific claims.

Second, Genesis has a divine author who completely specified its contents and wording. It is completely true, and needs to be received in a manner distinct from merely human documents from the past.

Third, Genesis has a genre distinct from most other documents in the ancient Near East. On a fine-grained level, it is unique. It is most closely related in genre to other Old Testament historical books, such as 1–2 Samuel and 1–2 Kings. These observations about genre help us to avoid improperly assimilating Genesis 1–3 to ancient Near Eastern myths.

Fourth, we should keep in mind the key role of *analogy* between God's acts of creation and his later acts of providence.

Getting Some Answers

When we keep these principles in mind, some of the principal disputes about Genesis 1–3 begin to resolve themselves. Genesis 1–3 is about events that happened in the real world—it is nonfiction. It makes understandable claims about the past, claims that can be understood even by ordinary people because of its use of analogies between God's acts of creation and our ordinary experience of providence.

Not Having All the Answers

At the same time, because the descriptions use analogy rather than pure identity, there remain many questions of detail that Genesis 1–3 does not answer. In particular, it does not give us firm guidelines for positive scientific reconstruction of the far past, because the reality of analogy with ordinary providence is not a guarantee that all the detailed regularities of providence, including regularities of a specialized kind uncovered by scientists, can be naively extrapolated into the far past. Creation is not providence.

The upshot is that we may be left without a single overarching solution to questions about harmonizing Genesis with speculative reconstruction of the past on the basis of an appeal to scientifically known regularities. We believe in God's truthfulness and in the intrinsic harmony between what he says in the Bible and how he rules in creation and providence. But we cannot completely *demonstrate* to the satisfaction of a skeptic how harmony is achieved, because both we and the skeptic have limited human knowledge.

And however much that knowledge may grow while we are on earth, God has not seen fit to give us a detailed basis for extrapolation into the far past, because creation is not providence. "And on the seventh day God finished his work . . ." (Gen. 2:2a). In this verse, we have a positive, personal revelation about God and his relation to history. That revelatory statement produces a divinely given limitation to dogmatism about the details of how God did his work during the six days. We know that God did what he says he did in Genesis 1–2. But beyond what Genesis 1–2 says, we do not know the details with certainty. Scientific attempts at reconstruction have a dimension of speculation, because they assume (beyond the sparse account in Genesis 1–2) that certain specific temporal and physical regularities can be extrapolated into the far past. Typically the regularities are projected back even to the first moment of creation, "in the beginning." Maybe basic physical regularities did occur as far back as the first moment of creation.[1] But we are making an assumption. We should acknowledge our limited knowledge.

For some, it is easy to underinterpret Genesis 1–3, partly because modern scientific claims put pressure on interpreters to diminish the implications of Genesis 1–3 in areas where scientists have made pronouncements. For others, it is easy to overinterpret Genesis 1–3, because in their minds analogy becomes near identity, and so they easily assume a more detailed system of continuous technical regularities than what Genesis 1–3 actually provides.

God really did create the world in six days. He really did create Adam and Eve as human beings, made in the image of God—two individuals whose actions and fall into sin have affected the whole human race. We can be confident about these things, not only because Genesis 1–3 sets them forth, but because they are confirmed by later biblical reflections based on Genesis 1–3. But we do well to respect the sparseness of the account in Genesis and to remain tentative at some points as to how we think these truths are to be connected with modern scientific claims.

---

1. In chap. 14, our tentative concordance between Genesis 1 and epochs in the mainstream scientific account has such an assumption in the background.

Appendix A

Genesis 1:1 Is the First Event, Not a Summary

Commentaries regularly discuss three main interpretations of Genesis 1:1 in relation to the subsequent verses.[1] (1) According to the first, traditional interpretation, Genesis 1:1 describes the initial event

---

1. Gordon J. Wenham, *Genesis 1–15*, Word Biblical Commentary 1 (Waco, TX: Word, 1987), 11–13; C. John Collins, *Genesis 1–4: A Linguistic, Literary, and Theological Commentary* (Phillipsburg, NJ: P&R, 2006), 50–55; Edward J. Young, "The Relation of the First Verse of Genesis One to Verses Two and Three," *Westminster Theological Journal* 21, no. 2 (May 1959): 133–46, reprinted in Edward J. Young, *Studies in Genesis One* (Philadelphia: Presbyterian and Reformed, 1964), 1–14; Bruce K. Waltke, "The Creation Account in Genesis 1:1–3: Part III: The Initial Chaos Theory and the Precreation Chaos Theory," *Bibliotheca Sacra* 132 (1975): 216–28. For an extensive discussion, see Joshua D. Wilson, "A Case for the Traditional Translation and Interpretation of Genesis 1:1 Based upon a Multi-Leveled Linguistic Analysis," PhD diss., Southern Baptist Theological Seminary, 2010.
   Waltke's article, "The Creation Account in Genesis 1:1–3: Part III," is the third of five articles in which he addresses aspects of Gen. 1:1–3. The others are Bruce K. Waltke, "The Creation Account in Genesis 1:1–3: Part I: Introduction to Biblical Cosmogony," *Bibliotheca Sacra* 132 (1975): 25–36; "The Creation Account in Genesis 1:1–3: Part II: The Restitution Theory," *Bibliotheca Sacra* 132 (1975): 136–44; "The Creation Account in Genesis 1:1–3: Part IV: The Theology of Genesis 1," *Bibliotheca Sacra* 132 (1975): 327–42; and "The Creation Account in Genesis 1:1–3: Part V: The Theology of Genesis 1—Continued," *Bibliotheca Sacra* 133 (1976): 28–41. An editorial note accompanying each of these articles says that they are "adapted" from the Bueermann-Champion Foundation Lectures at Western Conservative Baptist Seminary, Portland, Oregon, delivered Oct. 1–4, 1974, and published as *Creation and Chaos* (Portland, OR: Western Conservative Baptist Seminary, 1974). We will focus on the 1975–1976 articles rather than the 1974 book because the articles are more recent and more widely accessible. (The pieces seem to be almost, but not quite, identical in wording in both the book and the journal.)
   Part III in the series in *Bibliotheca Sacra* is especially relevant for the purposes of this appendix, and I will regularly cite it simply as "Waltke, 'Part III.'" Waltke's 2001 commentary (Bruce K. Waltke, with Cathi J. Fredricks, *Genesis: A Commentary* [Grand Rapids, MI: Zondervan, 2001], 58–59) maintains the same basic interpretation of Gen. 1:1, but contains only a short version of the first of his three main arguments set forth in 1975. A later work also contains a shorter version of the first argument and a piece of the second: Bruce K. Waltke, with Charles Yu, *An Old Testament Theology: An Exegetical, Canonical, and Thematic Approach* (Grand Rapids, MI: Zondervan, 2007), 179–81.

among God's acts of creation. Verse 2 then gives circumstantial information about the state of the earth at an early point. (2) According to the second interpretation, verse 1 functions as a temporal subordinate clause: "In the beginning, when God created the heaven and the earth, the earth was without form . . ." (3) According to the third interpretation, verse 1 is a summary of the entire sequence of divine acts described in verses 2–31. It does *not* describe the very first event that led to the creation of the earth and its unformed state in verse 2. Rather, the first act of making things starts with verse 3, and Genesis 1 offers no comment on how the unformed earth of verse 2 came into being.[2]

The second interpretation has had many advocates, but it seems to be fading, and it has received a number of convincing refutations.[3] For the sake of brevity, we will confine ourselves to the debate between the first and the third interpretations. The first says that Genesis 1:1 is the initial event, and accordingly may be designated the *initiation view*. The third says that Genesis 1:1 is a summary, and accordingly may be designated the *summary view*.

The initiation view was common among earlier Jewish and Christian interpreters,[4] but it is no longer in such favor. In his 1987 commentary, Gordon Wenham indicates that "the majority" of modern commentators favor the summary view.[5]

Beyond the three interpretations summarized in this paragraph, a fourth interpretation, sometimes called "the gap theory," now receives little attention. But it used to be advocated, and was popularized by the Scofield Bible note on Gen. 1:2. *The Scofield Reference Bible*, ed. C. I. Scofield, new and improved edition (New York: Oxford University Press, 1917), 3n3. The theory says that there is a time gap between verses 1 and 2. Verse 1 briefly describes God's creation of an initial good creation, while verse 2 describes a subsequent ruination ("the earth *became* without form and void") of that creation as an act of judgment. Verses 3–31 describe a re-creation after the ruination. In support of this idea, Scofield's note cites Jer. 4:23–26; Isa. 24:1; 45:18. But the gap theory is now largely abandoned because it is does not conform to the natural reading of the Hebrew in Gen. 1:2. The word order of verse 2 indicates that the verse introduces an accompanying circumstance rather than an advance in the main events in the narrative. For a critique of the gap theory, see Waltke, "The Creation Account in Genesis 1:1–3: Part II."

2. This appendix is a revision of Vern S. Poythress, "Genesis 1:1 Is the First Event, Not a Summary," *Westminster Theological Journal* 79, no. 1 (2017): 97–121. Used with permission.

3. Waltke, "Part III," 221–25; Collins, *Genesis 1–4*, 50–52; Victor P. Hamilton, *The Book of Genesis, Chapters 1–17* (Grand Rapids, MI: Eerdmans, 1990), 104–8; Young, "Relation," 133–39; Young, *Studies in Genesis One*, 1–7; Nicolai Winther-Nielsen, "'In the Beginning' of Biblical Hebrew Discourse," in *Language in Context: Essays for Robert E. Longacre*, ed. Shin Ja J. Hwang and William R. Merrifield (Dallas TX: The Summer Institute of Linguistics and the University of Texas at Arlington, 1992), 67–80, https://www.sil.org/system/files/reapdata/12/98/61/12986188336927782352102945248120690455031844.pdf; Wilson, "A Case," 60–112.

4. Waltke, "Part III," 217.

5. Wenham, *Genesis 1–15*, 12.

Major Arguments for the Initiation View

The initiation view still has its defenders. Commentaries by C. John Collins, Wenham, and others advocate it.[6] But because of space limitations, these commentaries interact only briefly with the summary view. I wish to engage more thoroughly with the summary view, focusing especially on its fullest articulation in a key article by Bruce K. Waltke.[7]

In this analysis, I will treat Genesis as a literary unity, as Waltke does. By contrast, the historical-critical tradition breaks Genesis apart, and usually finds layers of meanings at times earlier than the extant form of Genesis 1. I will not deal with this line of speculation.[8] For simplicity, I will mostly quote from the English Standard Version, but it is to be understood that the arguments are ultimately framed in terms of the underlying Hebrew text.

Let us begin by briefly noting the three main arguments for the initiation view.

1. *Cohesion between verses 1 and 2: the initial state of the earth as without form.*

The first argument appeals to the close connection between Genesis 1:1 and 2. The term *the earth* (הָאָרֶץ) occurs as the last term in verse 1 and the first main term in verse 2. The syntactic linkage between the two verses consists in a waw-conjunctive, which, when followed by a noun and then the main verb of the clause, customarily introduces circumstantial information.[9] (By contrast, the waw-consecutive plus imperfect is the usual way of introducing new main events in a narrative sequence.) Verse 2 is providing circumstantial information.

---

6. Collins, *Genesis 1–4*, 51–55; Wenham, *Genesis 1–15*, 12–13. Wenham also cites others; *Genesis 1–15*, 13.

7. Waltke, "Part III." Collins considers Waltke's article to be "the strongest case" for the summary view. Collins, *Genesis 1–4*, 54.

8. The commentaries on Genesis have voluminous discussion of source theories. Source theories can make a difference, because they often treat Gen. 1:2 as stemming from a primitive tradition that starts with chaos and thereby repudiates any idea of creation out of nothing. If someone accepts this assumption and treats verse 2 as still meaning what it meant at the earlier stage, he has already confined himself to only two options: either to say that verse 1 does not describe creation out of nothing or to say that it contradicts verse 2 because two disparate sources have not been satisfactorily united. My approach is to interpret the text as it stands and to presuppose that, even if there are sources behind it, the meaning of the text can differ from its sources (see chap. 6, p. 112). The completed text of Genesis is the inspired, inerrant Word of God.

9. Waltke agrees that Gen. 1:2 is circumstantial, and that "on syntactical grounds" it could be attached backward to verse 1. "Part III," 221. However, he thinks that it provides circumstantial information connecting it forward to verse 3. "Part III," 226–27. On circumstantial clauses, see Paul Joüon, *A Grammar of Biblical Hebrew* (Roma: Editrice Pontificio Istituto Biblico, 1996), §155nc.

The significant point here is what *kind* of circumstantial information is introduced in Genesis 1:2. It is information about the state of the earth. Since the earth has just been introduced in the preceding verse, the information specifies the state of the earth that was mentioned in verse 1. It follows that the act of creation mentioned in verse 1 results in an earth that is "without form and void." "The earth" is *not* the formed and filled earth at which the narrative arrives by verse 31, and which is summarized in 2:1: "Thus the heavens and the earth were *finished*, and all the *host* [the furnishings, implying that the earth was no longer empty or "void"] of them." The early unformed state of the earth is described by 1:2 *with reference to the earth of verse 1*. So verse 1 cannot be a summary. That is to say, the expression "the heavens and the earth" in verse 1 does not refer to the heavens and the earth in their completed form (2:1), as a summary might do. Rather, it refers to the heavens and the earth in an immature state.

2. *Theological purpose: the assertion of absolute divine sovereignty.*

A second argument focuses on the theological purpose of Genesis 1. It is clear that 1:1–2:3[10] as a whole strongly asserts the full and effective sovereignty of God. He is the one true God who controls and rules over everything that he has made. In its majestic monotheism, the passage contrasts strongly with the polytheism of the cultures of the ancient Near East. It also contrasts with ancient Near Eastern cosmogonic narratives that involve the birth of gods and conflicts between gods. In Genesis 1, there is no plurality of gods. There are no birth events. There is no mention of conflict. God personally rules and brings about his will.

It is therefore fitting that the narrative of creation should assert God's sovereignty not only over *some* of the things in the world, but over *all*. God's sovereignty must include not only ruling over the development of things that already exist, but controlling the very being and constitution of whatever exists. This comprehensive sovereignty must include the original earth, which is without form, and the deep. Otherwise, the earth is left as a potential *independent* entity. If God did not make it, if it is just eternally there, its original constitution escapes God's sovereignty, and God just has to do the best he can

---

10. On the literary division occurring between Genesis 2:3 and 4, see Collins, *Genesis 1–4*, 40–42.

with material that he did not originally specify. Moreover, according to those assumptions, the earth may be just as eternal as God himself. Anything coeternal with God, even an impersonal coeternal, is really a rival to complete sovereignty.[11] So it is fitting that the narrative in Genesis 1:1 closes this door to rivalry by indicating that the initial act of creation includes the creation of the earth and, by implication, the deep that covers its surface. By contrast, the summary view postulates that the earth and the deep are already there, without any explanation, *before* God begins to create in verse 3.[12] This postulate is in tension with the overall theological purpose of Genesis 1.

3. *Narrative structure: the use of the perfect verb for an antecedent event.*

A third argument focuses on the narrative structure in Genesis 1:1–2. Collins argues that the use of the Hebrew perfect tense at the commencement of a narrative normally refers to an antecedent event.[13] His case can be strengthened by observing two cases where such a structure occurs at the beginning of a whole book.

בִּשְׁנַת שָׁלוֹשׁ לְמַלְכוּת יְהוֹיָקִים מֶלֶךְ־יְהוּדָה בָּא נְבוּכַדְנֶאצַּר מֶלֶךְ־בָּבֶל יְרוּשָׁלַם וַיָּצַר עָלֶיהָ
(Dan. 1:1)

In the third year of the reign of Jehoiakim king of Judah, Nebuchadnezzar king of Babylon came to Jerusalem and besieged it.

The grammatical structure in Hebrew is parallel to Genesis 1:1:

בְּרֵאשִׁית בָּרָא אֱלֹהִים אֵת הַשָּׁמַיִם וְאֵת הָאָרֶץ

In the beginning, God created the heavens and the earth.

In Daniel 1:1, we first have a temporal marker ("In the third year of the reign of Jehoiakim king of Judah") parallel to the temporal marker "in the beginning" in Genesis 1:1.[14] Then, in the Hebrew word

11. Wayne A. Grudem, *Systematic Theology: An Introduction to Biblical Doctrine* (Grand Rapids, MI: Zondervan, 1994), 264.

12. Young advocates a form of the summary view, but also thinks that Gen. 1:1, though not directly focusing on the initial act of creation out of nothing, indirectly implies it. Young, "Relation," 141; *Studies in Genesis One*, 9.

13. Collins, *Genesis 1–4*, 51–52.

14. On the absence of the article in the Hebrew underlying "in the beginning," see Waltke, "Part III," 221–25; Alexander Heidel, *The Babylonian Genesis: The Story of Creation*, 2nd ed.,

order, comes a perfect verb ("came," בָּא), parallel to the perfect verb "created" (בָּרָא) in Genesis 1:1. Then comes the subject, "Nebuchadnezzar king of Babylon," which is parallel to the subject "God" in Genesis 1:1.

A similar example occurs in Ezra 1:1:

> In the first year [וּבִשְׁנַת אַחַת] of Cyrus king of Persia, that the word of the LORD by the mouth of Jeremiah might be fulfilled, the LORD stirred up [הֵעִיר יְהוָה] the spirit of Cyrus king of Persia, so that he made a proclamation throughout all his kingdom and also put it in writing.

Unlike Daniel 1:1, the verse begins with a waw-conjunctive. But then comes the temporal marker, "in the first year of Cyrus king of Persia," parallel to the expression "in the beginning" in Genesis 1:1. Then comes an infinitive clause of purpose, "that the word of the LORD by the mouth of Jeremiah might be fulfilled," which is an extra element in comparison with Genesis 1:1. Then comes a verb in the perfect, "stirred up" (הֵעִיר), and then the subject, "the LORD."

In both Daniel 1:1 and Ezra 1:1, the opening describes the first event rather than giving a summary of the subsequent narrative. The grammatical structure in both verses is parallel to Genesis 1:1. So, reasoning by analogy, we conclude that Genesis 1:1 describes the first event in relation to the narrative in verses 2–31.

The Summary View

Now we turn to the summary view of Genesis 1:1. The summary view has many advocates. For the sake of simplicity, and for the sake of allowing a fuller discussion, we focus on Waltke as the best representative of that view.[15] Waltke opposes each of the three arguments above with a corresponding counterargument. We shall consider each of them in turn.

The Heavens and the Earth as Already Ordered

The first counterargument is that the expression "the heavens and the earth" in Genesis 1:1 designates "the *organized* universe, the

---

3rd impression (Chicago/London: University of Chicago Press, 1963), 92–93; Collins, *Genesis 1–4*, 51n50; Hamilton, *Genesis, Chapters 1–17*, 103–8; Winther-Nielsen, "In the Beginning," 67–80.

15. Waltke, "Part III," 216–28. Waltke, *Genesis*, 58–59, and *Old Testament Theology*, 179–81, also contain shortened versions of some of the same arguments.

cosmos."[16] It is *not* the unorganized state described in verse 2. If the heavens and earth are organized in verse 1, it follows that the endpoint of God's activity of creating, as described in the verse, must be the same endpoint at which the narrative arrives in verse 31. This endpoint is then summarized in 2:1, "Thus the heavens and the earth were *finished*." So Genesis 1:1 gives in summary form the same sequence of activities that is expounded in detail in the rest of the chapter, verses 2–31.

In favor of this interpretation of the expression "the heavens and the earth," Waltke has three subpoints: (1) "the heaven(s) and the earth" is a merism, that is, a designation of the whole using two opposite polarities, so the expression must be considered *as a whole*; (2) the Hebrew expression always designates the ordered or organized cosmos; and (3) consequently, to postulate a distinct meaning in Genesis 1:1 would violate standard philology.

On the surface, this line of argument may sound reasonable. But with respect to each of the three points, there is some vagueness in the claims, and there are some slippery points in the arguments.

1. *A merism.*

The first subpoint is that the expression "the heavens and the earth" (אֵת הַשָּׁמַיִם וְאֵת הָאָרֶץ in the underlying Hebrew) is a merism.[17] Waltke elsewhere defines a merism as "a figure of speech involving opposites to indicate totality."[18] In discussing Genesis 1:1, Waltke illustrates with various expressions: "they came, great and small" and "the blessed man meditates in God's law 'day and night,' i.e., 'all the time.'"[19]

The appeal to merism is significant because Waltke thinks that it lays the groundwork for his second point about the reference to the organized universe. It is true that the key expression is a merism, but as we shall see, it does not help Waltke's case.

Many merisms are relatively "transparent" in meaning. The meaning of the whole can easily be inferred from the meaning of the two

---

16. Waltke, "Part III," 218 (emphasis added); *Old Testament Theology*, 179; so also Young, "Relation," 142n17; *Studies in Genesis One*, 10n17.
17. Waltke, "Part III," 218; *Old Testament Theology*, 179.
18. Bruce K. Waltke, *A Commentary on Micah* (Grand Rapids, MI: Eerdmans, 2007), 456.
19. Waltke, "Part III," 218. The first of the two illustrative merisms is quoted by Waltke from Cyrus H. Gordon, *The World of the Old Testament* (Garden City, NY: Doubleday, 1958), 35. See also Waltke, *Old Testament Theology*, 179.

opposites. For example, the expression "day and night" covers all the time if we allow that the expression could cover by implication times of transition between full daytime and full nighttime, that is, the times of twilight. Similarly, the classic merisms in the marriage vows, "for richer, for poorer" and "in sickness and in health," cover all the human conditions if we allow for situations that are intermediate (for example, recovering health after being sick). The expression "the heavens and the earth" in Hebrew is similar because "the heavens" usually refers to what is above and "the earth" refers to what is below us or at least lower down, below the heavens. Together, the two make up everything that we see. So the meaning of the compound expression "the heavens and the earth" is transparently composed from the meanings of the two main constituents, "the heavens" and "the earth."

Why is the transparency of meaning significant? Waltke says that the expression "the heavens and the earth" "is a compound phrase that must be studied as a unity."[20] But what does it mean for a compound to "be studied as a unity"? It could mean merely that the full import of the compound should not be deduced *merely* by taking the two main words "in isolation from one another."[21] But it could also mean that, once we see the unity of the compound, it must be studied in isolation from the two main words that compose it. In other words, we ignore all the occurrences of the words *heavens* and *earth* outside of the compound expression. We treat the compound expression as if it were completely equivalent to saying, "God made everything."

This is not a trivial issue. If, in Genesis 1:1, we replace the expression "the heavens and the earth" with some other expression, such as "all things" (John 1:3) or "visible and invisible" (Col. 1:16), we lose the key connection between "the earth" in Genesis 1:1 and "the earth" in verse 2, which is important for determining the state of the earth in verse 1. Similarly, if we assume that the compound expression in verse 1 must be isolated from the expression "the earth" in verse 2 (because the compound is somehow a seamless whole), we arrive at a similar result, wherein verse 2 is disconnected from verse 1. We fail

---

20. Waltke, "Part III," 218.
21. Waltke, "Part III," 218.

to do justice to the significance of the occurrence of the particular expression "the earth" in both verses. Waltke's argument never discusses this problem.[22]

Waltke quotes approvingly from Umberto Cassuto, who uses the English word *broadcast* to illustrate the principle that the meaning of a compound ("broadcast") cannot be deduced from the meaning of its parts ("broad" and "cast").[23] But the example does not prove what it is supposed to prove. The question is whether the compound "the heavens and the earth" works in the same way as the compound "broadcast." It does not. As I indicated, many merisms are, by their nature, transparent in meaning, as the examples "day and night" and "in sickness and in health" illustrate. In determining the meaning of a merism, it is necessary only to adjust to the fact that the two polar opposites, by being adjoined, are meant by implication to encompass any intermediates. So the meaning of a merism is deducible from the meaning of its constituents. This transparency of meaning allows us to multiply merisms indefinitely. For example, we can have any number of merisms to describe humanity: rich and poor, slave and free, big and small, young and old, strong and weak, short and tall, educated and uneducated, employed and unemployed, and so on. Given

---

22. Young, who advocates a form of the summary view, *does* notice the problem. In explanation, he writes:

> Verse two does obviously [!] connect with verse one and employs the word הָאָרֶץ in a sense different from that which it had in the first verse. (Young, "Relation," 142n17; *Studies in Genesis One*, 10n17)

Elsewhere Young further clarifies:

> [T]he word הָאָרֶץ does not have precisely the same connotation which it bore in verse one. In the first verse it went with the word הַשָּׁמַיִם to form a combination which designates the well-ordered world and universe that we now know. In verse two, however, it depicts the earth as being in an uninhabitable condition. (Edward J. Young, "The Interpretation of Genesis 1:2," *Westminster Theological Journal* 23, no. 2 [1961]: 168)

Rather than provide a supporting argument, Young's explanation seems only to illustrate the difficulty. On the one hand, he says that there is an obvious connection between Gen. 1:1 and 2. And we can see that the heart of the connection consists in the repetition of the term "the earth." On the other hand, he thinks there is a radical difference: "the earth" in verse 1 is the organized earth, while "the earth" in verse 2 is yet to be formed and organized.

Other analysts, such as Hermann Gunkel, escape the problem by postulating that verses 1 and 2 go back to distinct sources. Hermann Gunkel, *Genesis*, trans. Mark E. Biddle (Macon, GA: Mercer University Press, 1997), 104 (103 in the original German).

The difficulty is generated only if an interpreter—whether Waltke, Young, Gunkel, or another—decides that verse 1 is referring to the *organized*, completed heaven and earth. This move is a common mistake. How it came to be so common is revealed in our subsequent discussion.

23. Waltke, "Part III," 218, citing Umberto Cassuto, *A Commentary on the Book of Genesis*, 2 vols. (Jerusalem: Magnes, 1961), 1.22; Waltke, *Old Testament Theology*, 179, offers the example "*Butterfly* is quite different from *butter* and *fly*."

an appropriate context, discerning the meaning of the compound is easy. Our ability to discern the meaning is not significantly affected by whether the compound is already a common, well-known, fixed expression.

Note also that, while all the merisms for humanity have the same referent, namely, humanity, none is strictly synonymous with any other. "Rich and poor" draws attention to a financial polarity; "slave and free" draws attention to the polarity between freedom and non-freedom; and so on. The merism "educated and uneducated" might occur suitably in a context where naively it might be thought that education would affect people's situations, but where in fact it does not—all humanity, both educated and uneducated, belong together.

The same holds for the expression "the heavens and the earth." We can see that it refers to the whole world precisely because its two major inner constituents have polar meanings that are used to refer to the two major spatial regions of the world. Like many other merisms, the meaning of the whole is transparently derivable from the meanings of the two parts.

So let us look more carefully at how Waltke treats the compound expression "the heavens and the earth." Citing Cyrus Gordon with approval, Waltke uses the illustration that "in English, the expression 'they came, great and small' means that 'everybody came.'"[24] There is some vagueness here with the word *means*. The sample statement using the compound expression "great and small" *implies* that "everybody came." It "means" that, in a loose sense of the word *means*. But if we substitute "everybody" for "great and small," we change the sense subtly, precisely by eliminating the fact that the compound expression is transparent to its two inner components, "great" and "small," and operates by inviting us to conceive of humanity as composed of these two polar parts. The "meaning," in a more nuanced sense, includes a focus of attention on the two extremes—great and small—and then everyone in between. Likewise, the distinct meanings of *heavens* and *earth* do not totally disappear in the compound. They are still "visible"; they are "transparent" in their contribution to the full meaning of the compound expression.

---

24. Waltke, "Part III," 218, citing Cyrus H. Gordon, *The World of the Old Testament* (Garden City, NY: Doubleday, 1958), 35.

2. *The claim of an organized universe.*

A second element in Waltke's argumentation is the claim that the compound expression designates "the organized universe, the cosmos." But here we must be careful to distinguish the *sense* of an expression from its *referent*. For the sake of clarity, let us illustrate the difference between sense and referent. The expression "the father of Isaac" *refers* to Abraham, but the *sense* or *meaning* of the phrase "the father of Isaac" is roughly "the first-generation male parent of the person designated Isaac." The sense does not contain everything we know about the referent (Abraham). Similarly, we may refer to Philadelphia as "the largest city in Pennsylvania," as "the city where the Delaware River and the Schuylkill River flow together," as "the city where the Liberty Bell is," as "the place where the Declaration of Independence was signed," or as "the first U.S. capital." These expressions all have the same referent, but they differ in what sort of information they provide about that referent. They differ in *sense*.

Once we make this distinction, we can see that there is a potential problem with how we go about analyzing the expression "the heavens and the earth." We must distinguish the *sense* of the expression from what it *refers* to in any particular case of its use. The great majority of occurrences of this expression in the Old Testament *refer* to the world in an organized state. Why? Because, subsequent to the completion of God's work of creation, the world remains in an organized state (we may make a partial exception for the time of the flood of Noah). In addition, subsequent to Genesis 1–3, nearly every use of the expression refers to the world in a state of historical development brought about by human activities and human births and deaths. Therefore, if we are talking about the *referent*, we may say that in most cases the compound expression "the heavens and the earth" designates a world that already has undergone human historical development. We may also say that it designates a world that shows the effects of the fall.

But it would be erroneous to take all this information about the *referent* and read it back into the *sense* of the expression, as if the sense included the idea of historical development and the idea of effects of the fall. Such reading back would be just as mistaken as if I were to claim that the *sense* of the expression "the largest city in Pennsylvania" included all the voluminous information about the referent, namely, the actual city with all its material, structural, economic, and social dimensions. Likewise, we must ask with some care, "Does the *sense* of the expression 'the heavens and the earth' include the idea of *organization*, which idea certainly belongs to the referent, at least in the great majority of cases?" It will not do just to go through the various occurrences, noting that the *referent* is organized.

Is this an artificial problem? Waltke's own use of terminology is not reassuring, because it seems sometimes to focus on the referent and sometimes on the sense, without clearly distinguishing the two. Consider the following two paragraphs in Waltke's argument:

> So here, "the heavens and the earth" are antonyms to *designate* "everything," and more specifically "the organized universe, the cosmos." In fact, Wisdom of Solomon [11:17] uses the Greek words ὁ κόσμος to *refer* to Genesis 1:1.
>
> This is undoubtedly the *sense* of the compound in the summary statement concluding the creation account: "Thus the heavens and the earth were completed, and all their hosts" (Gen. 2:1). The compound occurs again in this *sense* in the summary statement introducing the stories about man [Gen. 2:4] . . . this compound never has the *meaning* of disorderly chaos but always of an orderly world.[25]

The shift from terms about reference ("designate," "refer") to terms about meaning ("sense," "meaning") does not show awareness of a distinction between reference and meaning. And the sentence discussing the Wisdom of Solomon is inexact. More precisely, it should say that the words ὁ κόσμος refer to the universe and allude to Genesis 1:1.

We can further illustrate the problem by dipping into the specific evidence concerning the usages of the expression "the heavens and the earth" and other textual expressions that have the pair *heaven* and *earth*. Waltke first mentions Genesis 2:1 in the quotation provided above. He writes, "This is *undoubtedly* the sense of the compound." But once we make the distinction between sense and reference, the evidence fails to have any force. In Genesis 2:1, the compound expression *refers* to the completed heavens and earth. But the *sense* may still turn out

---

25. Waltke, "Part III," 218 (emphasis added).

to be little more than "what is above" and "what is below," taken together. The sense does not automatically accumulate everything that we know about the state of the referent at the time to which the sentence refers when it uses the compound expression. In using the word *undoubtedly*, Waltke has passed over a difficulty. He does not note that the compound could have a fairly minimal *sense* and still *refer* to a universe that happened to be organized at the time to which the reference was made.

Even when we focus on the *referent* of Genesis 2:1 instead of the *sense*, we find a subtle difficulty. Genesis 2:1 mentions not only "the heavens and the earth," but also "all the host of them." The expression "all the host of them" refers to things in the sphere of the heavens, like the heavenly bodies and the birds, and things in the sphere of the earth, like the plants and the animals.[26] These hosts are distinguished from the heavens and the earth themselves. So the expression "the heavens and the earth" in this context focuses primarily on the spatial regions, in distinction from their "host" or inhabitants (compare Jer. 51:48). Consequently, "the heavens and the earth" is *not* simply a synonym for "everything." It would be odd to say, "Everything was completed, and all its host." "Everything" cannot have inhabitants distinct from "everything," because the inhabitants are already included in the referent of "everything."

In this respect, the compound expression "the heavens and the earth" has the same flexibility in its use as the constituent expression "the earth." "The earth" sometimes serves to designate the lower *region*, particularly the solid ground (Gen. 1:11, 28, 29; 7:3; 8:17, 19; 11:8; etc.), and sometimes to designate inclusively the region *together with* everything on it (Gen. 2:4; 6:11; 9:11, 13; Ex. 19:5; etc.). The flexibility in use confirms that the compound expression is not a rigid, technical term, but transparently reflects the flexibility in its constituent terms.

Another difficulty arises because of a certain vagueness in the idea of being "organized" or "ordered." How much organization is needed before we consider something organized? Well, it depends on the circumstances, the purposes, and interests of those who evaluate a

---

26. In some verses, "host" is the host of angels (1 Kings 22:19), but the word can also refer to human "hosts" (1 Sam. 17:46; Ps. 68:11, 18) or to the heavenly lights (Deut. 4:19).

particular object or region. In a minimal sense, the earth in Genesis 1:2 already shows organization. First, there is the deep, which has some kind of surface, but also involves a larger body of material of which the surface is the upper, exposed part. So the deep is "organized" into two parts, the surface and the depth beneath the surface. Second, the deep together with its surface is "organized" in relation to the space above it, in which the Spirit of God[27] is hovering. The space in question is distinct from the deep and is in place over it.

In addition, there is organized movement within this space. The Spirit is hovering. This description of hovering suggests that the space is like our normal space with three distinct dimensions, one of which is the up-and-down dimension. That in itself is a kind of "organization."

Moreover, as we learn from Genesis 1:9, a solid entity is already present underneath the liquidlike "deep." Verse 9 does not say that God made or created the dry land alongside the waters. Neither does it say that he caused the dry land to be congealed out of the waters. Rather, the waters were "gathered together" so that the dry land might "appear." This description implies that the solid material already existed underneath. If so, presumably it already existed in verse 2.

Therefore, in Genesis 1:2, the early stage of "the earth" has a vertical arrangement involving at least six distinct elements: the space over the Spirit, the Spirit himself, the space under the Spirit, the surface of the deep, the deep under the surface, and the solid ground underneath the deep. If we combine the space over and under the Spirit, and consider them as a single distinct element in the midst of which the Spirit is hovering, we still have five elements, and they are structurally organized in specific ways in relation to each other.

So the earth in Genesis 1:2 already has some degree of organization. While the earth is "without form and void," Collins points out that that is not equivalent to saying that it is total chaos. He explains, "'[W]ithout form and void' (Gen. 1:2) is not a term for 'disorderly chaos' but pictures the earth as 'an unproductive and uninhabited place.'"[28]

The scholars who insist on the meaning "organized universe" for the compound "the heavens and the earth" do not tell us how organized

---

27. Hamilton makes the case for the sense "Spirit of God." *Genesis, Chapters 1–17*, 111–14.
28. Collins, *Genesis 1–4*, 54.

the universe must be before it can appropriately be designated using the compound. If we push in one direction, the situation in Genesis 1:2 is already sufficiently organized, and Waltke's argument loses all force. Let us, therefore, try to push in the other direction. Let us specify that the universe has to be organized as completely as it is now in order to count as "organized." Then we create tension with Genesis 2:1. The verse says that "the heavens and the earth were *finished*," implying that they underwent a *process* to get to their finished state. If so, the implication would seem to be that they are appropriately called "the heavens and the earth" while they are still in the process. (Otherwise, the wording would presumably have been something like "the region above was completed, and the region below was completed, and so God made the heavens and the earth"—that is, the organized spaces are called "the heavens and the earth" only at the endpoint.) In reply to this point, the defender of the idea of complete organization could argue that the earlier stages are only indirectly or proleptically being treated as worthy of the appellation "the heavens and the earth." But even that is a partial concession.[29]

So the actual wording in Genesis 2:1 exhibits some tension with the idea that everything has to be "finished" in order for the whole to be called "the heavens and the earth." This tension further illustrates that Genesis 2:1 does not actually provide positive evidence (as opposed to neutral or negative evidence) for the thesis that the *meaning* of the merism includes as an essential feature the idea of organization.

We find a similar difficulty with Waltke's interpretation of Genesis 2:4. He cites this verse as a second indication that "the heavens and the earth" means the organized universe. But, as usual, the meaning needs to be distinguished from the referent. The meaning is not to be equated with everything that we know about the referent. Even if we suppose that the *referent* in Genesis 2:4 is as fully organized as we might want, yet that does not imply by itself that the *meaning* of the merism includes as an essential feature the idea of organization.

As for the referent for Genesis 2:4, it is once again not so clear how organized it has to be. We may see the difficulty by focusing on the expression "the day" in verse 4, that is, "the day that the LORD God

---

29. In another context in his article, Waltke rejects an explanation that appeals to proleptic use of the compound expression "the heavens and the earth." Waltke, "Part III," 219. His rejection of proleptic use only increases the difficulty that his view has with Gen. 2:1.

made the earth and the heavens." This period when God makes things may include the entire span of 1:1–31. In that case, the expression "the earth and the heavens" may be designating the universe as it exists all the way through the process, including its beginning as well as its end. So again, 2:4 does not support the theory that the compound expression includes the idea of organization in its meaning.

Waltke's interpretation has still another difficulty, which is even more serious. As we observed, the expression "the heavens and the earth" is transparently built out of its two main constituents, "the heavens" and "the earth." Both of these regions are referred to not only at the end, when they are fully organized, but several times in the course of the narrative in 1:2–31 (the heavens: 1:9, 14, 15, 17, 20, 26, 28, 30; the earth: 1:2, 11 [twice], 12, 15, 17, 20, 22, 24, 25, 26 [twice], 28 [twice], 29, 30 [twice]). And 1:2 provides clear information. The earth is appropriately designated "the earth" even while it is "without form and void." Since the meaning of the compound "the heavens and the earth" is built out of the constituent meanings of the parts, verse 2 represents clear evidence that the compound as well as its constituent parts does not innately contain, as an integral and essential element of its *sense*, the idea of a thorough organization. The idea that organization is included in its sense is an illusion created by a confusion between sense and reference.

Waltke summarizes his argument by saying:

> If this understanding [that the meaning is "organized universe"], based on its extensive and unambiguous usage in the creation account itself and elsewhere is allowed, then Genesis 1:2 cannot be construed as a circumstantial clause.[30]

This summary is not reassuring. Waltke talks about "extensive and unambiguous usage." He intends thereby to include in principle many other occurrences of the compound expression (he says, "and elsewhere"). But he has cited only two verses, Genesis 2:1 and 4. And neither verse is unambiguous in its evidence. In a careful analysis that distinguishes sense and referent, neither verse shows

---

30. Waltke, "Part III," 219. For proper punctuation, the quoted material should have an extra comma after "elsewhere." I have let it stand as it is printed in the article. Waltke, *Creation and Chaos*, 26, includes the extra comma.

any positive evidence that the idea of organization is an essential element of the sense, in distinction from the referent. Waltke has also ignored the evidence offered by 1:2. As for the many other occurrences of the compound expression within the Old Testament, we would have to look at them one by one to see just what evidence they offer. The evidence that has been offered through Genesis 2:1 and 4 is not convincing. In fact, in subtle ways, 2:1 and 4 both present problems for Waltke's thesis.

How, then, do we actually assess whether the idea of *organization* is an essential component of the sense of the expression "the heavens and the earth"? We have already done so by our previous observation that the meaning of the compound is transparently composed of the meaning of the parts. The idea of organization is not an essential component of the meaning of "the earth" in Genesis 1:2, so neither is it an essential component of the compound.[31]

Moreover, the compound, through its composition out of two polar opposites, functions like other merisms. It enables a reference to a larger whole precisely through the use of the opposites. The particular kind of opposition is still visible in the meaning of the whole. For example, as mentioned before, the merism "educated and uneducated" refers to humanity in terms of two parts distinguished by means of education. It thereby draws attention not to the age distinctions within humanity (young and old), the beauty or ugliness of humanity, or the "organization" of humanity, but to one criterion only, namely, education. Likewise, the merism "the heavens and the earth" refers to the world in terms of two parts distinguished as higher and lower regions within the whole. The focus, if any, is on the world as composed of regions, and the regions are located in two distinct vertical directions with reference to the observer. This focus on the regions and their locations actually counts against the idea that *organization* rather than *space* is essential to the meaning.

We could also go through all the occurrences of the expression "the heavens and the earth" and related expressions in the Old Testament. Many of these would have the organized universe as their *referent*. But because of the distinction between sense and referent, it would be

---

31. In favor of the idea of organization, Waltke ("Part III," 218–19) includes a supporting quote from John Skinner, *A Critical and Exegetical Commentary on Genesis* (Edinburgh: T&T Clark, 1910), 14. But Skinner provides no evidence for his claim.

a delicate task, not a trivial one, to show that this information about referent has any implications at all for incorporation of the idea of organization into the *sense*.

It is nevertheless informative to search through joint occurrences of *heavens* and *earth* to see the range of usage. We easily find many cases where the two terms occur in a paired way, but not in the exact expression "the heavens and the earth."

> May God give you of the dew of *heaven*
>> and of the fatness of the *earth*
>> and plenty of grain and wine. (Gen. 27:28)

> And I will break the pride of your power, and I will make your *heavens* like iron and your *earth* like bronze. (Lev. 26:19; cf. Deut. 28:23)

> Out of *heaven* he let you hear his voice, that he might discipline you. And on *earth* he let you see his great fire, and you heard his words out of the midst of the fire. (Deut. 4:36)

> Behold, to the LORD your God belong *heaven* and the heaven of heavens, the *earth* with all that is in it. (Deut. 10:14)

> . . . that your days and the days of your children may be multiplied in the land that the LORD swore to your fathers to give them, as long as the *heavens* are above the *earth*. (Deut. 11:21)

> The LORD your God, he is God in the *heavens* above and on the *earth* beneath. (Josh. 2:11b)

> On that day the LORD will punish
>> the host of *heaven, in heaven,*
>> and the kings of the *earth*, on the *earth*. (Isa. 24:21)

> Thus says the LORD:
> "*Heaven* is my throne,
>> and the *earth* is my footstool." (Isa. 66:1)

There is actually considerable variety. And in a number of instances, it is clear that the polarity between spatial locations, above and below, is very much operative.

We can also find passages with the expression "the heavens and the earth" that are quite similar to passages with a looser pairing between the two terms, *heavens* and *earth*. Compare, for example, Jeremiah 32:17a with 51:15:

Ah, Lord GOD! It is you who have made *the heavens and the earth* by your great power and by your outstretched arm! (Jer. 32:17a)

It is he who made the *earth* by his power,
   who established the world by his wisdom,
and by his understanding stretched out the *heavens*. (Jer. 51:15)

The similarities suggest that the expression "God made the heavens and the earth" is similar in meaning to "God made the heavens and God made the earth." The constituent expressions "the heavens" and "the earth" have their normal meanings in both contexts.

Consider also Deuteronomy 31:28 in relation to 32:1, which comes only a few verses later:

Assemble to me all the elders of your tribes and your officers, that I may speak these words in their ears and call *heaven and earth* [אֶת־הַשָּׁמַיִם וְאֶת־הָאָרֶץ] to witness against them. (Deut. 31:28)

Give ear, O *heavens* [הַשָּׁמַיִם], and I will speak,
   and let *the earth* [הָאָרֶץ] hear the words of my mouth.
     (Deut. 32:1)

Deuteronomy 31:28 contains the compound expression in its typical form. Deuteronomy 32:1 separates the two terms *heaven* and *earth*. But the two verses are talking about the same thing. In Deuteronomy 31:28, God says that he will call "heaven and earth" to witness. After the assembly is gathered (v. 30), in 32:1 God does just what he said he would do by commanding the heavens and the earth to listen to the succeeding words. In both 31:28 and 32:1, heaven and earth are personified. But given this figure of speech, the words *heaven* and *earth* have the same function inside and outside of the compound expression used in 31:28. So a comparison of these two verses in Deuteronomy supports the idea that the compound expression is transparent to the meanings of its two main constituents.

We can also find a few passages where heaven and the earth occur together with the sea, or with the sea and the dry land:

> For in six days the LORD made *heaven* and *earth*, the *sea*, and all that is in them, and rested on the seventh day. (Ex. 20:11)

> [God] made *heaven* and *earth*,
>   the *sea*, and all that is in them. (Ps. 146:6)

> I will shake the *heavens* and the *earth* and the *sea* and the *dry land*. (Hag. 2:6b)

These passages suggest that, even when they are paired, *heaven* and *earth* retain their normal function, according to which each designates a region.

Finally, we can find passages where the organization of the heavens and the earth is threatened:

> Therefore I will make the *heavens* tremble,
>   and the *earth* will be shaken out of its place,
> at the wrath of the LORD of hosts
>   in the day of his fierce anger. (Isa. 13:13)

> Lift up your eyes to the *heavens*,
>   and look at the *earth* beneath;
> for the *heavens* vanish like smoke,
>   the *earth* will wear out like a garment,
>   and they who dwell in it will die in like manner;
> but my salvation will be forever,
>   and my righteousness will never be dismayed. (Isa. 51:6)

> I looked on the *earth*, and behold, it was without form and void;
>   and to the *heavens*, and they had no light. (Jer. 4:23)

> The LORD roars from Zion,
>   and utters his voice from Jerusalem,
>   and the *heavens* and the *earth* quake. (Joel 3:16a)

> I am about to shake the *heavens* and the *earth*. (Hag. 2:21b)

The last two verses, Joel 3:16a and Haggai 2:21b, are particularly telling, because they have the compound expression (Joel 3:16a without definite articles in Hebrew) (cf. also Hag. 2:6). In all these verses, the threat to organization is compatible with the regions still being called "heavens" and "earth."

3. *The appeal to philology.*

In his wrap-up to his first argument, Waltke appeals to philology: "It is impossible to do so [take Gen. 1:2 as a further description of the result of verse 1] on philological grounds."[32] In some ways, this conclusion is only a summary of the subpoints we have already discussed. But it is still worthwhile to make two observations about the flexibility of language and the flexibility of meanings within a language.

First, the events described in Genesis 1 are unique in the whole history of the world. The world was created only once. It continues under God's providential rule for ages afterward. The events described in Genesis 1 include some involving origination, such as the creation of light, of plants, and of sea creatures. In their uniqueness, events of origination are necessarily *unlike* later events under the providential control of God. Moreover, the human beings who are addressed by the narrative in Genesis 1 have not themselves been eyewitnesses to the events of origination. So the only way of intelligibly describing such unique events is by way of analogy with events in providence (chap. 8). And analogy is not identity. Therefore, we must not expect that the descriptive usages in Genesis 1 will exactly match the later usages with respect to providential events. In particular, the fact that later references to heaven and earth speak of them in an organized state does not force an identical form of organization onto Genesis 1.

Second, word meanings in ordinary language include flexibility.[33] They do not function like technical terms, whose boundaries of meaning are precisely fixed. We can use old words in new contexts, and readers adjust.

Let us consider an example, with the English expression "the world." Among modern English words for referring to the universe, the word *world* is not often linked with discussions of the origin of the universe. Such discussions take place in the domain of technical

---

32. Waltke, "Part III," 221.
33. See the discussion of variation in Vern S. Poythress, *In the Beginning Was the Word: Language—A God-Centered Approach* (Wheaton, IL: Crossway, 2009), 154–55; Kenneth L. Pike, *Linguistic Concepts: An Introduction to Tagmemics* (Lincoln, NE/London: University of Nebraska Press, 1982), 52–59.

science (cosmology) and popularized science. In the context of science, expressions like "the universe" and "the cosmos" are customary. By contrast, the expression "the world" occurs in more commonplace contexts.[34] The result is that almost all the occurrences of the expression "the world" refer to the organized world familiar to us today, or some subdivision of it: "the world in which we live," "the world of finance," "the world of music," and so on. The expression also can refer to former ages, but still with the sense of the organization of human culture: "the world of ancient Greece" or "the world of the Renaissance."

But it takes only a moment to produce a discourse that stretches out beyond these more customary uses and refers to a less organized world:

> In the beginning God created the world. The world was without form and void, and darkness was all around. Then God said, "Let there be light."

The use of "the world" in the second sentence seems superficially to contradict the normal pattern in which the expression refers to the modern, organized world. But does the average reader see a contradiction? Or does he quickly adjust, by seeing that the author of the discourse has chosen to use the expression in a loose or more extended way?

The same reasoning applies by analogy to the Hebrew expression underlying "the heavens and the earth." The use of the expression "the heavens and the earth" in Genesis 1:1 can be taken in stride by a reader who is accustomed to frequent references to the world of providence subsequent to the completion of the days of creation. Thus, the philological problem that Waltke finds with the initiation view does not really exist.

---

34. One simple definition of *world* is: "the earth with its inhabitants and all things upon it." *Merriam-Webster's Collegiate Dictionary*, 11th ed. (Springfield, MA: Merriam-Webster, 2003), 1444. This definition, one of fourteen senses of *world* mentioned in the dictionary, clearly focuses on the organized world with people and things already in it. The mention of "inhabitants" and "all things" clearly has in mind a structured "world," more or less like the present. Another of the definitions is "the system of created things: universe." At first glance, this sense might seem to be synonymous with the word *universe*. But the word *system* gives the sense of an organized whole, and the word *created*—in the past tense—indicates that we are thinking of the world in something like the present state. None of the fourteen senses naturally brings to mind the kind of physical situation that existed long in the past, before the solar system was formed.

The irony is that, rightly assessed, philology weighs heavily *against* the summary view that Waltke champions "on philological grounds." A proper understanding of philology notes the transparency of meaning in most merisms, the necessity of analogical use in describing unique events, and the flexibility of meaning. Almost by itself, the first of these principles destroys the claim that the idea of organization is included in the *meaning* of the compound expression "the heavens and the earth." And that is at the heart of the argument against the initiation view.

The Theological Issue of God Creating a Formless Earth

In addition to the argument for the meaning "the organized universe," Waltke has two other supporting arguments in favor of the summary view of Genesis 1:1. One of these is an argument from theology. Waltke argues that it is theologically inappropriate to say that God would create a formless entity.

> 1. *Isaiah 45:18.*
> Waltke begins by discussing Isaiah 45:18:
>
> For thus says the LORD,
> who created the heavens
>   (he is God!),
> who formed the earth and made it
>   (he established it;
> he did not create it empty [לֹא־תֹהוּ בְרָאָהּ],
>   he formed it to be inhabited!):
> "I am the LORD, and there is no other."

Waltke claims that this verse is incompatible with the idea that God created the earth initially empty (תֹהוּ) in Genesis 1:2.[35]

Waltke's interpretation of Isaiah 45:18 is awkward. It is as if we were to take a single line out of the verse and treat it as a technical discussion. That is, we treat "he did not create it empty" as if it precisely targets the issue of an early, unformed state. According to such an interpretation, this poetic line precisely denies that the earth in Genesis 1:2 was the result of a creative act.

---

35. Waltke, "Part III," 220.

But Isaiah 45:18 is not a technical discussion. It is poetry. Within the key line, "create" is not to be construed narrowly as focusing solely on the initial act of bringing something into existence out of nothing. The parallels in the surrounding lines show that "create" is construed more broadly, as parallel to "formed" (twice), "made," and "established." In context, the key line is referring in broad fashion to the sequence of events that includes everything that God did over the course of the six days in order to prepare the earth to be a suitable environment for man. This broad scope is made particularly evident in the next-to-last line, "he formed it to be inhabited." By using the words *created* and *empty* together in the key line, the verse is making an allusion to Genesis 1:1–2. But that allusion functions as part of a verse that is commenting on "creation" in a broad sense, including, in principle, the entire sequence in Genesis 1:1–31.

Elsewhere in his articles, Waltke himself seems to agree that Isaiah 45:18 is speaking broadly about the entire process taking place in the six days, and that the endpoint of the process is the completed work of Genesis 1:31: "[h]e [God] did not end up with chaos, as Isaiah noted (Isa. 45:18)."[36] That is, Isaiah 45:18 is saying that chaos is not the *endpoint*. But that is consistent with saying that, at an *earlier point in time*, God might have brought into existence an earth that lacked much of the later organization. So there is no contradiction between Isaiah 45:18 and any part of Genesis 1, whether we hold the initiation view or the summary view of 1:1. Isaiah 45:18 is irrelevant to deciding between the two views.

2. *Formless and void.*
Next, Waltke appeals to the meaning of "formless and void":

Then too it has been demonstrated from Jeremiah 4:23 and Isaiah 34:11 that תהו ובהו denotes the antithesis of creation.[37]

But in this statement there is vagueness about the word *creation*, as well as difficulties with the related idea of being organized or unor-

---

36. Waltke, "The Creation Account in Genesis 1:1–3: Part IV," 342; also, "Isaiah 45:18 has reference to the completed creation at the end of six days." Waltke, "The Creation Account in Genesis 1:1–3: Part II," 144.

37. Waltke, "Part III," 220. Waltke provides a footnote referring readers back to Waltke, "The Creation Account in Genesis 1:1–3: Part II," 136–44.

ganized. In the quoted statement from Waltke, does the word *creation* focus on the initial act of creation? Or does the work of creation include every step in the overall transition, including the beginning of the work, the less organized states, and the final, well-organized state?

And what kind of antithesis do we have in view? To *undo* the present order of things and to return the world to a less organized state is, in *some respects*, the antithesis of building up multiple kinds of organization over the course of the six days of creation. It is the antithesis of creation as an overall transition. But how could it be the antithesis of the initial act of creation from nothing? Has Waltke's argument unconsciously slipped in the assumption that *creation* cannot mean creation out of nothing into a temporary situation that is relatively unorganized?

If God had left the created world in the situation described in Genesis 1:2, it *would* have been unsuitable for human habitation. Given that his purposes included human habitation, the situation in verse 2, as a static situation, apart from further development, is at odds with the endpoint that God has purposed. But of course it is a mistake to isolate verse 2 from the overall purposes of God involved in the entire narrative in Genesis 1. Once we have the entire narrative, we can see that the initial production of the earth in an uninhabitable state is quite in accord with his purposes. We must just be careful to take into account the theme of development, and to see that the state of verse 2 was intended by God and created by God, but never intended *just to stay* that way.

3. God's order.

Next, Waltke appeals to the fact "that elsewhere in Scripture it is said that God created everything by His Word"[38] (Ps. 33:6, 9; Heb. 11:3). But "no mention is made anywhere in Scripture that God called the unformed, dark, and water state of verse 3 [*sic*; v. 2] into existence."[39] This is an argument from silence, and a weak one at that. The verses that Waltke cites, Psalm 33:6, 9 and Hebrews 11:3, and others (Col. 1:15–17; John 1:3) imply that God made everything. The initial watery state of Genesis 1:2 is included *by implication* in "everything."

---

38. Waltke, "Part III," 220.
39. Waltke, "Part III," 221.

Next, Waltke appeals to the absence of sea and darkness in the new heaven and new earth. "This revelation about the new cosmos [Rev. 21:1, 25] suggests that the deep and darkness in verse 2 [of Genesis 1] are less than desirable and were not called into existence by the God of order and goodness."[40] Collins has discerningly replied that in the visionary context of Revelation, the sea and darkness are used "as symbols for what fallen man fears rather than as comments on the moral status of sea and night in themselves."[41] Moreover, Waltke's aspersions with regard to the deep and darkness are in danger of ignoring the importance of history and development. The deep and darkness are indeed "less than desirable" if they are regarded as *endpoints* in the development of creation. The earth in Genesis 1:2 does not *yet* present a suitable habitation for man. But what is undesirable as an endpoint may be fully in accord with the will and plan of God for an early stage.[42]

Waltke calls God "the God of order and goodness." Yes. But there is a wise temporal development to be found in Genesis 1:2, if we see it in relation to the subsequent narrative in Genesis 1. Verse 2 is one phase in the total process, and it cannot rightly be evaluated if we isolate it from the larger narrative in which it is embedded.

Waltke's language unfortunately opens the door to an unbiblical idea of God, according to which he is the sovereign Creator only with respect to *some* pieces of the total picture. Are we supposed to say that he brings about order but not disorder? I should hope not! Moreover, to say that God did not create the deep and the darkness directly contradicts a number of New Testament texts (Col. 1:16; Heb. 11:3; Rev. 4:11)[43] and distorts our conception of the sovereignty of God.

This particular argument by Waltke is not his best. Fortunately, in his 2001 commentary, Waltke shows a change in his position: he

---

40. Waltke, "Part III," 221. Waltke, however, wants to assert the complete sovereignty of God over the deep and the darkness. Waltke, "The Creation Account in Genesis 1:1–3: Part IV," 338–39. God exerts control over them, but Waltke still does not think that God originated them.

41. Collins, *Genesis 1–4*, 54n55.

42. Waltke is not alone in mistakenly assessing the state described in Gen. 1:2. He quotes approvingly from Brevard S. Childs, who notes, "It is rather generally acknowledged that the suggestion of God's first creating a chaos is a logical contradiction and must be rejected." Childs, *Myth and Reality in the Old Testament*, 2nd ed. (London: SCM, 1962), 30, quoted in Waltke, *Old Testament Theology*, 179. If such a view is "rather generally acknowledged," it is not a good sign for the state of Old Testament scholarship. Such a view appears to ignore the distinction between different kinds and degrees of organization, between complete chaos and being "without form and void," and between a permanent condition and a starting point for development. In addition, Childs's choice to use the language of "logical contradiction" is inappropriate.

43. Collins, *Genesis 1–4*, 53.

affirms that God "made everything."[44] This change removes the basis for his whole argument in 1975 concerning the alleged theological inappropriateness of God creating a formless earth.

4. *Parallels in ancient myths.*

In his key arguments, Waltke does not appeal directly to the theme of primeval chaos found in some ancient Near Eastern myths.[45] But other interpreters do appeal to this factor in order to argue that the ancient Near East has no concept of creation from nothing, and so such a concept cannot be found in Genesis 1:1. Genesis 1:2 therefore describes the original condition that is the starting point for creative activity. Interpreters may also appeal to later poetic biblical texts that use the imagery of God triumphing over the sea and over the sea monster, "Leviathan."

A brief reply may include four points. First, the true God may say and do something different from and even in contrast to the ancient Near East. Second, there is a partial parallel in some Egyptian texts that have Ptah producing everything, including the primeval waters.[46] Third, in dealing with the ancient Near Eastern myths, one must ask whether the sea or water god(dess) is genuinely primeval. In contexts where gods give birth to other gods, the sea god is not necessarily first. So the waters are not just "there," but come from something more ultimate. Fourth, the biblical texts that poetically invoke a picture of God defeating a sea monster must be used in a way that respects their poetic style: they are examples of imagery rather than theories about an initial chaos. Moreover, the specific terminology used in these texts often has connections with terms in later verses in Genesis 1—

---

44. Waltke, *Genesis*, 68. In its key section, the 2001 commentary on Genesis does not refer to Waltke's earlier articles in *Bibliotheca Sacra*. His change of position is therefore an inference, not a direct statement in his text. Waltke, *Old Testament Theology*, 180, published in 2007, seems to be more ambivalent, and on pp. 180–81, it revives pieces of the second argument found in Waltke, "Part III" (from 1975), the argument about theological inappropriateness.

45. However, Waltke does mention parallels in the fourth article of his series ("The Creation Account in Genesis 1:1–3: Part IV," 329) after he has finished the main arguments in "Part III." And he reviews ancient Near Eastern cosmogonies in the first article in the series ("The Creation Account in Genesis 1:1–3: Part I"). Moreover, Waltke, *Old Testament Theology*, 181–83, discusses the myths.

46. Wenham, *Genesis 1–15*, 13; Viktor Notter, *Biblischer Schöpfungsbericht und ägyptische Schöpfungsmythen* (Stuttgart: KBW, 1974), 23–26; Vincent Arieh Tobin, "Myths: Creation Myths," in *The Oxford Encyclopedia of Ancient Egypt*, ed. Donald B. Redford (Oxford: Oxford University Press, 2001), 2:471. Note, however, that the productions by Ptah appear to be similar to emanations, so there is no clear Creator-creature distinction. Nothing in ancient Near Eastern polytheism is truly parallel to the monotheism of Genesis 1.

the "seas" in verse 10 and "great sea creatures" in verse 21, both of which are clearly created by God and over which he is thoroughly sovereign.[47] So specific vocabulary choices in poetic biblical language actually count against the idea that Genesis 1 is playing with a theory of original chaos outside the creative activity of God.

Structural Evidence for Genesis 1:1 as a Summary

Waltke's third and final argument focuses on parallel structures.

1. A parallel with Genesis 2:4–7.

The most impressive parallel in Waltke's exposition is the one between Genesis 1:1–3 and 2:4–7. According to Waltke, each text is composed of three pieces:

1. "Introductory summary statement" (1:1; 2:4);
2. "*Circumstantial clause* of the pattern *waw* + noun + verb (היה) describing a negative state before creation" (1:2; 2:5–6);
3. "*Main clause* of the pattern *waw* consecutive + prefixed conjugation form describing the creation" (1:3; 2:7).[48]

This parallelism may look impressive. But we must recognize that (2) and (3) represent common ways of producing circumstantial

---

47. Waltke, *Old Testament Theology*, 181, discusses the theme of chaos and the primordial waters in the ancient Near East directly on the heels of an argument claiming that Genesis 1 does not reveal the origin of "the primordial water" (180). Both discussions fall under Waltke's section heading "Negative State of the Earth *before* Creation (1:2)" (emphasis added). So Waltke may be using the ancient Near East as an extra support for his summary view. As a biblical parallel to the ancient Near Eastern theme of chaos, Waltke quotes Ps. 74:12–17 and interprets the reference to "the sea" in verse 13 by inserting brackets: "[Yamm]" (181–82). He intends to indicate that verse 13 has a parallel in the role of the god "Yamm" in Canaanite myth. Yes, there may be allusion to such myths. But such allusion still does not imply that the Bible endorses a theory of original chaos. The Bible must be allowed to speak with its own voice. Unfortunately for the theory of original chaos, the Hebrew word in verse 13 corresponds to "seas" in Gen. 1:10. And the parallel line in the second half of the same verse has "the great sea creatures," the same word as in Gen. 1:21. The details in Ps. 74:13 actually fight against Waltke's suggested alignment of Ps. 74:13 with *initial* chaos. Waltke also cites Ps. 77:17 (English verse 16), where the word for "deep" occurs. But here the context provides a poetic recital concerning the exodus from Egypt, and the waters in question are the waters of the Red Sea, which Gen. 1:10 affirms to be part of the created order.

The argument for seeing Gen. 1:2 as precreation chaos has three doubtful steps. (1) First, read into the ancient Near East an affirmation of *initial* chaos. But in a polytheistic context, the sea god is not necessarily first. (2) Second, transfer the entire theory of initial chaos, rather than looser poetic imagery of triumph, from the myths into Old Testament poetry. (3) Third, project the Old Testament poetry back onto Gen. 1:2 rather than onto later events to which it may be more directly related—the exodus, the flood, the creation of seas (v. 10), and the creation of the great sea creatures (v. 21).

48. Waltke, "Part III," 226. The numbered points are not direct quotes, but a summary of Waltke's presentation using some of his phraseology.

clauses and main clauses, respectively. Because these grammatical con-structions are common, their reoccurrence is not weighty evidence for a genuine parallel. And, of course, Waltke's label for (1), "introductory summary statement," is fitting only if the summary view is correct.

There are also some differences between Genesis 1:1–3 and 2:4–7.

First, the material in Genesis 2:4 is not really a heading solely for events in which God creates new things. It is an introductory title for the entire section 2:5–4:26. As the outline and discussion in Waltke's commentary recognizes,[49] 2:4 is the first of several headings in the form "these are the generations of Noah" (6:9), "these are the genera-tions of Terah" (11:27), "these are the generations of Isaac" (25:19), and so on. (Gen. 5:1 is only slightly different in wording: "This is the *book* of the generations of Adam.") Each section introduced by a heading mainly contains not the account of the origin of the named person, that is, Noah, Terah, or Isaac, but the account of the subse-quent history (the "generations") involving the named person and his descendants. The word *these* points forward to the entire section. It signals that the sentence is a heading for the section. This key use of *these* is unlike Genesis 1:1, which does not contain the key word. Nothing in 1:1 clearly marks it out as a heading.

Note also that the section 2:5–4:26 gives no attention to the cre-ation of the heavens or heavenly lights. It is a more focused account. It is about the "generations" of the heavens and the earth, the history and the products that flow from them. So it does not run fully parallel to the creation account in 1:1–2:3. Thus, also, 2:5–6 is not "describing a negative state before creation" *of the world as a whole*, but an un-developed state before the creation of Adam and the garden of Eden.

Second, Genesis 1:1 has a main verb in the perfect. A clause with this structure can naturally be construed as describing the first event in a series unfolding in the subsequent verses. Genesis 2:4 does not have this feature.[50]

Third, the typical case in which Hebrew discourse supplies a head-ing has clear signals that it is a heading. The use of the word *these* in the headings to the sections of Genesis is such a signal. Similarly, we have "These are the names of the sons of Israel" (Ex. 1:1); "These are

---

49. Waltke, *Genesis*, 18.
50. At another point, Waltke carefully notes the differences. Waltke, "Part III," 225.

the words that Moses spoke to all Israel beyond the Jordan" (Deut. 1:1); and "These are the words of the letter that Jeremiah the prophet sent from Jerusalem" (Jer. 29:1). More simply, a heading may use a phrase instead of a clause: "The proverbs of Solomon, son of David, king of Israel" (Prov. 1:1); "The words of the Preacher, the son of David, king in Jerusalem" (Eccles. 1:1); and "The vision of Isaiah the son of Amoz" (Isa. 1:1). All of these expressions show by their special form that they are headings. In the absence of such special signals, Genesis 1:1 is to be construed as describing an initial event.

Fourth, as we have observed, the linkage between Genesis 1:1 and 2 through the key term "the earth" is naturally interpreted as an indication that verse 2 begins with a circumstantial clause linked *backward* to verse 1. The linkage between 2:4 and 5 is not as tight. It is true that the Hebrew for "earth" (ארץ) occurs twice in verse 4, twice in verse 5, and once in verse 6. (ESV translates it "the land" in 2:5–6 and includes an explanatory footnote.) But in all three occurrences in verses 5–6, the key word has a subordinate, inconspicuous role in the narrative. Verses 5–6 have in focus the lack of bushes, plants, rain, and man, and the presence of mist. They do not start off with the land itself as the subject. In addition, because 2:4 in its structure clearly identifies itself as a heading for the entire subsequent narrative, verses 5–6 can be construed only as circumstantial clauses linked forward to the main clause in verse 7. The same is not true concerning 1:1–3.

Fifth, Genesis 2:4–7 comes too late to affect the ordinary Israelite's interpretation of the basic meaning and syntax of Genesis 1:1–3. The reader has already found out what it means long before coming to 2:4–7. To read quite a different significance into the sequence of verses 1:1–3 on the basis of 2:4–7 is therefore suspect.

2. A parallel with Genesis 3:1.

Next, Waltke appeals to parallels between Genesis 1:1–3 and 3:1.[51] According to Waltke, in 3:1, the heading is supplied by 2:4. The circumstantial clause is 3:1a, and the main clause begins in 3:1b. But this is a weak analogy, because Waltke finds the heading for 3:1 all the way back in 2:4. Moreover, 2:4 is not the heading for 3:1–7 or 3:1–24 as such, but for the entire section, 2:5–4:26. So observations about 3:1

---

51. Waltke, "Part III," 227.

cannot have much relevance for determining whether 1:1 is the heading for what comes *immediately* after it.

3. *A parallel with the beginning of* Enuma Elish.

Waltke also appeals to the *Enuma Elish*, which begins with a circumstantial clause and then a main clause.[52] But there is no heading in the *Enuma Elish*. So this alleged parallel again does not help us to determine whether Genesis 1:1 is a heading.

In various cases describing development, it is natural to start with a description of a relatively undeveloped state. So the transitions from an undeveloped to a developed state are natural, quite apart from whether some preceding material functions as a heading, a summary, or an earlier event preceding the process of development.

In sum, the parallels that Waltke finds are too loose to serve as persuasive evidence.

Conclusion

In conclusion, all three of the main arguments for the summary view have superficial plausibility, but none has weight. In addition, as of 2001, Waltke himself no longer holds fully to the second argument contained in his earlier work (in 1974). The summary view is much weaker than many have taken it to be. By contrast, the initiation view makes good sense of the phrase meanings, theology, and syntax of Genesis 1:1–2 in relation to 1:1–2:3 as a whole, and beyond (the rest of Genesis and the rest of the Bible). I conclude that the initiation view is correct.

---

52. Waltke, "Part III," 227.

Appendix B

The Meaning of Accommodation

Let us consider the issue of "accommodation." God is infinite. Human recipients of God's Word are finite. How do we negotiate the relation between the infinite and the finite? Ultimately there is mystery. But how we think about God also affects how we think about what sort of communication we have in the Bible. And that, in turn, affects what we expect when we read Genesis 1–3.

For centuries, interpreters have used the word *accommodation* to describe God's communication with finite human beings. But a lot depends on what it means. Does it mean that God takes into account human capacities? That seems reasonable. But the word *accommodation* is sometimes used to postulate that the Bible is accommodated to mistaken notions of the cultures in the times when it was written in such a way that it affirms these notions along with a core of theological truth. So we must take time to think about the word *accommodation*.[1]

The doctrine of accommodation in God's revelation to man has had a long and venerable history, from the ancient church to the present.[2] On one level, it is a simple idea. But a closer inspection reveals mysteries and intractable depths.

---

1. Apart from the two opening paragraphs, this appendix is a minor revision of Vern S. Poythress, "Rethinking Accommodation in Revelation," *Westminster Theological Journal* 76, no. 1 (2014): 143–56. Used with permission.
2. John Henry Blunt, ed., "Accommodation," in *Dictionary of Doctrinal and Historical Theology* (London/Oxford/Cambridge: Rivingtons, 1871), 4; A. N. S. Lane, "Accommodation," in *New Dictionary of Theology*, ed. Sinclair B. Ferguson, David F. Wright, and J. I. Packer (Downers Grove, IL: InterVarsity Press, 1988), 3; John D. Woodbridge, *Biblical Authority: A Critique of the Rogers/McKim Proposal* (Grand Rapids, MI: Zondervan, 1982); Hoon Lee,

The Definition of Accommodation

Let us begin at the simple level. A. N. S. Lane summarizes the idea of accommodation by saying, "God speaks to us in a form that is suited to the capacity of the hearer."[3] God speaks to human beings in human languages and in a manner that is intelligible to them. This suitability has been called *condescension* or *accommodation*.[4] It is a simple and obvious idea in the sense that it is an obvious feature of Scripture and of the earlier oral communications from God to man that are recorded in Scripture (Gen. 3:9–13; 12:1–3; 15:1; etc.).

This kind of accommodation can be defined in at least two ways. In the narrower sense, it denotes the ways that God reveals *himself*.[5] That is, we focus not on all instances of revelation, but on those in which God himself is the subject matter being communicated. God is infinite and incomprehensible, but he makes himself known to human beings. As a result, they truly know him, but in accord with the limitations of their finiteness. Thus, we may say that his revelation of himself and his character is accommodated to the noetic abilities of human beings. For example, when Scripture says that God is king, the word *king* is intelligible partly because we know about human kings. God is not a king on the same level as human kings, but by analogy to human kings. The use of analogy functions in making scriptural teaching accessible to its readers, who know about human kings.

In a broader sense, *accommodation* denotes all the ways in which God produces revelation or communication to human beings in ways that suit their capacities.[6] In this sense, not only what God says directly about *himself* but what he says about anything at all is accommodated to the capacities of his hearers.

"Accommodation: Orthodox, Socinian, and Contemporary," *Westminster Theological Journal* 75, no. 2 (2013): 335–48.

3. Lane, "Accommodation," 3. The word *accommodation* is also sometimes used to describe progressive revelation: God's communication to his people at any one time in history suits the historical circumstances and the redemptive epoch in which the communication occurs. Earlier communication may lack the detail and specificity that God intends to provide later. The progress is from truth to deeper truth, not from error to truth. See Blunt, "Accommodation," 4–5.

4. Lane, "Accommodation," 3.

5. According to L. M. Sweet and G. W. Bromiley, accommodation is "the principle that God adapts His *self-revelation* to man." Sweet and Bromiley, "Accommodation," in *International Standard Bible Encyclopedia* (Grand Rapids, MI: Eerdmans, 1979), 1:24 (emphasis added).

6. Lane, "Accommodation," 3. Wick Broomall says, "[It] allows a writer, for purposes of simplification, to adjust his language to the limitations of his readers without compromising the truth in the process." Broomall, "Accommodation," in *Evangelical Dictionary of Theology*, ed. Walter A. Elwell (Grand Rapids, MI: Baker, 1984), 9.

This kind of suitability or accommodation surely makes sense. Theological discussions of accommodation may use the analogy of "a father addressing a small child or a teacher with a young pupil."[7] In an ordinary human situation, a wise person adjusts his speech to fit his hearers. Likewise, God, who is all wise, beyond any human wisdom, suits his speech to his hearers. In addition, subsequent to the fall of mankind into sin, God's communication takes into account the sinful condition of people and comes in a manner suited to that condition.[8]

Anthropomorphism

Biblical interpreters have appealed to the narrow sense of accommodation to explain features about biblical descriptions of God. For example, they may say that God describes himself according to human capacities when the Bible speaks of his arm, his eyes, or his being angry or grieved. These descriptions are "anthropomorphisms." Modern discussions of accommodation sometimes quote John Calvin on this point:

> The Anthropomorphites also, who dreamed of a corporeal God, because mouth, ears, eyes, hands, and feet are often ascribed to him in Scripture, are easily refuted. For who is so devoid of intellect as not to understand that God, in so speaking, *lisps with us as nurses are wont to do with little children*? Such modes of expression, therefore, do not so much express what kind of a being God is, as *accommodate* the knowledge of him to our feebleness. In doing so, he must of course *stoop* far below his proper height.[9]

A Variant View

Is there more than one concept of accommodation? Up until the Enlightenment, the classical idea of accommodation took care not to deny the full truthfulness of Scripture.[10] Accommodation did *not*

---

7. Lane "Accommodation," 3. Also, Rudolf Hofmann, "Accommodation," in *The New Schaff-Herzog Encyclopedia of Religious Knowledge*, ed. Samuel Macauley Jackson (Grand Rapids, MI: Baker, 1977), 1.22–23.

8. On the additional complications due to sin, see Sweet and Bromiley, "Accommodation," 26–27.

9. John Calvin, *Institutes of the Christian Religion*, trans. Henry Beveridge (Grand Rapids, MI: Eerdmans, 1970), 1.13.1 (emphasis added).

10. However, gnostics and Socinians put forward an idea of accommodation that included error. John M'Clintock and James Strong, *Cyclopedia of Biblical, Theological, and Ecclesiastical Literature* (New York: Harper, 1874), 1.46–47.

mean that God tolerated a process in which human writers of Scripture would include in their writings erroneous conceptions of their time in order to serve a higher theological purpose. Richard Muller summarizes:

> The Reformers and their scholastic followers all recognized that God must in some way condescend or accommodate himself to human ways of knowing in order to reveal himself. This *accommodatio* occurs specifically in the use of human words and concepts for the communication of the law and the gospel, but it in no way implies the loss of truth or the lessening of scriptural authority. The *accommodatio* or *condescensio* refers to the manner or mode of revelation, the gift of the wisdom of infinite God in finite form, not to the quality of the revelation or to the matter revealed.[11]

Muller goes on to note that a counterproposal involving accommodation that included error rose later in historical criticism.[12] It is with us to this day, and has penetrated ostensibly evangelical circles.[13] For our purposes, let us concentrate on the classical doctrine. We cannot include a full treatment of the heterodox idea of accommodation to error.[14]

Doctrinal Basis

At its core, the doctrine of accommodation seems to be little more than an expression of the implications of the Creator-creature distinction for the nature of revelation. God is the infinite Creator, and we are not. On the basis of biblical teaching, we make a distinction between what he knows and what we know. And we infer that his communication to us takes into account who we are as creatures. The doctrine guards against overestimating our knowledge and trying to treat it as if it were the ultimate standard into which God is required to fit.

---

11. Richard A. Muller, *Dictionary of Latin and Greek Theological Terms: Drawn Principally from Protestant Scholastic Theology* (Grand Rapids, MI: Baker, 1985), 19.

12. Muller, *Dictionary*, 19. Also Hofmann, "Accommodation," 1.23–24.

13. E.g., Kenton L. Sparks, *God's Word in Human Words: An Evangelical Appropriation of Critical Biblical Scholarship* (Grand Rapids, MI: Baker, 2008); Kenton L. Sparks, *Sacred Word, Broken Word: Biblical Authority and the Dark Side of Scripture* (Grand Rapids, MI: Eerdmans, 2012).

14. The classical defenses of the inerrancy of Scripture, cited in chap. 3, include discussion and refutation of the idea of error allegedly due to "accommodation." See also chap. 5 for a treatment of some aspects of the idea.

In addition to the Creator-creature distinction, the Bible teaches that man is made in the image of God, and that even human beings in rebellion continue to know him (Rom. 1:19–21). These affirmations guard against an opposite danger, namely, that we would *underestimate* the instruction given by Scripture and general revelation, and move in the antibiblical direction of saying that God is unknown or unknowable.[15]

So we might choose to leave it at that, and to say that the doctrine of accommodation is fairly straightforward and obvious. It is, if we confine ourselves to an introductory discussion. But if we look at the details, we find mysteries. And we find potential perils, because as sinners, we may be tempted to rush in too quickly on the basis of the assumption that we have understood all that there is to understand.

The Peril of False Transcendence

One peril arises from the temptation to practice a false transcendence. Such a temptation can enter even after someone has affirmed the transcendence of God using the Creator-creature distinction. The peril can be illustrated by starting from the common human depictions of accommodation mentioned above: a father with a young child or a teacher with a young pupil. We can watch the father or the teacher, and we understand what is going on. We appreciate the ways in which the father or the teacher knows more, and knows more deeply. We observe with appreciation all that the father or teacher is holding back in order to communicate in a simple fashion to the youngster.

So someone—let us call her Donna—imagines God doing the same thing. And, indeed, there is an analogy. But the analogy is only partial. Donna cannot actually become an observer of God, on his own level, in the same way that she can observe a human father. But she can try to imagine it, and then fall into the temptation of trying to figure out just what God is leaving out, compressing, and simplifying in the process of speaking to "childlike" human beings. Donna's speculation about what God is really doing may then function as a more ultimate authority than Scripture. Scripture only has the qualified authority of being for the childlike. And Donna? She has become godlike.

---

15. John M. Frame warns against both dangers in *The Doctrine of the Knowledge of God* (Phillipsburg, NJ: Presbyterian and Reformed, 1987), 13–40.

Something similar to Donna's approach actually arose historically in the case of gnosticism. The gnostics claimed that they had secret teachings for those who were "spiritual." By contrast, the overt teachings in the writings of the New Testament were at a lower level, suited to the capacity of ordinary Christians. The gnostics were saying, in effect, that the biblical writings were accommodated in a way that contrasted with the gnostics' allegedly deeper knowledge.

This route taken by Donna and by the gnostics illustrates the peril of false transcendence. Donna tries to transcend our human limitations in order to watch God over his shoulder, so to speak, and thereby to know the ways in which she can and cannot receive Scripture at full value. This move of Donna's can well result in a transition from accommodation in the classical sense to the modern historical-critical sense of accommodation of errors within Scripture. Even if it does not, at least not immediately, there has been a fateful transition to a new seat of authority. The new authority is Donna's personal vision of how God practices father-like condescension. That vision trumps the authority of Scripture itself. And so, by means of her personal vision, Donna has become her own ultimate master. She may still verbally confess that Scripture is inerrant, but internally, the ultimate authority has shifted. In like manner, the gnostics shifted authority toward their secret knowledge and secret writings.

The Peril of False Immanence

I have described Donna's approach as an instance of false transcendence. But it simultaneously involves a false understanding of God's immanence.[16] According to the biblical teaching about God, God's immanence implies, in the sphere of epistemology, that he makes himself known to us both in general revelation and in Scripture. As a substitute for this doctrine of immanence, Donna and the gnostics have their own claims to special knowledge. Donna's personal vision of the nature of God and the gnostics' claims to secret knowledge function as immanent authorities. Human ideas here function as a false source of

---

16. Frame's square on transcendence and immanence is valuable here in distinguishing between Christian and non-Christian views of transcendence and immanence. Frame, *The Doctrine of the Knowledge of God*, 14. Even those of us who have become Christians through the work of the Holy Spirit have some remaining sinfulness, and we are tempted to fall back into various compromises with non-Christian views.

insight. These key ideas claim to function as immanent and accessible knowledge concerning what God is "really" like or is "really" doing behind the veil offered by Scripture.

We can also fall into another form of false immanence. Let us say that a particular person—Joe—acknowledges in a basic way that Scripture is ultimate for all human understanding of God. He knows that he cannot "get behind" Scripture in the way that Donna imagines. However, Joe can still distort the idea of immanence by interpreting the accommodated character of Scripture as if it implied that he can *master* scriptural revelation. In taking this route, he is still admitting, on the basis of the Creator-creature distinction, that he cannot master God. But he thinks that (in principle) he can master Scripture, precisely because it is accommodated to us and therefore falls within the sphere of human control. He reasons that, unlike God himself, Scripture as accommodated language must be completely subject to human ideas of rationality. This move still maintains that God is unmasterable and infinite. But Joe may infer that his idea of God, given through Scripture, is masterable, since it belongs to him and to humanity. Then the "god" about which Joe is talking is finite, and he is worshiping an idol of his own conception.

Thus, we must hold together two sides: God, in communicating to us, suits his speech to our capacity (immanence), but it is God who speaks, with divine authority and power (transcendence). God's immanence implies that we can genuinely understand and absorb what he says, by the help of the Holy Spirit. God's transcendence implies that we cannot master his communication to us—or any part of it, since he is present in everything he says.

Perils in Underestimating Divine Power

The language describing accommodation is not perfectly precise. So the door remains open for misusing it in still other directions. One such direction involves underestimating divine capabilities.

Consider again the analogies involving a human father with his child or a teacher with his young pupil. These situations involve adjustments on the part of the father or the teacher, depending on the particular case.

In the case of a father with his child, the child is who he is, whether the father likes it or not. The father cannot sovereignly control who the child is or what his capacities are. The father may feel frustrated if the child has limited capacities. He may feel frustrated by not being able to say more. He may be frustrated because, even after effort, he fails to communicate some idea that is important to him. He does the best he can, but he is limited by circumstances outside his control.

If we put too much stock in this illustration, the temptation arises to drag the same connotations into our picture of God. We infer that God is like a human father, and so he is hemmed in, against his will, by the circumstances and limits of human capacities. But that is not correct. God is not limited like a human father, because he creates all the "circumstances," according to the doctrine of creation. Sin violates God's order, to be sure, but it is an intruder.[17] In the original situation of creation, man as a creature cannot "frustrate" God's desire to communicate, because God created man and is completely in charge.

God did not create man in isolation from a later purpose to communicate. It is not as if he created man first, and then, as an afterthought, asked himself whether it might not be good to establish communication, and on what terms communication might be possible. Rather, God created man already having in mind the purposes of communication. Consequently, there can be no frustration on God's part due to what human beings are. By contrast, a human being might make a bicycle, and then be frustrated that it is not stronger or faster than it is. God is not frustrated, because he is God. He does not have to "adjust" to a situation outside his control or to human capacities that he did not specify. Precisely because God is the absolute Creator, human finiteness offers no resistance, no problem, for communication. Contrary to the thinking into which we are prone to fall, the distinction between infinite and finite minds, and between cognitive capacities, is not a problem for God. It is not something that he must puzzle over in order to adapt his communication to unfortunate, uncontrollable limitations.

Thus, the words *accommodation* and *adaptation* are not altogether helpful. Both can suggest that God is accommodating or adapting to a situation that he cannot control, more or less the way we as human beings adapt to our circumstances or accommodate ourselves

---

17. On "accommodation" in a situation of sin, see Sweet and Bromiley, "Accommodation," 1.26–27.

to situations beyond our control. So how else can we describe what God does? More guardedly, we might describe God as communicating in a way *suited to* or *fitting for* his hearers. But even with these new expressions, it is possible to import the idea that God must mold himself or his word into shape, so to speak, in order to "fit in" to circumstances outside his control. This kind of concession undermines the authority of God's word, because it implies that God is only partly responsible for what he says, and that part of the responsibility goes to allegedly autonomous circumstances that constrain the limits of what he is able to say.

Peril Concerning Improper Inference of Defects

In addition, the analogy with a human father suggests a certain kind of defect in the communication. Communication between two adults is richer than communication between a father and a child. But is the latter "defective"? Some people might say so. However, there is a time and place for everything. Father-child communication is not defective if we have a robust view of family life, and of the positive role of child-rearing and those early opportunities for communication. Even communication early in the life of a child may still be completely true and robustly edifying. Communicative adequacy and success are not to be judged by artificial standards of perfection, but ultimately by divine design and conformity to divine standards. Divine standards positively approve the kind of communication in which a father takes into account his child's present capacities.

But suppose that the child is in an accident that causes permanent brain damage. The child never reaches mental adulthood during this life. Might we say that the communication between the father and child is now impaired? It is, in a sense, defective in a way that the father is powerless to remedy.

How might such a situation relate to our situation with God? Over time, human beings are meant to grow, both as individuals and as a race. But they never outgrow humanity in order to become God. We can appreciate the growth of God's people through progressive revelation, as well as an individual's growth in spiritual knowledge as he continues to study Scripture over a period of time. But we continue to be human, not God. According to the analogy, we never outgrow "childhood." Is this a defect? Only if it is measured against the sinful human desire to be God. Our knowledge at the consummation will still be fully human. And that is OK.

Perils Concerning Quick Dismissal or Underestimation of Meaning That Looks Accommodated

Another kind of peril involves an underestimation of the mystery of Scripture in its details. Consider the concept of accommodation in the narrow sense, where it deals with how God reveals himself, that is, his own character. This kind of accommodation, it is said, explains anthropomorphic language about God. But does it? A closer look shows that there are continuing mysteries.

Consider an example. Exodus 15:6b says, "Your right hand, O Lord, shatters the enemy." The stock explanation of this description of God is that it is an accommodation to human capacities through anthropomorphism. Yes, it is an anthropomorphism. But does this verse really have much to do with the concept of accommodation? If we were to reckon with the immediate context, we could observe that verse 6 is part of a poetic song. The song is full of metaphors and figures of speech. The Lord does not have a physical body with a physical right hand. Consequently, it is clear that the expression is a metaphor, in keeping with the context. It means that the Lord acts to shatter the enemy as a human being might shatter a thing with his right hand.

This truth *could* be expressed in other ways, without the use of a vivid metaphor. For example, as an alternative we could say, "The Lord exercises his power to defeat the enemy utterly." That way of saying it is not colorful, not poetic, and not rhetorically engaging. But it says some of the same things that the poetic expression does. Thus, the Lord could have spoken without using vivid anthropomorphisms. But he did not. Why not? The doctrine of accommodation, by itself, says only that God addresses human beings according to their capacities. Both metaphorical and nonmetaphorical forms of expression meet this criterion. Indeed, any intelligible human language meets the criterion! Accommodation says only that Scripture is intelligible. It does not explain why the Lord chooses one particular kind of intelligible speech in contrast to many other alternatives. Thus, accommodation does not really explain anthropomorphism or any of the particulars. If we use it as an explanation where it is not appropriate, we run the danger of overlooking the particulars. Our appeal to accommodation may become a recipe for glossing over the particulars and implying that they are not significant.

One peril arising in this connection is the temptation unconsciously to "discount" and devalue figurative language. We can start to think that figurative language is not "the real thing," but only an ornament, due to accommodation. So the "unaccommodated" truth will be truth stripped of ornamentation. If we take this route in our minds, we label metaphor and figurative language as nonserious. We substitute our own ideas of what should have been said for what God actually said, perhaps because we are embarrassed by what he said or because we think it is just for theological children and not for us. Simultaneously, we fall victim to false transcendence by imagining that we know the unaccommodated truth. The remedy, as usual, is to submit to what God said rather than be embarrassed by it. He knows what he is saying. He is utterly comfortable with metaphors, even though human sin tempts us to misunderstand them.

Perils of Overestimating Our Control over Language and Thought

Another peril concerns the temptation to overestimate the depth of what we know or underestimate remaining mysteries. We say to ourselves, "I know what a right hand is. It is a physical hand, on the right side of the body, with four fingers and a thumb. God does not have a right hand. Therefore, Exodus 15:6 is an accommodation."

Do we really know what a right hand is? The description I just gave is partial, because it focuses wholly on the shape, position, and physical constitution of the hand. Do we think that is all there is to it? Then we are ignoring the functions of the right hand. We do things with our hands. We touch, we grab, we gesture. We are ignoring also the potential for using the right hand as a metaphor for something.

Why do we as human beings have right hands? Within a biblical framework, the answer surely includes observing that God made us that way. He did so out of his bounty. For example, Sue has a right hand because God gave her one. And why did he do it? Partly, at least, so that she could praise him for her right hand. Partly so that she could do things with it. Her power to do things imitates God's original power. So it is an aspect of the image of God.

God is the original, the Creator who is all-powerful. Sue has power derivative from and imitative of God's power. Her hands are expressions of that imitation. We may take the next step and say that the original for Sue's right hand is God's power to make, to shape, and to protect. If so, Sue's right hand is metaphorical. It is a figure within creation for God's power. God's power is the original "right hand."

But Sue's right hand is not only an image of God's power. It embodies God's power. God is present to empower Sue whenever she moves her hand. So when Sue moves her hand, we observe not only Sue's power but God's power, right there in her right hand. Without his sustaining power, Sue could do nothing.

If we then say that Exodus 15:6 is *merely* accommodation, in an attempt to explain away a metaphor, are we not also engaged in explaining away depth of meaning in the significance of Sue's right hand? And does not such an attempt display overweening and dangerous arrogance, which tempts us to think that we have already grasped all that is important when we focus exclusively on a hand as a physically structured object, and when we in our minds ignore the presence of God filling the heavens and the earth, and therefore also Sue's hand?

Consider another example. The doctrine of accommodation can be used to say that "God (of course) is not really angry; the Bible's statements about God's anger are instances of accommodation."

This analysis, like the analysis of God's right hand, exposes temptations to minimizing. To begin with, instead of saying that God is not angry, one could propose that God's anger is analogous to human anger, but is not on the same level. So the word *angry* would be used metaphorically or figuratively. But we could also attempt the same kind of reversal as we observed with God's right hand. Where does the human ability to get angry come from? It comes from the Creator, who made us in his image. There can be sinful human anger, of course, but that is a perversion and a sinful twisting of righteous anger, which ought to engage us when we see injustice, and which stirs us up to pray, work, and fight against injustice. Where did we get these abilities? We got them from God, who has the archetypal ability because he is the God of justice. God's character is fully just, and he is powerful in acting for justice. His being is engaged, as it were, in its depths. It is not just that he has a proposition in his mind, the proposition "This is unjust." God's commitment in evaluating and judging injustice is the original anger. Our anger is the shadowy imitation. So which is the "real" anger and which is only "metaphorical" anger?

As with the right hand, so here—our anger is not only imitative of God's anger, but, when it is righteous, involves God's work in us. We have fellowship with God, and our anger is an expression of the Holy Spirit's work in us. God is expressing *his* anger in ours (though we must be careful not to deify ourselves or excuse cases of unrighteous anger). So there is no such thing as "merely human" anger. It is always also a testimony to the character of God. J. I. Packer said once that it is not that God is anthropomorphic, but that man is theomorphic— made in the image of God.[18] Even in the case of unrighteous and un- believing anger, people do not escape the God who made them. They are twisting the image of God, not escaping it. So what is anger? We do not really know much about what we are saying until we realize that knowledge of anger is bound up with knowledge of God, which travels out into unfathomable mystery.

The Peril of Treating the World as Nonmysterious

A related peril arises from the decision (understandable in one respect) to focus on accommodation with respect only to descriptions of God, and not with respect to descriptions of anything else. This distinctive focus can easily tempt us to infer that our knowledge of the world— of right hands, anger, eyes, fire, wind, human love—is nonmysterious. We evaporate the mystery of the presence of God in the world and the testimony of the world to God.

So let us consider the broader use of the word *accommodation*, where the word applies not only to God's descriptions of himself, but to all of Scripture. All of Scripture comes to us in human languages through human authors, and originates within the context of human circumstances in history. What God says suits these contexts. To use the traditional term, all of Scripture is "accommodated."

As before, the same peril arises of thinking of accommodation as a kind of human adaptation to circumstances beyond an individual's

---

18. I remember hearing this point orally from J. I. Packer.

control. We then introduce ideas that are not appropriate to God, given his comprehensive control, from creation onward.

The Peril of Treating Some Scripture as "More" Accommodated

If all of Scripture is accommodated, we have to include the literal statements as well as the figurative ones. Anthropomorphic language about God is no more and no less accommodated than the affirmation that God is "immortal, invisible" (1 Tim. 1:17b) or that "Erastus remained at Corinth" (2 Tim. 4:20a). But a single general principle of accommodation that explains everything is in danger of explaining nothing in particular. In practice, we run the danger of considering some things in Scripture as accommodated and others as not. But then we are in danger of producing a canon within the canon, and also producing a false transcendence with respect to what allegedly can be treated in practice as if it were unaccommodated.

Prioritizing Reason, General Revelation, and Other Extrascriptural Sources

The language of accommodation, when applied to all of Scripture, opens the door to still another peril. If Scripture is accommodated, perhaps something outside Scripture is not. Human reason will not serve as an allegedly unaccommodated source because it is surely related to finite human capacities. And yet, people have been tempted to consider human reason as a window onto the divine. According to this view, reason is virtually a divine spark within us, and therefore identical to divine reason. Then reason becomes lord over Scripture, as took place in deism.

Even if this route is rejected, people may still plausibly think that God's word governing creation (Ps. 33:9; Heb. 1:3) is unaccommodated. It is not addressed to us, so it need not have the restrictions involved in communicating to human beings. It is untrammeled and unlimited. Therefore, people may be tempted to treat it as a source allegedly superior to Scripture. Given the impressive triumphs of modern science, the danger is real and growing.

But theologically speaking, the general principle of accommodation applies to God's speech governing creation in a way analogous to what we have said concerning speech addressed to human beings.

The speech of God with respect to creation calls for a response on the part of the created things that obey God's commands. So by analogy with God's speech to human beings, we may infer that God's commands suit or fit the created things to which they are addressed. Since we ourselves are not these created things, we know little about how such accommodation would work. In the end, the details are highly mysterious. We are in a worse position to understand these words of God, partly because we are not among the immediate hearers (God is not immediately addressing us in these cases) and partly because we do not have access to these words in verbal form. Scientists can only infer, guess at, and approximate what God says, and these guesses constitute what scientists think about the "laws of nature."

In this respect, scientific thinking about the laws of nature is thrice accommodated. God's speech concerning creation suits creation. That speech includes the first step in accommodation, namely, accommodation to the created things being addressed. Second, creation becomes a source of information to scientists. It "reveals" clues about how things work. This information from creation, though nonverbal in character, suits the capacities of scientists. That suitability is a second accommodation. Third, the scientific interpretations undertaken by scientists suit their capacities. Their own reflections constitute an accommodation to their thoughts and predispositions. Thus, the products of human science, in the form of theories, hypotheses, and summaries of "facts," are thrice accommodated. The same goes, *mutatis mutandis* ("once the necessary changes have been made"), for historical investigation.

A thrice-accommodated human project offers us a view through a dark glass. Neither science nor historical investigation can become a source from which we build a stable, solid platform that allegedly would be superior to Scripture. The reason should be plain. It is a case of "Physician, heal yourself." The proposed platform could be built only if we first "healed" the effects of triple accommodation on science and the study of history.

This path eventually reveals that a sound view of accommodation ought never to become an excuse for seeking a superior viewpoint outside a scriptural foundation. The person who seeks a superior viewpoint has tacitly abandoned, somewhere in the process, the conviction that Scripture is actually God's speech, accommodated or not.

The Peril of Leaving Out God as Recipient

Finally, simplistic thinking about accommodation runs the danger of neglecting a full reckoning with covenantal revelation. The implications of covenant need some explanation. We may begin with a human treaty (or "covenant") between two parties. The treaty is written not for the sake of one party alone, but for both. Both parties make binding commitments to the treaty (e.g., Gen. 31:44–54). When God makes his covenants with human beings, the covenants address and bind the human beings. But God is the second party. He binds himself, as it were, to his own words (cf. Heb. 6:13). He hears what he says. We can see this implication by observing that God told Moses to deposit the documents of the Mosaic covenant in the Most Holy Place, in and beside the ark, in the presence of God (Deut. 10:5; 31:24–26). Their location symbolically expresses the fact that God is aware of their contents and will faithfully fulfill the commitments that he has made as one party of the covenant. This placing of covenantal words in the presence of God comes to full realization when God addresses God in John 17, in words that are also accessible to us.[19]

John 17 is a very special case. But even in its special character, it can illustrate by analogy what is true of all Scripture. All of Scripture is covenantal in a broad sense. In it, God addresses us, but he also addresses himself as the second party. The Holy Spirit stands with us, indwelling us, as we receive Scripture. And that implies that the Spirit is hearer as well as speaker.

Thus, the usual reasoning about accommodation has a potential flaw. It can suggest the assumption that Scripture has us human beings as the *only* hearers. If we are the only hearers, Scripture is accommodated to us, but not to God. That is false. Like the treaty, Scripture speaks both to God and to us. To put it more elaborately, God is speaking to God, in the mystery of the Trinity, and to us as well. If so, what it means to God is beyond calculation. Therefore, Scripture itself is beyond calculation.[20] Its accommodation to us is an additional feature, not a subtraction from the fullness of divine meaning.

---

19. Vern S. Poythress, *God-Centered Biblical Interpretation* (Phillipsburg, NJ: P&R, 1999), 19–25.
20. Poythress, *God-Centered Biblical Interpretation*, 19–25.

Since we are considering the matter deeply, let us observe that the Son communicates to the Father in John 17 in the context of the indwelling of the Holy Spirit. The communion between two persons of the Trinity always *suits* the context of the third person, as well as the context of each person who is giving and receiving love. The archetype for accommodation or contextual fit is the Trinity.

Do you understand it? No. It is incomprehensible. Those who would make it comprehensible undertake to destroy God, or to become God themselves.

Consequences

The attempt to destroy God cannot succeed. Neither can the attempt to rationalize accommodation (essentially, to rationalize the Creator-creature distinction). To rationalize accommodation would mean to accommodate the doctrine of accommodation to the capacity of human autonomous rationality. Such an attempt has consequences. God does not hold him guiltless who takes his name in vain (Ex. 20:7). The attempt to destroy God turns back against itself, and may damage the image of God, the one who makes the attempt.

Some kinds of postmodernism illustrate the process. Some postmodernists reject supernatural revelation because they think they can see that supernatural revelation cannot actually be received by a finite human being within a finite language and a finite culture around him. They are, in effect, accommodationists, for whom accommodation means the inevitable absorption and dissolution of any alleged revelation within the sea of finite language and culture. As a consequence, they think that any alleged revelation, once accommodated to human finiteness, inherits some of the errors and failings of its environment.

Such false views have consequences. The same false reasoning can be applied to science. When the postmodernist theory of accommodation is applied to science, the triple accommodation in science leads to the conclusion that science is a social construct whose function is to maintain the power and prestige of scientists. And if the reasoning goes this far, it can then attack the foundations of social science and the sociology of knowledge as well as natural science. This attack finally undermines postmodernism itself, because postmodernism builds on modern social scientific insights about language and culture. The postmodernist victim may travel out into an epistemic void with only the will to power left at the core of his being—raw desire for autonomy.

Conclusion

Rightly understood, accommodation is an expression of the Creator-creature distinction. But sin tempts us in many ways to distort the meaning of accommodation in favor of false transcendence and false immanence. We must be on our guard and avoid thinking that the concept of accommodation dissolves the fundamental mysteries in divine communication and divine covenants. Instead, it reasserts them.

Appendix C

A Misunderstanding of Calvin on Genesis 1:6–8 and 1:5

In his commentary on Genesis, John Calvin had some interesting things to say about Genesis 1:6–8.[1] I want to reexamine them, because there is a dispute about their meaning. In addition, I will examine a related problem concerning Genesis 1:5. Both cases have implications for the doctrine of Scripture and the nature of "accommodation." So they have more than historical interest.[2]

Kenton Sparks's book *God's Word in Human Words* (2008) includes comments on Calvin's interpretation of Genesis 1:6–8.[3] But as we shall see, Sparks misunderstands Calvin. Moreover, Sparks uses Calvin's remarks in a significant way as a building block on his way to constructing an overall approach to Scripture. Sparks's overall approach says that the Bible may incorporate erroneous ancient views about the cosmos—and errors of other kinds as well. He claims that Calvin thought in a similar way. Problems belong both to Sparks's position and to his use of Calvin to support it.[4]

1. John Calvin, *Commentaries on the First Book of Moses Called Genesis* (Grand Rapids, MI: Baker, 1979), 1.78–81.
2. This appendix is a revision of Vern S. Poythress, "A Misunderstanding of Calvin's Interpretation of Genesis 1:6–8 and 1:5 and Its Implications for Ideas of Accommodation," *Westminster Theological Journal* 76, no. 1 (2014): 157–66. Used with permission.
3. Kenton L. Sparks, *God's Word in Human Words: An Evangelical Appropriation of Critical Biblical Scholarship* (Grand Rapids, MI: Baker, 2008), 235.
4. On the broader issue of Calvin's views on biblical authority, see John D. Woodbridge, *Biblical Authority: A Critique of the Rogers/McKim Proposal* (Grand Rapids, MI: Zondervan, 1982), 49–52, 56–67. Note also the bibliography from p. 56n32 and 56n33, found on pp. 177–78,

An evangelical scholar recently repeated in his own words Sparks's misunderstanding of what Calvin said about Genesis 1:6–8. This shows that other people are making the same mistake that Sparks made. So it is time to set to rest this misreading of Calvin.

Calvin and Sparks

Let us begin with Calvin's exposition of Genesis 1:6–8 and then compare it with Sparks's. For a sense of context, it is worthwhile reading all of Calvin's remarks on Genesis 1:6–8. For convenience, we start with the most salient portion, which lies in the middle of his exposition:

> Moses describes the special use of this expanse, "to divide the waters from the waters," from which words arises a great difficulty. For it appears opposed to common sense, and quite incredible, that there should be waters above the heaven. Hence some resort to allegory, and philosophize concerning angels; but quite beside the purpose. For, to my mind, this is a certain principle, that nothing is here treated of but the visible form of the world. He who would learn astronomy, and other recondite arts, let him go elsewhere. Here the Spirit of God would teach all men without exception; and therefore what Gregory declares falsely and in vain respecting statues and pictures is truly applicable to the history of the creation, namely, that it is the book of the unlearned. The things, therefore, which he relates, serve as the garniture of that theatre which he places before our eyes. Whence I conclude, that the waters here meant are such as the rude and unlearned may perceive. The assertion of some, that they embrace by faith what they have read concerning the waters above the heavens, notwithstanding their ignorance respecting them, is not in accordance with the design of Moses. And truly a longer inquiry into a matter open and manifest is superfluous. We see that the clouds suspended in the air, which threaten to fall upon our heads, yet leave us space to breathe. They who deny that this is effected by the wonderful providence of God, are vainly inflated

and the discussion of Calvin on Genesis on p. 61. For Calvin's views on "accommodation," see Glenn S. Sunshine, "Accommodation in Calvin and Socinus: A Study of Contrasts," MA thesis, Trinity Evangelical Divinity School, 1985; Clinton M. Ashley, "John Calvin's Utilization of the Principle of Accommodation and Its Continuing Significance for an Understanding of Biblical Language," PhD diss., Southwestern Baptist Theological Seminary, 1972; Martin I. Klauber and Glenn S. Sunshine, "Jean-Alphonse Turrettini on Biblical Accommodation: Calvinist or Socinian?" *Calvin Theological Journal* 25, no. 1 (1990): 7–27, and the further bibliography in 9n4.

with the folly of their own minds. We know, indeed, that the rain is naturally produced; but the deluge sufficiently shows how speedily we might be overwhelmed by the bursting of the clouds, unless the cataracts of heaven were closed by the hand of God.[5]

In his book, Sparks quotes the middle part of this passage.[6] He then interprets Calvin as follows:

One should not, Calvin says, believe "by faith" that there are waters above the firmament when one knows good and well that this is not the case. Genesis merely accommodates itself to *the ancient view* that such waters existed.[7]

Calvin's Meaning

Sparks's interpretation misses widely what Calvin is saying. Sparks thinks that Calvin is saying that there are no waters above the firmament.[8] But this is directly contradicted by Calvin's repeated references to these very waters (emphasis added in each case):

Whence I conclude, that *the waters here meant* are such as the rude and unlearned [i.e., ordinary people in Calvin's time, as well as in ancient Israel] may perceive [i.e., the waters are something obvious, not something "recondite" as in astronomy].

We see that the *clouds* suspended in the air, which threaten to fall upon our heads, yet leave us space to breathe.

We know, indeed, that the *rain* is naturally produced; but the deluge [i.e., the flood of Noah] sufficiently shows how speedily we might be overwhelmed by the bursting of the *clouds*, unless the *cataracts of heaven* [a figurative reference to the water above] were closed by the hand of God.

Calvin is saying that the water in the clouds is the "water above the expanse," and the lower air is the expanse.

---

5. Calvin, *First Book of Moses*, 1.78–81.

6. Sparks, *God's Word*, 235. Sparks's quotation begins with the words "For, to my mind . . . ," elides the sentence about Gregory, and ends with the sentence "And truly a longer inquiry into a matter open and manifest is superfluous."

7. Sparks, *God's Word*, 235 (emphasis added).

8. ". . . one knows good and well that this [that there are waters above the firmament] is not the case." Sparks, *God's Word*, 235.

The surrounding text in Calvin's commentary confirms that this is what Calvin has in mind. Before coming to the middle part of his exposition (already quoted), Calvin argues that the key Hebrew word *rakia'* ("firmament" or "expanse") includes the lower atmosphere:

> Moreover, the word רקיע, (*rakia,*) comprehends not only the whole region of the air, but whatever is open above us: as the word heaven is sometimes understood by the Latins. Thus the arrangement, as well of the heavens as of the lower atmosphere, is called רקיע, (*rakia,*) without discrimination between them [i.e., between the heavens and the lower atmosphere], but sometimes the word signifies both together, sometimes one part only, as will appear more plainly in our progress [i.e., Calvin's discussion still to come]. I know not why the Greeks have chosen to render the word στερέωμα, which the Latins have imitated in the term *firmamentum*; for literally it means *expanse* [*expansio*].[9]

Calvin claims that the key word *rakia'* ("expanse") can include both "the heavens" and "the lower atmosphere," but can also be used for "one part only." This claim paves the way for Calvin later on to interpret the "expanse" in Genesis 1:6 as referring to the lower atmosphere, that is, the air separating the clouds from the earth.

After the middle part of the exposition that we quoted above, Calvin continues to explain:

> Since, therefore, God has created the clouds, and assigned them a region above us [i.e., in the general region of the expanse], it ought not to be forgotten that they are restrained by the power of God, lest, gushing forth with sudden violence, they should swallow us up: and especially since no other barrier is opposed to them than the liquid and yielding air, which would easily give way unless this word [God's word of command given in Gen. 1:6] prevailed, "Let there be an expanse between the waters."[10]

---

9. Calvin, *First Book of Moses*, 1.79. It should be noted that Calvin provides his own translation of the text of Gen. 1:1–31. He renders *rakia'* (רקיע) variously: *extensio* ("extension," v. 6), *expansio* ("expanse, expansion," vv. 7, 8, 15, 17), and *firmamentum* ("firmament," v. 14). Calvin, *First Book of Moses*, 1.67–68. By contrast, the Latin Vulgate consistently uses *firmamentum*.

10. Calvin, *First Book of Moses*, 1.80–81.

Here Calvin's final sentence uses the key word *expanse* (*extensio*) as part of its quotation of Genesis 1:6. Calvin implies that God's word of command concerning the expanse causes the air not to "give way." He thereby identifies the expanse with the air, which functions as a "barrier." He implies that this air, like a barrier, separates the waters below from the waters above the expanse. If the air did give way, the water from the clouds would be "gushing forth with sudden violence." Thus, he identifies the clouds with the waters above the expanse, that is, with the waters that are above the "barrier" of the air.

This entire paragraph, be it noted, makes good sense in the light of Calvin's principle: "For, to my mind, this is a certain principle, that nothing is here [in Genesis 1] treated of but the visible form of the world."[11] The clouds and the air are both observable. Calvin interprets Genesis 1:6–8 as referring to them. A theoretically postulated, invisible, recondite body of "waters above the heavens" would be *out of accord* with the principle that Calvin thinks is operative throughout Genesis 1. He therefore rejects such speculative views, even though they piously appeal to faith:

> The assertion of some, that they embrace by faith what they have read concerning the waters above the heavens, notwithstanding their ignorance respecting them [an ignorance due to the fact that they have in mind waters that they believe to constitute an invisible body of which they have never had any experience], is not in accordance with the design of Moses [i.e., it does not match Moses's purpose to address "the rude and unlearned," and to confine himself to "the visible form of the world."][12]

Calvin is rejecting a speculative construction in favor of one that says that Genesis 1:6–8 is referring to "the visible form of the world," in this case, to the air and the clouds.[13]

---

11. Calvin, *First Book of Moses*, 1.79. Cf. John Calvin, *Institutes of the Christian Religion*, 1.14.3: "Moses, in accommodation to the ignorance of the generality of men, does not in the history of the creation make mention of any other works of God than *those which meet our eye*" (emphasis added); cited in Klauber and Sunshine, "Turrettini," 10.

12. Calvin, *First Book of Moses*, 1.80.

13. So also Scott M. Manetsch, "Problems with the Patriarchs: John Calvin's Interpretation of Difficult Passages in Genesis," *Westminster Theological Journal* 67, no. 1 (2005): 1–21; with respect to the same passage, 11–13.

Calvin thinks that his meaning is what Moses intended ("the design of Moses"). In his own view, Calvin is not making any alteration in meaning, as if hypothetically such an alteration were needed in the light of more modern knowledge. The meaning is the same for the ancient Israelites and for Calvin himself. It has this stable function over time because the passage is discussing what is visible to all (including "the rude and unlearned"). Calvin repeatedly indicates that Genesis 1:6–8 is referring to perceivable aspects of the world, so that all people may grasp what is in view: "the *visible* form of the world"; "teach *all* men without exception"; "the book of the *unlearned*"; "he places before *our eyes*"; "such as the *rude and unlearned* may *perceive*"; "a matter *open and manifest*"; and "We *see* that the clouds suspended in the air . . ."[14]

A Further Puzzle

There remains one part of Calvin's exposition that might still puzzle modern readers. He says, "For it appears opposed to common sense, and quite incredible, that there should be waters above the heaven."[15] Does Calvin here repudiate the existence of "waters above the heavens" because it is "opposed to common sense"? No. To understand what Calvin is saying, it is best to proceed sentence by sentence. His sentence about "common sense" is immediately preceded by words that Calvin uses to introduce to his readers a "difficulty": "from which words arises a great difficulty." At this comparatively early point in his exposition, he is preparing to discuss why interpreters perceive a difficulty. These other interpreters—not Calvin—cannot figure out what these waters might be in a way that would agree with common sense.[16] Calvin does not directly say so, but their difficulty involves the fact that they understand "the heaven" (i.e., the "expanse") to mean high heaven. Calvin does not so understand it. Earlier in his exposition, he has already begun to expound this part of his view by explaining the flexibility of the use of *rakia'* (the "expanse"). The Hebrew word for "expanse" can refer to the air, and so Calvin has avoided the difficulty that confronts these other interpreters.

---

14. Calvin, *First Book of Moses*, 1.79–80 (emphasis added).
15. Calvin, *First Book of Moses*, 1.79.
16. Manetsch, "Problems," 11.

Following his sentence about "common sense," Calvin next explains the routes these other interpreters take in order to deal with their difficulty: "Hence some resort to allegory, and philosophize concerning angels; but quite beside the purpose." Calvin rejects these interpretations with the words "quite beside the purpose." Why are these routes "beside the purpose"? Calvin explains in the next sentence: "For, to my mind, this is a certain principle, that nothing is here treated of but the visible form of the world." Here Calvin reveals his own stance. The other interpreters have gone astray into speculations because they suppose that the "waters above the heavens" must refer to something invisible or recondite. If, instead, we realize that this and other expressions in Genesis 1 refer to things that are observable, the difficulty dissolves. And indeed, in the subsequent discussion, Calvin does dissolve them, at least to his own satisfaction.

Thus, in the key sentence about "common sense," Calvin is *not* repudiating the existence of the "waters above the heavens." Rather, he is posing an *apparent* difficulty. This difficulty has steered other interpreters into allegory. But Calvin himself thinks that the solution can be found once we see that Genesis 1:6 is talking about "the visible form of the world." We then see that the text is talking about water in the clouds, separated from the earth by the air.

Not everyone will agree with every detail in Calvin's interpretation. But his interpretation makes good sense, given his starting orientation, his assumptions about "the design of Moses," his understanding of the "expanse," and his assumptions about the divine authority of Scripture.

Sparks's Misunderstanding

Sparks, by contrast, introduces a profound disjunction between two distinct times, namely, the time of Calvin and the time during which there prevailed what Sparks calls "the ancient view." According to Sparks, "the ancient view" is one to which "Genesis merely accommodates itself." He says that Calvin, as a modern interpreter, knowingly deviates from the ancient view, because he "knows good and well that this is not the case."[17] But Sparks is mistaken. His disjunction between two times is completely foreign to Calvin's words. In fact, it

---

17. Sparks, *God's Word*, 235.

contradicts what Calvin says about "the design of *Moses*," which is to speak about clouds, rain, and the lower atmosphere. There is no distinct "ancient view" in Calvin's thinking. Sparks has unconsciously read it in.

How did Sparks fall into this mistake? We do not know. Perhaps Sparks thinks he knows what this ancient view is and is convinced that we can no longer hold to it.[18] Sparks himself would doubtless say, "One should not . . . believe 'by faith' that there are waters above the firmament when one knows good and well that this is not the case." He attributes his own thought to Calvin. But Calvin is saying almost exactly the opposite, namely, that in interpreting Genesis 1:6–8, one must determine a meaning for "waters above the expanse" that is in accord with Moses's design. Then one must appreciate how true it is and to what practical lessons it leads.[19] Calvin thinks that one should believe what Moses describes. Sparks says that one should not (because "one knows good and well that this is not the case"). He thinks that there are no waters above the firmament. Calvin thinks that there are, and identifies the waters as the rainwater in the clouds.

Sparks's Treatment of Time (Gen. 1:5)

As long as we are considering Calvin in relation to Sparks's interpretation of him, we should consider a second claim about Calvin that Sparks introduces on the same page as the first. Sparks says:

> Calvin similarly argued that accommodation was at work in the chronological system used to enumerate the various creation days of Genesis 1. Because the text reflects an accommodation to the ancient view of time, says Calvin, "It is useless to dispute whether this is the best and legitimate order or not." In other words, for Calvin, accommodation was a useful interpretive tool because it made irrelevant in such cases any questions about the Bible's correctness.[20]

In the middle of this paragraph, Sparks offers us a direct quote of Calvin's words. Sparks's footnote indicates that Calvin's words come

---

18. Sparks, *God's Word*, 234.
19. "Having established the correct interpretation of Gen. 1:6, Calvin the preacher finally proceeds to application." Manetsch, "Problems," 12.
20. Sparks, *God's Word*, 235.

from pages 1.79–80 of his commentary on Genesis.[21] The words actually come from page 1.77. My English edition of Calvin's commentary has slightly different wording: "It is to no purpose to dispute whether this be the best and the legitimate order or not."

Calvin's Meaning

What is at issue here? It is important to discern Calvin's meaning because there is more than one possible understanding of "accommodation."

To understand Calvin, we must consider the larger context. Calvin is discussing Genesis 1:5, with its mention of the evening and the morning, day one. He writes:

> What Moses says [in Gen. 1:5], however, admits a double interpretation; either that this was the evening and morning belonging to the first day, or that the first day consisted of the evening and the morning. Whichever interpretation be chosen, it makes no difference in the sense, for he simply understands the day to have been made up of two parts. Further, he begins the day, according to the custom of his nation [i.e., Israel], with the evening. *It is to no purpose to dispute whether this* [i.e., beginning the day at evening] *be the best and the legitimate order or not.* . . . Although Moses did not intend here to prescribe a rule which it would be criminal to violate; yet (as we have now said) he accommodated his discourse to the received custom [of the Jews]. Wherefore, as the Jews foolishly condemn all the reckonings of other people, as if God had sanctioned this alone [i.e., that the reckoning of the beginning of a day *must* begin with evening]; so again are they equally foolish who contend that this mode of reckoning [i.e., the Jewish way of beginning with evening], which Moses approves, is preposterous.[22]

In part, Calvin is discussing the significance of the word order in Genesis 1:5: "evening," then "morning." The last sentence in the quoted material is especially illuminating. It makes clear that Calvin is aware of a dispute. Some of the Jews insist that their way of reckoning, which begins the day at evening, is the only proper ("sanctioned") way. Others reject this Jewish way as "preposterous," thereby impugning

21. Sparks, *God's Word*, 235n19.
22. Calvin, *First Book of Moses*, 1.77–78 (emphasis added).

what "Moses approves." Calvin maintains that either way is OK. This clarifies what he means when he says earlier, "It is to no purpose to *dispute* whether this [the Jewish way] be the best and the legitimate order or not."

Calvin also uses the word *accommodated* at one point: Moses "accommodated [*accommodavit*] his discourse to the received custom." This use of the word is about as innocuous as it can be. Calvin simply means that Moses wrote in a way that took into account "received custom"—the normal way that the Jews expressed themselves.

Sparks's Explication

Now we turn to Sparks's remarks on Calvin. They have some peculiarities. To begin with, he uses the expression "the ancient view of time." This expression makes it sound as if there were only one ancient view. But Calvin does not say this. He discusses more narrowly how the Jews treated the description of a day. He makes no claim that their way was universal in ancient times, and he mentions "all the reckonings of other people." The word *all* (*omnes*) suggests that he may be including various ancient people as well as those of his own time. In addition, he is aware that some people think that the Jewish way is "preposterous." To say the least, he is aware of multiple points of view here.

For Calvin, there is no question of one way being the "correct" way. Rather, it would be possible to begin with the morning or with midnight, as well as with the evening. Calvin does not really need an elaborate theory of accommodation to achieve this result. He happens to use a Latin word that is translated as "accommodated," but the point would be plain even without it. Different people may have different customary ways of looking at the sequence of daylight and nighttime. More than one might serve, without generating a dispute. "It is to no purpose to dispute."

Unfortunately, it is easy for a reader of Sparks's comments to misunderstand the implications of what Calvin is saying. Sparks speaks about "the chronological system used to enumerate the various creation days of Genesis 1." In this system, says Sparks, Calvin "argued that accommodation was at work." A reader who listens to Sparks but does not read through Calvin's entire discussion could easily believe that Calvin views the *entire system of a sequence of six days* as an accommodation. As it is, all Calvin is actually saying is that the repeated refrain "and there was evening and there was morning" is in line with a Jewish way of reckoning, in which the commencement of a day comes at evening.

Sparks's quote from Calvin also includes the key expression "the best and the legitimate order." Apart from a larger context, this expression can easily be misunderstood. Modern interpreters are likely to think that it refers to the chronological order of events that occur in the creation week, because that is one area now in dispute. But the word *order* in Calvin has a very different reference, namely, to whether one uses the order evening to morning, morning to evening, or even midnight to midnight in counting one day. He is not discussing the chronological order of *events*. He is discussing what one chooses to call the "beginning" of a daily cycle. The chronological sequence is the same for everyone: dawn, morning, noon, afternoon, evening, and night, repeated in a cycle. Calvin is implying that it is legitimate to commence the cycle at any point one chooses.

Calvin's Comments on the System of Six Days

Right after the discussion concerning evenings and mornings, Calvin comments on the sequence of six days. He rejects the view that "the world was made in a moment." Instead, he says, "Let us rather conclude that God himself took the space of six days, for the purpose of accommodating [*temperaret*] his works to the capacity of men."[23]

Here again we meet language concerning accommodation. But note what it means. Calvin implies that God *could have* made the world "in a moment." Instead, he "took the space of six days." Calvin clearly believes that the words in Genesis 1 describe a series of works that took six days. What he calls an accommodation is the decision on God's part to do it in this way, that is, to spread his works over "the space of six days." God did so, Calvin thinks, because a process spread over time would be easier for human beings to take in and digest. It suited "the capacity of men." Hence, according to Calvin, the accommodation lies in the fact that God spreads out his works in time, *not* in the language in Genesis 1 describing those works.

---

23. Calvin, *First Book of Moses*, 1.78.

Modern scholars, by contrast, are greatly interested in the disputes about the chronological length of the days of Genesis 1 and whether the various works described are given in chronological order. For the sake of reconciliation with mainstream accounts in modern science, some modern interpreters say that God "accommodated" the *language* of Genesis 1 to a framework of six days, even though the works being described belong to an entirely different order of time.[24]

Again, whether a modern interpreter agrees with Calvin is not my point. My point is that Calvin's approach should be recognized for what it is. In affirming "the space of six days," Calvin is advocating nearly the opposite of the point of view that alleges that a radical kind of "accommodation" is taking place in the *language* about six days. Calvin thinks that the language in Genesis 1 actually describes six days of God's works, but accommodation takes place in the way God accomplishes *the works* themselves. If we translate it anachronistically into modern terms, we could almost say that Calvin is talking about accommodation in what science researches (the works), while modern interpreters are talking about an alleged accommodation in the language—the verbal deposit in Genesis 1. According to these modern interpreters, the wording in Genesis 1 sets forth a literary framework that talks about six days for the purpose of accommodating the description to a graspable framework, but Genesis 1 refers to events that belong to another order of time.[25] Or, going a step further, modern interpreters may say that the entire scheme of events, as well as the framework of six days, is a literary invention useful (as a accommodation) in describing God as the ground for the existence of the world.

---

24. Sparks's own view of Calvin's remarks on Genesis 1:5 is not clear. It is possible that Sparks has misunderstood Calvin. In the case of Genesis 1:5, however, it seems more likely that Sparks has correctly understood Calvin's narrow focus on the dispute over when a day begins. At the same time, he has worded his description in such a way as to suggest broader implications. But a description that tries simultaneously to address Calvin's meaning and broader implications easily becomes unclear about both. In addition, it fails to establish whether the one leads to the other. In fact, Calvin's own focused treatment of Jewish custom does not provide grounds for the broad reinterpretive treatment that some modern interpreters would like to apply to the *whole system* of chronology of six days. Quite the contrary.

25. I do not intend here to criticize every form of the framework hypothesis for Genesis 1; for a further evaluation of the framework view, see Vern S. Poythress, *Redeeming Science: A God-Centered Approach* (Wheaton, IL: Crossway, 2006), 143–47, 341–45. Rather, I am merely saying that Calvin's approach to Gen. 1:5 cannot be used to launch a framework view. Moreover, we should distinguish between (1) a dismissal of textual details on the basis of a loose general principle of "accommodation" and (2) a serious engagement with the details, on the basis of which an interpreter tries to argue in favor of a framework view as Moses's meaning.

Meanings of *Accommodation*

Distinct kinds of accommodation are quite different, and it does not help to roll all the uses together. In particular, we obscure an important dispute if, in discussing Genesis 1:5, we do not distinguish a careful use of language according to "received custom" (Calvin) from a global reorganization of chronological order (modern desire). Likewise, earlier in this appendix we uncovered two vastly different approaches to Genesis 1:6–8. Calvin attempts to interpret the language of Genesis 1:6–8 as a *true* description of "the visible form of the world." By contrast, Sparks depreciates the same biblical language because it allegedly represents a *mistaken* "ancient view." He says, "Genesis merely accommodates itself to the ancient view that such waters existed."[26]

Both of these stratagems, Calvin's and Sparks's, have been described with the word *accommodation*. But in Calvin, God accommodates to the needs of his addressees by describing the visible form of the world and thereby making sure that his communication makes sense to ordinary people ("the unlearned"). Accommodation in this sense serves the truth by expressing it in an accessible manner. In Sparks's view, God allegedly accommodates erroneous ancient views by incorporating them into the text that he endorses. Accommodation in this second sense serves confusion. Many in our day think there is no real alternative to such confusion because of the limitations of language and culture that God confronts.[27] Ironically, the very places where Sparks appeals to Calvin count against this pessimistic view of communication. Even if Calvin is wrong in some details, he at least shows how a clear meaning *could* be communicated from God to man, namely, by talking about the observable world in ordinary ways. That is what God does in Genesis 1.

---

26. Sparks, *God's Word*, 235.
27. A lot of assumptions lie behind postmodern conceptions of "limitation" with respect to language, culture, and human psychology. See Vern S. Poythress, *Inerrancy and Worldview: Answering Modern Challenges to the Bible* (Wheaton, IL: Crossway, 2012).

Appendix D

Multiple Interpretations of Ancient Texts

For the sake of further illustration of chapter 5, we continue with two more instances that show the challenge of interpreting ancient Near Eastern texts.[1]

Egyptian Pictures of the Sky Goddess

The first example comes from Egypt, which has a number of pictorial representations of Nut, the goddess of the sky, with the front of her body facing downward. The body as a whole forms a kind of tent-like shape, with her trunk as the roof, her arms and hands as the sloping side to the right, and her legs and feet as the sloping side to the left.[2] Her body is held up by the uplifted hands of the air god Shu. Lying at Shu's feet is the earth god Geb. In some of the representations, Shu's arms are propped up on either side by the uplifted arms of two images of Heh, the androgynous deity/deities of eternity.

---

1. This appendix is a revision of part of Vern S. Poythress, "Three Modern Myths in Interpreting Genesis 1," *Westminster Theological Journal* 76, no. 2 (2014): 321–50.
2. See, e.g., the photograph from the Greenfield Papyrus (the Book of the Dead of Nesitanebtashru) by the British Museum, available online at http://en.wikipedia.org/wiki/File:Geb,_Nut,_Shu.jpg. The same picture appears in James B. Pritchard, *The Ancient Near East in Pictures Relating to the Old Testament* (Princeton, NJ: Princeton University Press, 1969), 183, #542. Another picture of Nut can be found in James P. Allen, *Genesis in Egypt: The Philosophy of Ancient Egyptian Creation Accounts* (New Haven, CT: Yale Egyptological Seminar, Department of Near Eastern Language and Civilizations, The Graduate School, Yale University, 1988), 115, Plate I, with discussion, 1–7.

Physicalistic Interpretation

Student A offers a physicalistic interpretation:

> Lacking modern science, the Egyptians explained such things by a primitive substitute. They said that the material composition of the sky was the body of a goddess. They explained the physical structure of the sky by saying that it was formed into a tent-like shape by the bends in the goddess's body, and that it was held up both by the hands and feet of the goddess herself and by the hands of the air god.

Critique. Like the earlier interpretation of Tiamat (chap. 5), this interpretation suffers the weakness of injecting into ancient Egypt the questions about material composition and physical structure that are of interest to modern science. It may have postulated, against the background of scientistic metaphysics, that such questions must reveal the most ultimate realities, and that the Egyptians, in searching for ultimate reality, must have been trying to answer these questions, but in a confused way.

An additional weakness lies in the fact that this interpretation has to put into the background the personal interactions among the gods and between the gods and humans, both of which have roles in Egyptian thinking. According to various Egyptian stories, Geb and Nut were the offspring of Shu and Tefnut, and the two of them produced further gods (Osiris, Isis, Seth, and Nephthys) as offspring.[3] These interactions must be interpreted as only a primitive way of leading up to answering the "real" questions about physical structure.

The physicalistic interpretation is also weakened by the presence of Shu, the air god, and Heh, representing eternity, because it is implausible to think that the Egyptians were giving an ultimately mechanistic account involving literal physical props from the "hands" of air and eternity to hold up the sky. Air and eternity are not the kind of things that could serve as physical props.

In addition, there are features in the picture that have no visible counterpart in the sky. For example, where in the visible sky can one see the eyes, ears, hair, and mouth of Nut? Where in the sky is the line of division between her two arms or two legs? Where in the sky

---

3. See Vincent Arieh Tobin, "Myths: An Overview," in *The Oxford Encyclopedia of Ancient Egypt*, ed. Donald B. Redford (New York: Oxford University Press, 2001), 2.464–65, concerning the "Heliopolitan tradition"; Veronica Ions, *Egyptian Mythology*, new rev. ed. (New York: Peter Bedrick, 1982), 45, 48–50, 56.

are her feet, toes, hands, and fingers? These features suggest that we have an imaginative representation of a goddess in human form, not a physical, literal representation of parts of the sky. The goddess as a spiritual reality is represented spatially, but the pictorial representation is symbolic. Thus, a modern physicalistic interpretation may be missing the nature of imagistic representation in Egypt:

> The Egyptian gods, unlike the anthropomorphic gods of the Greeks, were not understood to be limited to the forms in which iconography portrayed them.[4]

Spiritistic Interpretation

Student B offers a spiritistic interpretation:

> In Egyptian thinking, sky, air, and earth are not composed of "matter" as we know it. Rather, they are the visible manifestations of the gods and goddesses of sky, air, and earth, respectively. The picture is a metaphorical representation of the reality.

> *Critique.* In this interpretation, the world is composed of spirits. It has plausibility, since the focus is on the gods and their activities.

Dualistic Interpretation

Student C offers a dualistic interpretation:

> The regions of nature are composed of matter and spirit, dualistically conceived. The matter of sky, air, and earth is animated by the corresponding spirit/gods.

> *Critique.* This interpretation also has plausibility, but suffers from the weakness that it may unwittingly have read into the Egyptian picture a body/soul dualism that is characteristic only of later cultures more familiar to us.

Monistic Interpretation

Student D offers a monistic interpretation:

> The gods flow into the realities of sky, air, and earth with no sharp distinction between gods and visible realities.

---

4. Tobin, "Myths: An Overview," 2.464.

Sociological-Functional Interpretation and Allegorical Interpretation

We could also consider sociological-functional and allegorical interpretations that would discount some of the mythic elements. We will pass over these, since the pattern should be evident.

The Making of Mankind from the Blood of Kingu

As our second example, we may consider another piece from *Enuma Elish*, concerning the making of mankind:

> They [the assembly of the gods] imposed on him [the god Kingu]
>   his guilt
>   [for inciting the rebellion] and severed his blood (vessels).
> Out of his blood they fashioned mankind.
> He [Ea?] imposed the service and let free the gods.
> After Ea, the wise, had created mankind,
>   Had imposed upon it the service of the gods—[5]

Physicalistic Interpretation

Since the description of the severed blood vessels and blood sounds physicalistic, this description seems to offer an opening for student A's physicalistic interpretation:

> We have an account of the origin of mankind, with Kingu's blood as the material composition of mankind.

Critique. This interpretation has the weakness that the bodies of human beings are quite obviously composed of skin and bones (mentioned in *Enuma Elish* VI.5) as well as blood. The interpretation therefore has to include an additional inference, perhaps that the "fashioning" by the gods transforms blood into other materials. The tablet also does not make clear whether the immediate result of creation consists of a single individual man, a pair, or a large group. It does not go into detail about the process. Neither does it answer the question as to why blood is singled out.

---

5. James B. Pritchard, ed., *Ancient Near Eastern Texts Relating to the Old Testament* (Princeton, NJ: Princeton University Press, 1969), 68, VI.32–36; also William W. Hallo, ed., *The Context of Scripture*, 2 vols. (New York: Brill, 1997–2002), 1.401, with minor variations in the translation.

Spiritistic Interpretation

This omission gives space for a spiritistic interpretation from student B:

> The blood represents the life of Kingu, as a spirit. His spirit is transmuted into the spirit animating mankind. Man as a spiritual being has within him a divine spark, deriving from Kingu's divine being. Like the rest of the poem, this description of creation has a sustained focus on spirits, not on "matter."

Dualistic Interpretation

Student C may similarly produce a dualistic interpretation:

> The blood of Kingu is a part of his body, but simultaneously a metaphorical representation of his spirit. Thus, we infer that the poem is saying that both the body (the blood as literal stuff) and the spirit of Kingu are transmuted (by "fashioning") into the bodies and spirits of mankind.

Sifting among Interpretations

These examples should suffice to indicate that physicalistic interpretations are not the only ones possible. The physicalistic interpretation is the only one that finds in these ancient texts and pictures evidence for a full-blown physicalistic cosmology. The variety of other interpretations makes it clear that the physicalistic interpretation is in danger of reading into the texts the focus of modern science on material explanation. This reading-in can easily take place because of the influence of the myth that we can understand cultures from facts.

All of this is not to say that the ancient Near Eastern cultures had no physicalistic theories about material composition, physical structure, and physical causation. Perhaps they did. But do we *know* that they did? Even if they did, they may have had multiple theories, not one. In addition, we may doubt whether the genre of cosmonomic myth is suited to reveal underlying physicalistic theories. If, as Vincent Tobin believes, the myths are about "symbolic articulations" of meaning, they move in other directions.[6]

---

6. Vincent Arieh Tobin, "Myths: Creation Myths," in *The Oxford Encyclopedia of Ancient Egypt*, 2.469.

Our purpose is not to debate these questions in further detail, but to show that discerning the actual character of cultures is more difficult than it appears at first. A simple summary taken from sources, either primary, secondary, or both, may communicate only an armchair knowledge of a culture. The danger increases when such summaries are presented for popular consumption. The myth of easy understanding then remains unchallenged.

Bibliography

Alexander, T. D. *From Paradise to Promised Land: An Introduction to the Pentateuch*. 2nd ed. Grand Rapids, MI: Baker, 2002.

Allen, James P. *Genesis in Egypt: The Philosophy of Ancient Egyptian Creation Accounts*. New Haven, CT: Yale Egyptological Seminar, Department of Near Eastern Language and Civilizations, The Graduate School, Yale University, 1988.

Ambrose. *Hexaemeron*. In *Saint Ambrose: Hexameron, Paradise, and Cain and Abel*. Washington, DC: Catholic University of America Press, 1961.

Anderson, James N. "Can We Trust the Bible over Evolutionary Science?" *Reformed Faith & Practice* 1, no. 3 (December 2016): 6–23. http://journal .rts.edu/article/can-we-trust-the-bible-over-evolutionary-science/.

Averbeck, Richard. "A Literary Day, Inter-Textual, and Contextual Reading of Genesis 1–2." In *Reading Genesis 1–2: An Evangelical Conversation*, edited by J. Daryl Charles, 7–34. Peabody, MA: Hendrickson, 2013.

Axe, Douglas D. "Estimating the Prevalence of Protein Sequences Adopting Functional Enzyme Folds." *Journal of Molecular Biology* 341, no. 5 (Aug. 27, 2004): 1295–1315.

Balserak, Jon. "The God of Love and Weakness: Towards an Understanding of God's Accommodating Relationship with His People." *Westminster Theological Journal* 62, no. 2 (2000): 177–95.

Barr, James. *The Semantics of Biblical Language*. London: Oxford University Press, 1961.

Barrett, Matthew, and Ardel B. Caneday, eds. *Four Views on the Historical Adam*. Grand Rapids, MI: Zondervan, 2013.

Barrick, William D. "A Historical Adam: Young-Earth Creation View." In *Four Views on the Historical Adam*, edited by Matthew Barrett and Ardel B. Caneday, 197–227. Grand Rapids, MI: Zondervan, 2013.

Basil the Great of Caesarea. *Hexaemeron.* In *A Select Library of Nicene and Post-Nicene Fathers of the Christian Church,* 2nd series, edited by Philip Schaff. Grand Rapids: Eerdmans, 1978.

Beale, G. K. *The Temple and the Church's Mission: A Biblical Theology of the Dwelling Place of God.* Downers Grove, IL: InterVarsity Press, 2004.

Beckson, Karl, and Arthur Ganz. *Literary Terms: A Dictionary.* New York: Farrar, Straus and Giroux, 1975.

Behe, Michael J. *Darwin's Black Box: The Biochemical Challenge to Evolution.* New York: Free Press, 1996.

———. *The Edge of Evolution: The Search for the Limits of Darwinism.* New York: Free Press, 2007.

Bergen, Robert. "Text as a Guide to Authorial Intention: An Introduction to Discourse Criticism." *Journal of the Evangelical Theological Society* 30, no. 3 (1987): 327–36.

Blunt, John Henry, ed. "Accommodation." In *Dictionary of Doctrinal and Historical Theology,* 4–5. London/Oxford/Cambridge: Rivingtons, 1871.

Boettner, Loraine. *The Reformed Doctrine of Predestination.* Grand Rapids, MI: Eerdmans, 1936.

Bromiley, Geoffrey W., et al., eds. *International Standard Bible Encyclopedia.* Rev. ed. 4 vols. Grand Rapids, MI: Eerdmans, 1979–1988.

Broomall, Wick. "Accommodation." In *Evangelical Dictionary of Theology,* edited by Walter A. Elwell, 9. Grand Rapids, MI: Baker, 1984.

Brown, Francis, S. R. Driver, and Charles A. Briggs. *A Hebrew and English Lexicon of the Old Testament.* Oxford: Oxford University Press, 1953.

Budge, E. A. Wallis. *The Babylonian Legends of Creation.* London: British Museum, 1921. Internet Sacred Text Archive. http://www.sacred-texts.com/ane/blc/blc11.htm.

———. *The Book of the Dead: The Papyrus of Ani in the British Museum: The Egyptian Text with Interlinear Transliteration and Translation, a Running Translation, Introduction, etc.* London: Longmans, 1895. Internet Sacred Text Archive. http://www.sacred-texts.com/egy/ebod/.

Cabal, Theodore J., and Peter J. Rasor, II. *Controversy of the Ages: Why Christians Should Not Divide over the Age of the Earth.* Ashland, OH: Weaver, 2017.

Calvin, John. *Commentaries on the First Book of Moses Called Genesis.* 2 vols. Grand Rapids, MI: Baker, 1979.

————. *Institutes of the Christian Religion.* Trans. Henry Beveridge. Grand Rapids, MI: Eerdmans, 1970.

Carson, D. A., and John D. Woodbridge, eds. *Scripture and Truth.* Grand Rapids, MI: Baker, 1992.

Charles, J. Daryl, ed. *Reading Genesis 1–2: An Evangelical Conversation.* Peabody, MA: Hendrickson, 2013.

Clifford, Richard J. *Creation Accounts in the Ancient Near East and in the Bible.* Washington, DC: Catholic Biblical Association of America, 1994.

Collins, C. John. *Did Adam and Eve Really Exist? Who They Were and Why You Should Care.* Wheaton, IL: Crossway, 2011.

————. *Genesis 1–4: A Linguistic, Literary, and Theological Commentary.* Phillipsburg, NJ: P&R, 2006.

————. *Reading Genesis Well: Navigating History, Poetry, Science, and Truth in Genesis 1–11.* Grand Rapids, MI: Zondervan, 2018.

————. "Reading Genesis 1–2 with the Grain: Analogical Days." In *Reading Genesis 1–2: An Evangelical Conversation*, edited by J. Daryl Charles, 73–92. Peabody, MA: Hendrickson, 2013.

————. "The Evolution of Adam." The Gospel Coalition. April 26, 2012. https://www.thegospelcoalition.org/reviews/the_evolution_of_adam/.

Currid, John D. *Ancient Egypt and the Old Testament.* Grand Rapids, MI: Baker, 1997.

Denton, Michael. *Evolution: Still A Theory in Crisis.* Seattle: Discovery Institute, 2016.

Duncan, J. Ligon, III, and David W. Hall. "The 24-Hour View." In *The Genesis Debate: Three Views on the Days of Creation*, edited by David G. Hagopian, 21–66. Mission Viejo, CA: Crux, 2001.

Eichrodt, Walther. *Theology of the Old Testament.* Philadelphia: Westminster, 1967.

Einstein, Albert. *Relativity: The Special and General Theory.* New York: Henry Holt, 1920.

Enns, Peter. *Inspiration & Incarnation: Evangelicals and the Problem of the Old Testament.* Grand Rapids, MI: Baker, 2005.

Frame, John M. *The Doctrine of God.* Phillipsburg, NJ: P&R, 2002.

————. *The Doctrine of the Knowledge of God.* Phillipsburg, NJ: Presbyterian and Reformed, 1987.

————. *The Doctrine of the Word of God.* Phillipsburg, NJ: P&R, 2010.

————. "God and Biblical Language: Transcendence and Immanence." In *God's Inerrant Word: An International Symposium on the Trustwor-*

thiness of Scripture, edited by John W. Montgomery, 159–177. Minneapolis: Bethany Fellowship, 1974. http://www.frame-poythress.org/god-and-biblical-language-transcendence-and-immanence/.

Futato, Mark. "Because It Had Rained: A Study of Gen 2:5–7 with Implications for Gen 2:4–25 and Gen 1:1–2:3." *Westminster Theological Journal* 60, no. 1 (1998): 1–21.

Gaster, T. H. "Cosmogony." In *Interpreter's Dictionary of the Bible*, edited by George Arthur Buttrick, 1.702–9. New York: Abingdon, 1962.

Gauger, Ann, Douglas Axe, and Casey Luskin. *Science and Human Origins*. Seattle: Discovery Institute, 2012.

Gelb, Ignace J., et al., eds. *Assyrian Dictionary*. Chicago: University of Chicago Press, 1956–2010.

Gladkoff, Michael. "Writing Speeches Using Similes, Metaphors, and Analogies for Greater Impact." Word Nerds. https://www.word-nerds.com.au/writing-speeches-using-similes-metaphors-and-analogies/.

Gonzales, Robert R., Jr. "Predation & Creation: Animal Death before the Fall?" Evangelical Theological Society paper, March 23, 2013.

Griffiths, J. Gwyn. "Myths: Solar Cycle." In *The Oxford Encyclopedia of Ancient Egypt*, edited by Donald B. Redford, 2.476–80. New York: Oxford University Press, 2001.

Grudem, Wayne A. *Systematic Theology: An Introduction to Biblical Doctrine*. Grand Rapids, MI: Zondervan, 1994.

Hagopian, David G., ed. *The Genesis Debate: Three Views on the Days of Creation*. Mission Viejo, CA: Crux, 2001.

Hallo, William W., ed. *The Context of Scripture*. 3 vols. New York: Brill, 1997–2002.

Hamilton, Victor P. *The Book of Genesis, Chapters 1–17*. Grand Rapids, MI: Eerdmans, 1990.

Harris, R. Laird, Gleason L. Archer Jr., and Bruce K. Waltke, eds. *Theological Wordbook of the Old Testament*. 2 vols. Chicago: Moody Press, 1981.

Harrison, R. K. "Firmament." In *The International Standard Bible Encyclopedia*, rev. ed., edited by Geoffrey W. Bromiley, et al., 2.306–7. Grand Rapids, MI: Eerdmans, 1979.

Headland, Thomas, Kenneth Pike, and Marvin Harris, eds. *Emics and Etics: The Insider/Outsider Debate*. Newbury Park, CA: Sage, 1990.

Heidel, Alexander. *The Babylonian Genesis: The Story of Creation*. 2nd ed. 3rd impression. Chicago/London: University of Chicago Press, 1963.

Hersey, Oliver. "Hammering Out the Meaning of *Rāqîaʿ* and 'Waters Above' in Gen. 1:6–8 against Its Ancient Near Eastern and Biblical Context," unpublished manuscript.

Hodge, Archibald A., and Benjamin B. Warfield. *Inspiration.* With introduction by Roger R. Nicole. Grand Rapids, MI: Baker, 1979.

Hofmann, Rudolf. "Accommodation." In *The New Schaff-Herzog Encyclopedia of Religious Knowledge*, edited by Samuel Macauley Jackson, 1.22–24. Grand Rapids, MI: Baker, 1977.

Horowitz, Wayne. *Mesopotamian Cosmic Geography.* Winona Lake, IN: Eisenbrauns, 1998.

Ions, Veronica. *Egyptian Mythology.* New rev. ed. New York: Peter Bedrick, 1982.

Jacobsen, Thorkild. *The Sumerian King List.* Chicago: University of Chicago Press, 1939.

Jastrow, Marcus. *A Dictionary of the Targumim, the Talmud Babli and Yerushalmi, and the Midrashic Literature.* New York: Pardes, 1950.

Josephus. *Jewish Antiquities.* Translated by H. St. J. Thackeray. London: Heinemann; Cambridge: Harvard University Press, 1967. http://www.biblestudytools.com/history/flavius-josephus/antiquities-jews/.

Keathley, Kenneth D., and Mark F. Rooker. *40 Questions about Creation and Evolution.* Grand Rapids, MI: Kregel, 2014.

Kidner, Derek. "Gen 2:5–6, Wet or Dry?" *Tyndale Bulletin* 17 (1966): 109–14.

———. *Genesis: An Introduction and Commentary.* Leicester, England: Inter-Varsity; Downers Grove, IL: InterVarsity Press, 1967.

King, L. W., ed. *The Seven Tablets of Creation, or the Babylonian and Assyrian Legends concerning the Creation of the World and of Mankind.* London: Luzac, 1902.

Klein, Jacob. "Enki and Ninmaḫ." In *The Context of Scripture*, edited by William Hallo, 1.517–18. Leiden/New York/Köln: Brill, 1997.

Kline, Meredith G. *Images of the Spirit.* Grand Rapids, MI: Baker, 1980.

Kuhn, Thomas S. *The Copernican Revolution: Planetary Astronomy in the Development of Western Thought.* Cambridge: Harvard University Press, 1992.

Kuhn, Thomas S. *The Structure of Scientific Revolutions.* Chicago: University of Chicago Press, 1970.

Lamoureux, Denis O. *I Love Jesus & I Accept Evolution.* Eugene, OR: Wipf & Stock, 2009.

Lane, A. N. S. "Accommodation." In *New Dictionary of Theology*, edited by Sinclair B. Ferguson, David F. Wright, and J. I. Packer. Downers Grove, IL: InterVarsity Press, 1988.

Langdon, S. *The Babylonian Epic of Creation: Restored from the Recently Recovered Tablets of Aššur: Transcription, Translation & Commentary*. Oxford: Clarendon, 1923.

Lee, Hoon. "Accommodation: Orthodox, Socinian, and Contemporary." *Westminster Theological Journal* 75, no. 2 (2013): 335–48.

Leopold, H. C. *Exposition of Genesis*. Grand Rapids, MI: Baker, 1965.

Letham, Robert. "'In the Space of Six Days': The Days of Creation from Origen to the Westminster Assembly." *Westminster Theological Journal* 61 (1999): 149–74.

Lewis, C. S. *The Pilgrim's Regress: An Allegorical Apology for Christianity, Reason, and Romanticism*. 3rd ed. Grand Rapids, MI: Eerdmans, 1943.

Liddell, Henry George, Robert Scott, and Henry Stuart Jones. *A Greek-English Lexicon*. 9th ed., with supplement. Oxford: Oxford University Press, 1968.

Lillback, Peter A., and Richard B. Gaffin Jr., eds. *Thy Word Is Still Truth: Essential Writings on the Doctrine of Scripture from the Reformation to Today*. Philadelphia: Westminster Seminary Press; Phillipsburg, NJ: P&R, 2013.

Long, V. Philips. *The Art of Biblical History*. Grand Rapids, MI: Zondervan, 1994. Reprinted in Moisés Silva, ed. *Foundations of Contemporary Interpretation*. Six Volumes in One. Grand Rapids, MI: Zondervan, 1996.

———. *The Reign and Rejection of King Saul: A Case for Literary and Theological Coherence*. Atlanta: Scholars Press, 1989.

Longacre, Robert E. *An Anatomy of Speech Notions*. Lisse, Netherlands: Peter de Ridder, 1976.

———. *Discourse, Paragraph, and Sentence Structure in Selected Philippine Languages: Volume I: Discourse and Paragraph Structure*. Santa Ana, CA: Summer Institute of Linguistics, 1968.

———. *Joseph: A Story of Divine Providence: A Text Theoretical and Textlinguistic Analysis of Genesis 37 and 39–48*. Winona Lake, IN: Eisenbrauns, 1989.

Machen, J. Gresham. *Christianity and Liberalism*. New ed. Grand Rapids, MI: Eerdmans, 2009. Originally published New York: Macmillan, 1923.

Madueme, Hans, and Michael Reeves, eds. *Adam, the Fall, and Original Sin: Theological, Biblical, and Scientific Perspectives.* Grand Rapids, MI: Baker, 2014.

M'Clintock, John, and James Strong. *Cyclopedia of Biblical, Theological, and Ecclesiastical Literature.* New York: Harper, 1874.

Merriam-Webster's Collegiate Dictionary. 11th ed. Springfield, MA: Merriam-Webster, 2003.

Meyer, Stephen C. *Darwin's Doubt: The Explosive Origin of Animal Life and the Case for Intelligent Design.* New York: HarperOne, 2013.

———. *Signature in the Cell: DNA and the Evidence for Intelligent Design.* New York: HarperOne, 2009.

Moreland, J. P., et al., eds. *Theistic Evolution: A Scientific, Philosophical, and Theological Critique.* Wheaton, IL: Crossway, 2017.

Muller, Richard A. *Dictionary of Latin and Greek Theological Terms: Drawn Principally from Protestant Scholastic Theology.* Grand Rapids, MI: Baker, 1985.

Murray, John. "The Attestation of Scripture." In *The Infallible Word: A Symposium By Members of the Faculty of Westminster Theological Seminary*, 3rd rev. printing, edited by N. B. Stonehouse and Paul Woolley, 1–54. Philadelphia: Presbyterian and Reformed, 1967.

Muss-Arnolt, William. *Assyrisch-englisch-deutsches Handwörterbuch.* Berlin: Reuther & Reichard; New York: Lemcke & Büchner, 1905.

The New Encyclopaedia Britannica: Macropaedia. 15th ed. Chicago/London/Geneva/Sydney/Tokyo/Manila/Seoul/Johannesburg: Helen Hemingway Benton, 1974.

Newman, Robert C. "The Biblical Teaching on the Firmament." ThM thesis, Biblical Theological Seminary, 1972.

Orr, James, ed. *International Standard Bible Encyclopedia.* 5 vols. Grand Rapids, MI: Eerdmans, 1955.

Packer, J. I. "Hermeneutics and Genesis 1–11." *Southwestern Journal of Theology* 44, no. 1 (2001): 4–21.

Pike, Kenneth L. *Language in Relation to a Unified Theory of the Structure of Human Behavior.* 2nd ed. The Hague/Paris: Mouton, 1967.

———. *Linguistic Concepts: An Introduction to Tagmemics.* Lincoln, NE/London: University of Nebraska Press, 1982.

Porter, J. B. "Old Testament Historiography." In *Tradition and Interpretation: Essays by Members of the Society for Old Testament Study*, edited by G. W. Anderson, 125–62. Oxford: Clarendon Press, 1979.

Poythress, Vern S. "Adam versus Claims from Genetics." *Westminster Theological Journal* 75, no. 1 (2013): 65–82. http://www
.frame-poythress.org/adam-versus-claims-from-genetics/.

———. *Chance and the Sovereignty of God: A God-Centered Approach to Probability and Random Events.* Wheaton, IL: Crossway, 2014.

———. "Correlations with Providence in Genesis 1." *Westminster Theological Journal* 77, no. 1 (2015): 71–99.

———. "Correlations with Providence in Genesis 2." *Westminster Theological Journal* 78, no. 1 (2016): 29–48.

———. "Dealing with the Genre of Genesis and Its Opening Chapters." *Westminster Theological Journal* 78, no. 2 (2016): 217–30.

———. *Did Adam Exist?* Phillipsburg, NJ: P&R; Philadelphia: Westminster Seminary Press, 2014.

———. "Dispensing with Merely Human Meaning: Gains and Losses from Focusing on the Human Author, Illustrated by Zephaniah 1:2–3." *Journal of the Evangelical Theological Society* 57, no. 3 (2014): 481–99.

———. "Evaluating the Claims of Scientists." *New Horizons* 33, no. 3 (March 2012): 6–8. http://www.opc.org/nh.html?article_id=739; also http://www.frame-poythress.org/evaluating-the-claims-of-scientists/.

———. "Genesis 1:1 Is the First Event, Not a Summary." *Westminster Theological Journal* 79, no. 1 (2017): 97–121.

———. *God-Centered Biblical Interpretation.* Phillipsburg, NJ: P&R, 1999.

———. *In the Beginning Was the Word: Language—A God-Centered Approach.* Wheaton, IL: Crossway, 2009.

———. *Inerrancy and the Gospels: A God-Centered Approach to the Challenges of Harmonization.* Wheaton, IL: Crossway, 2012.

———. *Inerrancy and Worldview: Answering Modern Challenges to the Bible.* Wheaton, IL: Crossway, 2012.

———. *The Lordship of Christ: Serving Our Savior All of the Time, in All of Life, with All of Our Heart.* Wheaton, IL: Crossway, 2016.

———. "A Misunderstanding of Calvin's Interpretation of Genesis 1:6–8 and 1:5 and Its Implications for Ideas of Accommodation." *Westminster Theological Journal* 76, no. 1 (2014): 157–66.

———. "Problems for Limited Inerrancy." *Journal of the Evangelical Theological Society* 18, no. 2 (1975): 93–102.

———. "Rain Water versus a Heavenly Sea in Genesis 1:6–8." *Westminster Theological Journal* 77, no. 2 (2015): 181–91.

———. *Reading the Word of God in the Presence of God: A Handbook for Biblical Interpretation*. Wheaton, IL: Crossway, 2016.

———. *Redeeming Philosophy: A God-Centered Approach to the Big Questions*. Wheaton, IL: Crossway, 2014.

———. *Redeeming Science: A God-Centered Approach*. Wheaton, IL: Crossway, 2006.

———. "Rethinking Accommodation in Revelation." *Westminster Theological Journal* 76, no. 1 (2014): 143–56.

———. *Symphonic Theology: The Validity of Multiple Perspectives in Theology*. Reprint. Phillipsburg, NJ: P&R, 2001.

———. "Three Modern Myths in Interpreting Genesis 1." *Westminster Theological Journal* 76, no. 2 (2014): 321–50.

———. "Time in Genesis 1." *Westminster Theological Journal* 79, no. 2 (2017): 213–41.

———. *Understanding Dispensationalists*. 2nd ed. Phillipsburg, NJ: P&R Publishing, 1994.

Pratt, John H. *Scripture and Science Not at Variance*. 7th ed. London: Hatchards, 1872.

Pritchard, James B. *The Ancient Near East in Pictures Relating to the Old Testament*. Princeton, NJ: Princeton University Press, 1969.

———, ed. *Ancient Near Eastern Texts Relating to the Old Testament*. Princeton, NJ: Princeton University Press, 1969.

Provan, Iain. *Discovering Genesis: Content, Interpretation, Reception*. Grand Rapids, MI: Eerdmans, 2016.

Ramm, Bernard. *The Christian View of Science and Scripture*. Grand Rapids, MI: Eerdmans, 1954.

Ryken, Philip G. "Pastoral Reflection 2: We Cannot Understand the World or Our Faith without a Real, Historical Adam." In *Four Views on the Historical Adam*, edited by Matthew Barrett and Ardel B. Caneday, 267–79. Grand Rapids, MI: Zondervan, 2013.

Sanford, John, Wesley Brewer, Franzine Smith, and John Baumgardner. "The Waiting Time Problem in a Model Hominin Population." *Theoretical Biology and Medical Modelling* 12, no. 18 (2015).

Scofield, C. I., ed. *The Scofield Reference Bible*. New and improved ed. New York: Oxford University Press, 1917.

Seely, Paul. "The Firmament and the Water Above: Part I: The Meaning of *raqia'* in Gen 1:6–8." *Westminster Theological Journal* 53, no. 2 (1991): 227–40.

———. "The Firmament and the Water Above: Part II: The Meaning of 'The Water above the Firmament' in Gen 1:6–8." *Westminster Theological Journal* 54, no. 1 (1992): 31–46.

Skilton, John H. "The Transmission of the Scriptures." In *The Infallible Word: A Symposium by Members of the Faculty of Westminster Theological Seminary*, 3rd rev. printing, edited by N. B. Stonehouse and Paul Woolley, 141–95. Philadelphia: Presbyterian and Reformed, 1967.

Sparks, Kenton L. *God's Word in Human Words: An Evangelical Appropriation of Critical Biblical Scholarship*. Grand Rapids, MI: Baker, 2008.

———. *Sacred Word, Broken Word: Biblical Authority and the Dark Side of Scripture*. Grand Rapids, MI: Eerdmans, 2012.

Sterchi, D. A. "Does Genesis 1 Provide a Chronological Sequence?" *Journal of the Evangelical Theological Society* 39 (1996): 529–36.

Stonehouse, N. B., and Paul Woolley, eds. *The Infallible Word: A Symposium By Members of the Faculty of Westminster Theological Seminary*. 3rd rev. printing. Philadelphia: Presbyterian and Reformed, 1967.

Sweet, L. M., and G. W. Bromiley. "Accommodation." In *International Standard Bible Encyclopedia*, 1:24–28. Grand Rapids, MI: Eerdmans, 1979.

Throntveit, Mark A. "Are the Events in the Genesis Creation Account Set Forth in Chronological Order? No." In *The Genesis Debate: Persistent Questions about Creation and the Flood*, edited by R. F. Youngblood, 36–55. Grand Rapids, MI: Baker, 1990.

Tobin, Vincent Arieh. "Myths: Creation Myths." In *The Oxford Encyclopedia of Ancient Egypt*, edited by Donald B. Redford, 2.269–72. New York: Oxford University Press, 2001.

———. "Myths: An Overview." In *The Oxford Encyclopedia of Ancient Egypt*, edited by Donald B. Redford, 2.264–69. New York: Oxford University Press, 2001.

Tsumura, David Toshio. *The Earth and the Waters in Genesis 1 and 2: A Linguistic Investigation*. Journal for the Study of the Old Testament, Supplement Series 83. Sheffield: Sheffield Academic, 1989.

Versteeg, J. P. *Adam in the New Testament: Mere Teaching Model or First Historical Man?* translated by Richard B. Gaffin Jr. Phillipsburg, NJ: P&R, 2012.

Waltke, Bruce K. *A Commentary on Micah*. Grand Rapids, MI: Eerdmans, 2007.

———. "The Creation Account in Genesis 1:1–3: Part I: Introduction to Biblical Cosmogony." *Bibliotheca Sacra* 132 (1975): 25–36.

———. "The Creation Account in Genesis 1:1–3: Part II: The Restitution Theory." *Bibliotheca Sacra* 132 (1975): 136–44.

———. "The Creation Account in Genesis 1:1–3: Part III: The Initial Chaos Theory and the Precreation Chaos Theory." *Bibliotheca Sacra* 132 (1975): 216–28.

———. "The Creation Account in Genesis 1:1–3: Part IV: The Theology of Genesis 1." *Bibliotheca Sacra* 132 (1975): 327–42.

———. "The Creation Account in Genesis 1:1–3: Part V: The Theology of Genesis 1—Continued." *Bibliotheca Sacra* 133 (1976): 28–41.

———. *Creation and Chaos*. Portland, OR: Western Conservative Baptist Seminary, 1974.

Waltke, Bruce K., with Cathi J. Fredricks. *Genesis: A Commentary*. Grand Rapids, MI: Zondervan, 2001.

Waltke, Bruce K., with Charles Yu. *An Old Testament Theology: An Exegetical, Canonical, and Thematic Approach*. Grand Rapids, MI: Zondervan, 2007.

Walton, John H. *Genesis 1 as Ancient Cosmology*. Winona Lake, IN: Eisenbrauns, 2011.

———. "A Historical Adam: Archetypal Creation View." In *Four Views on the Historical Adam*, edited by Matthew Barrett and Ardel B. Caneday, 89–118. Grand Rapids, MI: Zondervan, 2013.

———. *The Lost World of Genesis One: Ancient Cosmology and the Origins Debate*. Downers Grove, IL: InterVarsity Press, 2009.

Warfield, Benjamin Breckinridge. *The Inspiration and Authority of the Bible*. Edited by Samuel G. Craig. Philadelphia: Presbyterian and Reformed, 1967.

Weeks, Noel. "The Ambiguity of Biblical 'Background.'" *Westminster Theological Journal* 72, no. 2 (2010): 219–36.

———. "Cosmology in Historical Context." *Westminster Theological Journal* 68, no. 2 (2006): 283–93.

———. "Problems in Interpreting Genesis: Part 1." Creation 2, no. 3 (June 1979): 27–32. http://creation.com/problems-in-interpreting-genesis-part-1.

———. *Sources and Authors: Assumptions in the Study of Hebrew Bible Narrative*. Piscataway, NJ: Gorgias, 2011.

Wenham, Gordon J. *Genesis 1–15*. Word Biblical Commentary 1. Waco, TX: Word, 1987.

"What Is Analogy?" ThoughtCo. https://grammar.about.com/od/ab/g
/analogy.htm.

Wilson, Joshua Daniel. "A Case for the Traditional Translation and Interpretation of Genesis 1:1 Based upon a Multi-Leveled Linguistic
Analysis." PhD diss., Southern Baptist Theological Seminary, 2010.

Winther-Nielsen, Nicolai. "'In the Beginning' of Biblical Hebrew Discourse." In *Language in Context: Essays for Robert E. Longacre*,
edited by Shin Ja J. Hwang and William R. Merrifield, 67–80. Dallas
TX: The Summer Institute of Linguistics and the University of Texas
at Arlington, 1992. https://www.sil.org/system/files/reapdata/12/98/61
/129861883369277823521029452481206904550/31844.pdf.

Woodbridge, John D. *Biblical Authority: A Critique of the Rogers/McKim
Proposal.* Grand Rapids, MI: Zondervan, 1982.

Young, Edward J. "The Interpretation of Genesis 1:2." *Westminster
Theological Journal* 23, no. 2 (1961): 151–78.

Young, Edward J. *An Introduction to the Old Testament.* Revised edition.
Grand Rapids, MI: Eerdmans, 1960.

———. "The Relation of the First Verse of Genesis One to Verses Two
and Three." *Westminster Theological Journal* 21, no. 2 (May 1959):
133–46.

———. *Studies in Genesis One.* Philadelphia: Presbyterian and Reformed,
1964.

Youngblood, Ronald. *The Book of Genesis: An Introductory Commentary.* Grand Rapids, MI: Baker, 1991.

Subject Index

Scripture Index

Also Available from
Vern Poythress

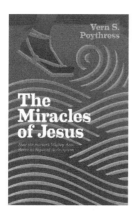

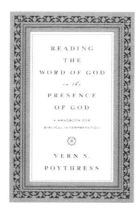

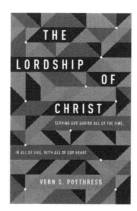

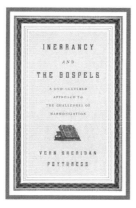

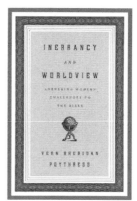

For more information, visit **crossway.org**.